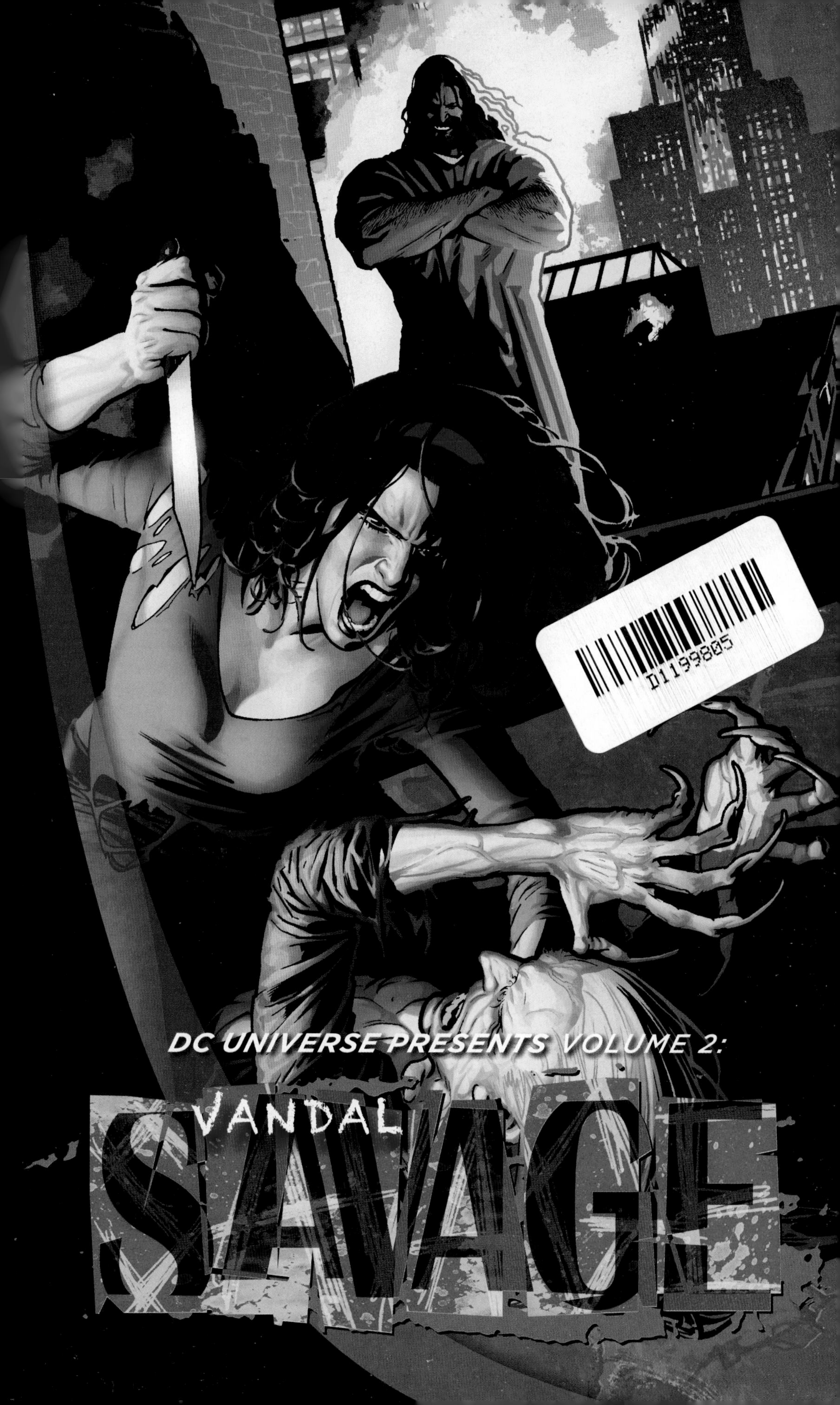
DC UNIVERSE PRESENTS VOLUME 2:
VANDAL
SAVAGE

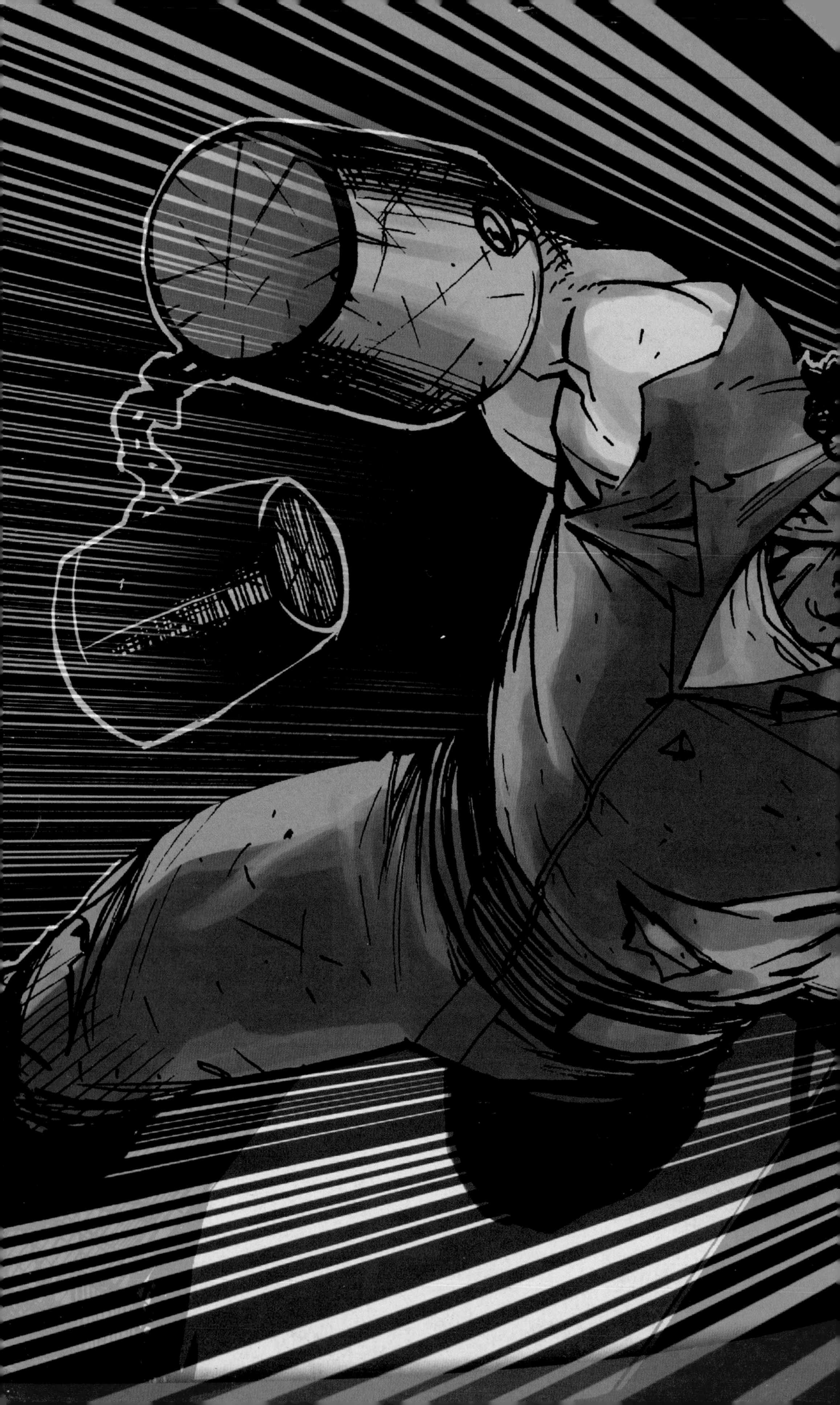

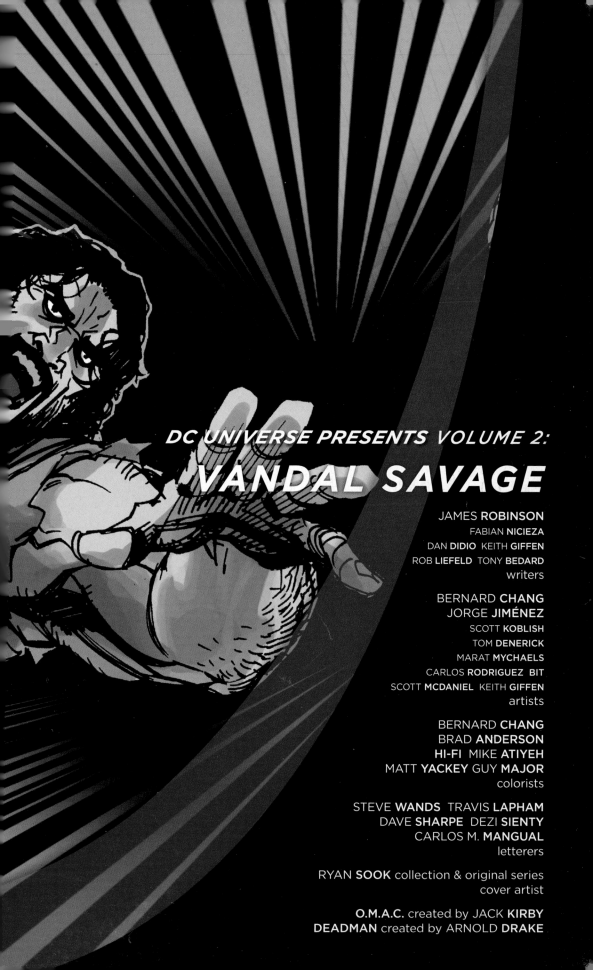

DC UNIVERSE PRESENTS VOLUME 2:
VANDAL SAVAGE

JAMES **ROBINSON**
FABIAN **NICIEZA**
DAN **DIDIO** KEITH **GIFFEN**
ROB **LIEFELD** TONY **BEDARD**
writers

BERNARD **CHANG**
JORGE **JIMÉNEZ**
SCOTT **KOBLISH**
TOM **DENERICK**
MARAT **MYCHAELS**
CARLOS **RODRIGUEZ** BIT
SCOTT **MCDANIEL** KEITH **GIFFEN**
artists

BERNARD **CHANG**
BRAD **ANDERSON**
HI-FI MIKE **ATIYEH**
MATT **YACKEY** GUY **MAJOR**
colorists

STEVE **WANDS** TRAVIS **LAPHAM**
DAVE **SHARPE** DEZI **SIENTY**
CARLOS M. **MANGUAL**
letterers

RYAN **SOOK** collection & original series
cover artist

O.M.A.C. created by JACK **KIRBY**
DEADMAN created by ARNOLD **DRAKE**

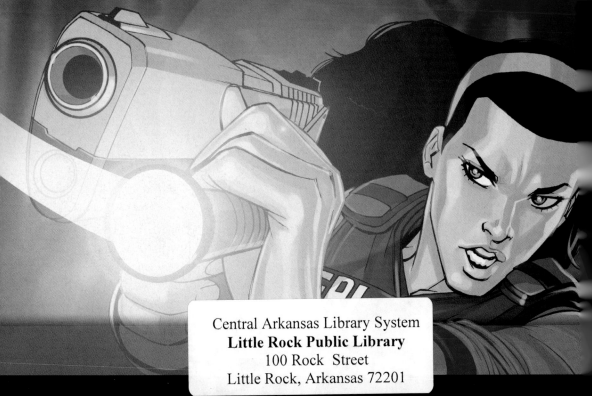

EDDIE BERGANZA WIL MOSS HARVEY RICHARDS JOEY CAVALIERI RACHEL GLUCKSTERN CHRIS CONROY Editors – Original Series
DARREN SHAN KATE STEWART RICKEY PURDIN Assistant Editors – Original Series RACHEL PINNELAS Editor
ROBBIN BROSTERMAN Design Director – Books ROBBIE BIEDERMAN Publication Design

BOB HARRAS Senior VP – Editor-in-Chief, DC Comics

DIANE NELSON President DAN DIDIO and JIM LEE Co-Publishers
GEOFF JOHNS Chief Creative Officer
JOHN ROOD Executive VP – Sales, Marketing and Business Development
AMY GENKINS Senior VP – Business and Legal Affairs NAIRI GARDINER Senior VP – Finance
JEFF BOISON VP – Publishing Planning MARK CHIARELLO VP – Art Direction and Design
JOHN CUNNINGHAM VP – Marketing TERRI CUNNINGHAM VP – Editorial Administration
ALISON GILL Senior VP – Manufacturing and Operations HANK KANALZ Senior VP – Vertigo & Integrated Publishing
JAY KOGAN VP – Business and Legal Affairs, Publishing JACK MAHAN VP – Business Affairs, Talent
NICK NAPOLITANO VP – Manufacturing Administration SUE POHJA VP – Book Sales
COURTNEY SIMMONS Senior VP – Publicity BOB WAYNE Senior VP – Sales

DC UNIVERSE PRESENTS VOLUME 2: VANDAL SAVAGE

Published by DC Comics. Cover and compilation Copyright © 2013 DC Comics. All Rights Reserved.

Originally published in single magazine form in DC UNIVERSE PRESENTS 0, 9-12, TEEN TITANS 11-12.
Copyright © 2012, 2013 DC Comics. All Rights Reserved. All characters, their distinctive likenesses and related elements
featured in this publication are trademarks of DC Comics. The stories, characters and incidents featured in
this publication are entirely fictional. DC Comics does not read or accept unsolicited ideas, stories or artwork.

DC Comics, 1700 Broadway, New York, NY 10019
A Warner Bros. Entertainment Company.
Printed by RR Donnelley, Salem, VA, USA. 7/19/13. First Printing.
ISBN: 978-1-4012-4076-9

Library of Congress Cataloging-in-Publication Data

Robinson, James Dale, author.
DC Universe Presents. Volume 2, Vandal savage / James Robinson, Bernard
Chang.
pages cm. — (DC Universe Presents)
"Originally published in single magazine form in DC UNIVERSE PRESENTS
0, 9-12, Teen Titans 11-2."
ISBN 978-1-4012-4076-9
1. Graphic novels. I. Chang, Bernard, 1972- illustrator. II. Title.
III. Title: Vandal savage.
PN6728.D35334R63 2013
741.5'973—dc23
                        2013010702

SUSTAINABLE
FORESTRY
INITIATIVE

Certified Chain of Custody
At Least 20% Certified Forest Content
www.sfiprogram.org
SFI-01042
APPLIES TO TEXT STOCK ONLY

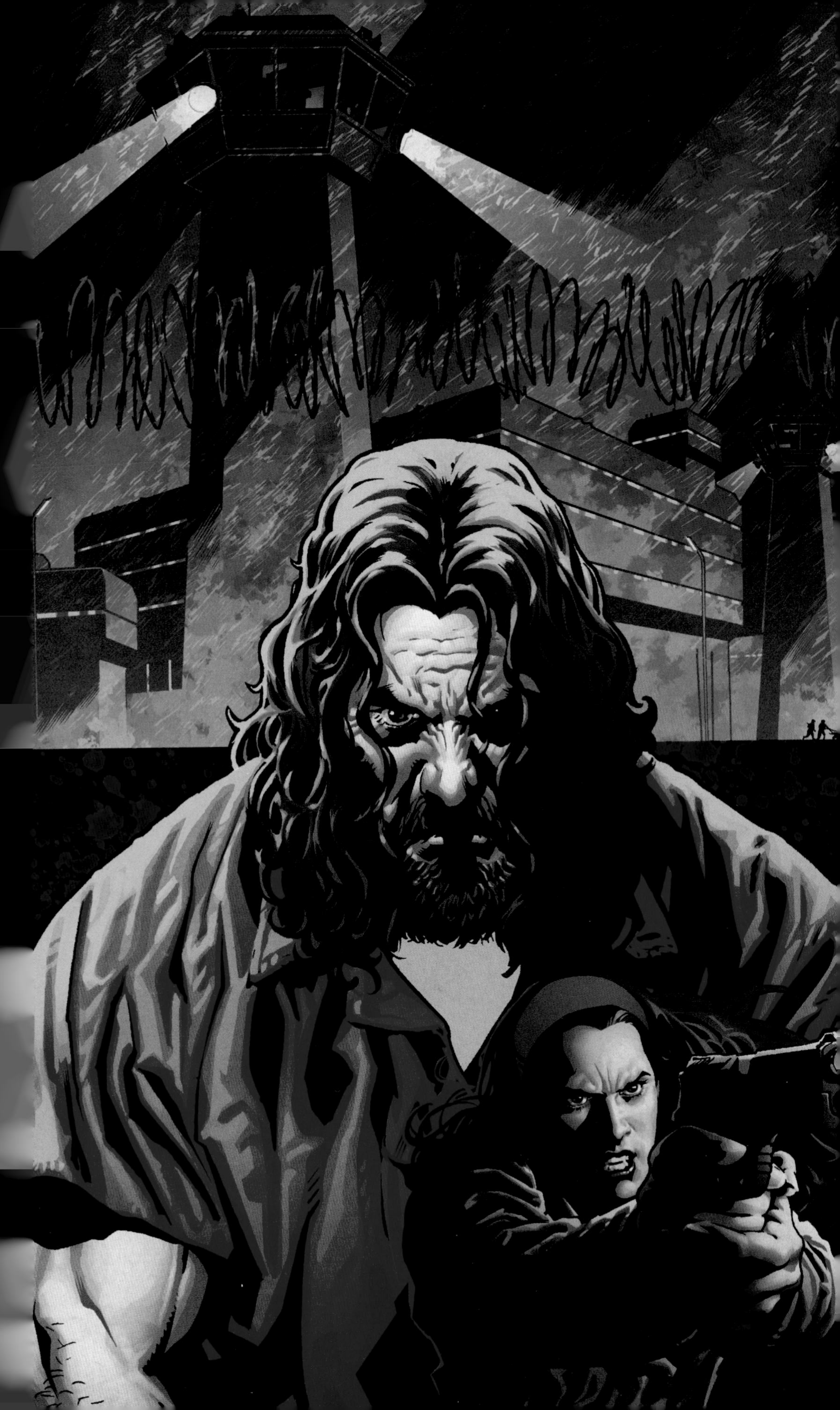

PART ONE: DADDY'S LITTLE GIRL

JAMES ROBINSON writer BERNARD CHANG artist

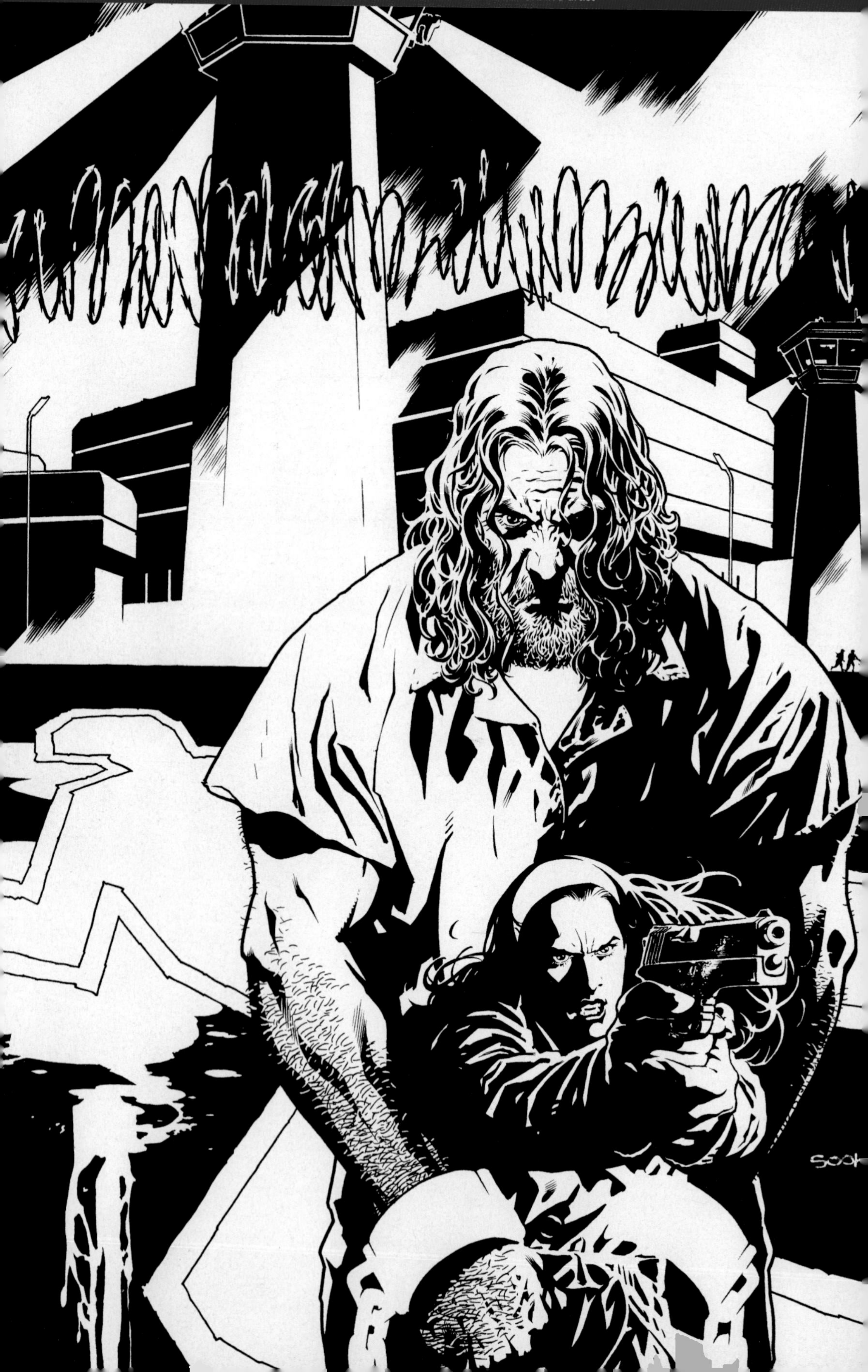
SOOK

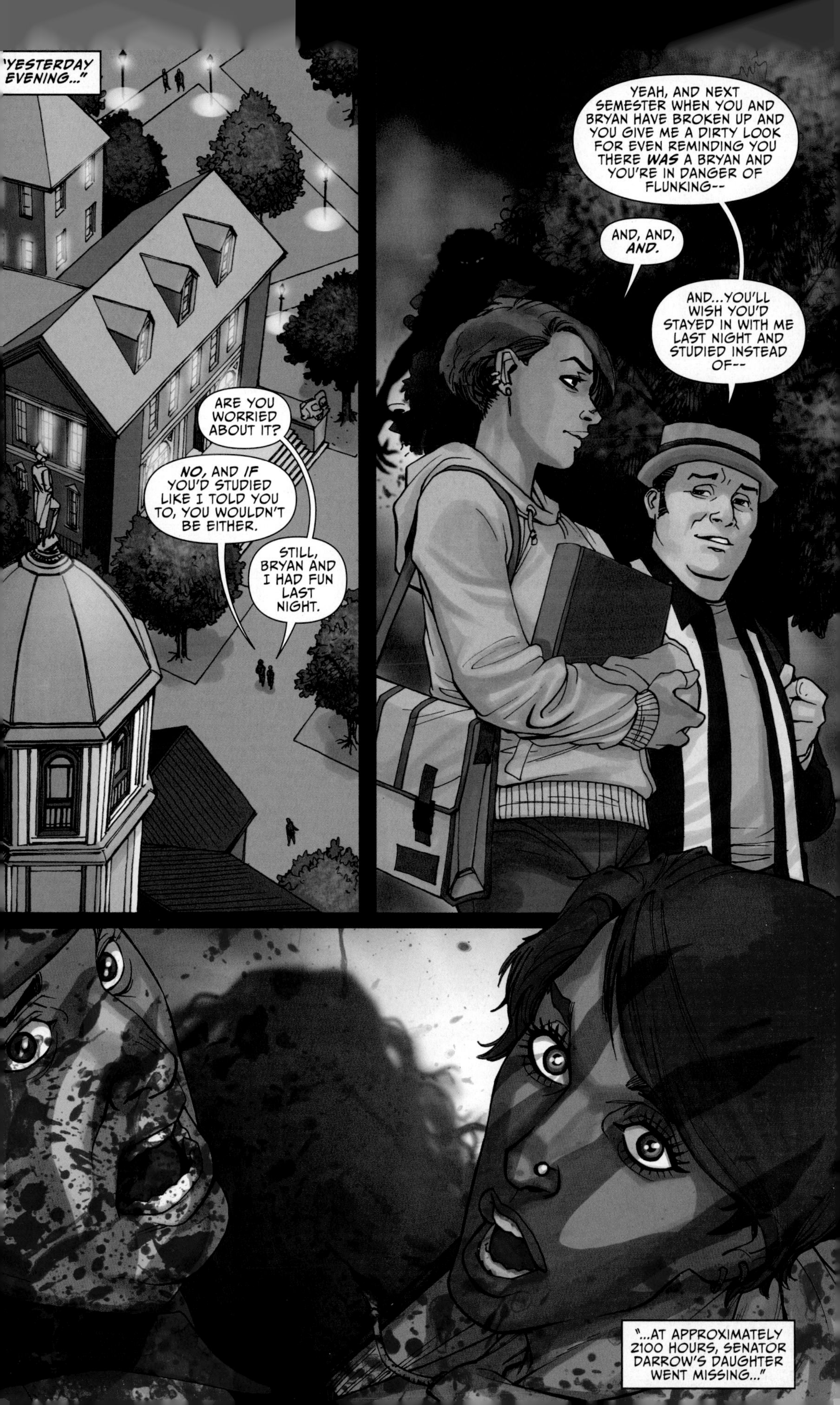
"YESTERDAY EVENING..."
ARE YOU WORRIED ABOUT IT?
NO, AND IF YOU'D STUDIED LIKE I TOLD YOU TO, YOU WOULDN'T BE EITHER.
STILL, BRYAN AND I HAD FUN LAST NIGHT.
YEAH, AND NEXT SEMESTER WHEN YOU AND BRYAN HAVE BROKEN UP AND YOU GIVE ME A DIRTY LOOK FOR EVEN REMINDING YOU THERE WAS A BRYAN AND YOU'RE IN DANGER OF FLUNKING--
AND, AND, AND.
AND...YOU'LL WISH YOU'D STAYED IN WITH ME LAST NIGHT AND STUDIED INSTEAD OF--
"...AT APPROXIMATELY 2100 HOURS, SENATOR DARROW'S DAUGHTER WENT MISSING..."

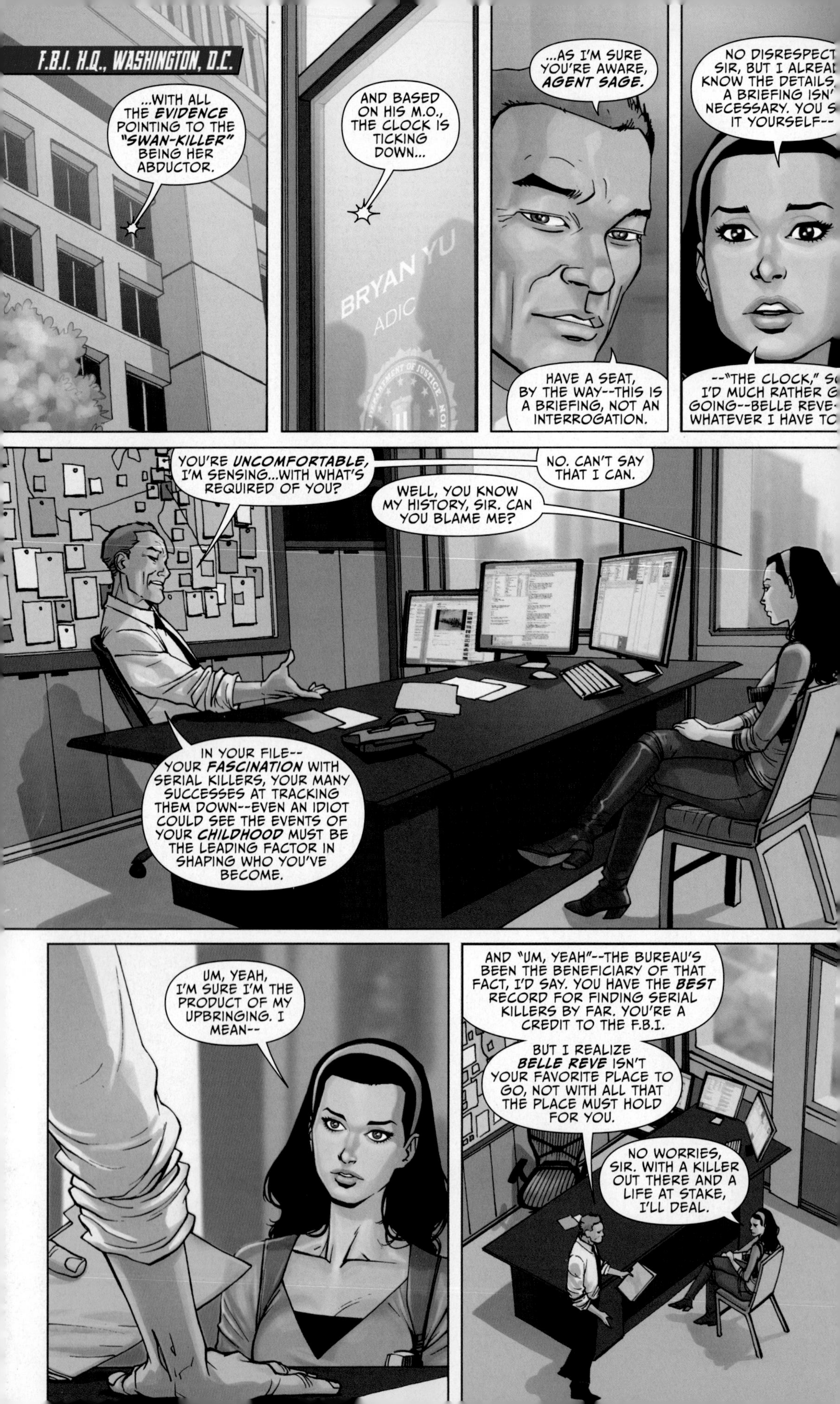
F.B.I. H.Q., WASHINGTON, D.C.
...WITH ALL THE EVIDENCE POINTING TO THE "SWAN-KILLER" BEING HER ABDUCTOR.
AND BASED ON HIS M.O., THE CLOCK IS TICKING DOWN...
BRYAN YU
ADIC
...AS I'M SURE YOU'RE AWARE, AGENT SAGE.
HAVE A SEAT, BY THE WAY--THIS IS A BRIEFING, NOT AN INTERROGATION.
NO DISRESPECT SIR, BUT I ALREA KNOW THE DETAILS. A BRIEFING ISN' NECESSARY. YOU S IT YOURSELF--
--"THE CLOCK," S I'D MUCH RATHER G GOING--BELLE REVE- WHATEVER I HAVE TO
YOU'RE UNCOMFORTABLE, I'M SENSING...WITH WHAT'S REQUIRED OF YOU?
NO. CAN'T SAY THAT I CAN.
WELL, YOU KNOW MY HISTORY, SIR. CAN YOU BLAME ME?
IN YOUR FILE--YOUR FASCINATION WITH SERIAL KILLERS, YOUR MANY SUCCESSES AT TRACKING THEM DOWN--EVEN AN IDIOT COULD SEE THE EVENTS OF YOUR CHILDHOOD MUST BE THE LEADING FACTOR IN SHAPING WHO YOU'VE BECOME.
UM, YEAH, I'M SURE I'M THE PRODUCT OF MY UPBRINGING. I MEAN--
AND "UM, YEAH"--THE BUREAU'S BEEN THE BENEFICIARY OF THAT FACT, I'D SAY. YOU HAVE THE BEST RECORD FOR FINDING SERIAL KILLERS BY FAR. YOU'RE A CREDIT TO THE F.B.I.
BUT I REALIZE BELLE REVE ISN'T YOUR FAVORITE PLACE TO GO, NOT WITH ALL THAT THE PLACE MUST HOLD FOR YOU.
NO WORRIES, SIR. WITH A KILLER OUT THERE AND A LIFE AT STAKE, I'LL DEAL.

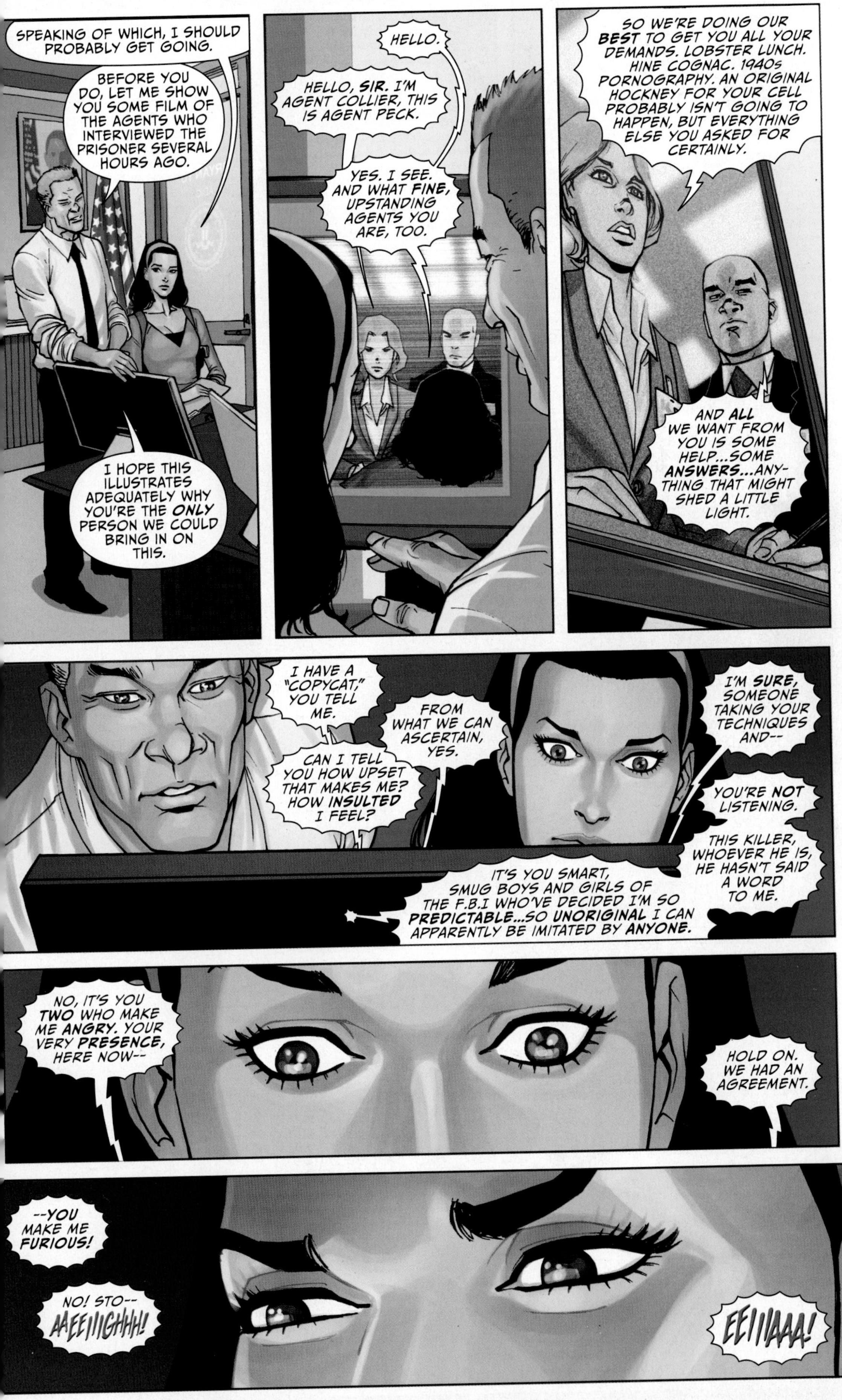

SPEAKING OF WHICH, I SHOULD PROBABLY GET GOING.
BEFORE YOU DO, LET ME SHOW YOU SOME FILM OF THE AGENTS WHO INTERVIEWED THE PRISONER SEVERAL HOURS AGO.
I HOPE THIS ILLUSTRATES ADEQUATELY WHY YOU'RE THE ONLY PERSON WE COULD BRING IN ON THIS.
HELLO.
HELLO, SIR. I'M AGENT COLLIER, THIS IS AGENT PECK.
YES. I SEE. AND WHAT FINE, UPSTANDING AGENTS YOU ARE, TOO.
SO WE'RE DOING OUR BEST TO GET YOU ALL YOUR DEMANDS. LOBSTER LUNCH. HINE COGNAC. 1940s PORNOGRAPHY. AN ORIGINAL HOCKNEY FOR YOUR CELL PROBABLY ISN'T GOING TO HAPPEN, BUT EVERYTHING ELSE YOU ASKED FOR CERTAINLY.
AND ALL WE WANT FROM YOU IS SOME HELP...SOME ANSWERS...ANYTHING THAT MIGHT SHED A LITTLE LIGHT.
I HAVE A "COPYCAT," YOU TELL ME.
FROM WHAT WE CAN ASCERTAIN, YES.
CAN I TELL YOU HOW UPSET THAT MAKES ME? HOW INSULTED I FEEL?
IT'S YOU SMART, SMUG BOYS AND GIRLS OF THE F.B.I WHO'VE DECIDED I'M SO PREDICTABLE...SO UNORIGINAL I CAN APPARENTLY BE IMITATED BY ANYONE.
I'M SURE, SOMEONE TAKING YOUR TECHNIQUES AND--
YOU'RE NOT LISTENING.
THIS KILLER, WHOEVER HE IS, HE HASN'T SAID A WORD TO ME.
NO, IT'S YOU TWO WHO MAKE ME ANGRY. YOUR VERY PRESENCE, HERE NOW--
HOLD ON. WE HAD AN AGREEMENT.
--YOU MAKE ME FURIOUS!
NO! STO-- AAEEIIIGHHH!
EEIIIAAA!

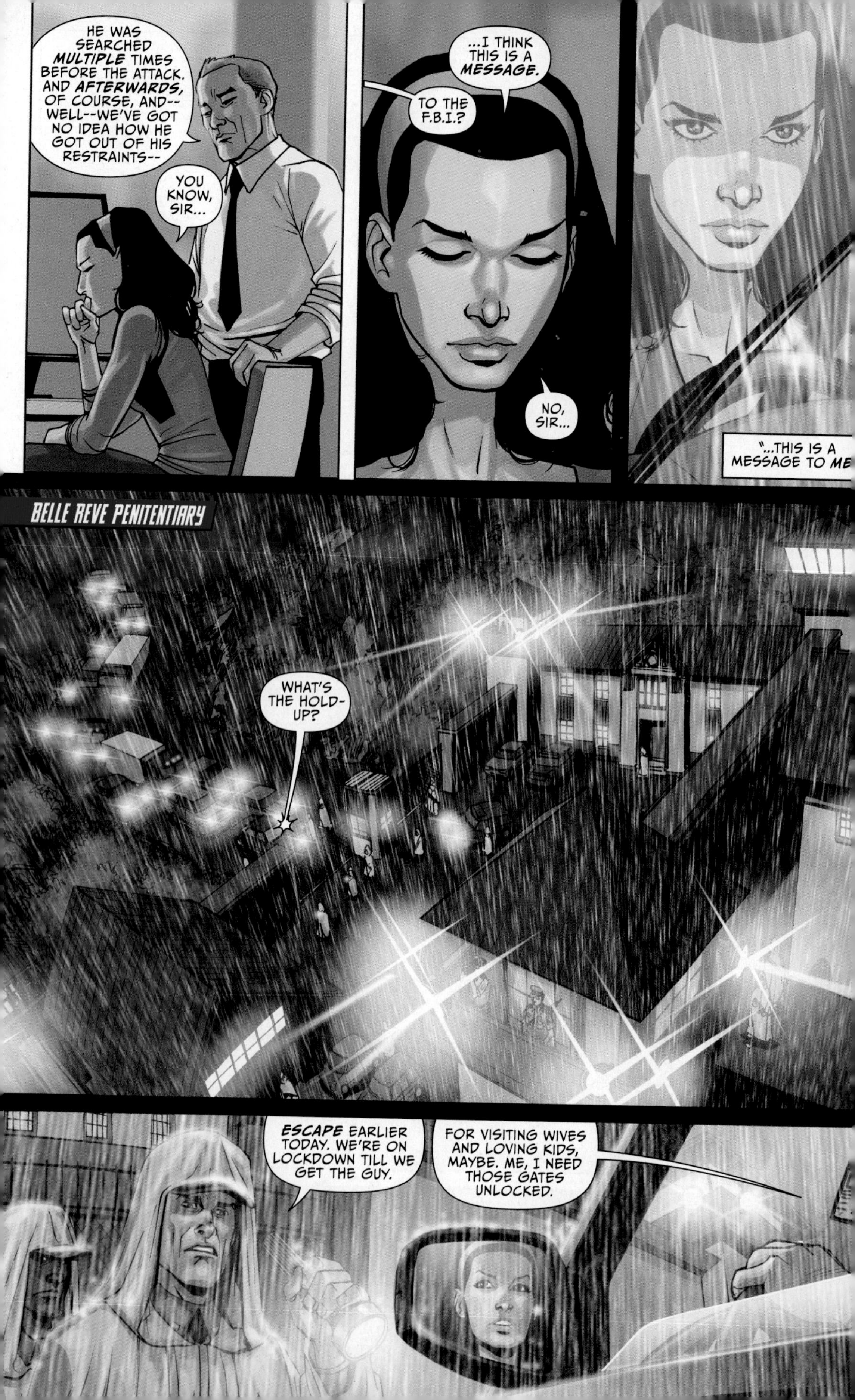
HE WAS SEARCHED MULTIPLE TIMES BEFORE THE ATTACK. AND AFTERWARDS, OF COURSE, AND-- WELL--WE'VE GOT NO IDEA HOW HE GOT OUT OF HIS RESTRAINTS--
YOU KNOW, SIR...
...I THINK THIS IS A MESSAGE.
TO THE F.B.I.?
NO, SIR...
"...THIS IS A MESSAGE TO ME
BELLE REVE PENITENTIARY
WHAT'S THE HOLD-UP?
ESCAPE EARLIER TODAY. WE'RE ON LOCKDOWN TILL WE GET THE GUY.
FOR VISITING WIVES AND LOVING KIDS, MAYBE. ME, I NEED THOSE GATES UNLOCKED.

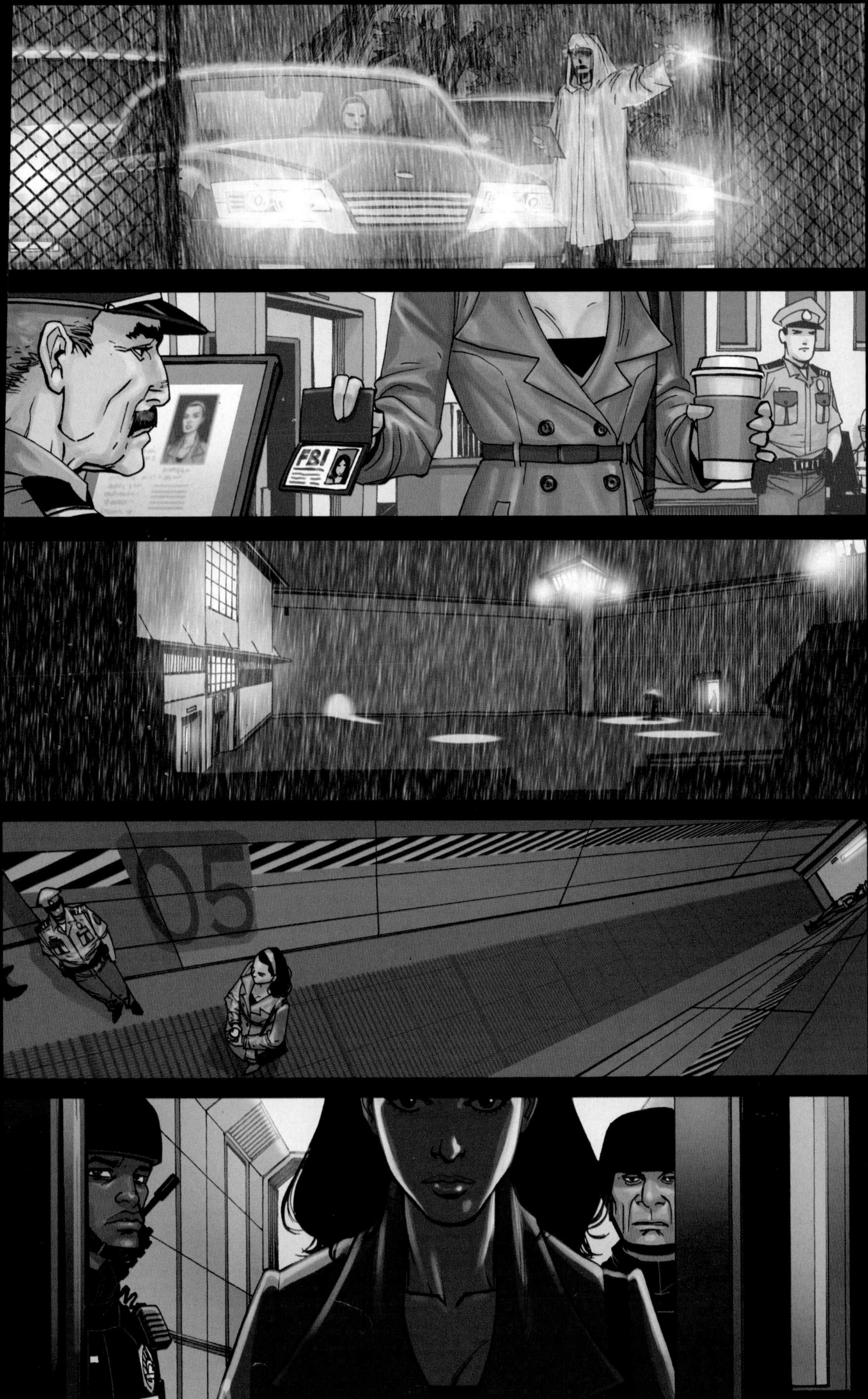
FBI
05

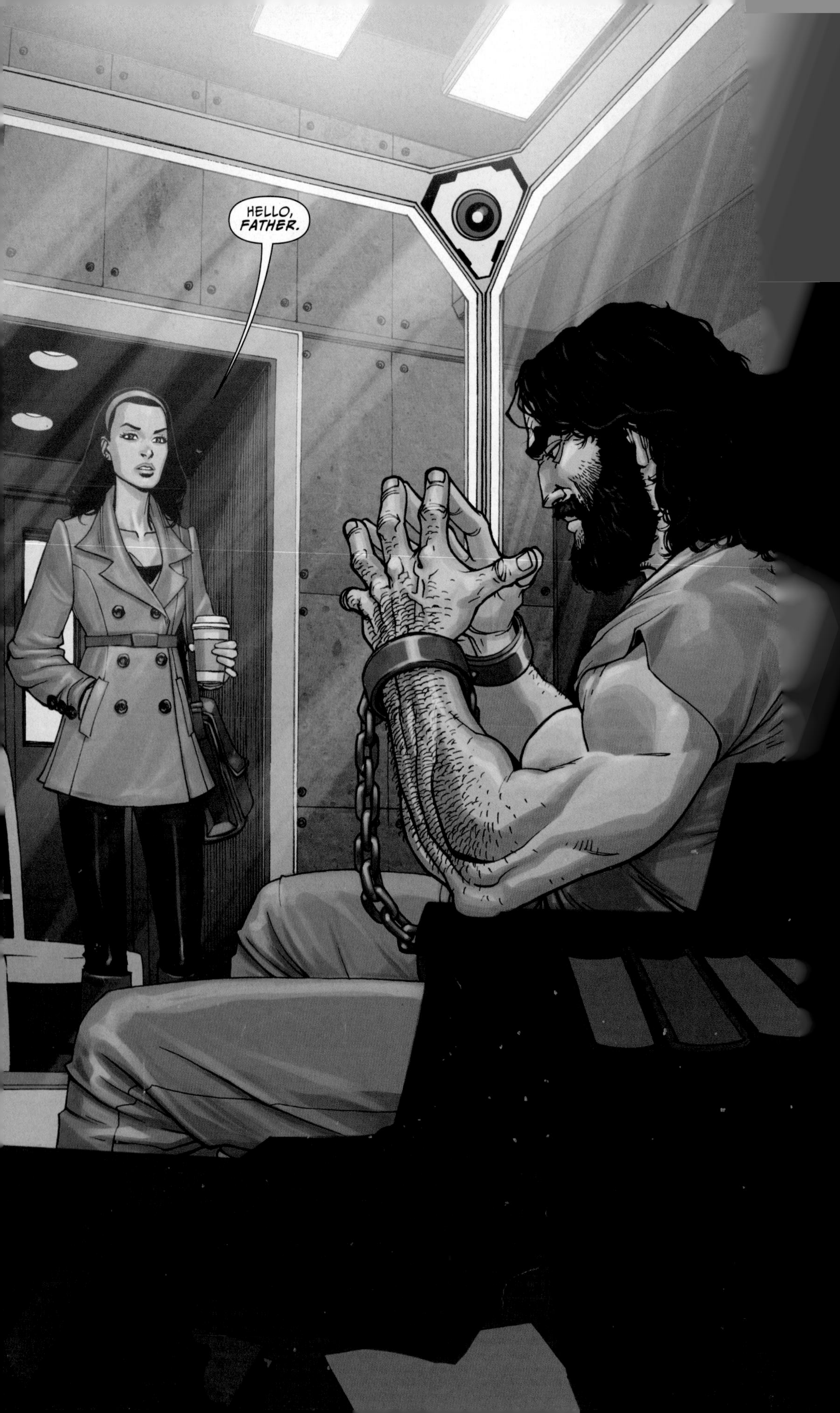
HELLO, FATHER.

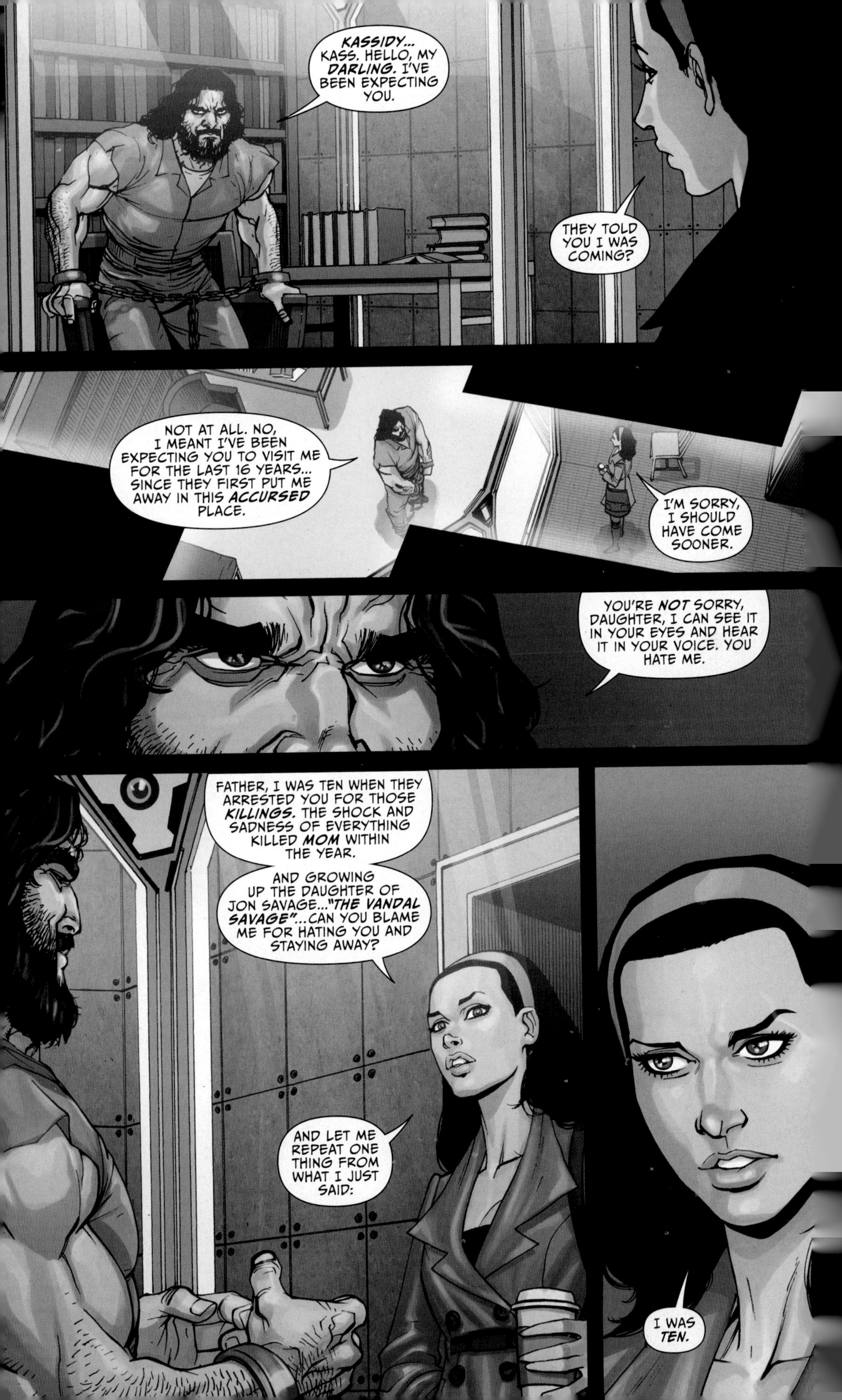
KASSIDY... KASS. HELLO, MY DARLING. I'VE BEEN EXPECTING YOU.
THEY TOLD YOU I WAS COMING?
NOT AT ALL. NO, I MEANT I'VE BEEN EXPECTING YOU TO VISIT ME FOR THE LAST 16 YEARS... SINCE THEY FIRST PUT ME AWAY IN THIS ACCURSED PLACE.
I'M SORRY, I SHOULD HAVE COME SOONER.
YOU'RE NOT SORRY, DAUGHTER, I CAN SEE IT IN YOUR EYES AND HEAR IT IN YOUR VOICE. YOU HATE ME.
FATHER, I WAS TEN WHEN THEY ARRESTED YOU FOR THOSE KILLINGS. THE SHOCK AND SADNESS OF EVERYTHING KILLED MOM WITHIN THE YEAR.
AND GROWING UP THE DAUGHTER OF JON SAVAGE..."THE VANDAL SAVAGE"...CAN YOU BLAME ME FOR HATING YOU AND STAYING AWAY?
AND LET ME REPEAT ONE THING FROM WHAT I JUST SAID:
I WAS TEN.

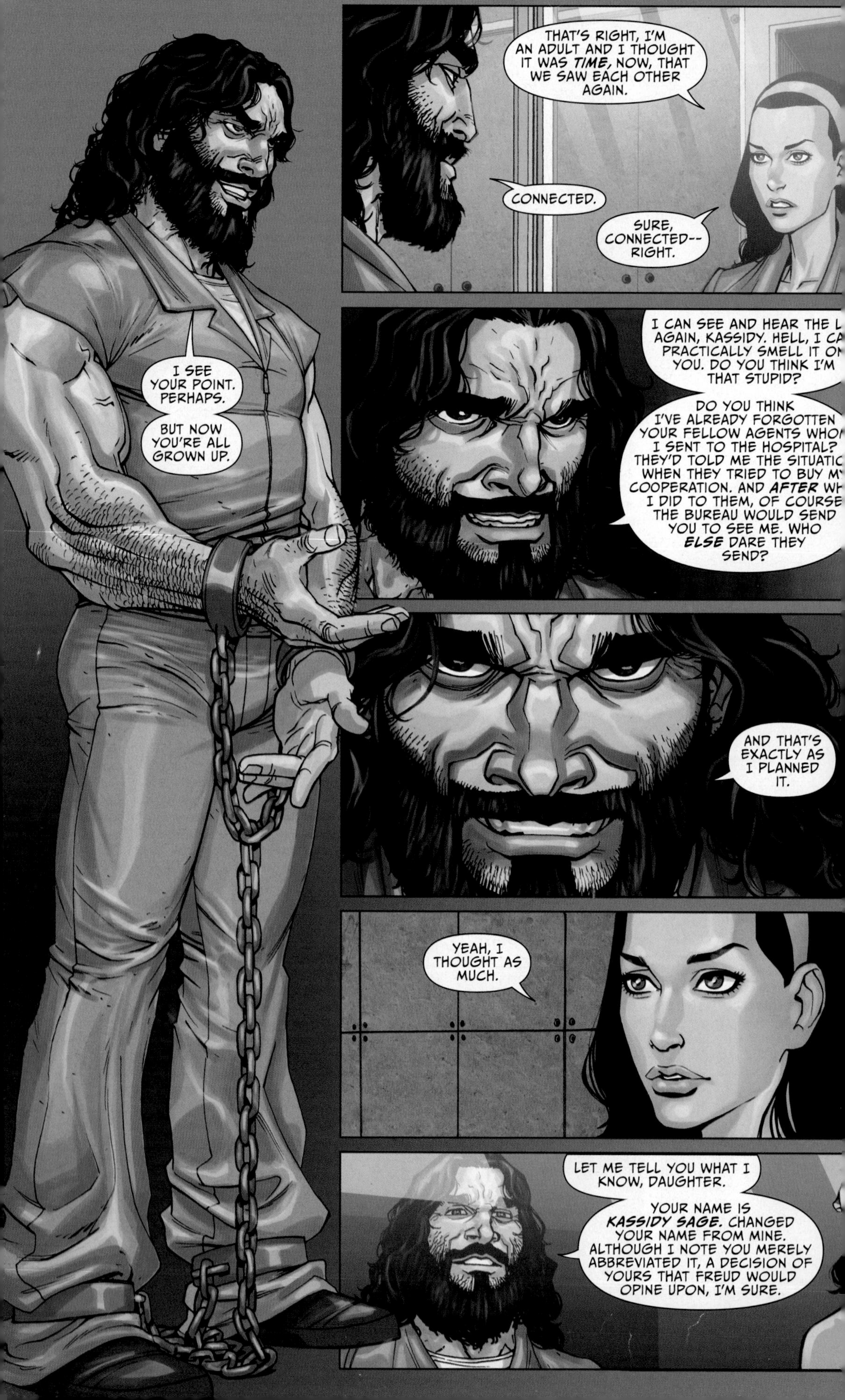
I SEE YOUR POINT. PERHAPS.
BUT NOW YOU'RE ALL GROWN UP.
THAT'S RIGHT, I'M AN ADULT AND I THOUGHT IT WAS TIME, NOW, THAT WE SAW EACH OTHER AGAIN.
CONNECTED.
SURE, CONNECTED-- RIGHT.
I CAN SEE AND HEAR THE L AGAIN, KASSIDY. HELL, I CA PRACTICALLY SMELL IT ON YOU. DO YOU THINK I'M THAT STUPID?
DO YOU THINK I'VE ALREADY FORGOTTEN YOUR FELLOW AGENTS WHOM I SENT TO THE HOSPITAL? THEY'D TOLD ME THE SITUATIC WHEN THEY TRIED TO BUY M COOPERATION. AND AFTER WH I DID TO THEM, OF COURSE THE BUREAU WOULD SEND YOU TO SEE ME. WHO ELSE DARE THEY SEND?
AND THAT'S EXACTLY AS I PLANNED IT.
YEAH, I THOUGHT AS MUCH.
LET ME TELL YOU WHAT I KNOW, DAUGHTER.
YOUR NAME IS KASSIDY SAGE. CHANGED YOUR NAME FROM MINE. ALTHOUGH I NOTE YOU MERELY ABBREVIATED IT, A DECISION OF YOURS THAT FREUD WOULD OPINE UPON, I'M SURE.

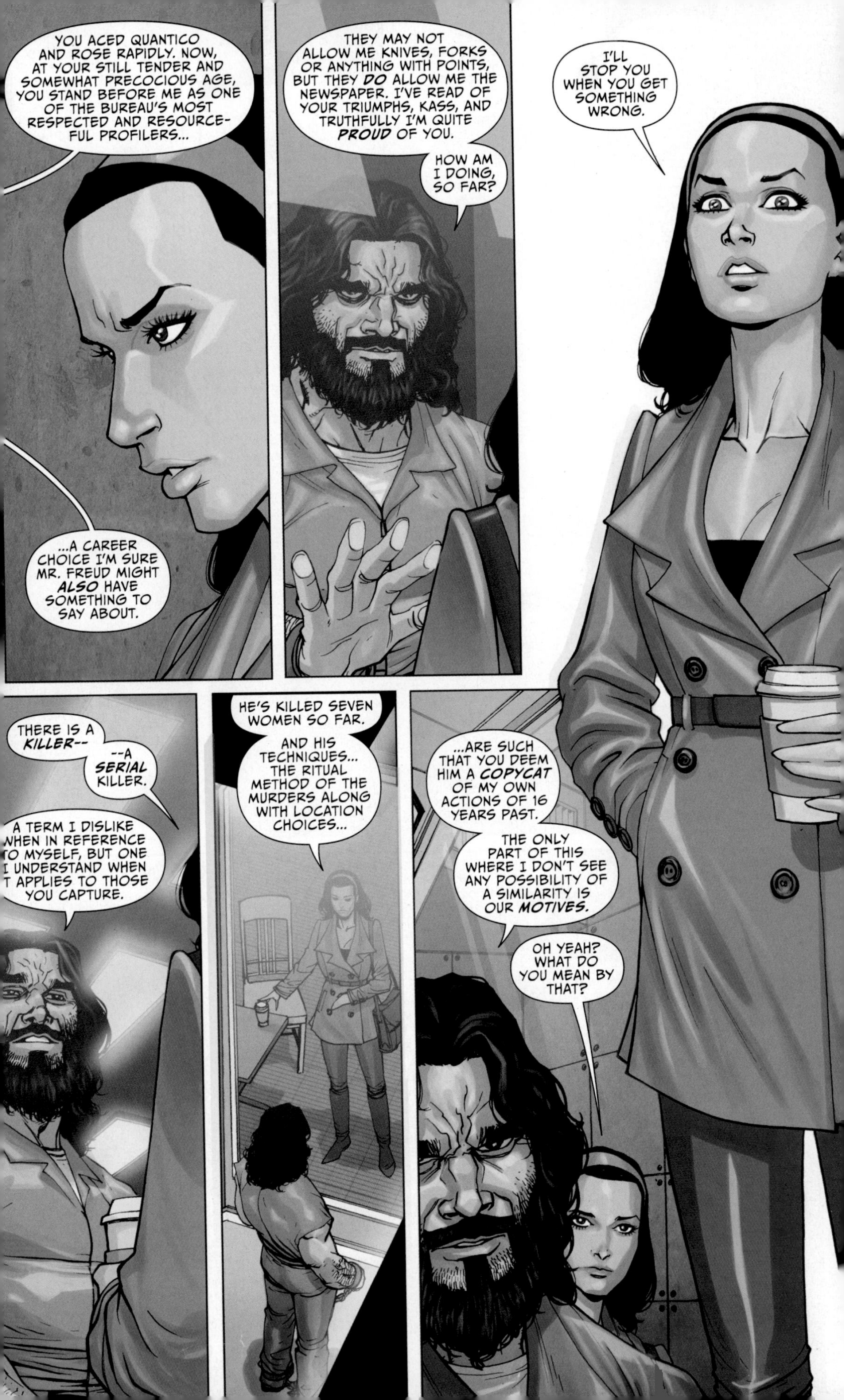
YOU ACED QUANTICO AND ROSE RAPIDLY. NOW, AT YOUR STILL TENDER AND SOMEWHAT PRECOCIOUS AGE, YOU STAND BEFORE ME AS ONE OF THE BUREAU'S MOST RESPECTED AND RESOURCEFUL PROFILERS...
...A CAREER CHOICE I'M SURE MR. FREUD MIGHT ALSO HAVE SOMETHING TO SAY ABOUT.
THEY MAY NOT ALLOW ME KNIVES, FORKS OR ANYTHING WITH POINTS, BUT THEY DO ALLOW ME THE NEWSPAPER. I'VE READ OF YOUR TRIUMPHS, KASS, AND TRUTHFULLY I'M QUITE PROUD OF YOU.
HOW AM I DOING, SO FAR?
I'LL STOP YOU WHEN YOU GET SOMETHING WRONG.
THERE IS A KILLER--
--A SERIAL KILLER.
A TERM I DISLIKE WHEN IN REFERENCE TO MYSELF, BUT ONE I UNDERSTAND WHEN IT APPLIES TO THOSE YOU CAPTURE.
HE'S KILLED SEVEN WOMEN SO FAR.
AND HIS TECHNIQUES... THE RITUAL METHOD OF THE MURDERS ALONG WITH LOCATION CHOICES...
...ARE SUCH THAT YOU DEEM HIM A COPYCAT OF MY OWN ACTIONS OF 16 YEARS PAST.
THE ONLY PART OF THIS WHERE I DON'T SEE ANY POSSIBILITY OF A SIMILARITY IS OUR MOTIVES.
OH YEAH? WHAT DO YOU MEAN BY THAT?

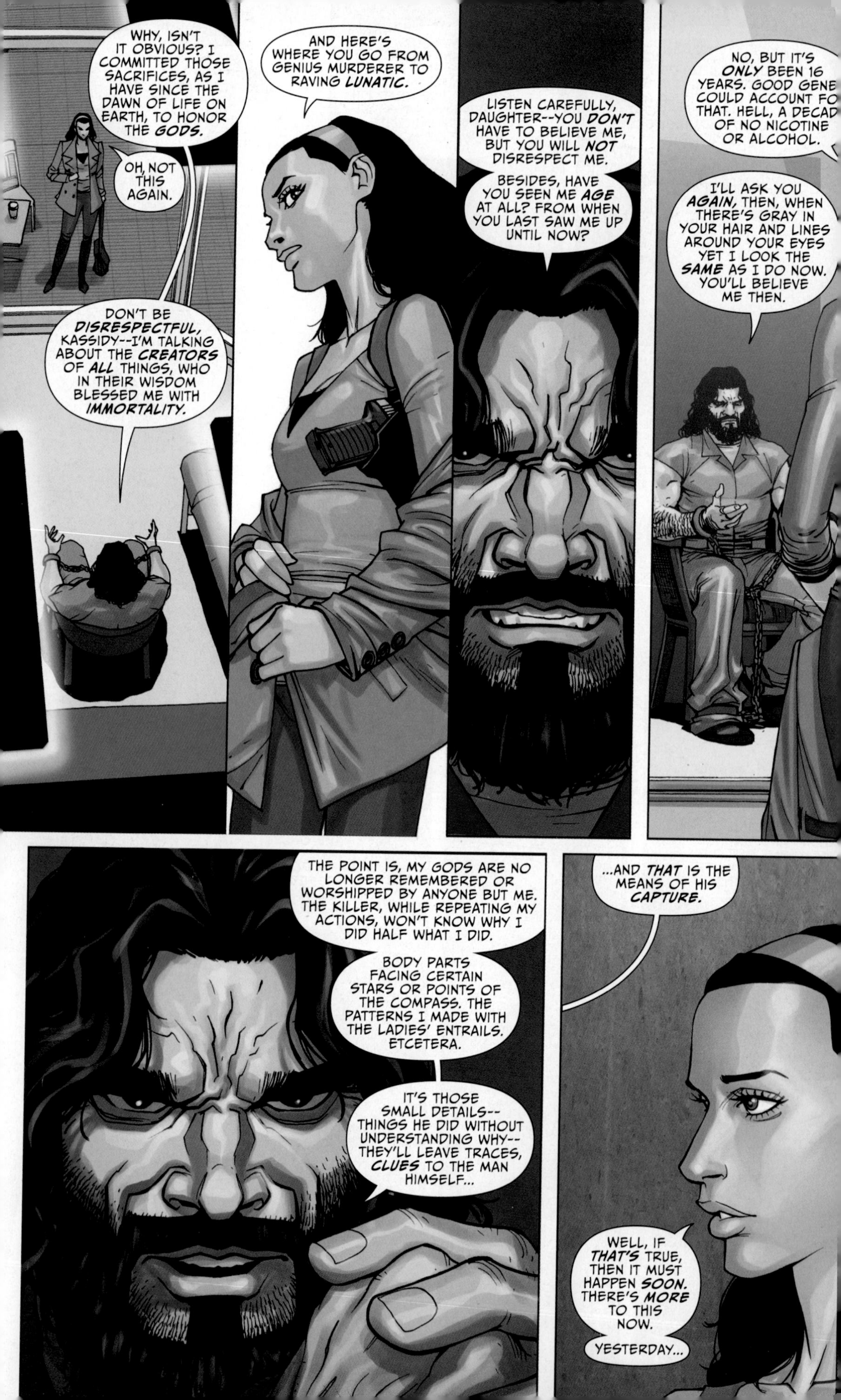

WHY, ISN'T IT OBVIOUS? I COMMITTED THOSE SACRIFICES, AS I HAVE SINCE THE DAWN OF LIFE ON EARTH, TO HONOR THE GODS.
OH, NOT THIS AGAIN.
DON'T BE DISRESPECTFUL, KASSIDY--I'M TALKING ABOUT THE CREATORS OF ALL THINGS, WHO IN THEIR WISDOM BLESSED ME WITH IMMORTALITY.
AND HERE'S WHERE YOU GO FROM GENIUS MURDERER TO RAVING LUNATIC.
LISTEN CAREFULLY, DAUGHTER--YOU DON'T HAVE TO BELIEVE ME, BUT YOU WILL NOT DISRESPECT ME.
BESIDES, HAVE YOU SEEN ME AGE AT ALL? FROM WHEN YOU LAST SAW ME UP UNTIL NOW?
NO, BUT IT'S ONLY BEEN 16 YEARS. GOOD GENE COULD ACCOUNT FO THAT. HELL, A DECAD OF NO NICOTINE OR ALCOHOL.
I'LL ASK YOU AGAIN, THEN, WHEN THERE'S GRAY IN YOUR HAIR AND LINES AROUND YOUR EYES YET I LOOK THE SAME AS I DO NOW. YOU'LL BELIEVE ME THEN.
THE POINT IS, MY GODS ARE NO LONGER REMEMBERED OR WORSHIPPED BY ANYONE BUT ME. THE KILLER, WHILE REPEATING MY ACTIONS, WON'T KNOW WHY I DID HALF WHAT I DID.
BODY PARTS FACING CERTAIN STARS OR POINTS OF THE COMPASS. THE PATTERNS I MADE WITH THE LADIES' ENTRAILS. ETCETERA.
IT'S THOSE SMALL DETAILS--THINGS HE DID WITHOUT UNDERSTANDING WHY--THEY'LL LEAVE TRACES, CLUES TO THE MAN HIMSELF...
...AND THAT IS THE MEANS OF HIS CAPTURE.
WELL, IF THAT'S TRUE, THEN IT MUST HAPPEN SOON. THERE'S MORE TO THIS NOW.
YESTERDAY...

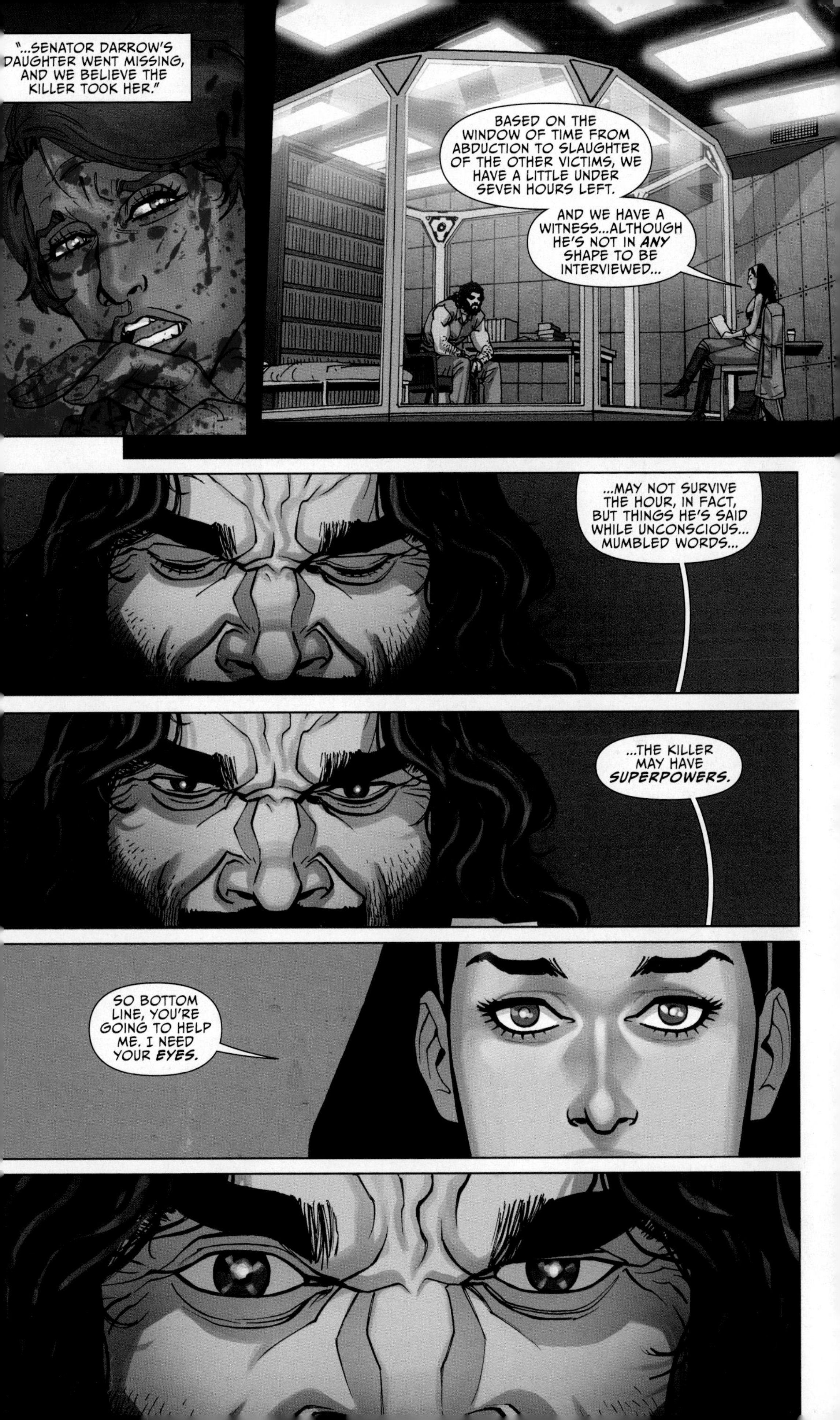
"...SENATOR DARROW'S DAUGHTER WENT MISSING, AND WE BELIEVE THE KILLER TOOK HER."
BASED ON THE WINDOW OF TIME FROM ABDUCTION TO SLAUGHTER OF THE OTHER VICTIMS, WE HAVE A LITTLE UNDER SEVEN HOURS LEFT.
AND WE HAVE A WITNESS...ALTHOUGH HE'S NOT IN ANY SHAPE TO BE INTERVIEWED...
...MAY NOT SURVIVE THE HOUR, IN FACT, BUT THINGS HE'S SAID WHILE UNCONSCIOUS... MUMBLED WORDS...
...THE KILLER MAY HAVE SUPERPOWERS.
SO BOTTOM LINE, YOU'RE GOING TO HELP ME. I NEED YOUR EYES.

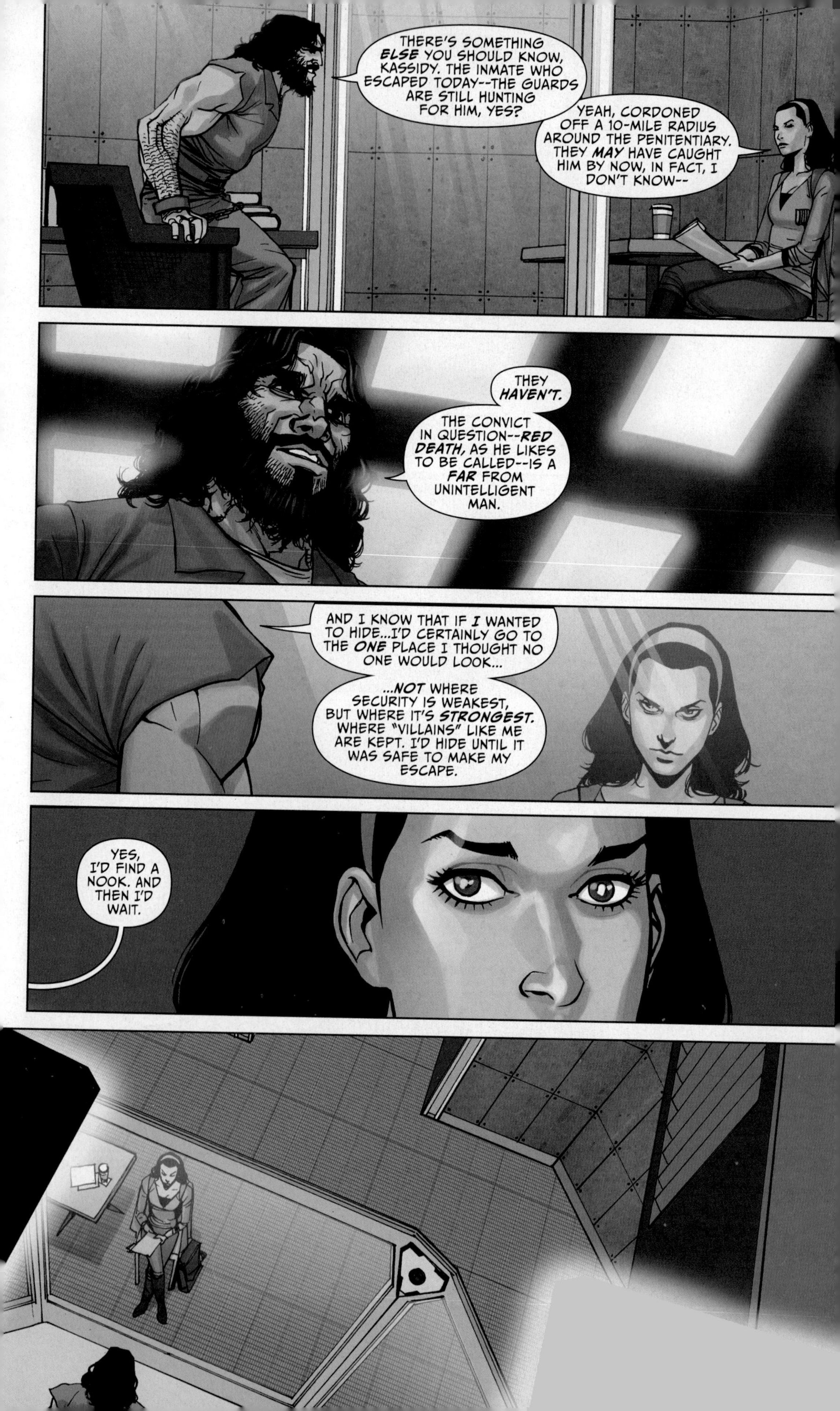
THERE'S SOMETHING ELSE YOU SHOULD KNOW, KASSIDY. THE INMATE WHO ESCAPED TODAY--THE GUARDS ARE STILL HUNTING FOR HIM, YES?
YEAH, CORDONED OFF A 10-MILE RADIUS AROUND THE PENITENTIARY. THEY MAY HAVE CAUGHT HIM BY NOW, IN FACT, I DON'T KNOW--
THEY HAVEN'T.
THE CONVICT IN QUESTION--RED DEATH, AS HE LIKES TO BE CALLED--IS A FAR FROM UNINTELLIGENT MAN.
AND I KNOW THAT IF I WANTED TO HIDE...I'D CERTAINLY GO TO THE ONE PLACE I THOUGHT NO ONE WOULD LOOK...
...NOT WHERE SECURITY IS WEAKEST, BUT WHERE IT'S STRONGEST. WHERE "VILLAINS" LIKE ME ARE KEPT. I'D HIDE UNTIL IT WAS SAFE TO MAKE MY ESCAPE.
YES, I'D FIND A NOOK. AND THEN I'D WAIT.

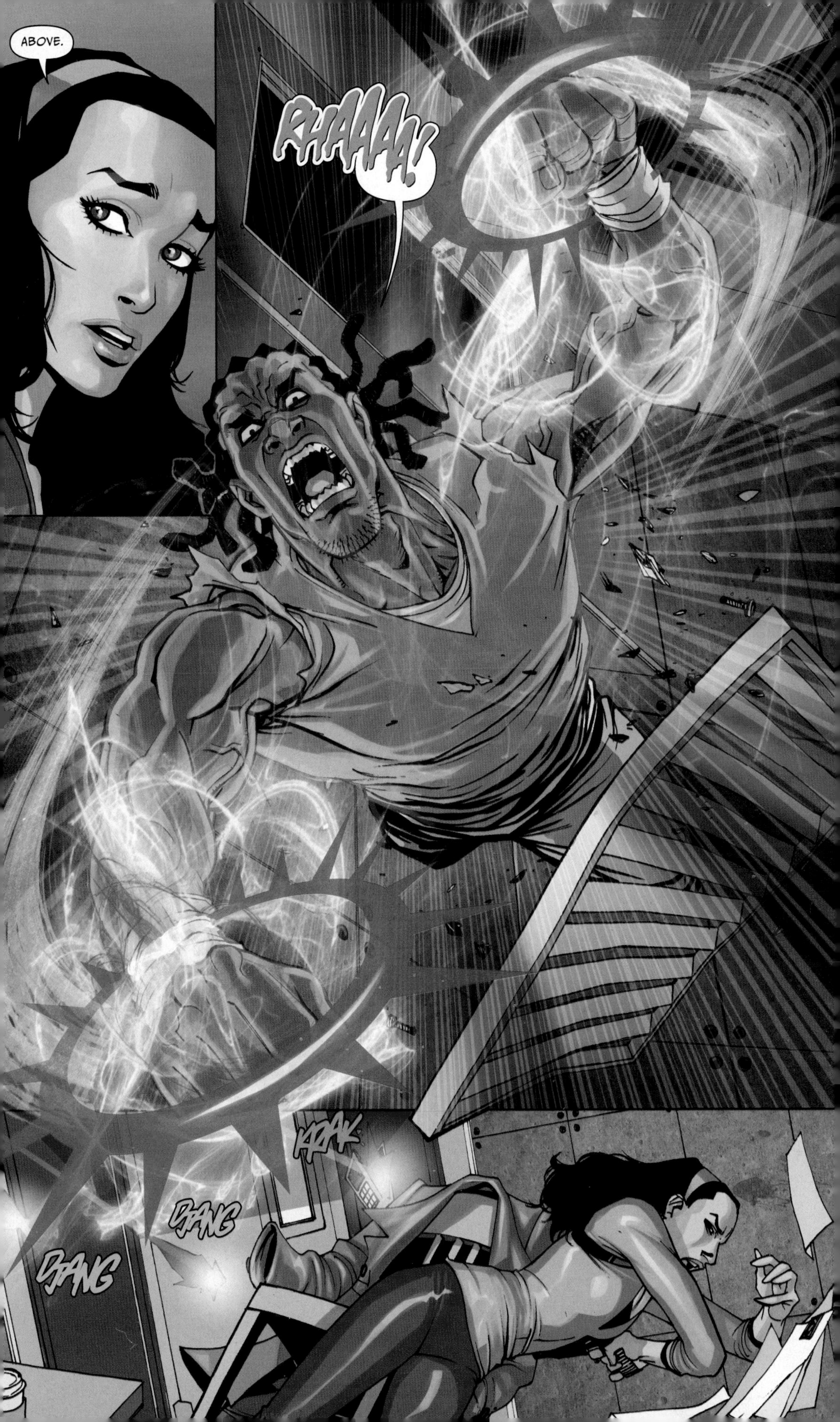
ABOVE.
RHAAAAA!
KRAK
DJANG
DJANG

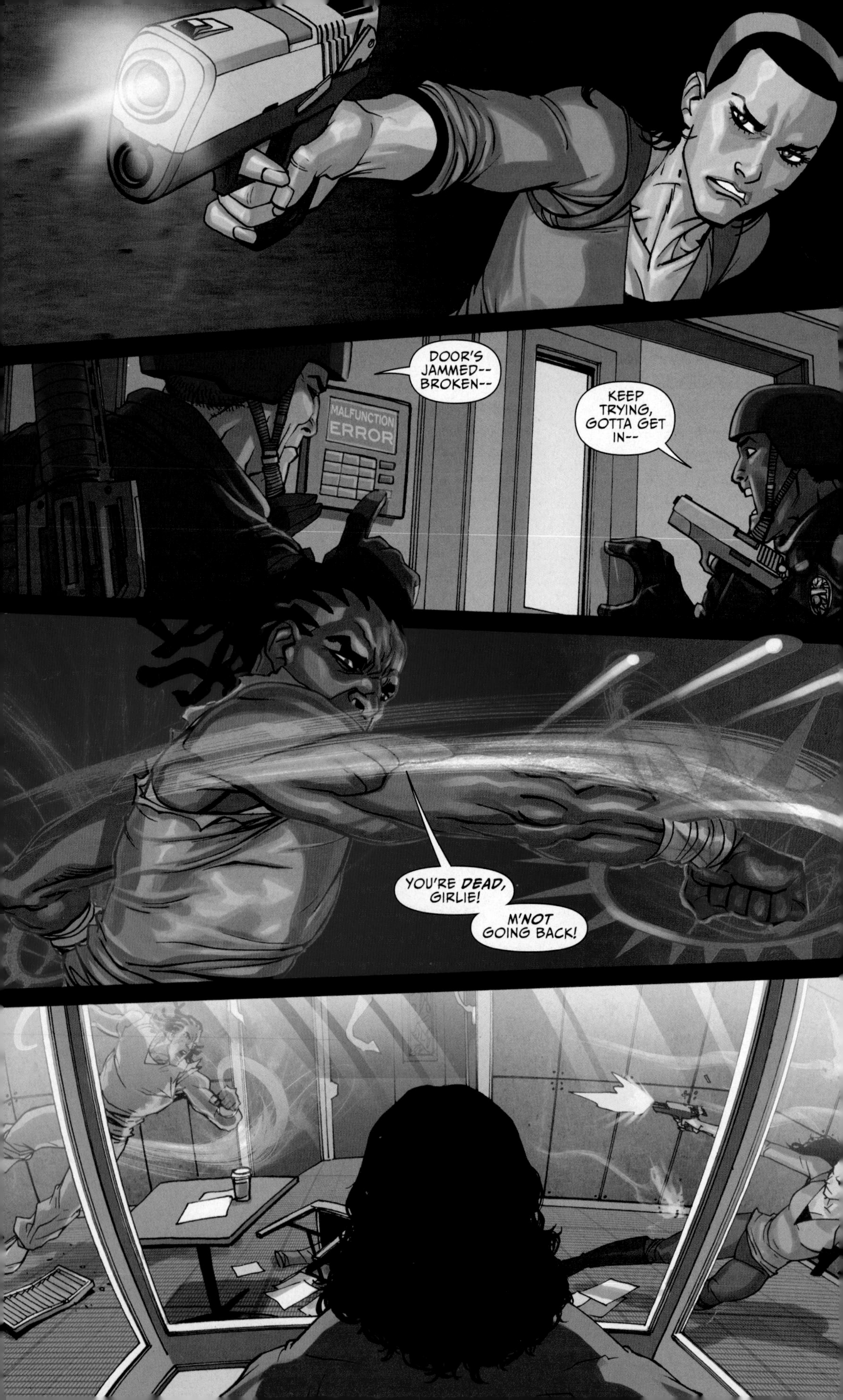
DOOR'S JAMMED-- BROKEN--
MALFUNCTION ERROR
KEEP TRYING, GOTTA GET IN--
YOU'RE *DEAD,* GIRLIE!
M'*NOT* GOING BACK!

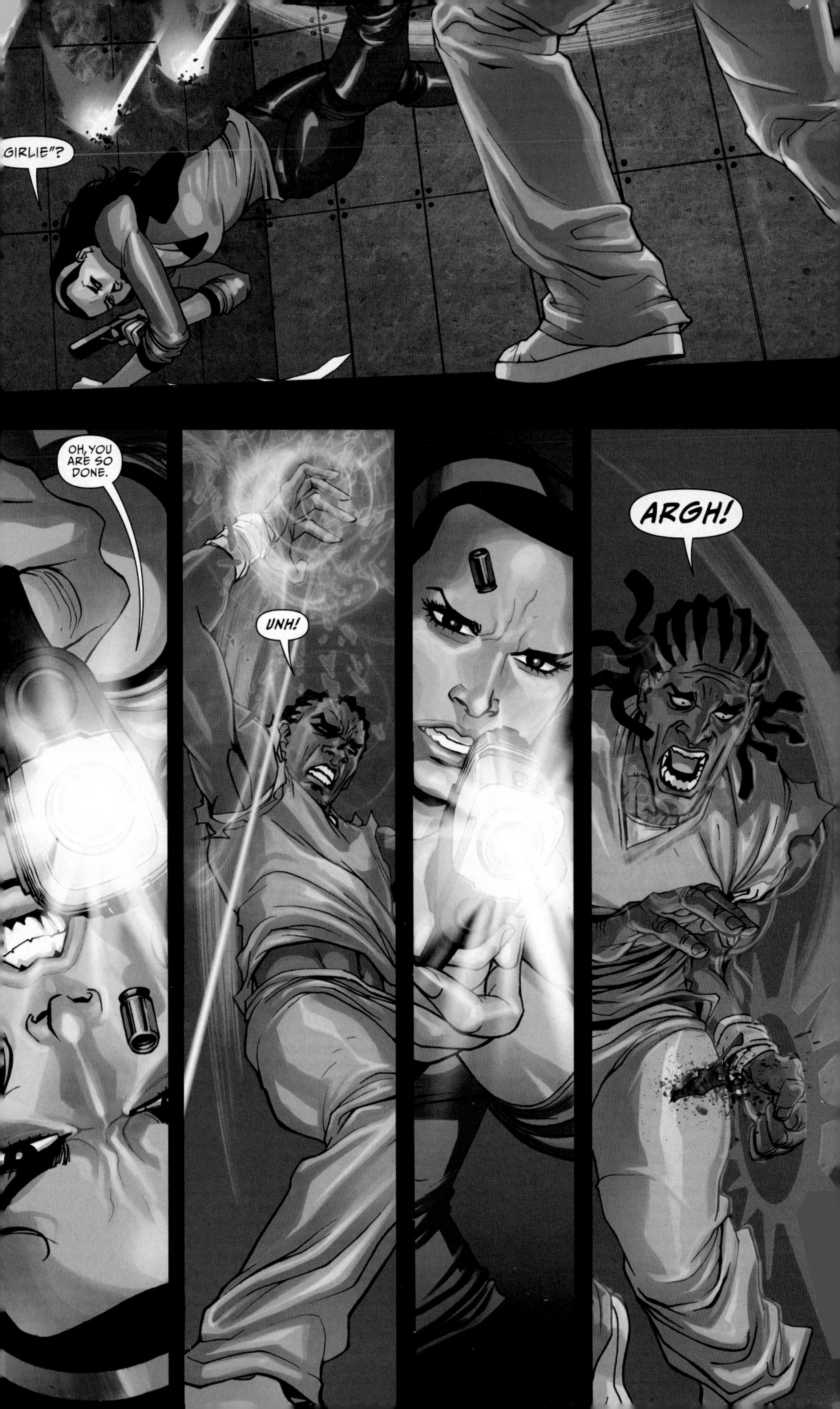
GIRLIE"?
OH, YOU ARE SO DONE.
UNH!
ARGH!

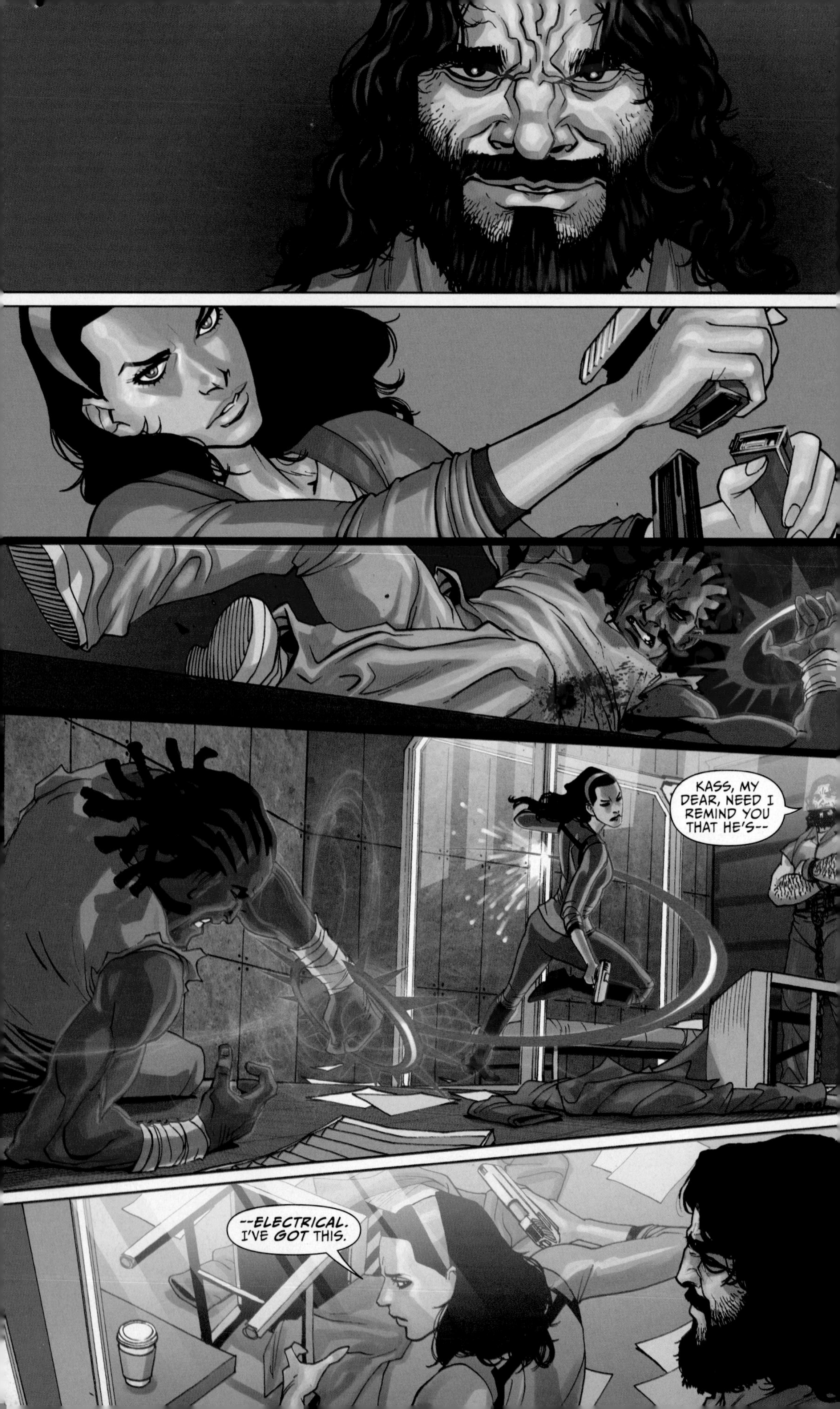
KASS, MY DEAR, NEED I REMIND YOU THAT HE'S--
--ELECTRICAL. I'VE GOT THIS.

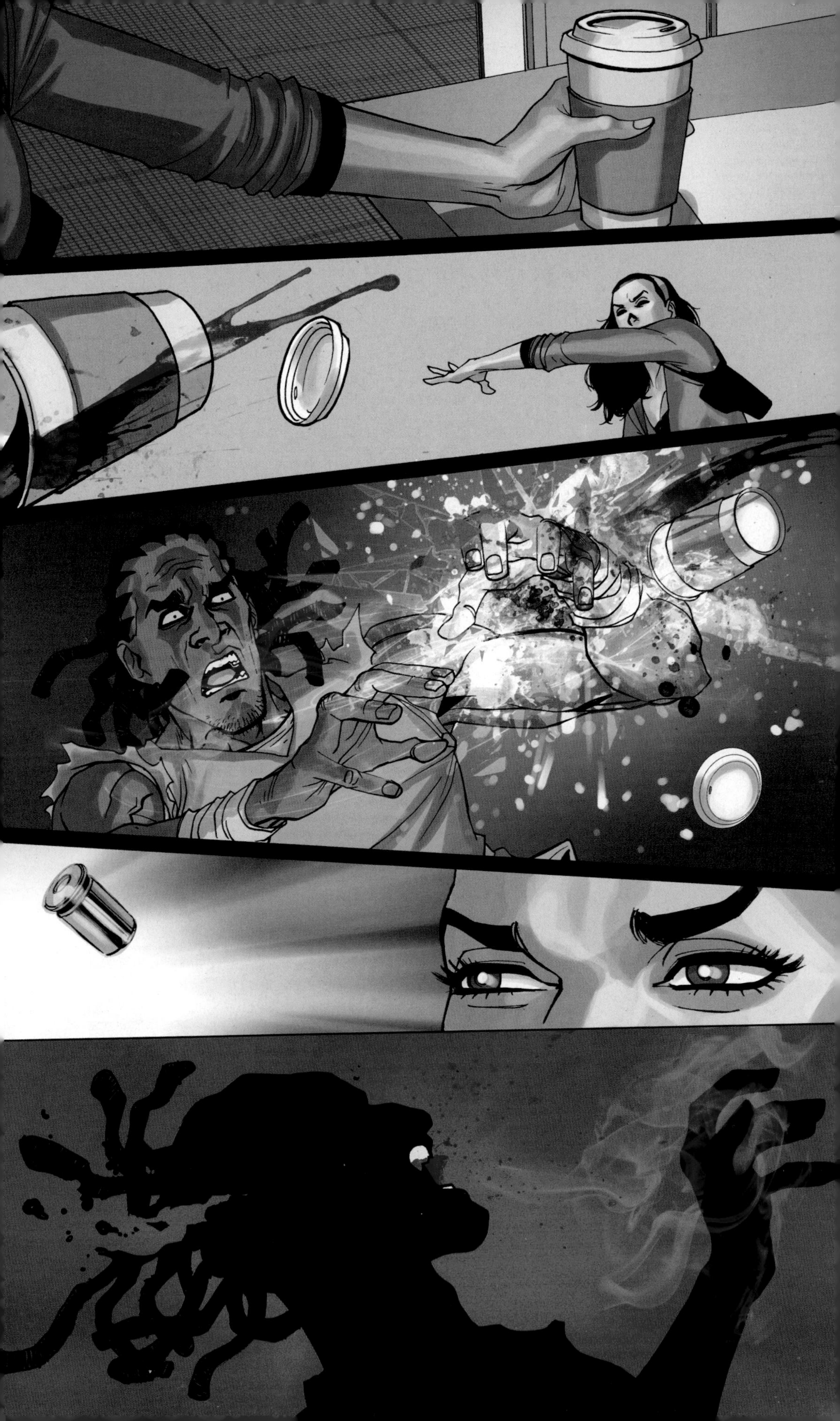

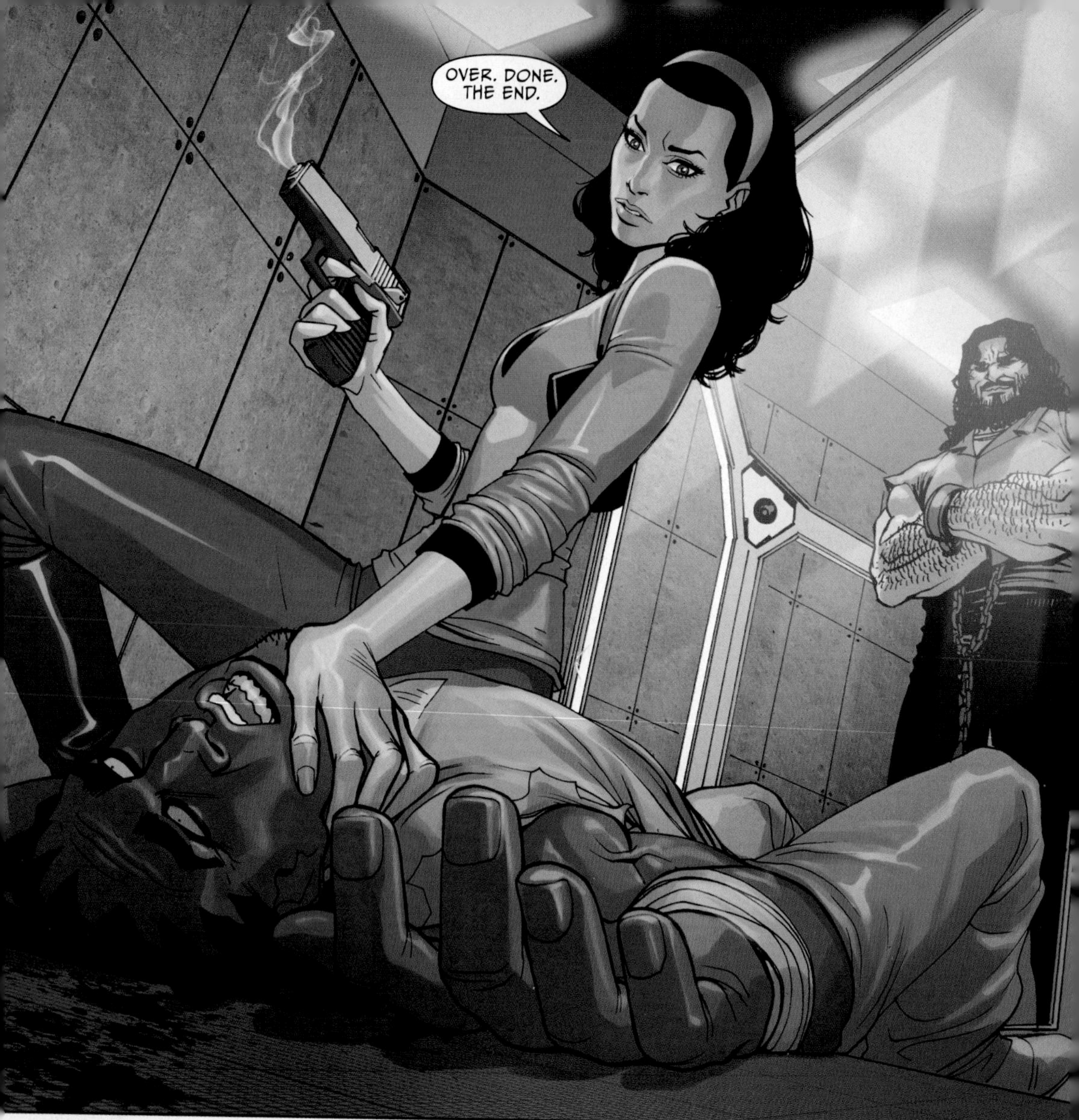
OVER. DONE. THE END.

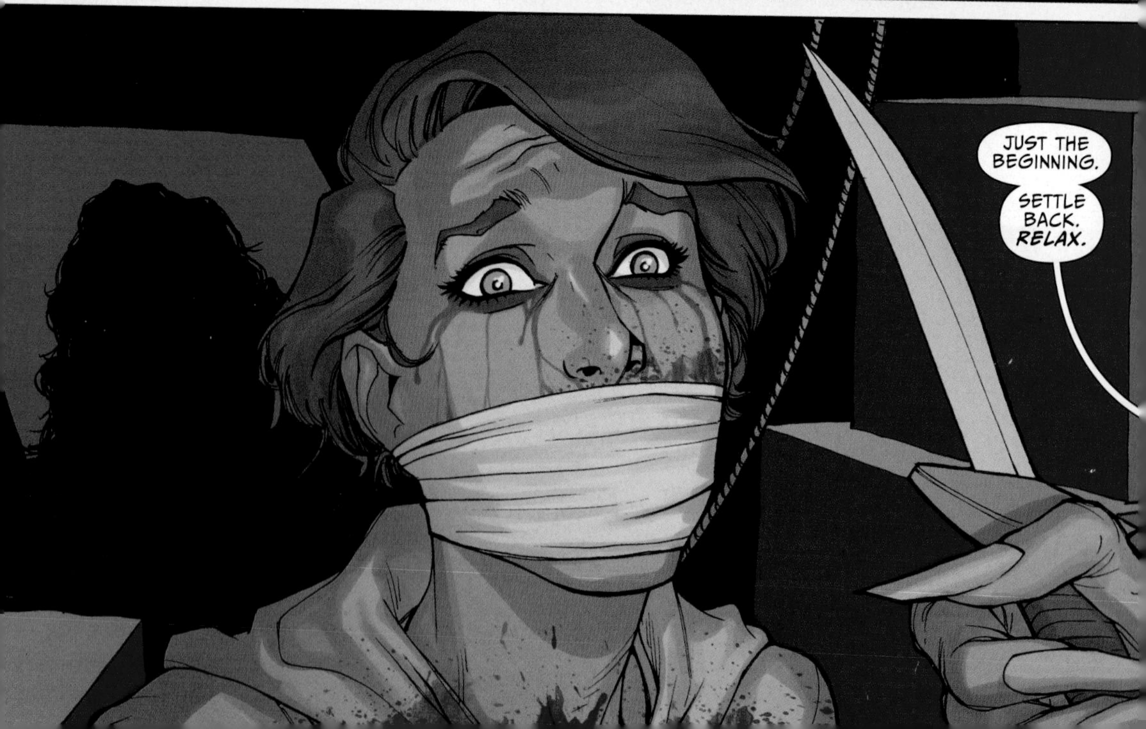
JUST THE BEGINNING.
SETTLE BACK. RELAX.

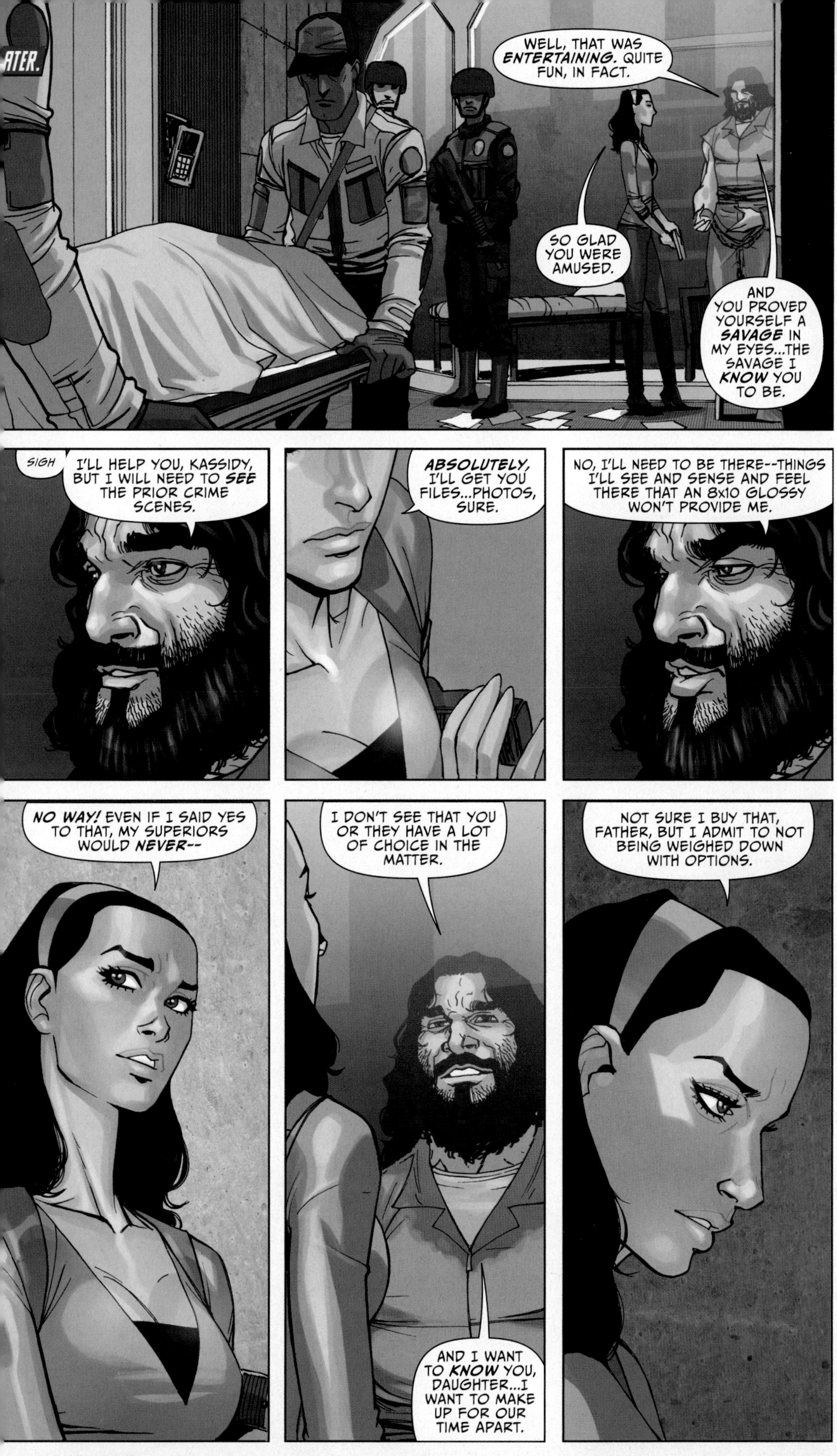
ATER.
WELL, THAT WAS ENTERTAINING. QUITE FUN, IN FACT.
SO GLAD YOU WERE AMUSED.
AND YOU PROVED YOURSELF A SAVAGE IN MY EYES...THE SAVAGE I KNOW YOU TO BE.
SIGH
I'LL HELP YOU, KASSIDY, BUT I WILL NEED TO SEE THE PRIOR CRIME SCENES.
ABSOLUTELY, I'LL GET YOU FILES...PHOTOS, SURE.
NO, I'LL NEED TO BE THERE--THINGS I'LL SEE AND SENSE AND FEEL THERE THAT AN 8x10 GLOSSY WON'T PROVIDE ME.
NO WAY! EVEN IF I SAID YES TO THAT, MY SUPERIORS WOULD NEVER--
I DON'T SEE THAT YOU OR THEY HAVE A LOT OF CHOICE IN THE MATTER.
AND I WANT TO KNOW YOU, DAUGHTER...I WANT TO MAKE UP FOR OUR TIME APART.
NOT SURE I BUY THAT, FATHER, BUT I ADMIT TO NOT BEING WEIGHED DOWN WITH OPTIONS.

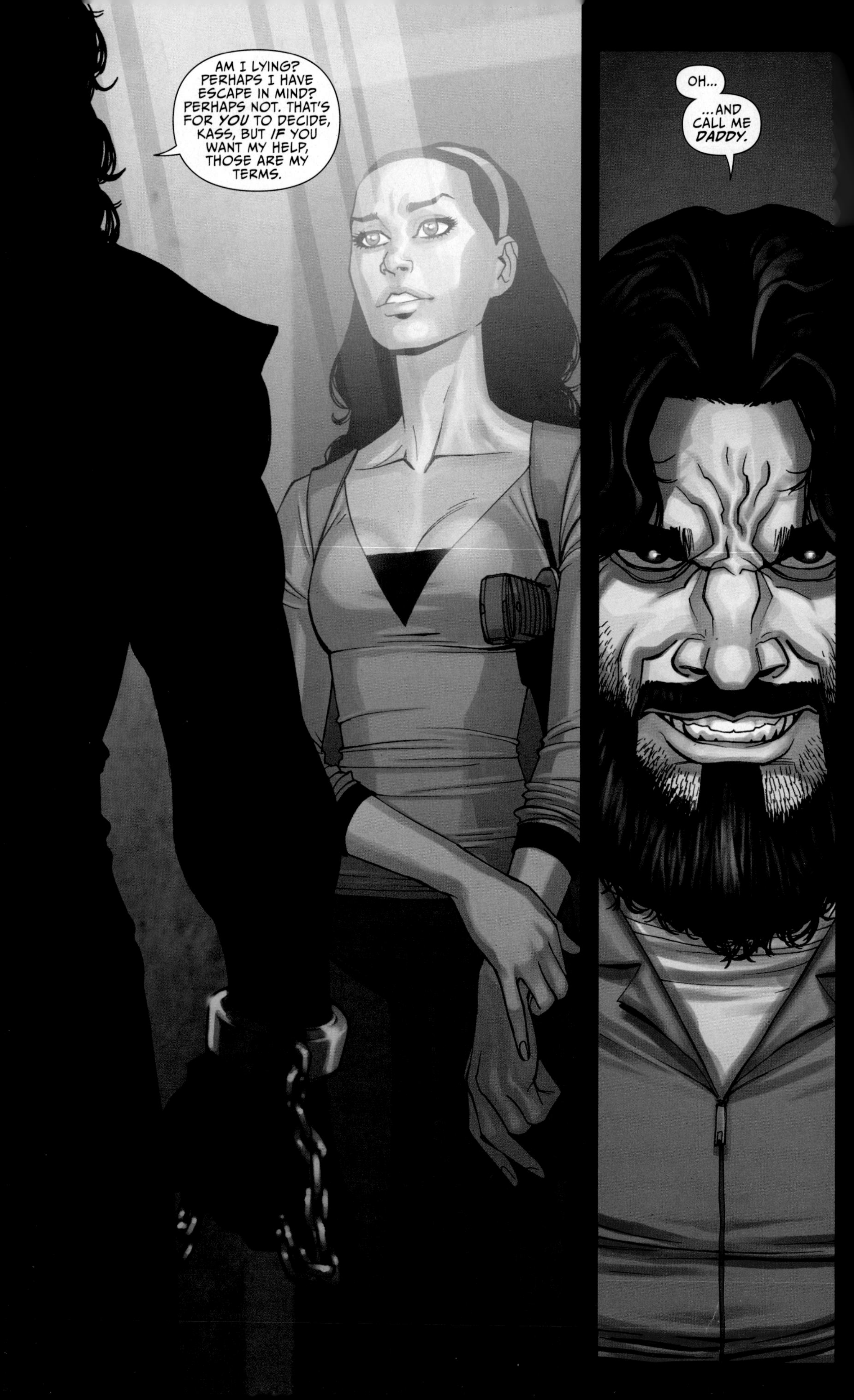
AM I LYING? PERHAPS I HAVE ESCAPE IN MIND? PERHAPS NOT. THAT'S FOR *YOU* TO DECIDE, KASS, BUT *IF* YOU WANT MY HELP, THOSE ARE MY TERMS.
OH...
...AND CALL ME *DADDY*.

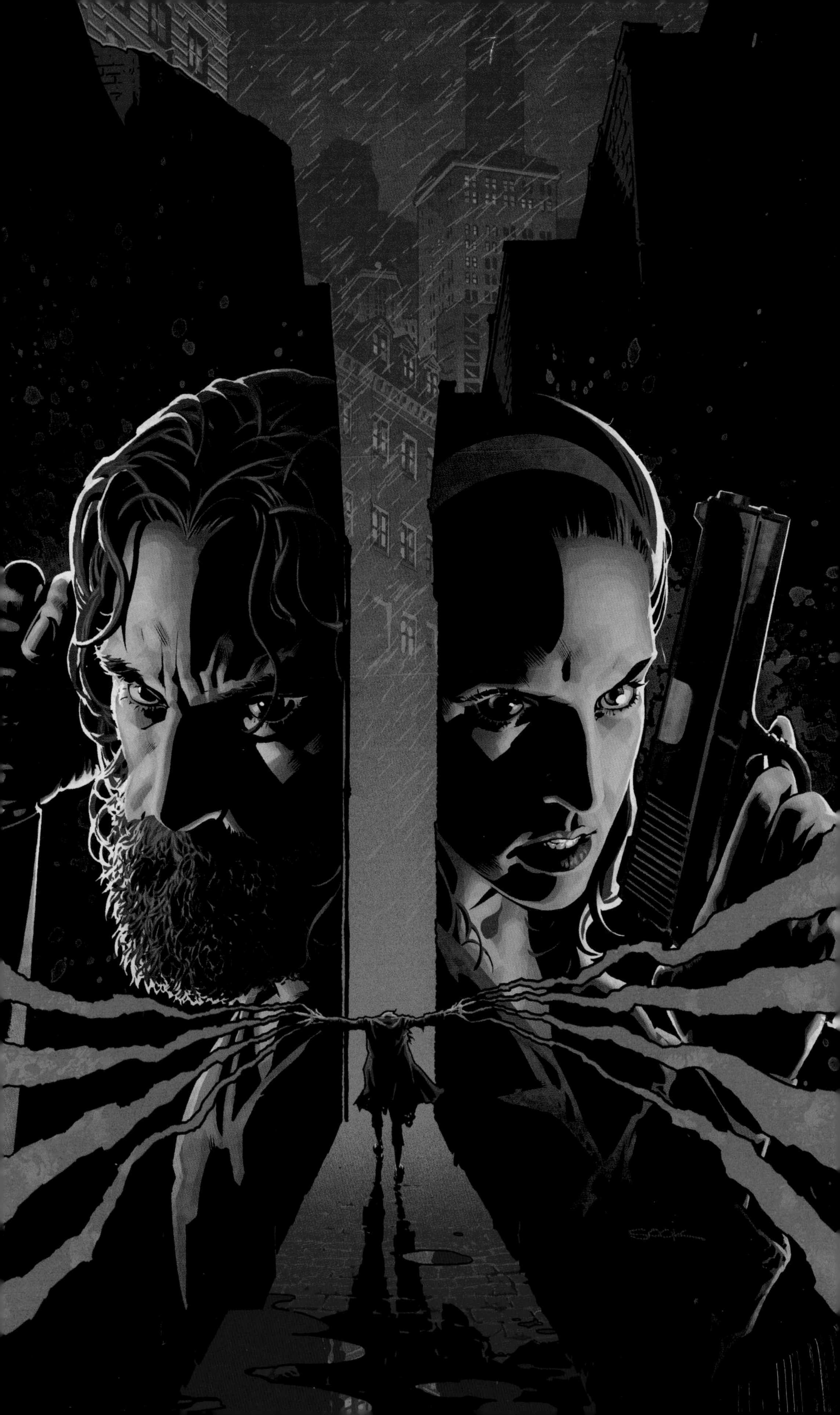

PART TWO: FATHER'S DAY OUT

JAMES ROBINSON writer BERNARD CHANG artist

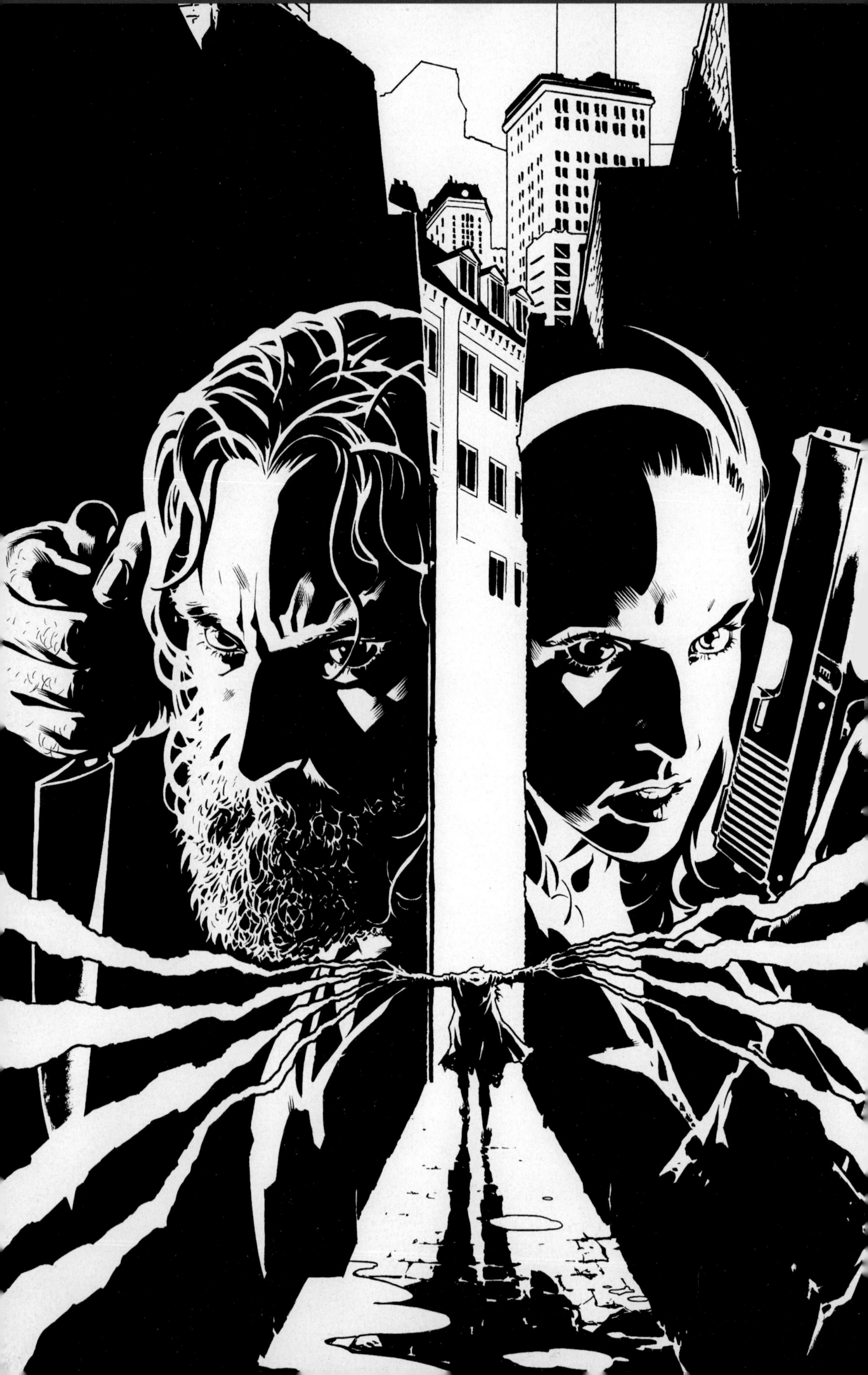

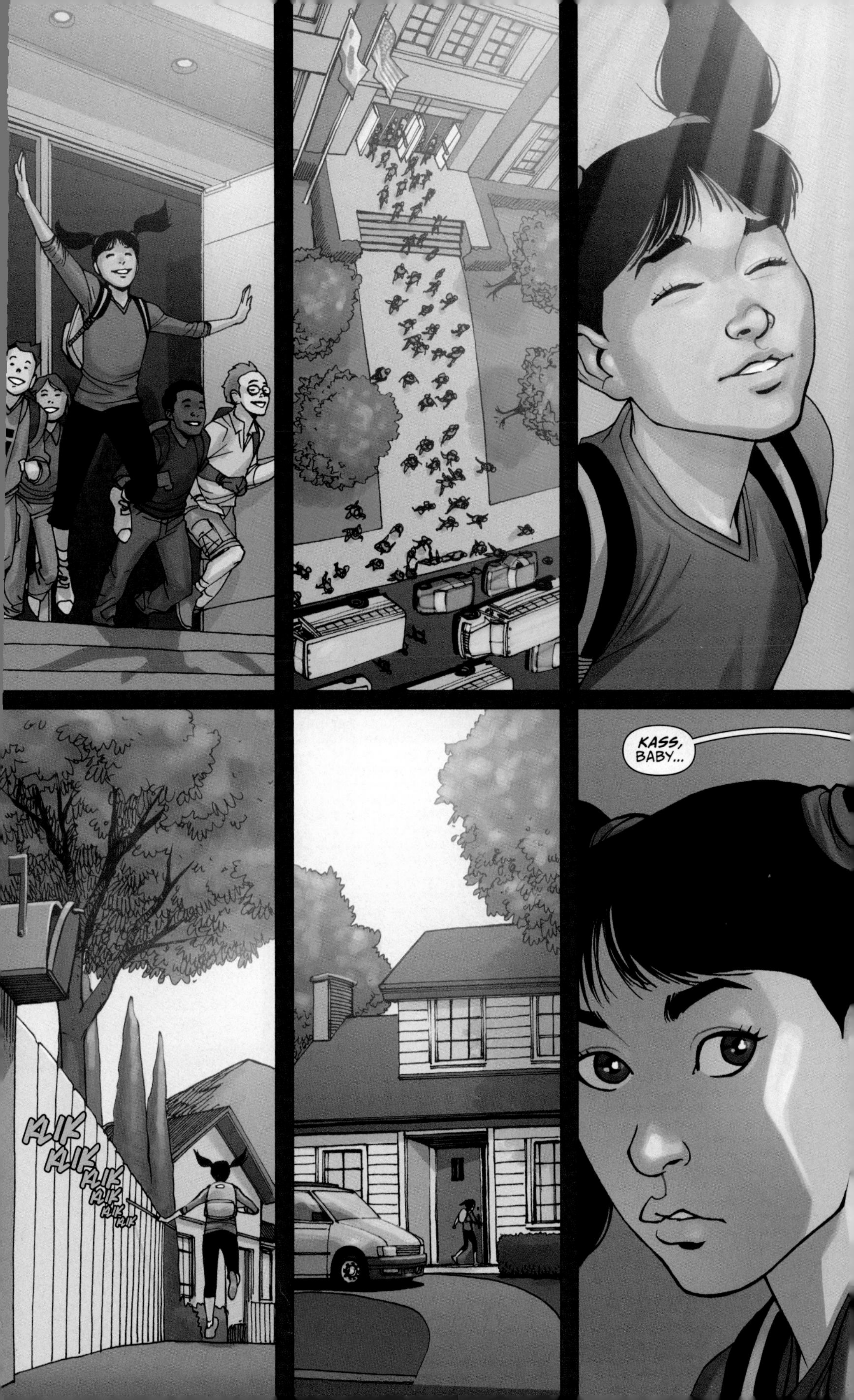
KLIK
KLIK
KLIK
KLIK
KLIK
KLIK
KASS, BABY...

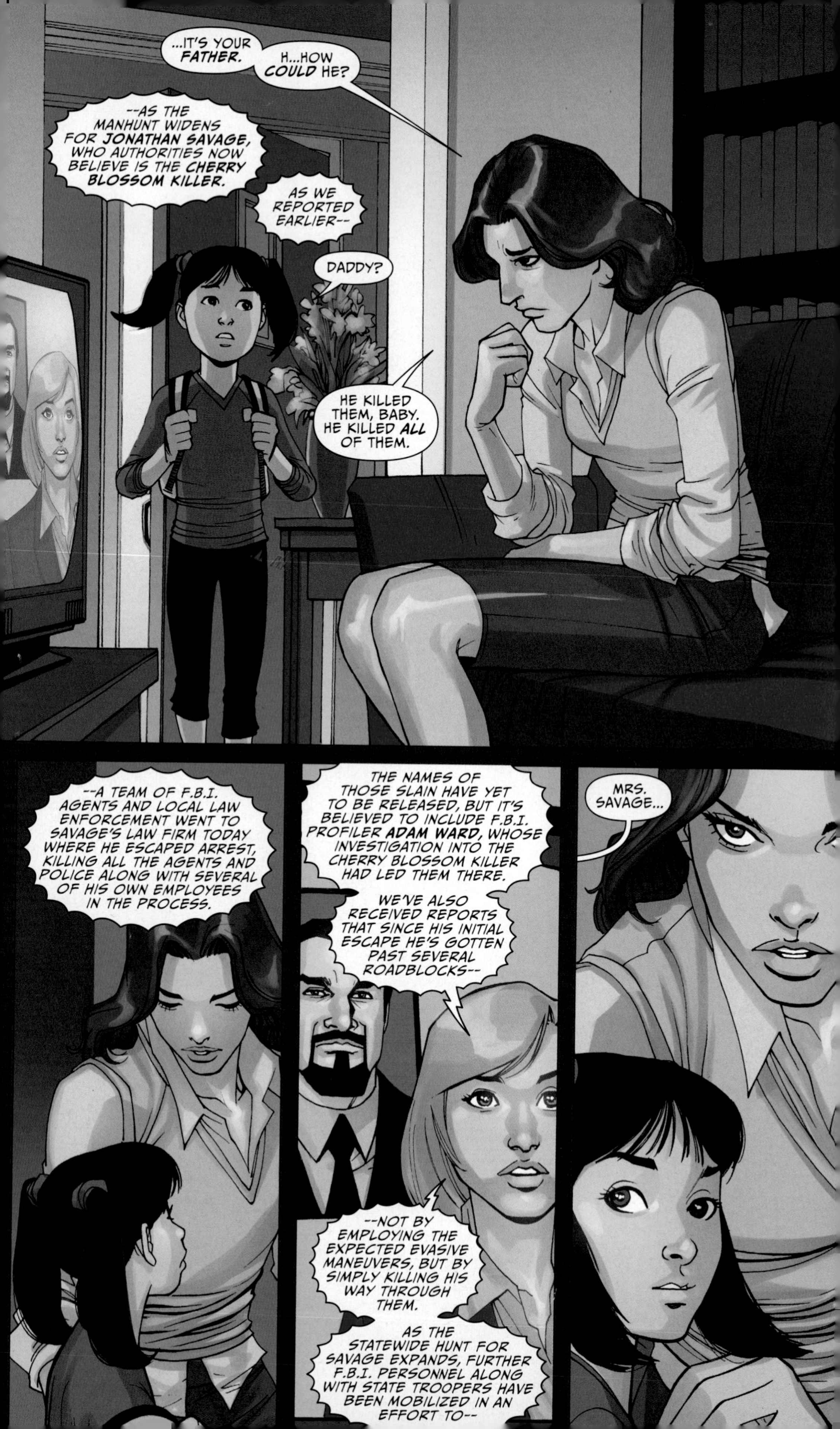
...IT'S YOUR FATHER.
H...HOW COULD HE?
--AS THE MANHUNT WIDENS FOR JONATHAN SAVAGE, WHO AUTHORITIES NOW BELIEVE IS THE CHERRY BLOSSOM KILLER.
AS WE REPORTED EARLIER--
DADDY?
HE KILLED THEM, BABY. HE KILLED ALL OF THEM.
--A TEAM OF F.B.I. AGENTS AND LOCAL LAW ENFORCEMENT WENT TO SAVAGE'S LAW FIRM TODAY WHERE HE ESCAPED ARREST, KILLING ALL THE AGENTS AND POLICE ALONG WITH SEVERAL OF HIS OWN EMPLOYEES IN THE PROCESS.
THE NAMES OF THOSE SLAIN HAVE YET TO BE RELEASED, BUT IT'S BELIEVED TO INCLUDE F.B.I. PROFILER ADAM WARD, WHOSE INVESTIGATION INTO THE CHERRY BLOSSOM KILLER HAD LED THEM THERE.
WE'VE ALSO RECEIVED REPORTS THAT SINCE HIS INITIAL ESCAPE HE'S GOTTEN PAST SEVERAL ROADBLOCKS--
--NOT BY EMPLOYING THE EXPECTED EVASIVE MANEUVERS, BUT BY SIMPLY KILLING HIS WAY THROUGH THEM.
AS THE STATEWIDE HUNT FOR SAVAGE EXPANDS, FURTHER F.B.I. PERSONNEL ALONG WITH STATE TROOPERS HAVE BEEN MOBILIZED IN AN EFFORT TO--
MRS. SAVAGE...

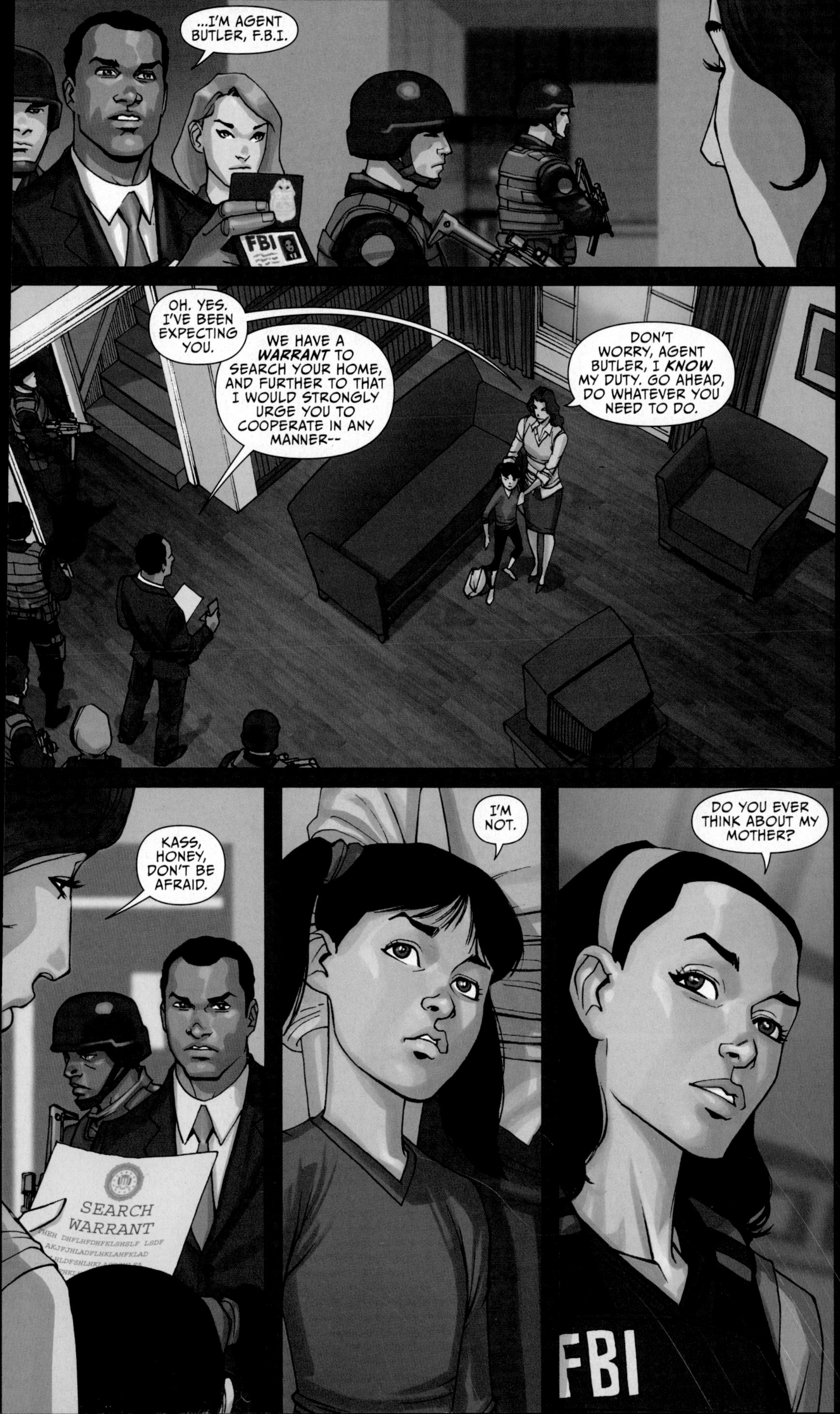
...I'M AGENT BUTLER, F.B.I.
FBI
OH. YES. I'VE BEEN EXPECTING YOU.
WE HAVE A WARRANT TO SEARCH YOUR HOME, AND FURTHER TO THAT I WOULD STRONGLY URGE YOU TO COOPERATE IN ANY MANNER--
DON'T WORRY, AGENT BUTLER, I KNOW MY DUTY. GO AHEAD, DO WHATEVER YOU NEED TO DO.
KASS, HONEY, DON'T BE AFRAID.
SEARCH WARRANT
I'M NOT.
DO YOU EVER THINK ABOUT MY MOTHER?
FBI

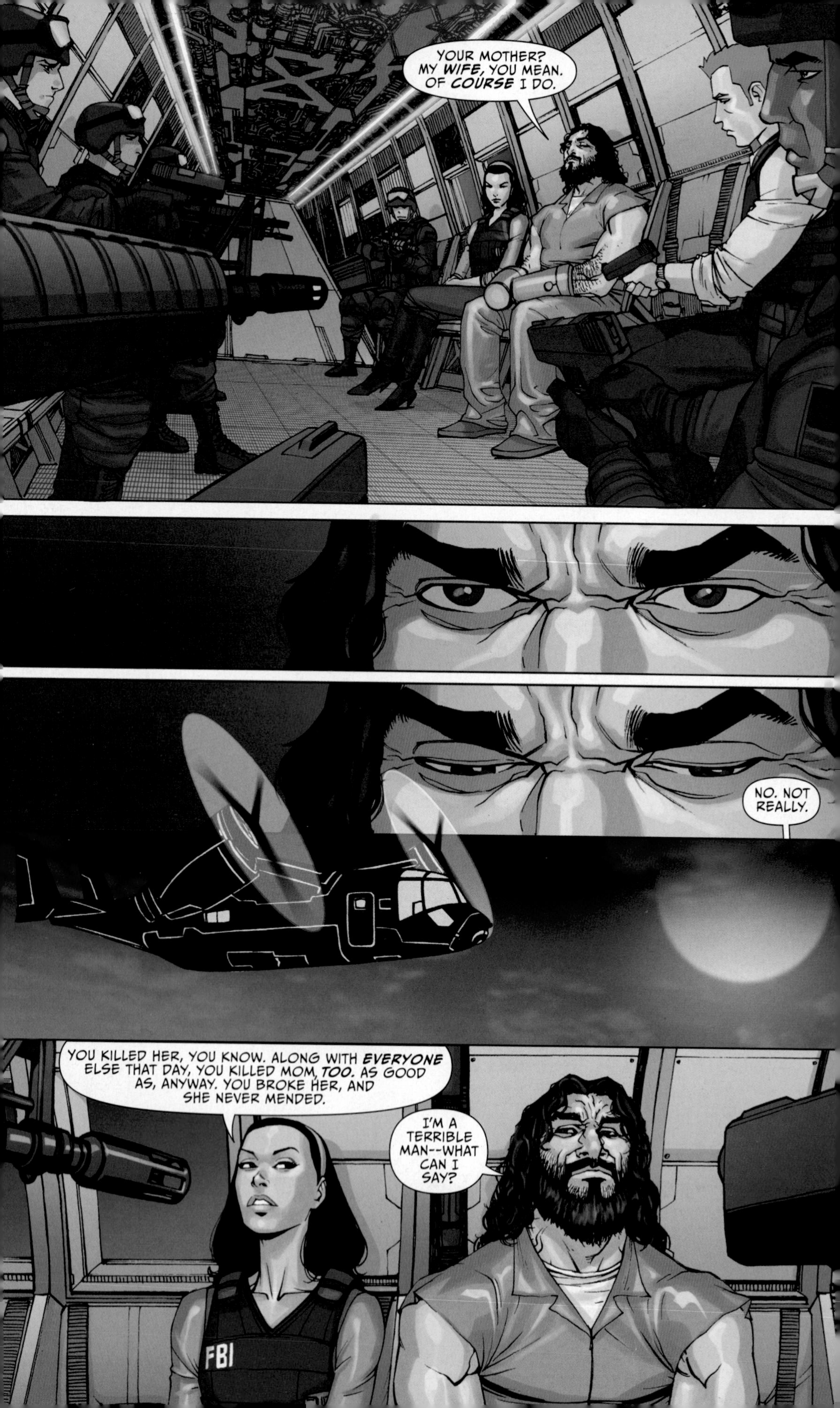
YOUR MOTHER? MY *WIFE,* YOU MEAN. OF *COURSE* I DO.
NO. NOT REALLY.
YOU KILLED HER, YOU KNOW. ALONG WITH *EVERYONE* ELSE THAT DAY, YOU KILLED MOM, *TOO.* AS GOOD AS, ANYWAY. YOU BROKE HER, AND SHE NEVER MENDED.
I'M A TERRIBLE MAN--WHAT CAN I SAY?
FBI

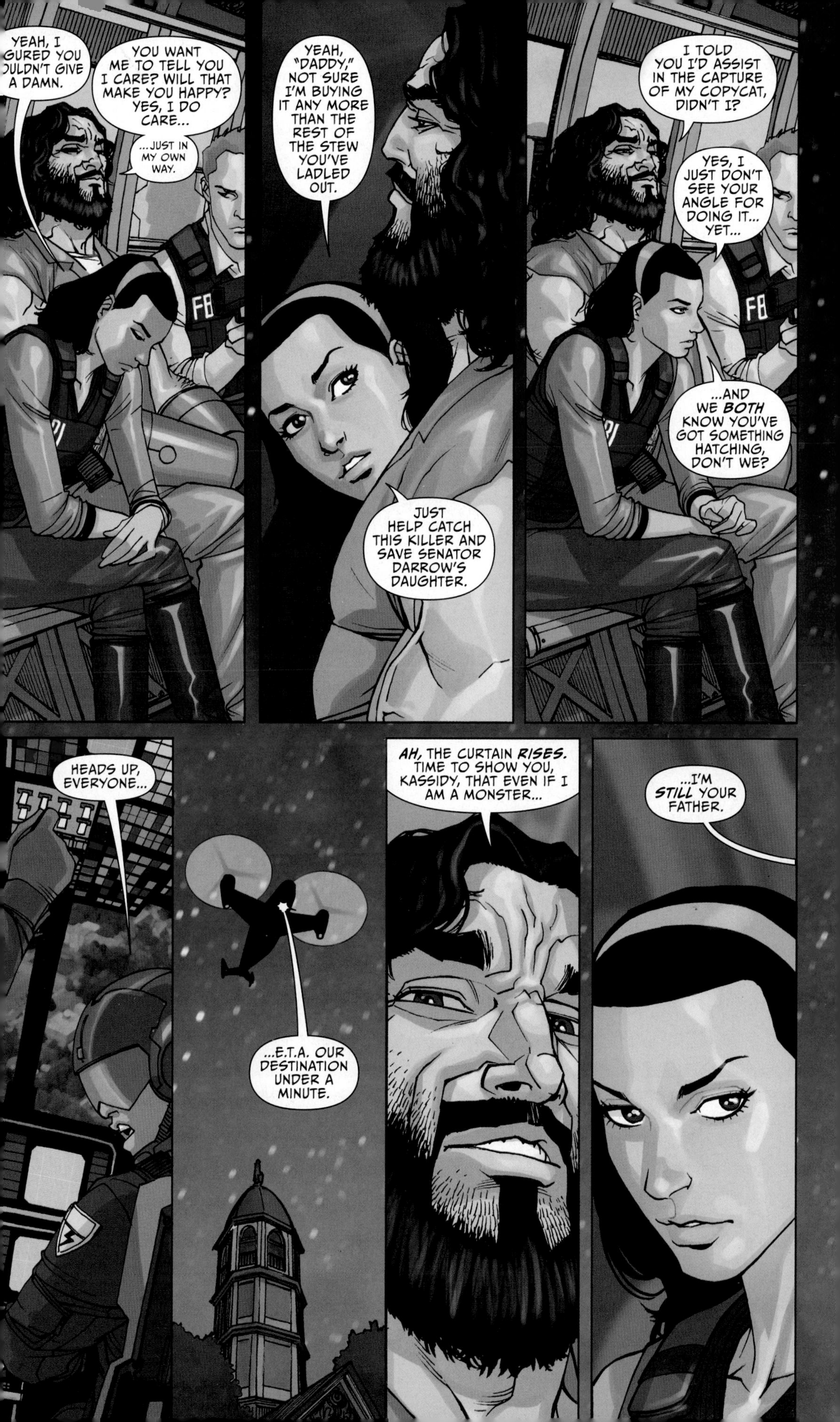
YEAH, I GURED YOU OULDN'T GIVE A DAMN.
YOU WANT ME TO TELL YOU I CARE? WILL THAT MAKE YOU HAPPY? YES, I DO CARE...
...JUST IN MY OWN WAY.
YEAH, "DADDY," NOT SURE I'M BUYING IT ANY MORE THAN THE REST OF THE STEW YOU'VE LADLED OUT.
JUST HELP CATCH THIS KILLER AND SAVE SENATOR DARROW'S DAUGHTER.
I TOLD YOU I'D ASSIST IN THE CAPTURE OF MY COPYCAT, DIDN'T I?
YES, I JUST DON'T SEE YOUR ANGLE FOR DOING IT... YET...
...AND WE BOTH KNOW YOU'VE GOT SOMETHING HATCHING, DON'T WE?
HEADS UP, EVERYONE...
...E.T.A. OUR DESTINATION UNDER A MINUTE.
AH, THE CURTAIN RISES. TIME TO SHOW YOU, KASSIDY, THAT EVEN IF I AM A MONSTER...
...I'M STILL YOUR FATHER.

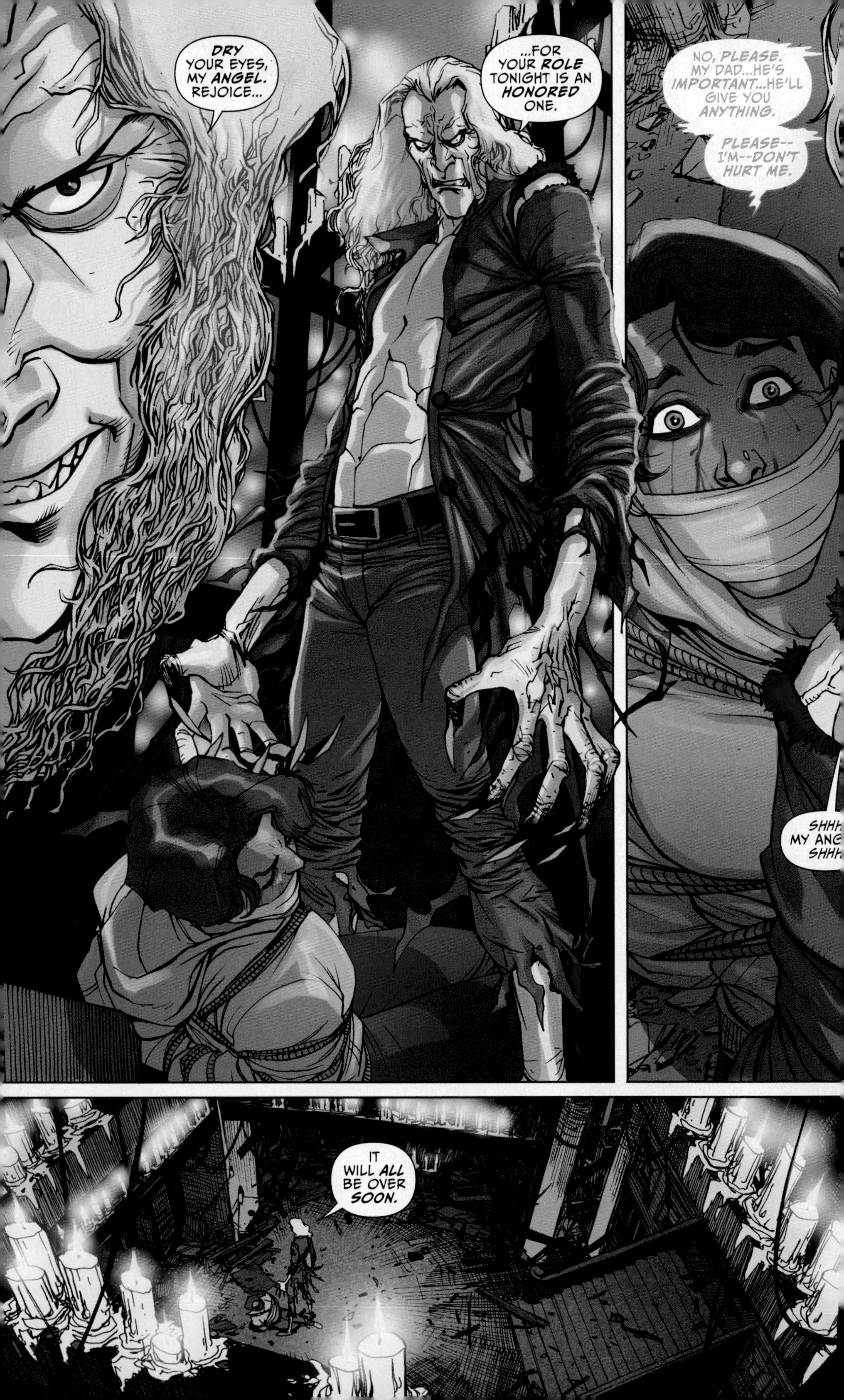
DRY YOUR EYES, MY ANGEL. REJOICE...
...FOR YOUR ROLE TONIGHT IS AN HONORED ONE.
NO, PLEASE. MY DAD...HE'S IMPORTANT...HE'LL GIVE YOU ANYTHING.
PLEASE-- I'M--DON'T HURT ME.
IT WILL ALL BE OVER SOON.

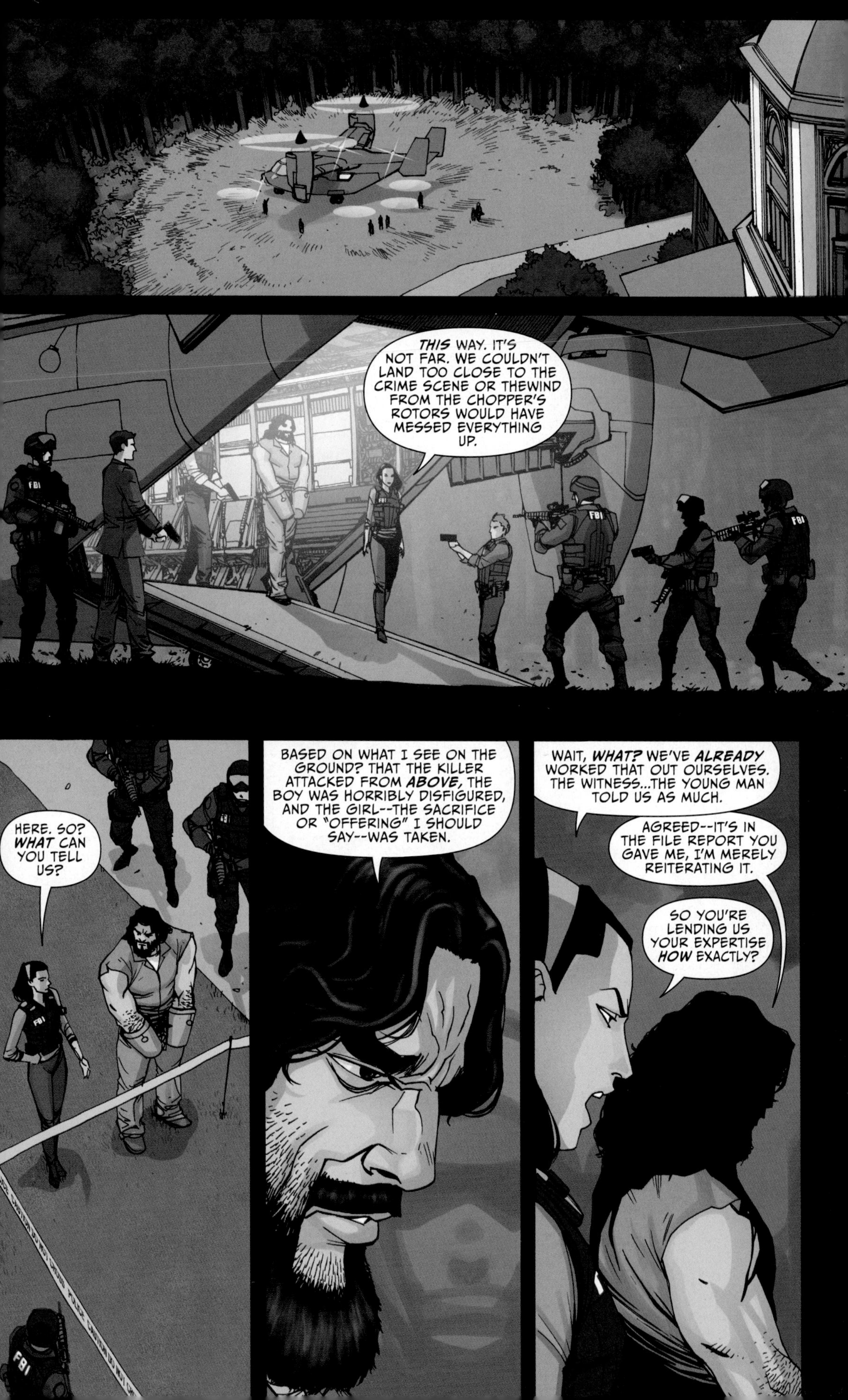
THIS WAY. IT'S NOT FAR. WE COULDN'T LAND TOO CLOSE TO THE CRIME SCENE OR THEWIND FROM THE CHOPPER'S ROTORS WOULD HAVE MESSED EVERYTHING UP.
HERE. SO? WHAT CAN YOU TELL US?
BASED ON WHAT I SEE ON THE GROUND? THAT THE KILLER ATTACKED FROM ABOVE, THE BOY WAS HORRIBLY DISFIGURED, AND THE GIRL--THE SACRIFICE OR "OFFERING" I SHOULD SAY--WAS TAKEN.
WAIT, WHAT? WE'VE ALREADY WORKED THAT OUT OURSELVES. THE WITNESS...THE YOUNG MAN TOLD US AS MUCH.
AGREED--IT'S IN THE FILE REPORT YOU GAVE ME, I'M MERELY REITERATING IT.
SO YOU'RE LENDING US YOUR EXPERTISE HOW EXACTLY?

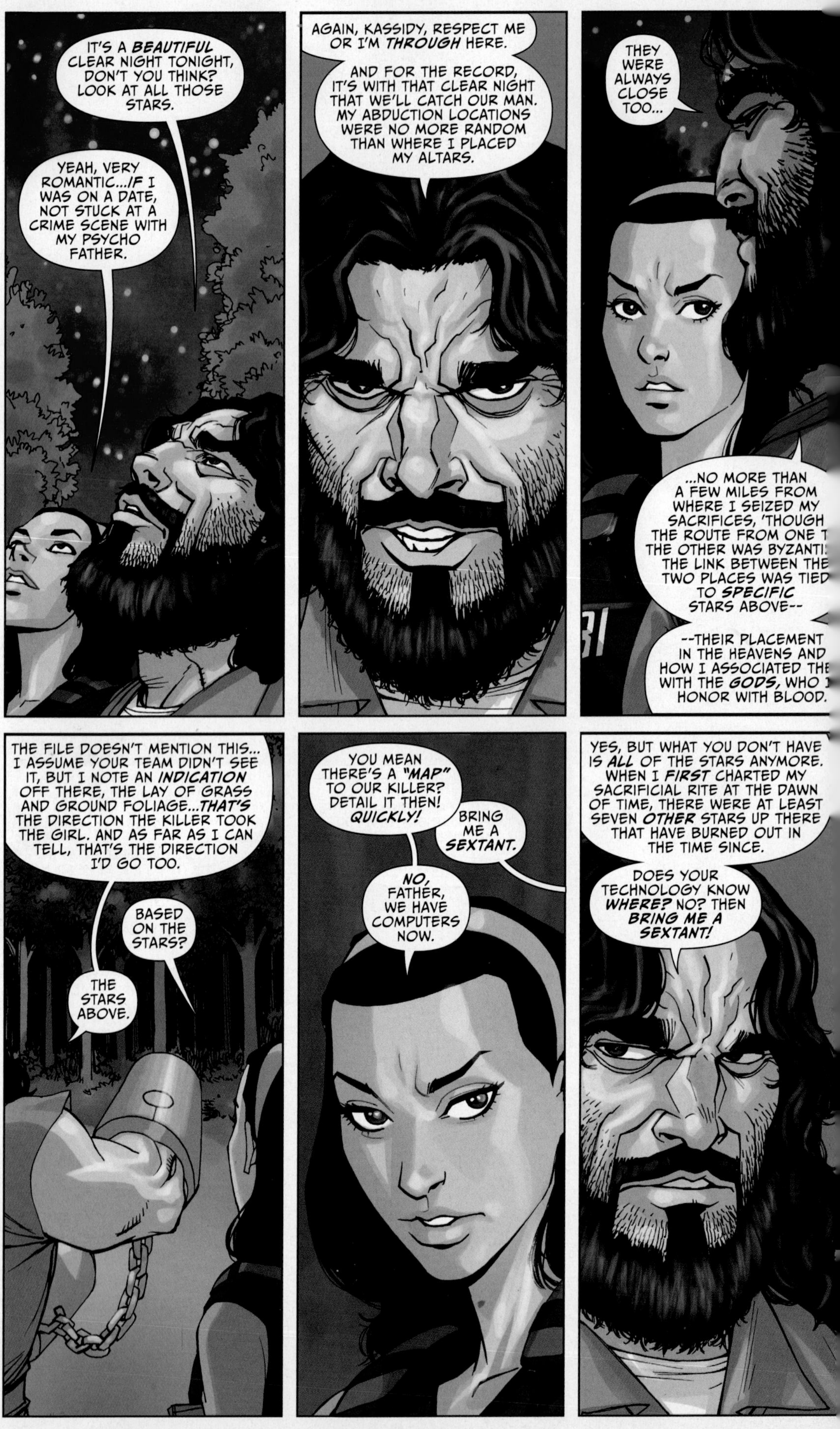
IT'S A BEAUTIFUL CLEAR NIGHT TONIGHT, DON'T YOU THINK? LOOK AT ALL THOSE STARS.
YEAH, VERY ROMANTIC...IF I WAS ON A DATE, NOT STUCK AT A CRIME SCENE WITH MY PSYCHO FATHER.
AGAIN, KASSIDY, RESPECT ME OR I'M THROUGH HERE.
AND FOR THE RECORD, IT'S WITH THAT CLEAR NIGHT THAT WE'LL CATCH OUR MAN. MY ABDUCTION LOCATIONS WERE NO MORE RANDOM THAN WHERE I PLACED MY ALTARS.
THEY WERE ALWAYS CLOSE TOO...
...NO MORE THAN A FEW MILES FROM WHERE I SEIZED MY SACRIFICES, 'THOUGH THE ROUTE FROM ONE T THE OTHER WAS BYZANTI THE LINK BETWEEN THE TWO PLACES WAS TIED TO SPECIFIC STARS ABOVE--
--THEIR PLACEMENT IN THE HEAVENS AND HOW I ASSOCIATED THE WITH THE GODS, WHO I HONOR WITH BLOOD.
THE FILE DOESN'T MENTION THIS... I ASSUME YOUR TEAM DIDN'T SEE IT, BUT I NOTE AN INDICATION OFF THERE, THE LAY OF GRASS AND GROUND FOLIAGE...THAT'S THE DIRECTION THE KILLER TOOK THE GIRL. AND AS FAR AS I CAN TELL, THAT'S THE DIRECTION I'D GO TOO.
BASED ON THE STARS?
THE STARS ABOVE.
YOU MEAN THERE'S A "MAP" TO OUR KILLER? DETAIL IT THEN! QUICKLY!
BRING ME A SEXTANT.
NO, FATHER, WE HAVE COMPUTERS NOW.
YES, BUT WHAT YOU DON'T HAVE IS ALL OF THE STARS ANYMORE. WHEN I FIRST CHARTED MY SACRIFICIAL RITE AT THE DAWN OF TIME, THERE WERE AT LEAST SEVEN OTHER STARS UP THERE THAT HAVE BURNED OUT IN THE TIME SINCE.
DOES YOUR TECHNOLOGY KNOW WHERE? NO? THEN BRING ME A SEXTANT!

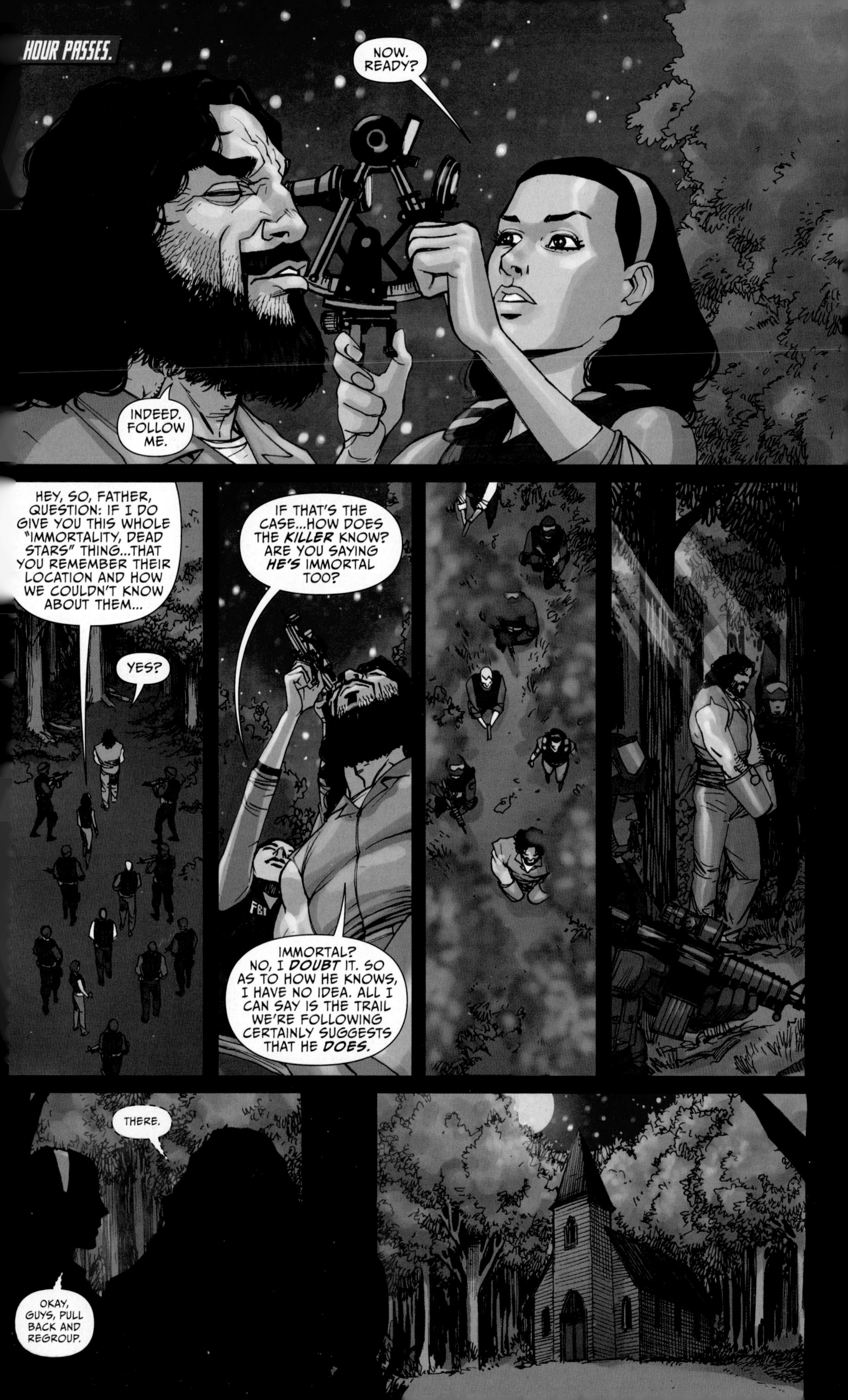

HOUR PASSES.
NOW. READY?
INDEED. FOLLOW ME.
HEY, SO, FATHER, QUESTION: IF I DO GIVE YOU THIS WHOLE "IMMORTALITY, DEAD STARS" THING...THAT YOU REMEMBER THEIR LOCATION AND HOW WE COULDN'T KNOW ABOUT THEM...
YES?
IF THAT'S THE CASE...HOW DOES THE KILLER KNOW? ARE YOU SAYING HE'S IMMORTAL TOO?
FBI
IMMORTAL? NO, I DOUBT IT. SO AS TO HOW HE KNOWS, I HAVE NO IDEA. ALL I CAN SAY IS THE TRAIL WE'RE FOLLOWING CERTAINLY SUGGESTS THAT HE DOES.
THERE.
OKAY, GUYS, PULL BACK AND REGROUP.

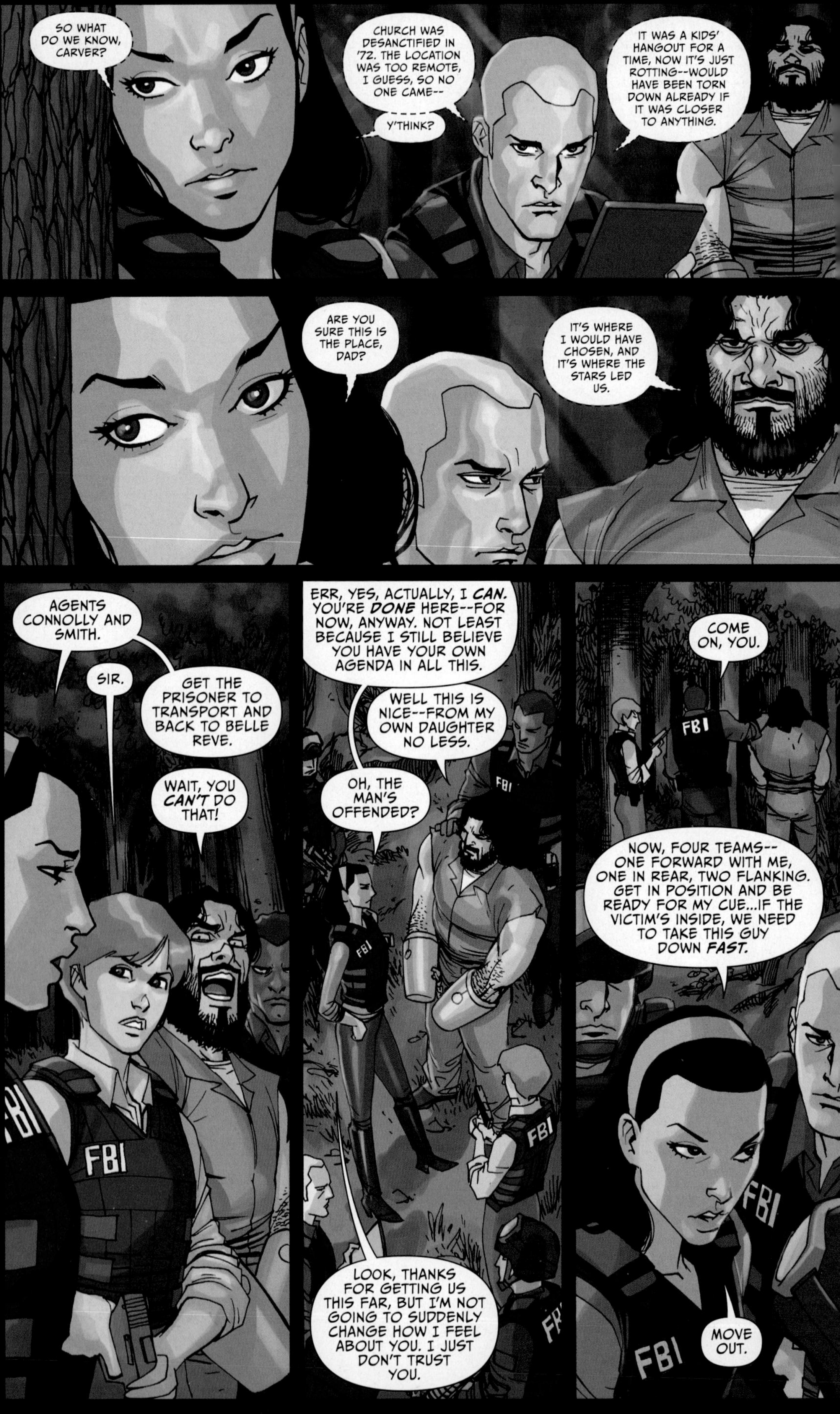
SO WHAT DO WE KNOW, CARVER?
CHURCH WAS DESANCTIFIED IN '72. THE LOCATION WAS TOO REMOTE, I GUESS, SO NO ONE CAME--
Y'THINK?
IT WAS A KIDS' HANGOUT FOR A TIME, NOW IT'S JUST ROTTING--WOULD HAVE BEEN TORN DOWN ALREADY IF IT WAS CLOSER TO ANYTHING.
ARE YOU SURE THIS IS THE PLACE, DAD?
IT'S WHERE I WOULD HAVE CHOSEN, AND IT'S WHERE THE STARS LED US.
AGENTS CONNOLLY AND SMITH.
SIR.
GET THE PRISONER TO TRANSPORT AND BACK TO BELLE REVE.
WAIT, YOU CAN'T DO THAT!
ERR, YES, ACTUALLY, I CAN. YOU'RE DONE HERE--FOR NOW, ANYWAY. NOT LEAST BECAUSE I STILL BELIEVE YOU HAVE YOUR OWN AGENDA IN ALL THIS.
WELL THIS IS NICE--FROM MY OWN DAUGHTER NO LESS.
OH, THE MAN'S OFFENDED?
LOOK, THANKS FOR GETTING US THIS FAR, BUT I'M NOT GOING TO SUDDENLY CHANGE HOW I FEEL ABOUT YOU. I JUST DON'T TRUST YOU.
COME ON, YOU.
NOW, FOUR TEAMS--ONE FORWARD WITH ME, ONE IN REAR, TWO FLANKING. GET IN POSITION AND BE READY FOR MY CUE...IF THE VICTIM'S INSIDE, WE NEED TO TAKE THIS GUY DOWN FAST.
MOVE OUT.

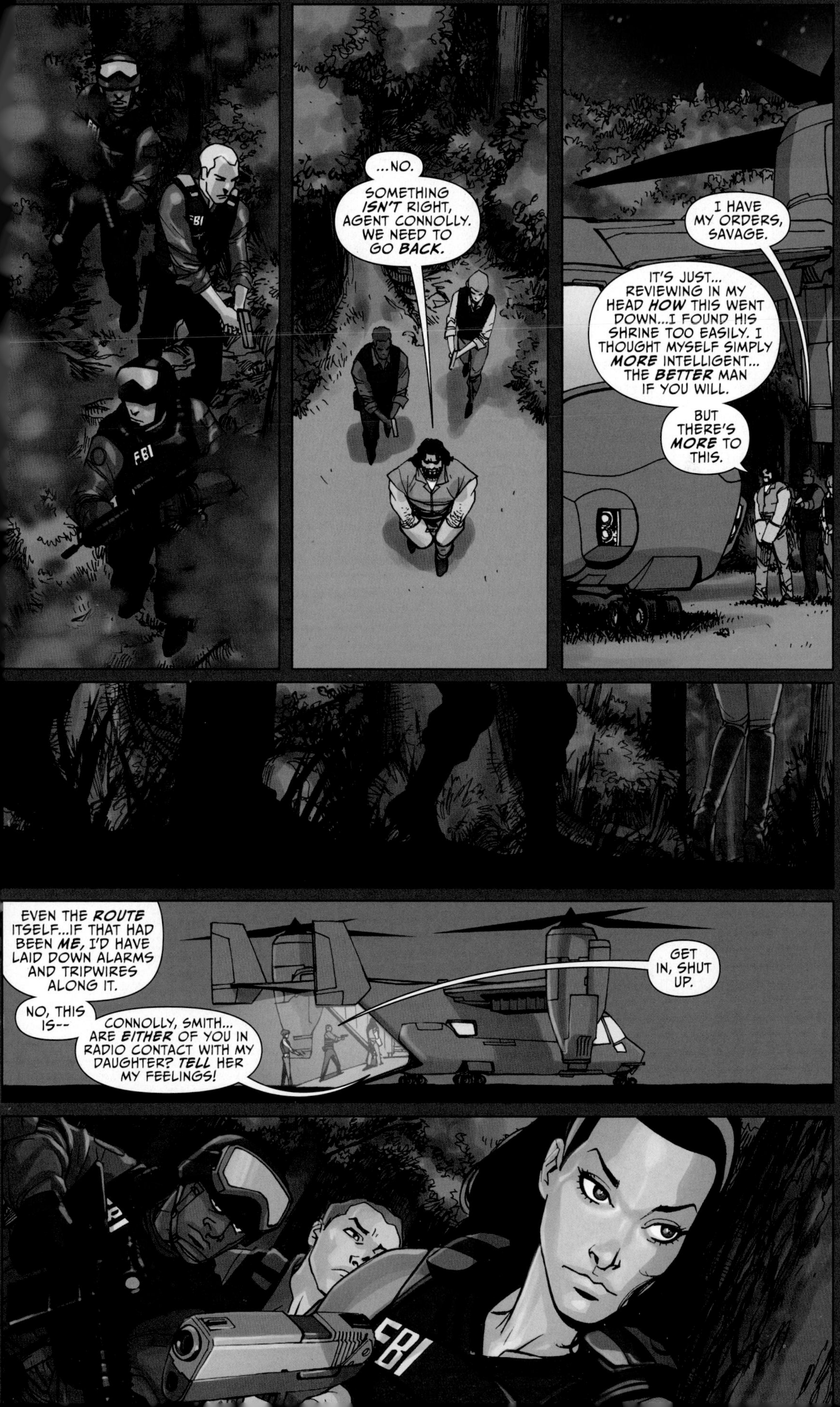

...NO.
SOMETHING ISN'T RIGHT, AGENT CONNOLLY. WE NEED TO GO BACK.
I HAVE MY ORDERS, SAVAGE.
IT'S JUST... REVIEWING IN MY HEAD HOW THIS WENT DOWN...I FOUND HIS SHRINE TOO EASILY. I THOUGHT MYSELF SIMPLY MORE INTELLIGENT... THE BETTER MAN IF YOU WILL.
BUT THERE'S MORE TO THIS.
EVEN THE ROUTE ITSELF...IF THAT HAD BEEN ME, I'D HAVE LAID DOWN ALARMS AND TRIPWIRES ALONG IT.
NO, THIS IS--
GET IN, SHUT UP.
CONNOLLY, SMITH... ARE EITHER OF YOU IN RADIO CONTACT WITH MY DAUGHTER? TELL HER MY FEELINGS!

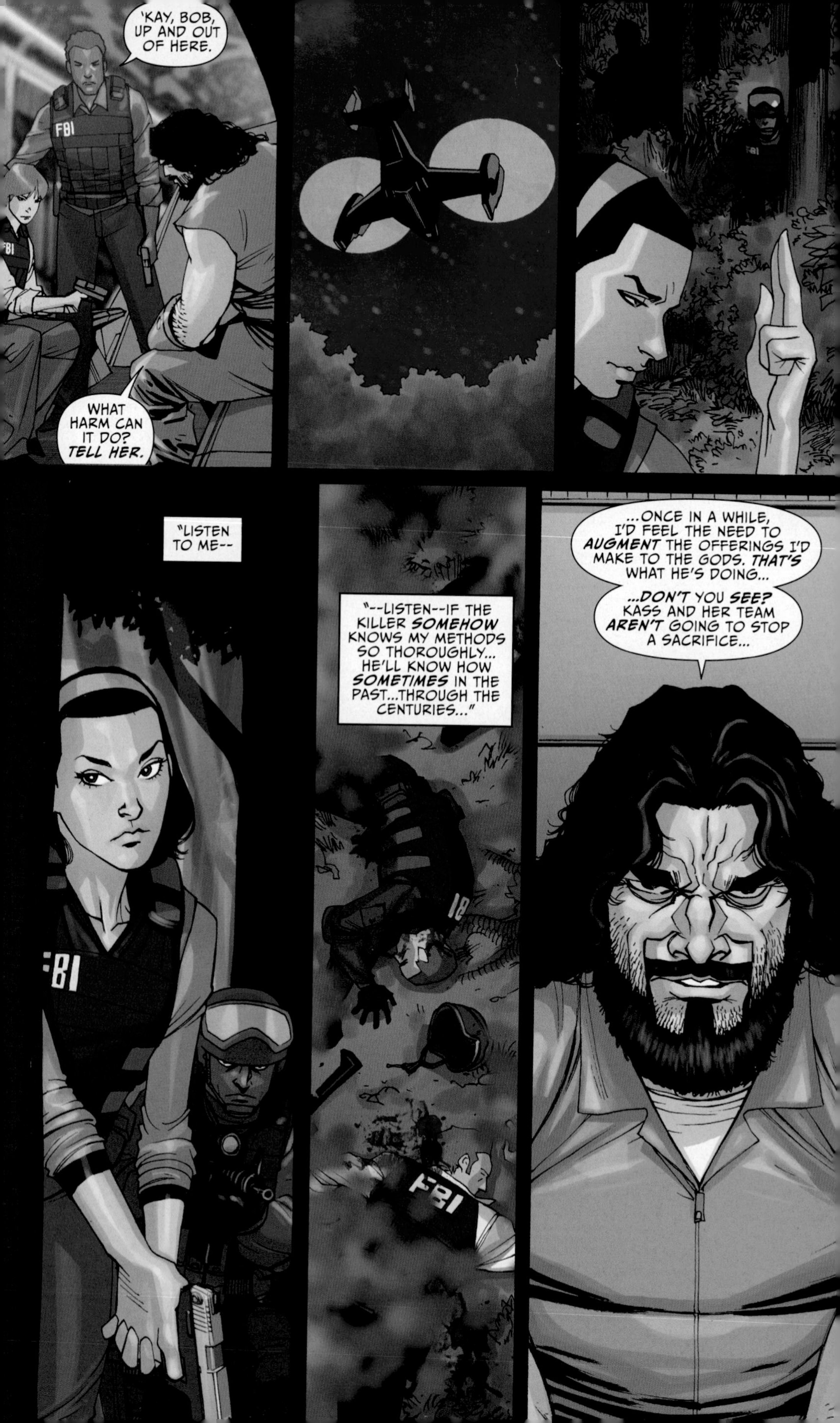
'KAY, BOB, UP AND OUT OF HERE.
WHAT HARM CAN IT DO? TELL HER.
"LISTEN TO ME--
"--LISTEN--IF THE KILLER SOMEHOW KNOWS MY METHODS SO THOROUGHLY... HE'LL KNOW HOW SOMETIMES IN THE PAST...THROUGH THE CENTURIES..."
...ONCE IN A WHILE, I'D FEEL THE NEED TO AUGMENT THE OFFERINGS I'D MAKE TO THE GODS. THAT'S WHAT HE'S DOING...
...DON'T YOU SEE? KASS AND HER TEAM AREN'T GOING TO STOP A SACRIFICE...

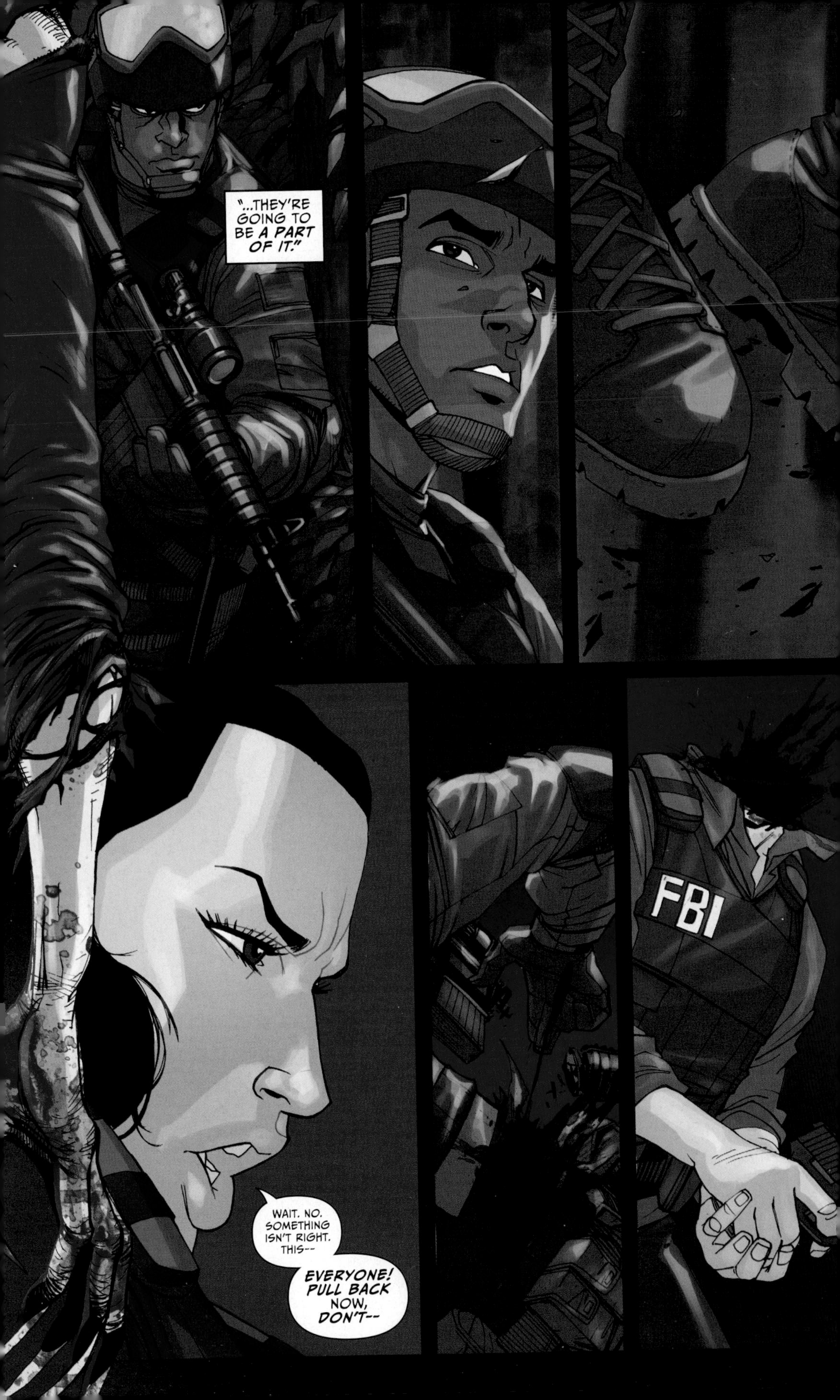
"...THEY'RE GOING TO BE A PART OF IT."
WAIT. NO. SOMETHING ISN'T RIGHT. THIS--
EVERYONE! PULL BACK NOW, DON'T--
FBI

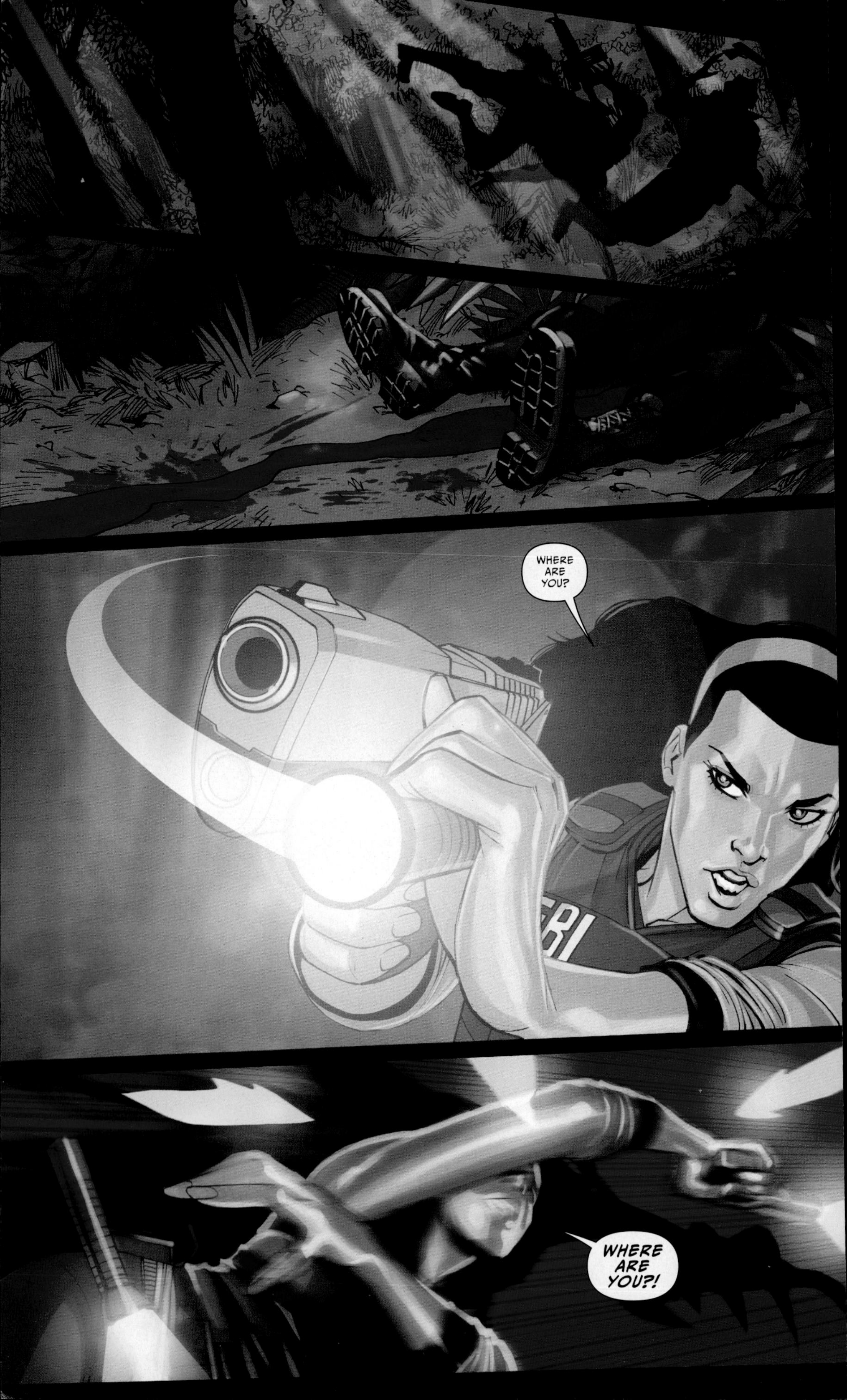
WHERE ARE YOU?
WHERE ARE YOU?!

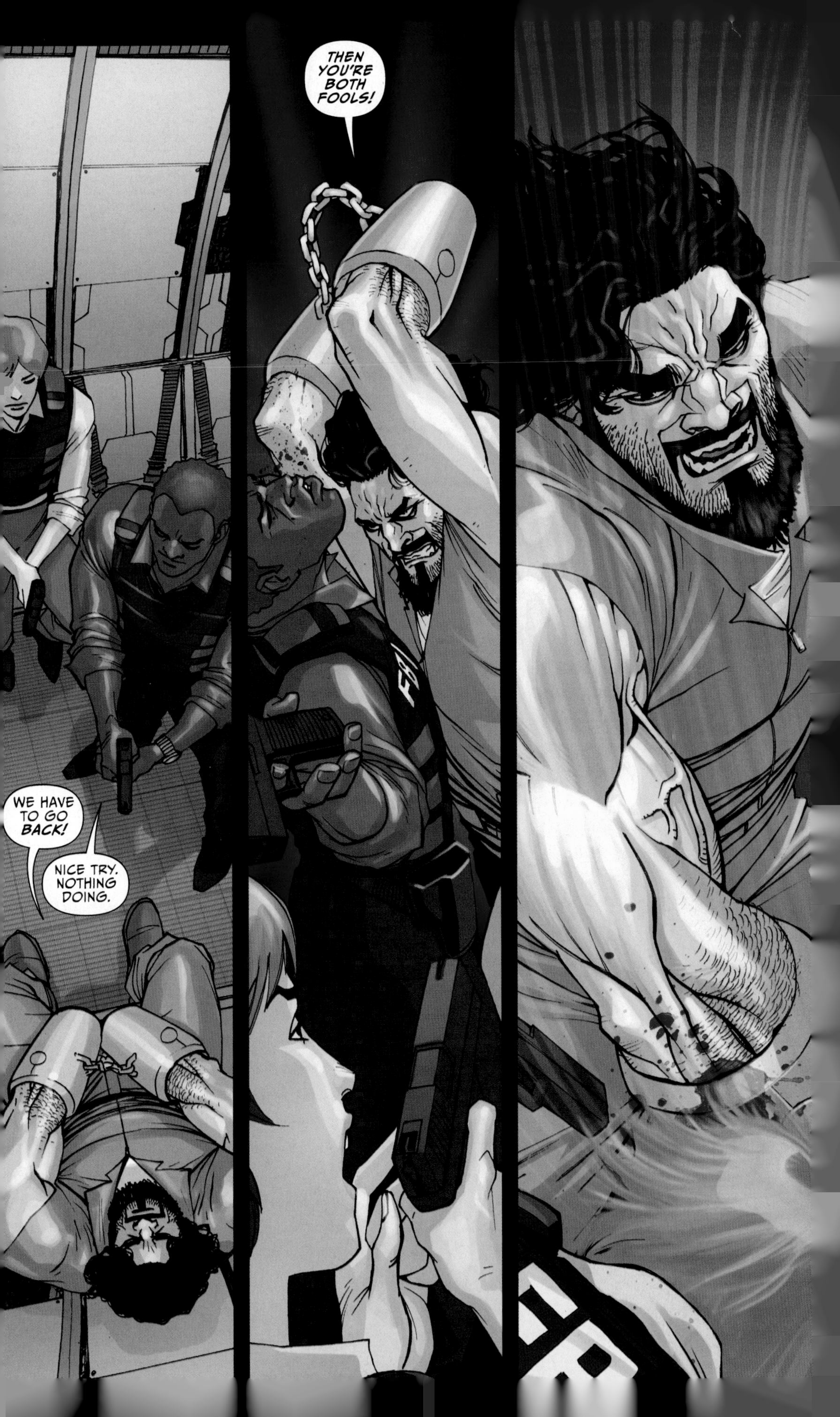
WE HAVE TO GO BACK!
NICE TRY. NOTHING DOING.
THEN YOU'RE BOTH FOOLS!

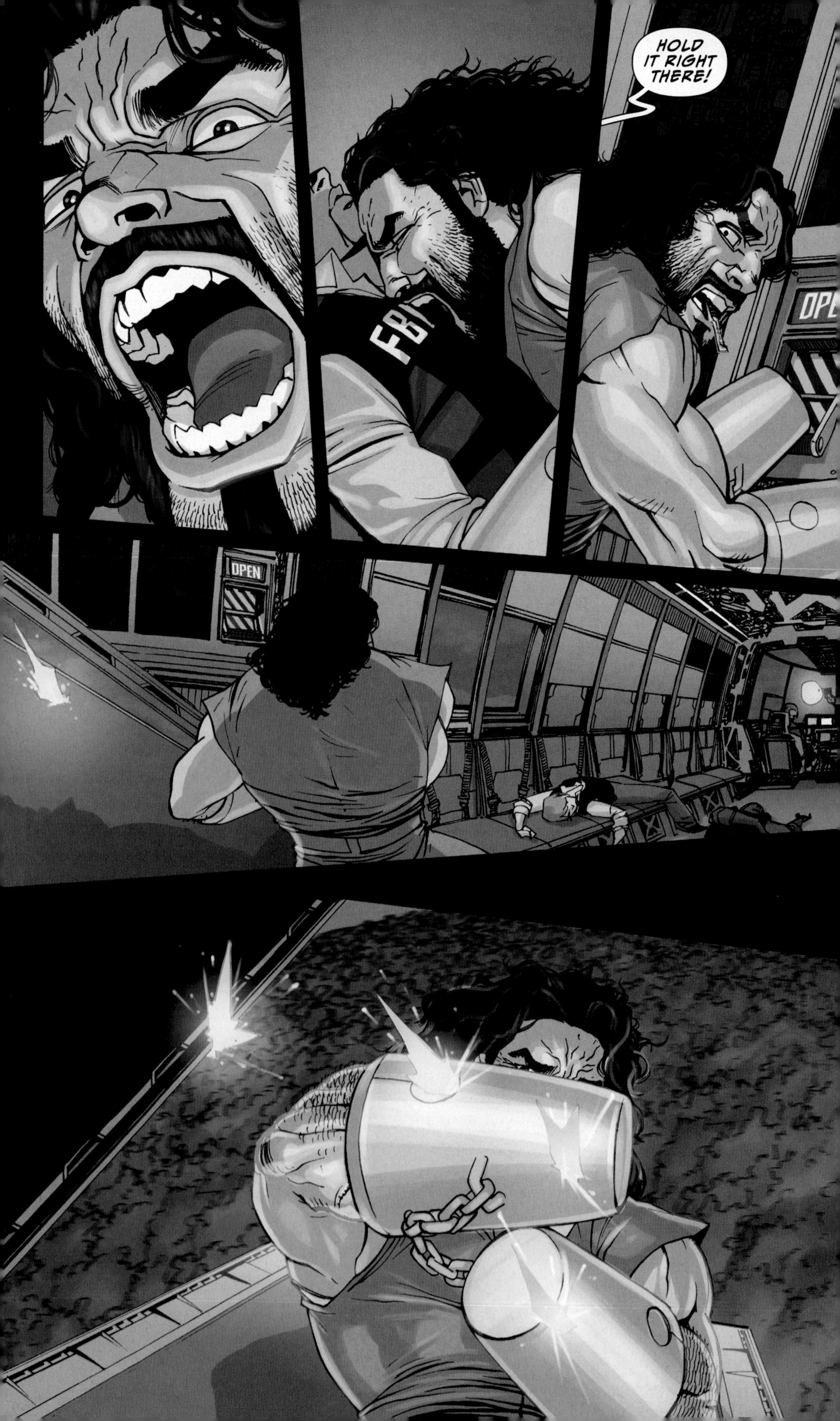
HOLD IT RIGHT THERE!
FBI
OPE
OPEN

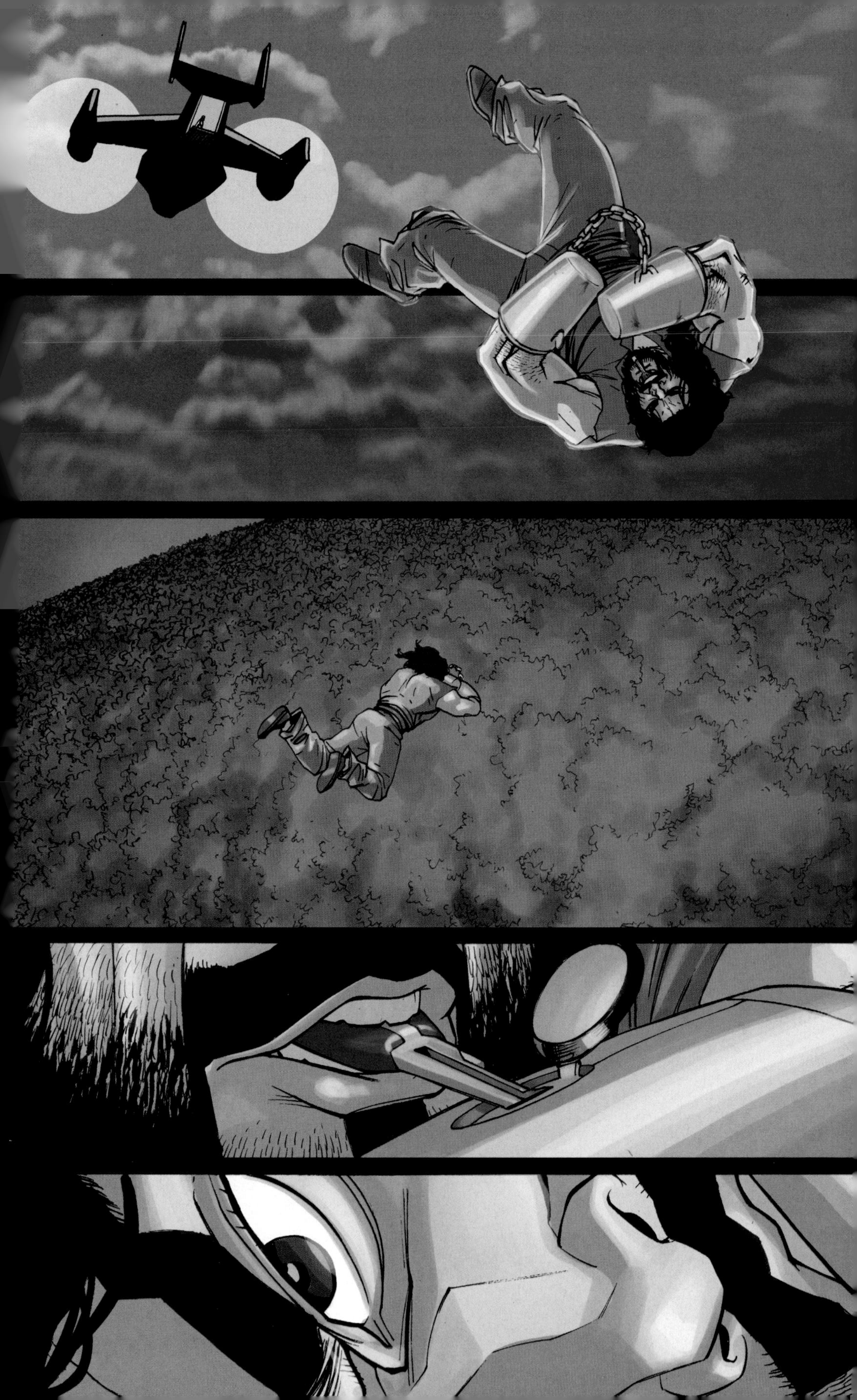

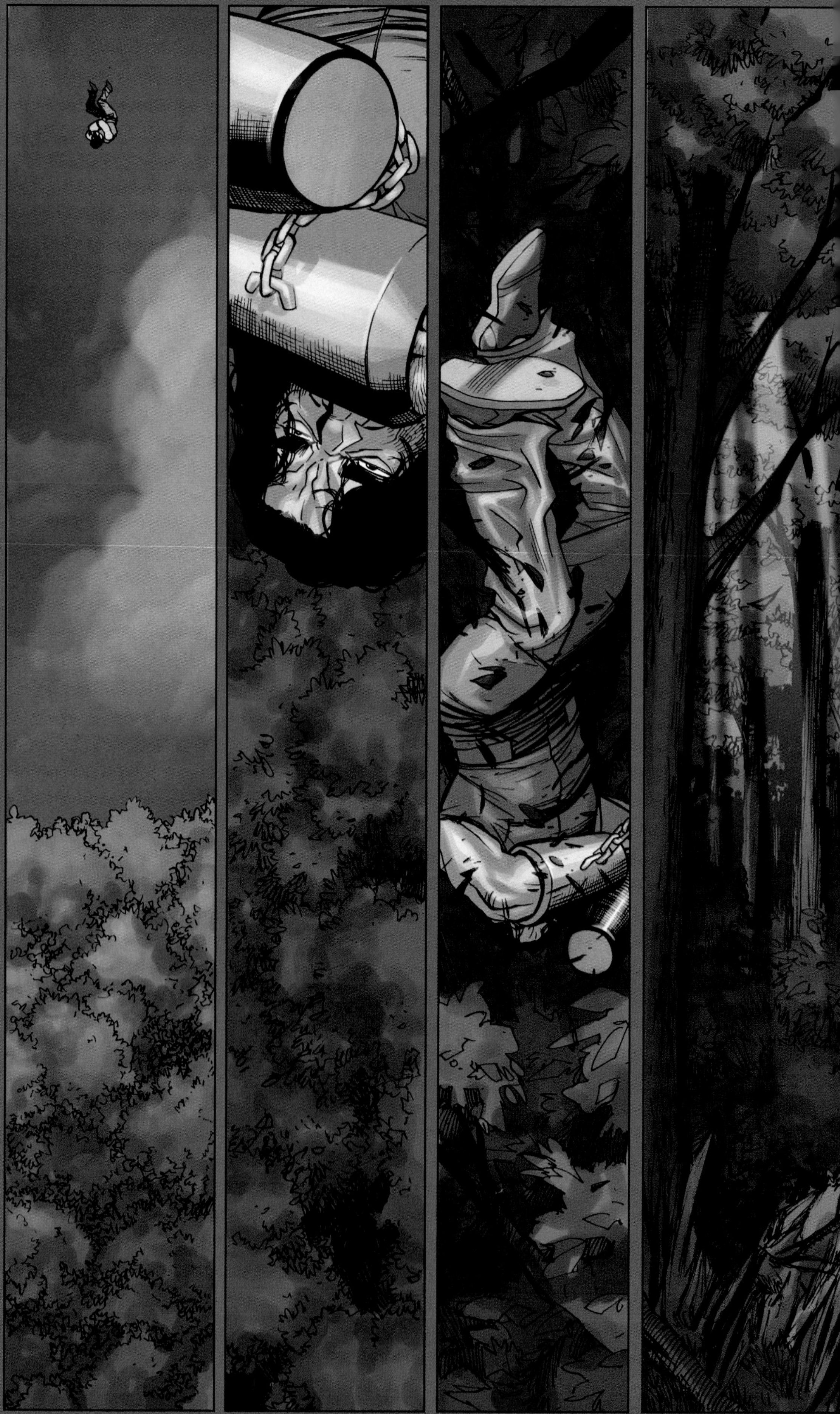

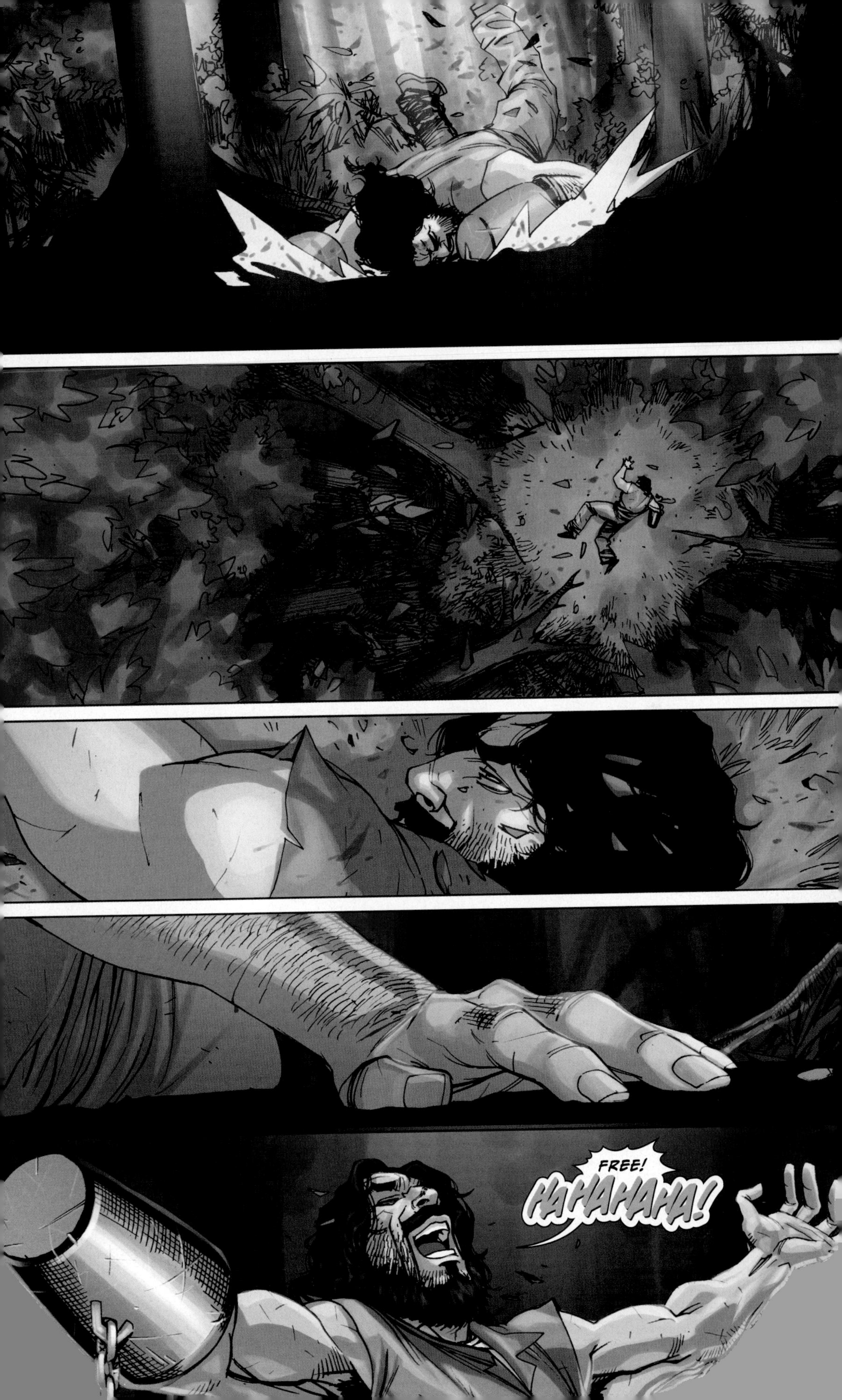
FREE!
HAHAHAHA!

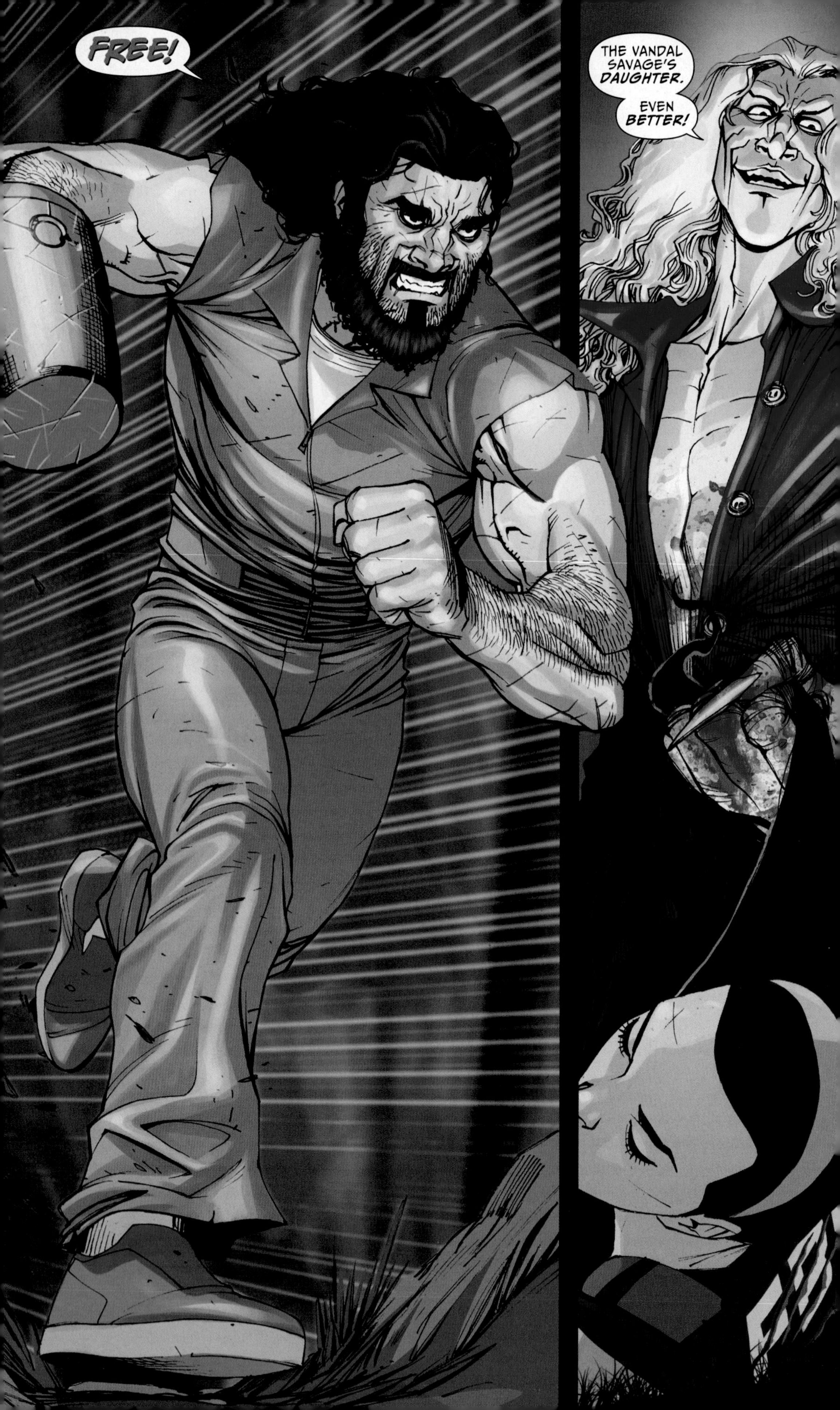
FREE!
THE VANDAL SAVAGE'S DAUGHTER.
EVEN BETTER!

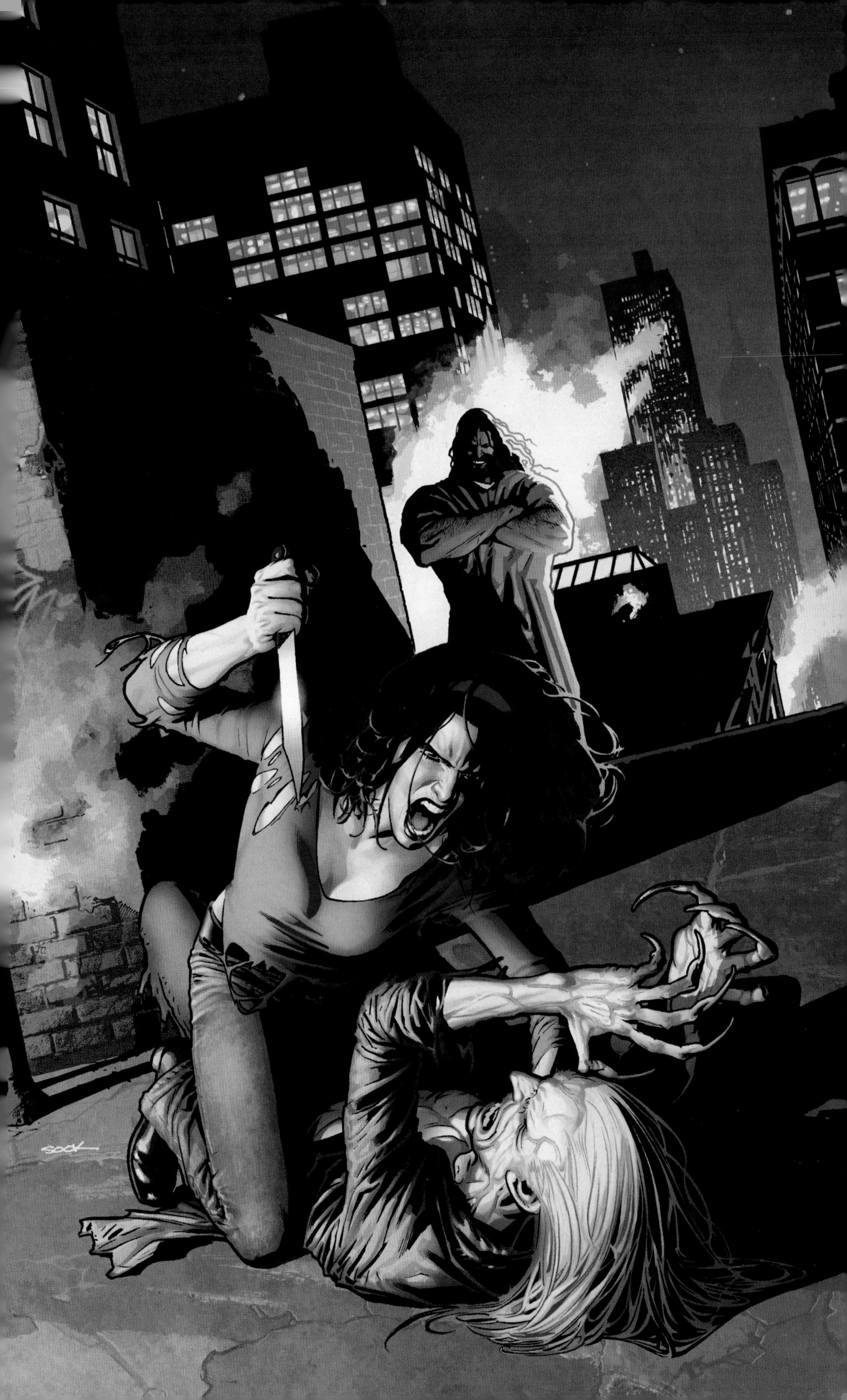
SOOK

PART THREE: BLOOD LOSS

JAMES ROBINSON writer **BERNARD CHANG** artist

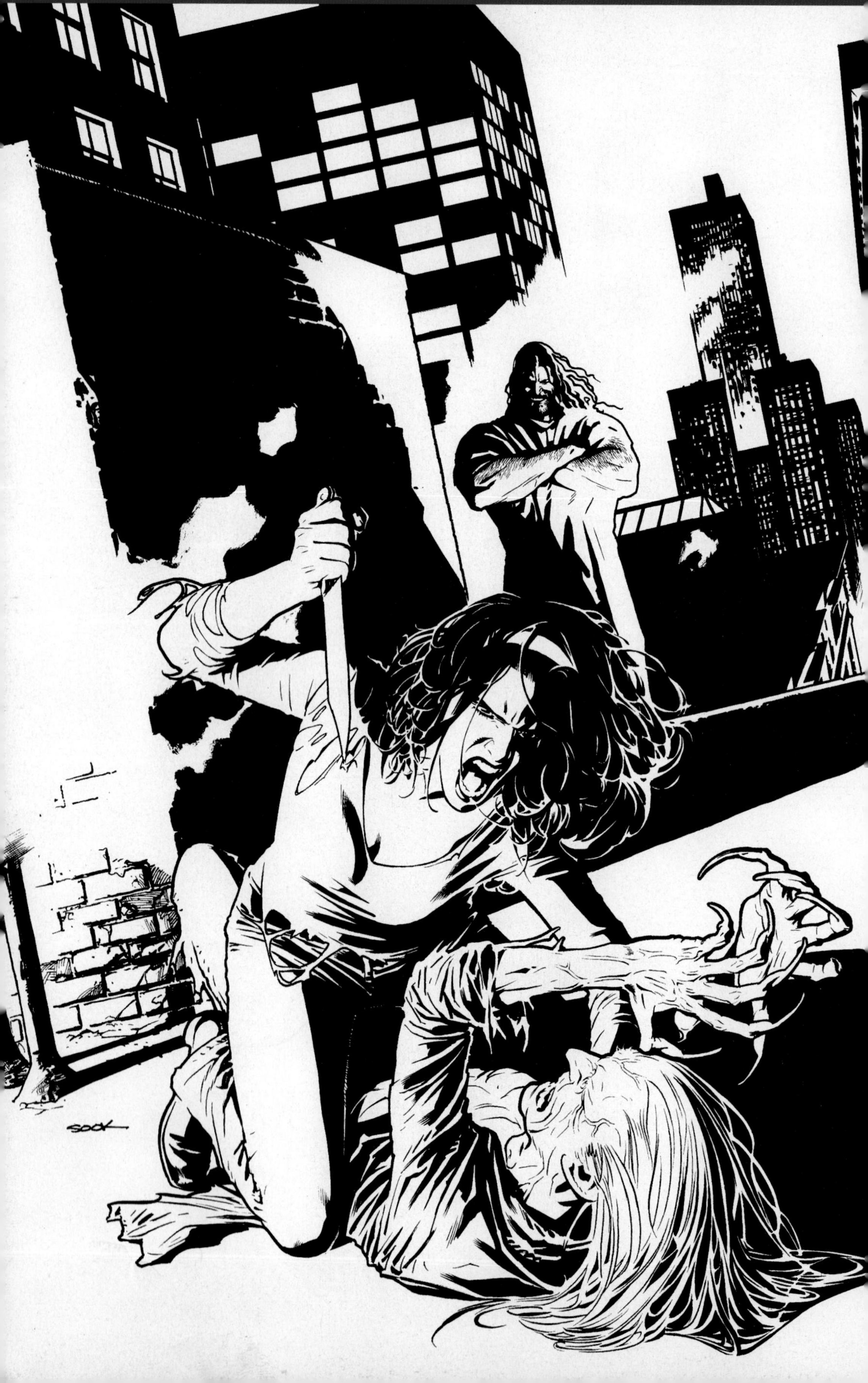
SOOK

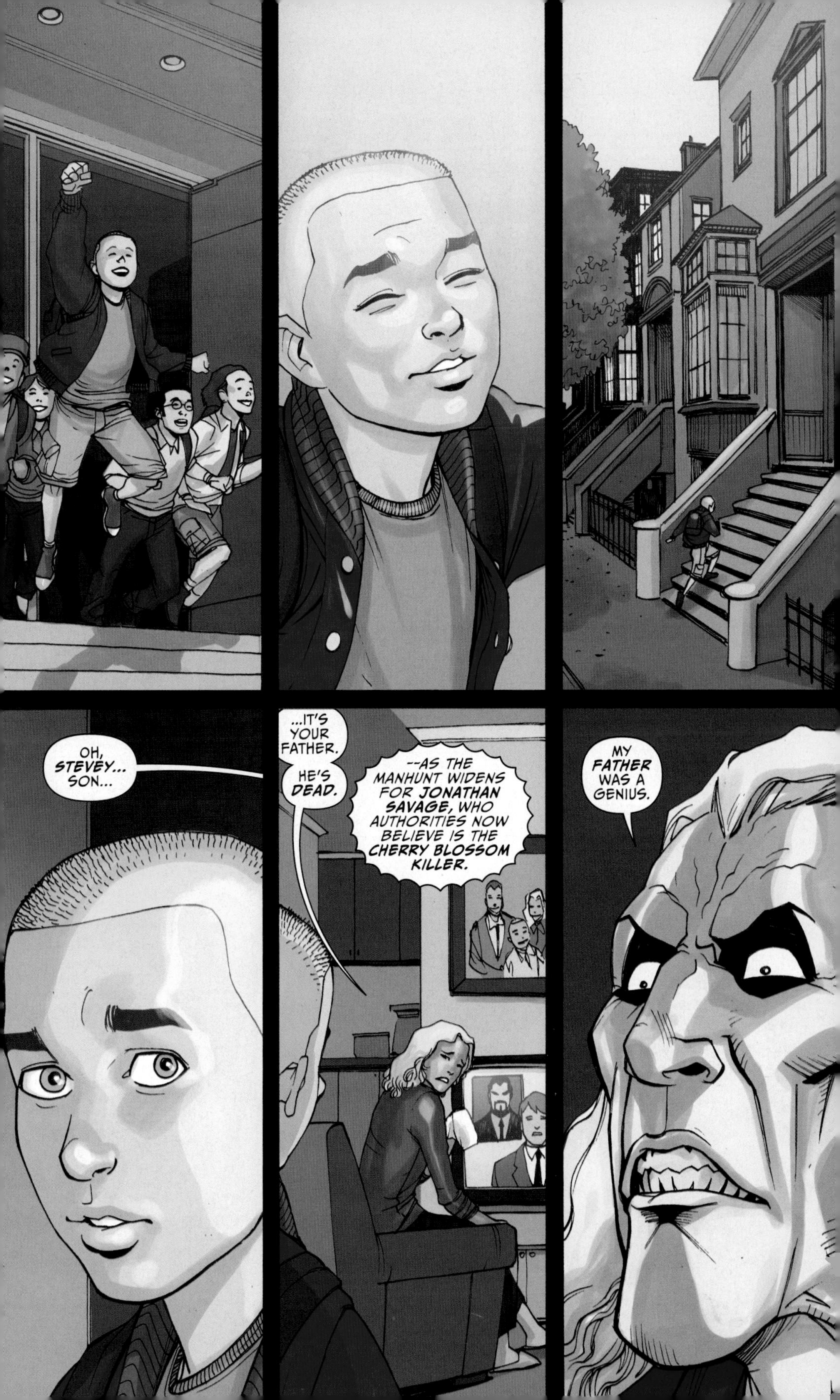
OH, STEVEY... SON...
...IT'S YOUR FATHER.
HE'S DEAD.
--AS THE MANHUNT WIDENS FOR JONATHAN SAVAGE, WHO AUTHORITIES NOW BELIEVE IS THE CHERRY BLOSSOM KILLER.
MY FATHER WAS A GENIUS.

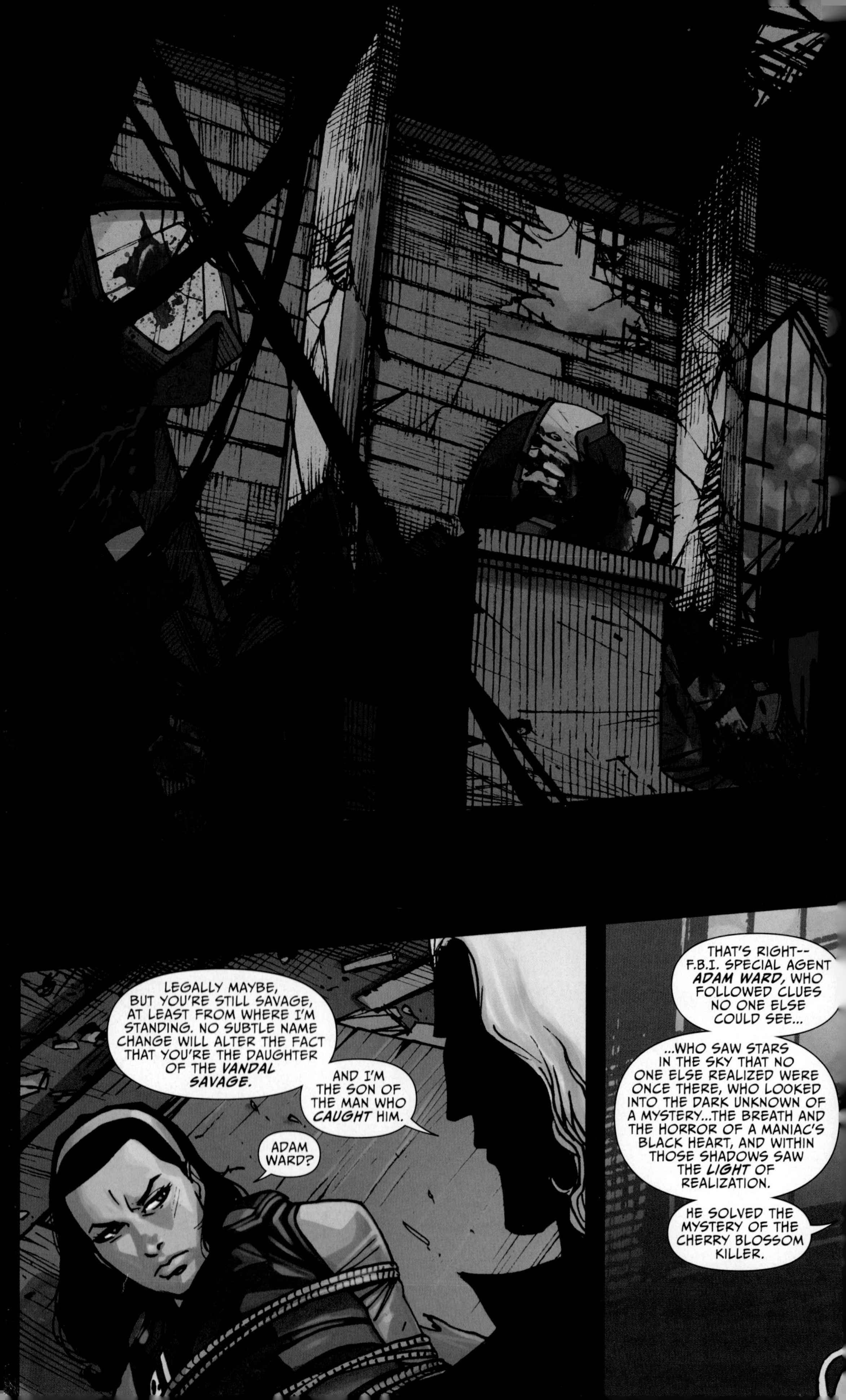
LEGALLY MAYBE, BUT YOU'RE STILL SAVAGE, AT LEAST FROM WHERE I'M STANDING. NO SUBTLE NAME CHANGE WILL ALTER THE FACT THAT YOU'RE THE DAUGHTER OF THE VANDAL SAVAGE.
AND I'M THE SON OF THE MAN WHO CAUGHT HIM.
ADAM WARD?
THAT'S RIGHT-- F.B.I. SPECIAL AGENT ADAM WARD, WHO FOLLOWED CLUES NO ONE ELSE COULD SEE...
...WHO SAW STARS IN THE SKY THAT NO ONE ELSE REALIZED WERE ONCE THERE, WHO LOOKED INTO THE DARK UNKNOWN OF A MYSTERY...THE BREATH AND THE HORROR OF A MANIAC'S BLACK HEART, AND WITHIN THOSE SHADOWS SAW THE LIGHT OF REALIZATION.
HE SOLVED THE MYSTERY OF THE CHERRY BLOSSOM KILLER.

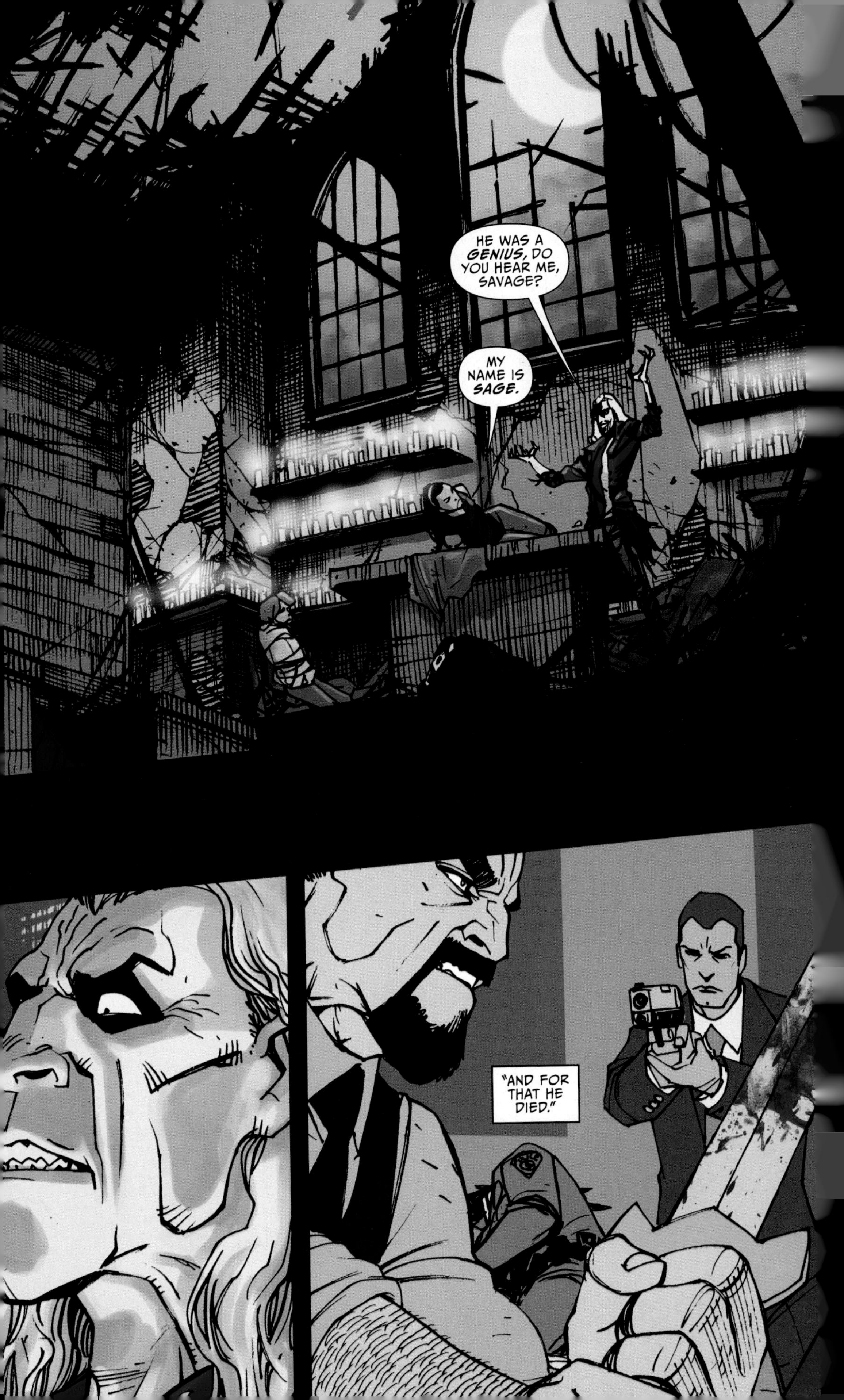
HE WAS A GENIUS, DO YOU HEAR ME, SAVAGE?
MY NAME IS SAGE.
"AND FOR THAT HE DIED."

I DON'T KNOW IF IT WAS THE *SHOCK* OF LEARNING MY FATHER WAS DEAD...

OR ADOLESCENCE... PUBERTY...BUT IT WASN'T LONG AFTERWARDS THAT I BEGAN TO GROW AND CHANGE...BECOME WHAT YOU SEE NOW.

SO ADAM WARD'S SON...THAT MAKES YOU *STEVEN,* RIGHT?

OH, YOU KNOW OF ME THEN.

ONCE YOU TOLD ME WHO YOUR FATHER WAS, SURE. I'VE STUDIED HIM...

...HELL, *EVERY* AGENT COMING OUT OF QUANTICO HAS--THERE'S A WHOLE CLASS ON HIS ACHIEVEMENTS AND THE ADVANCEMENTS IN SCIENTIFIC DEDUCTION THAT HE SPEARHEADED.

DOESN'T EXPLAIN THIS THOUGH, STEVEN.

DOESN'T EXPLA OR *EXCUSE* A THE MURDERS YOU'VE COMMITT DOESN'T *BEG* TO.

PLEASE...

...I JUST WANT TO GO HOME.

SO DO *I,* BELIEVE ME. JUST HANG TIGHT, 'KAY?

YOU WANT AN *EXPLANATION?* I'VE SPENT MY LIFE HATING *MYSELF* FOR THE GROTESQUE CREATURE I'VE TURNED INTO, AND *EQUALLY* I *HATE* THE MAN WHO TOOK MY FATHER FROM ME.

BUT I'M *SMART* TOO. I THINK THAT W A GIFT FROM MY DAD. THE *OTHER* G WAS HIS CASEBOOKS--CODED, I MIG ADD--THROUGH WHICH I WAS AB TO FOLLOW THE PATH OF HIS REASONING AND DEDUCTIONS...

...AND THEREBY *IMITATE* THE SACRIFICIAL MURDERS OF THE VANDAL SAVAGE.

FINE. YOU HATE MY FATHER, *CAN'T* SAY I BLAME YOU, BUT I DON'T SEE HOW IMITATING HIM MAKES IT BETTER.

ALL I KNOW IS IT *HAS* TO *STOP*--ALL THE MURDERS...THE INNOCENT GIRLS WHOSE LIVES YOU'VE TAKEN.

OH, THE KILLINGS MEAN *NOTHING* TO ME. I GET NOTHING FROM THEM, PER SE. I'M NOT WORSHIPPING FORGOTTEN GODS--I DON'T BELIEVE IN *ANY* GOD.

COME ON, SAVAGE, YOU'RE *SUPPOSED* TO BE INTELLIGENT TOO. DON'T YOU SEE *WHAT* I'VE BEEN DOING THIS *WHOLE TIME?*

OH. YEAH. OF *COURSE* I SEE.

ALL THIS MAYHEM WAS A CHESS GAME. YOU GAMBLED THAT IF YOU DID THIS, WE'D RELEASE MY FATHER TO HELP FIND YOU.

YES, THE MURDERS WERE JUST MOVES ON THE BOARD.

YOU EXPECTED JONATHAN SAVAGE TO COME...THAT WE'D RELEASE HIM FROM PRISON, THE ONE PLACE YOU COULDN'T REACH HIM, AND THAT HE'D BE HERE.

SO I COULD *KILL* HIM, THAT'S RIGHT. SO I COULD SMELL THE WARM IRON OF HIS INSIDES ONCE I'D *GUTTED* HIM.

OH, AND WITH MY MURDERS BEING *ALL* A MEANS TO GET HIM *HERE*-- IN A WAY YOU MIGHT SAY *HE'S* THE CAUSE OF *THESE* KILLINGS TOO. IF HE HADN'T KILLED MY DAD, *NONE* OF THIS WOULD HAVE HAPPENED. DO YOU *REALIZE* THAT?

IT CROSSED MY MIND, BELIEVE ME. FROM THE MOMENT I KNEW THERE WAS A COPYCAT. *OTHER* THING I REALIZE--WE'VE GOT OURSELVES A PROBLEM.

I'D SAY *YOU* HAVE. ABSOLUTELY.

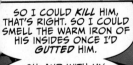

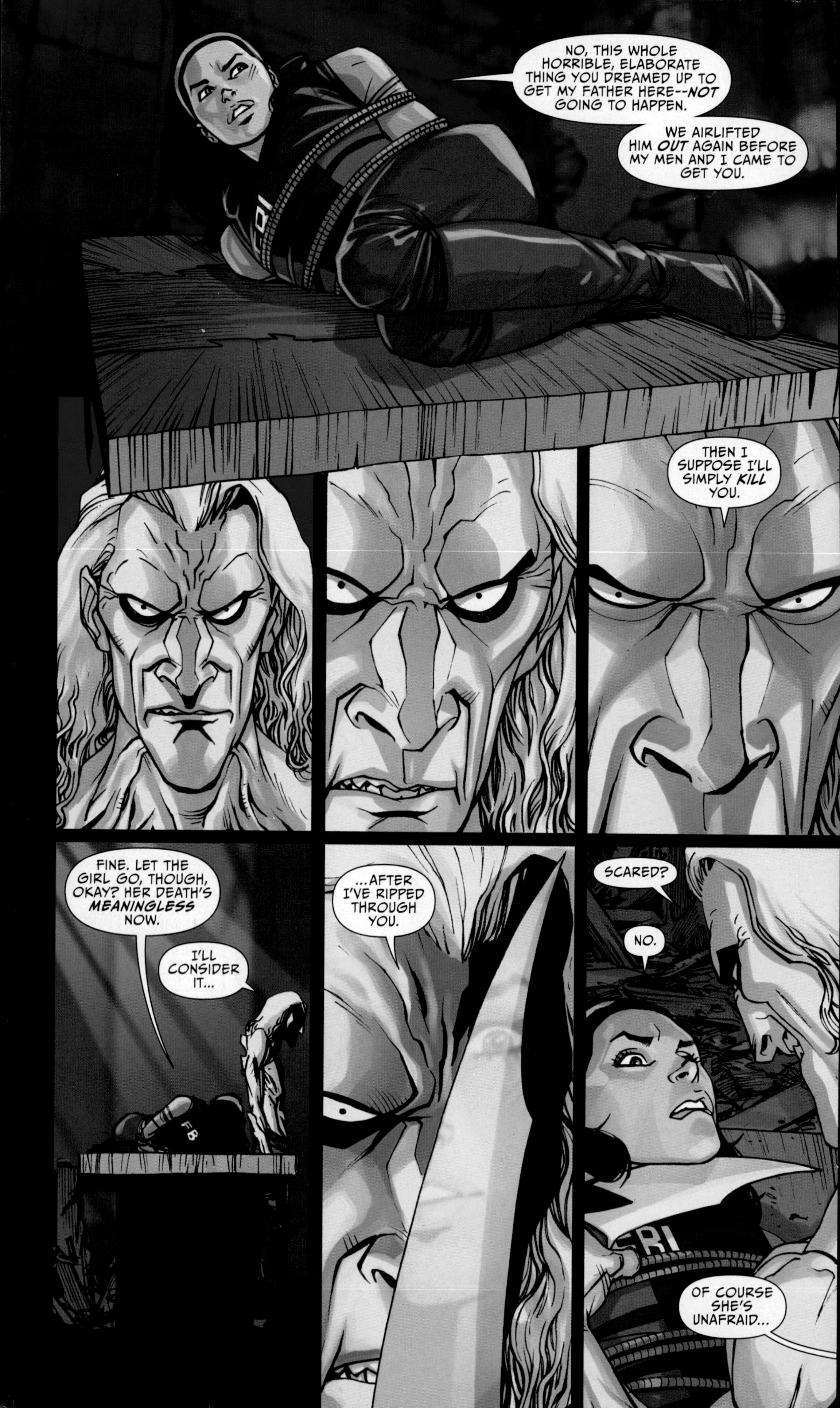
NO, THIS WHOLE HORRIBLE, ELABORATE THING YOU DREAMED UP TO GET MY FATHER HERE--NOT GOING TO HAPPEN.
WE AIRLIFTED HIM OUT AGAIN BEFORE MY MEN AND I CAME TO GET YOU.
THEN I SUPPOSE I'LL SIMPLY KILL YOU.
FINE. LET THE GIRL GO, THOUGH, OKAY? HER DEATH'S MEANINGLESS NOW.
I'LL CONSIDER IT...
...AFTER I'VE RIPPED THROUGH YOU.
SCARED?
NO.
OF COURSE SHE'S UNAFRAID...

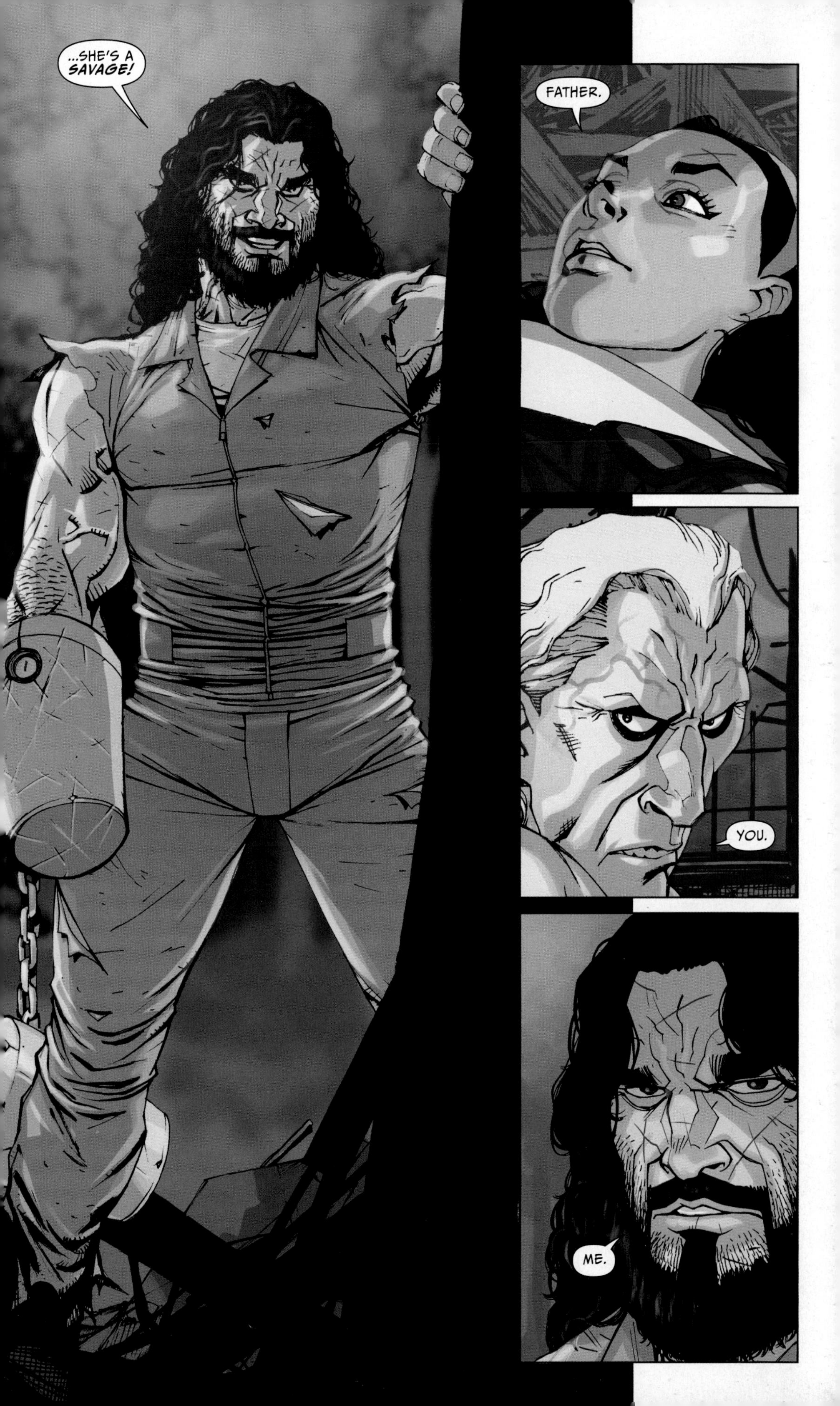

...SHE'S A SAVAGE!
FATHER.
YOU.
ME.

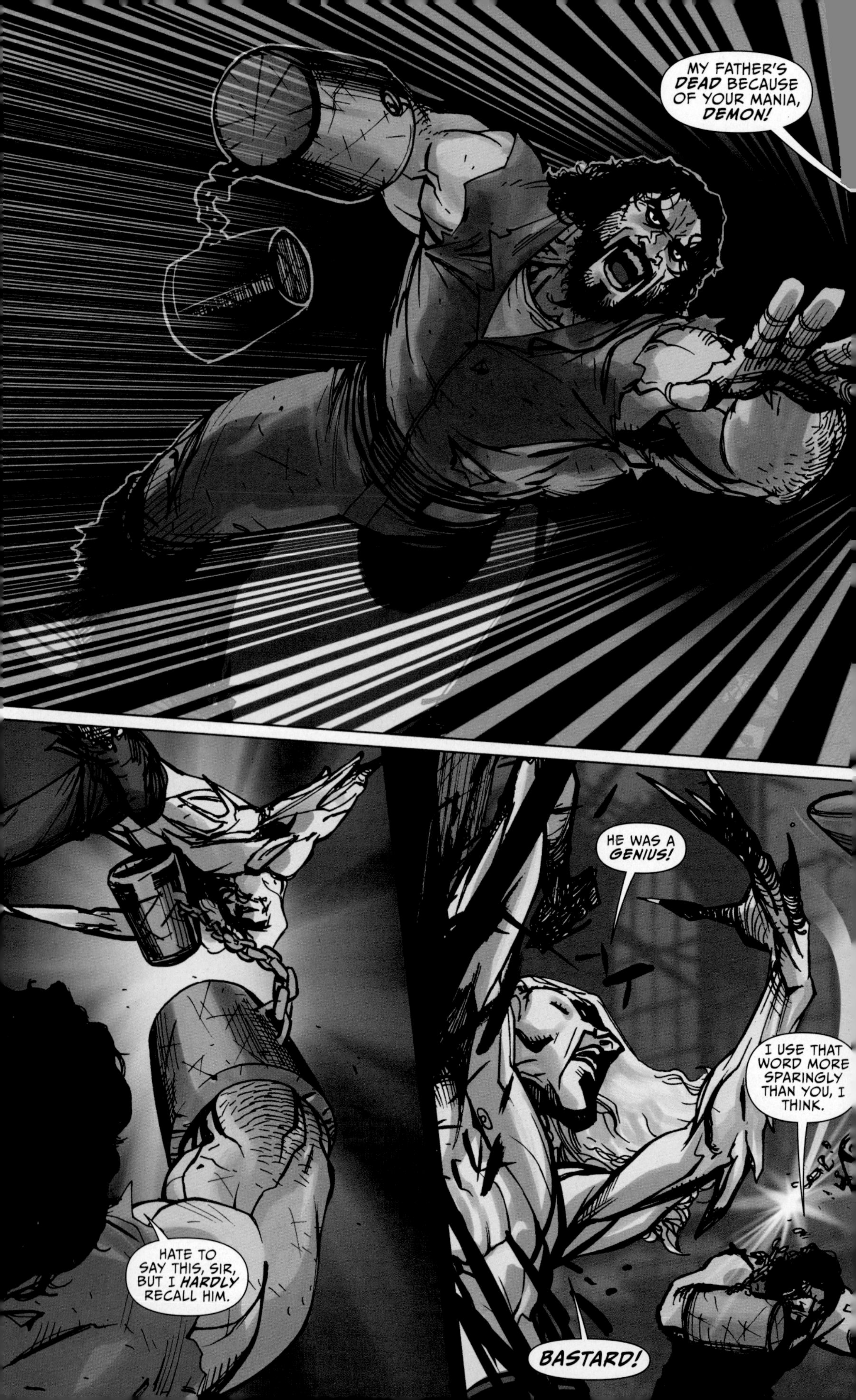
MY FATHER'S DEAD BECAUSE OF YOUR MANIA, DEMON!
HE WAS A GENIUS!
I USE THAT WORD MORE SPARINGLY THAN YOU, I THINK.
HATE TO SAY THIS, SIR, BUT I HARDLY RECALL HIM.
BASTARD!

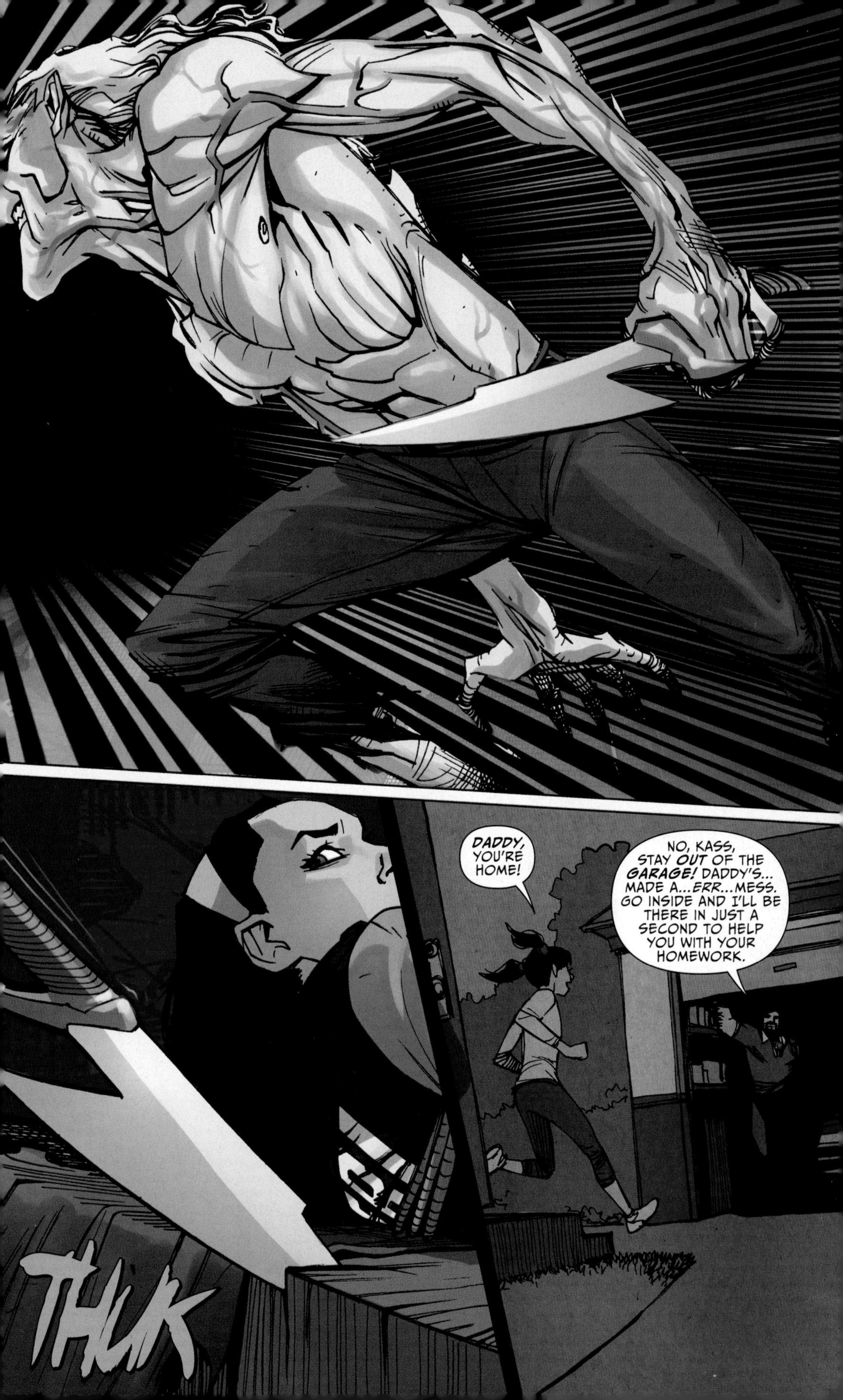
DADDY, YOU'RE HOME!
NO, KASS, STAY OUT OF THE GARAGE! DADDY'S... MADE A...ERR...MESS. GO INSIDE AND I'LL BE THERE IN JUST A SECOND TO HELP YOU WITH YOUR HOMEWORK.
THUK

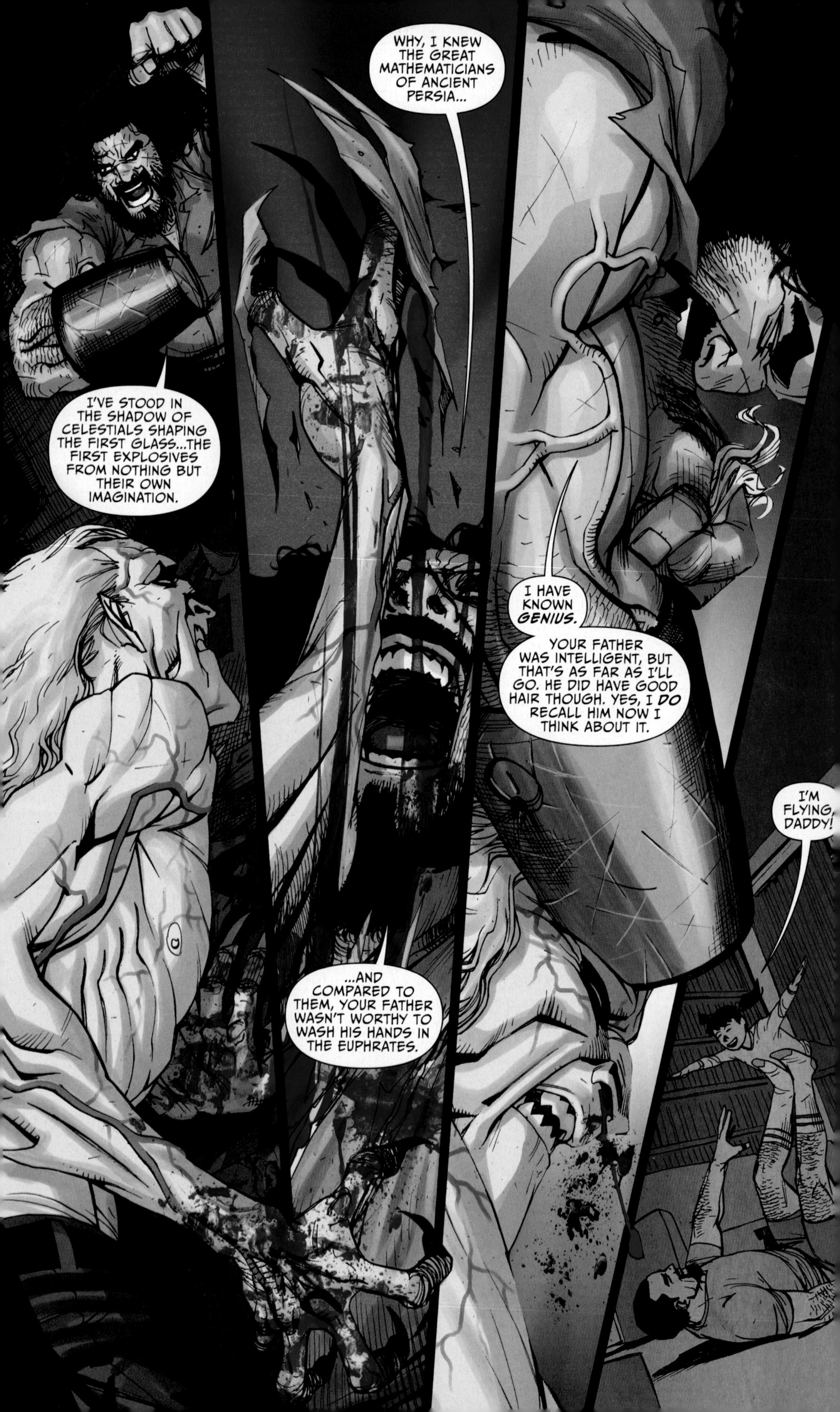
I'VE STOOD IN THE SHADOW OF CELESTIALS SHAPING THE FIRST GLASS...THE FIRST EXPLOSIVES FROM NOTHING BUT THEIR OWN IMAGINATION.
WHY, I KNEW THE GREAT MATHEMATICIANS OF ANCIENT PERSIA...
...AND COMPARED TO THEM, YOUR FATHER WASN'T WORTHY TO WASH HIS HANDS IN THE EUPHRATES.
I HAVE KNOWN ***GENIUS.***
YOUR FATHER WAS INTELLIGENT, BUT THAT'S AS FAR AS I'LL GO. HE DID HAVE GOOD HAIR THOUGH. YES, I ***DO*** RECALL HIM NOW I THINK ABOUT IT.
I'M FLYING, DADDY!

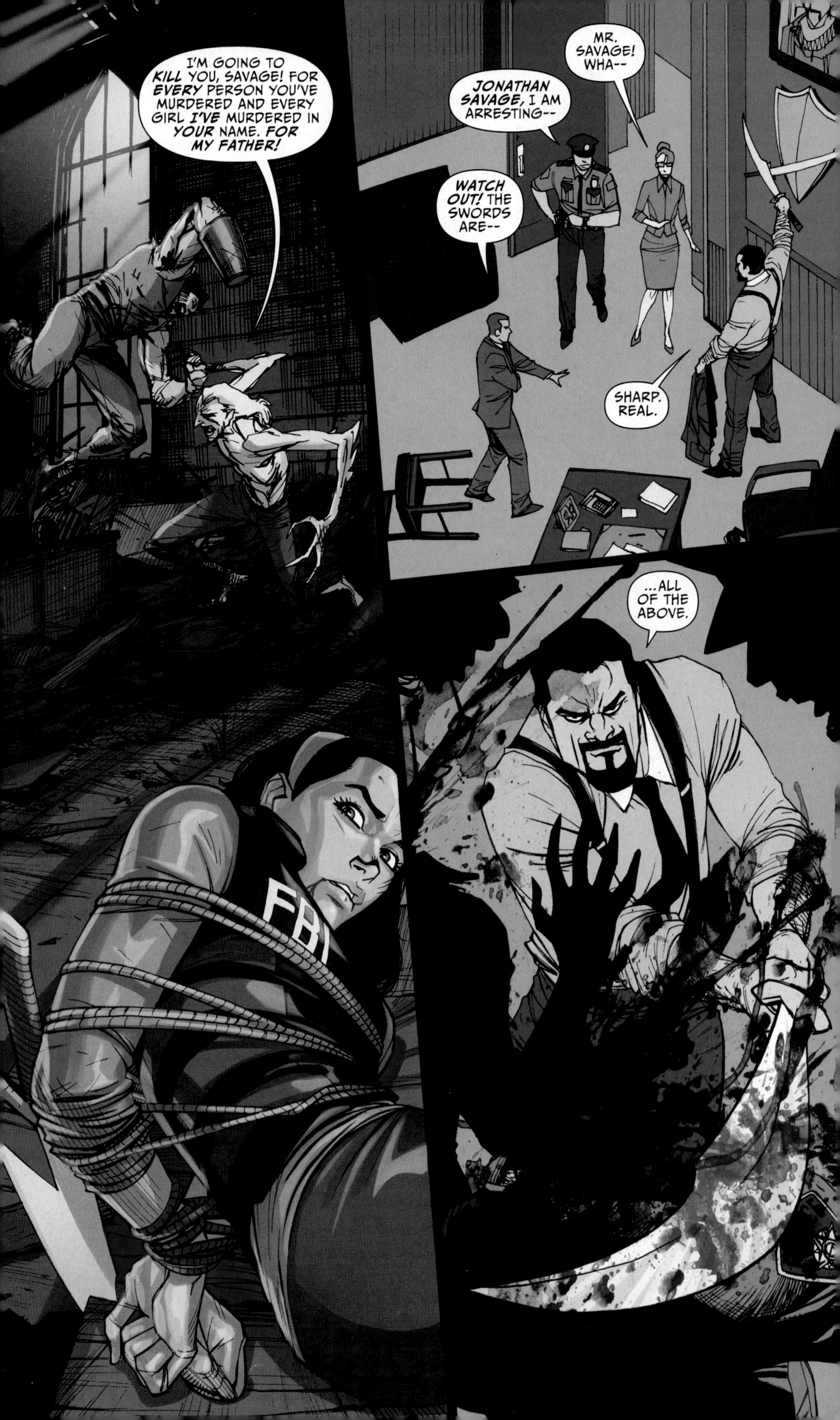
I'M GOING TO KILL YOU, SAVAGE! FOR EVERY PERSON YOU'VE MURDERED AND EVERY GIRL I'VE MURDERED IN YOUR NAME. FOR MY FATHER!
MR. SAVAGE! WHA--
JONATHAN SAVAGE, I AM ARRESTING--
WATCH OUT! THE SWORDS ARE--
SHARP. REAL.
...ALL OF THE ABOVE.
FBI

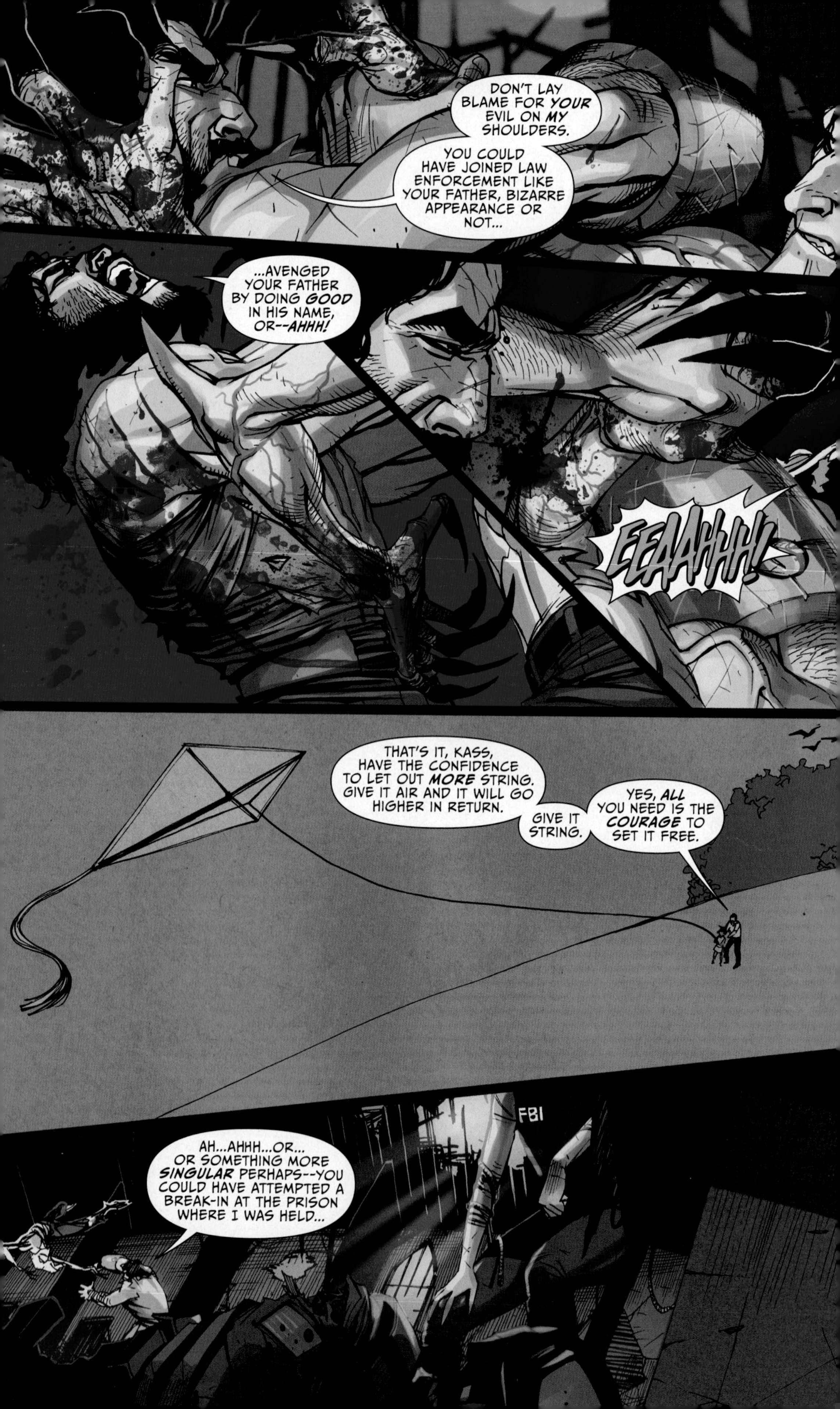
DON'T LAY BLAME FOR YOUR EVIL ON MY SHOULDERS.
YOU COULD HAVE JOINED LAW ENFORCEMENT LIKE YOUR FATHER, BIZARRE APPEARANCE OR NOT...
...AVENGED YOUR FATHER BY DOING GOOD IN HIS NAME, OR--AHHH!
EEAAHHH!
THAT'S IT, KASS, HAVE THE CONFIDENCE TO LET OUT MORE STRING. GIVE IT AIR AND IT WILL GO HIGHER IN RETURN.
GIVE IT STRING.
YES, ALL YOU NEED IS THE COURAGE TO SET IT FREE.
FBI
AH...AHHH...OR... OR SOMETHING MORE SINGULAR PERHAPS--YOU COULD HAVE ATTEMPTED A BREAK-IN AT THE PRISON WHERE I WAS HELD...

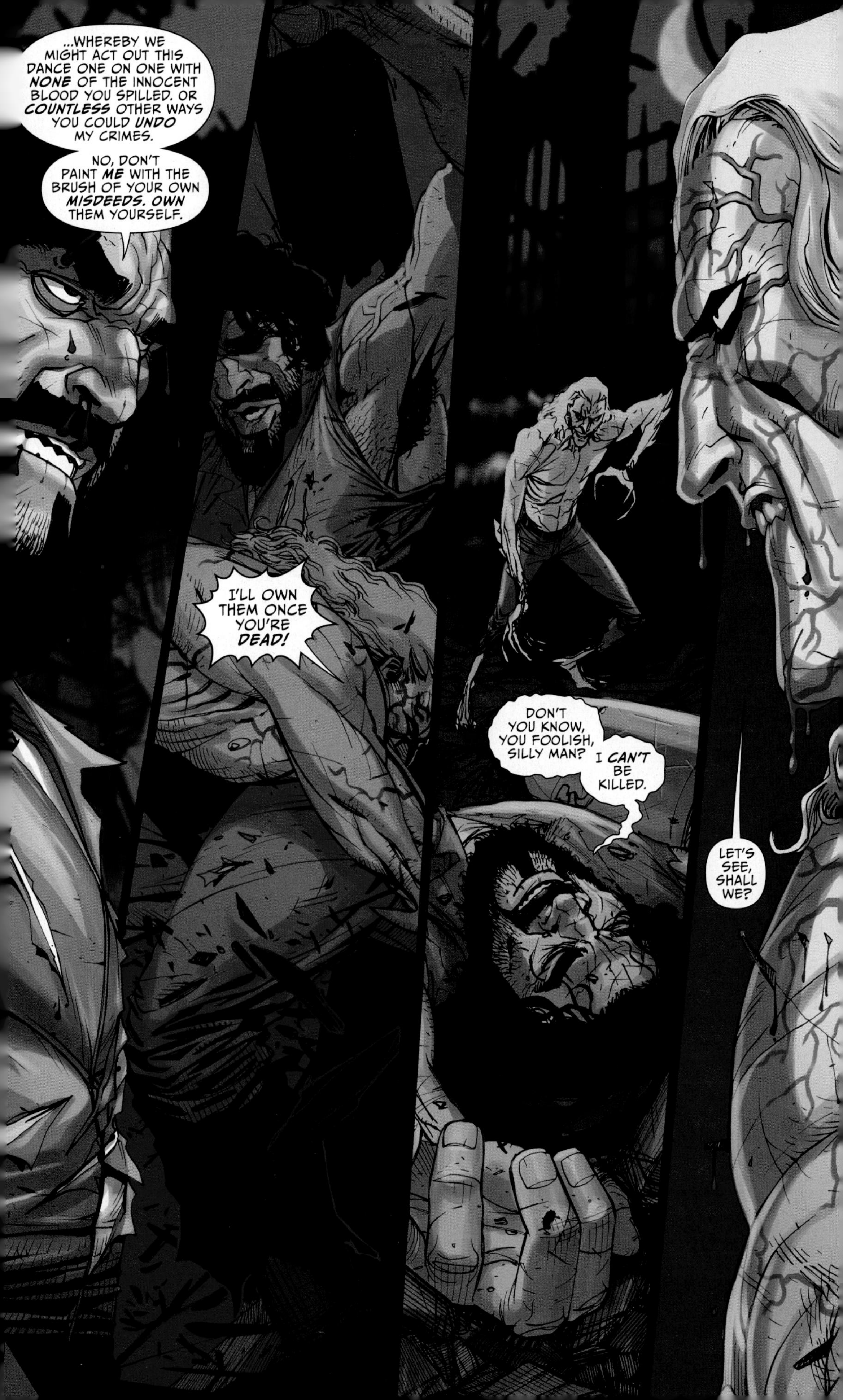

...WHEREBY WE MIGHT ACT OUT THIS DANCE ONE ON ONE WITH NONE OF THE INNOCENT BLOOD YOU SPILLED. OR COUNTLESS OTHER WAYS YOU COULD UNDO MY CRIMES.
NO, DON'T PAINT ME WITH THE BRUSH OF YOUR OWN MISDEEDS. OWN THEM YOURSELF.
I'LL OWN THEM ONCE YOU'RE DEAD!
DON'T YOU KNOW, YOU FOOLISH, SILLY MAN?
I CAN'T BE KILLED.
LET'S SEE, SHALL WE?

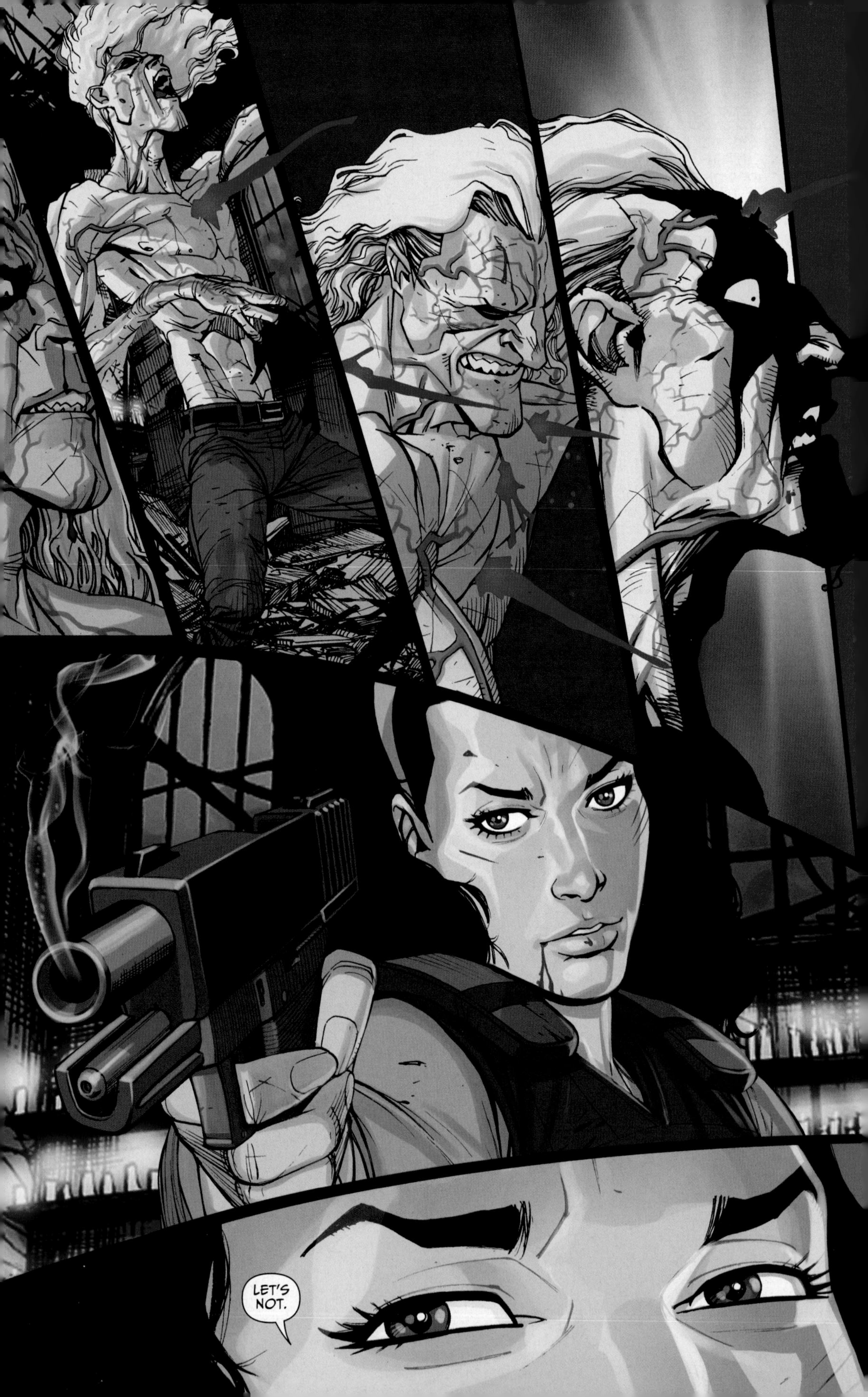
LET'S NOT.

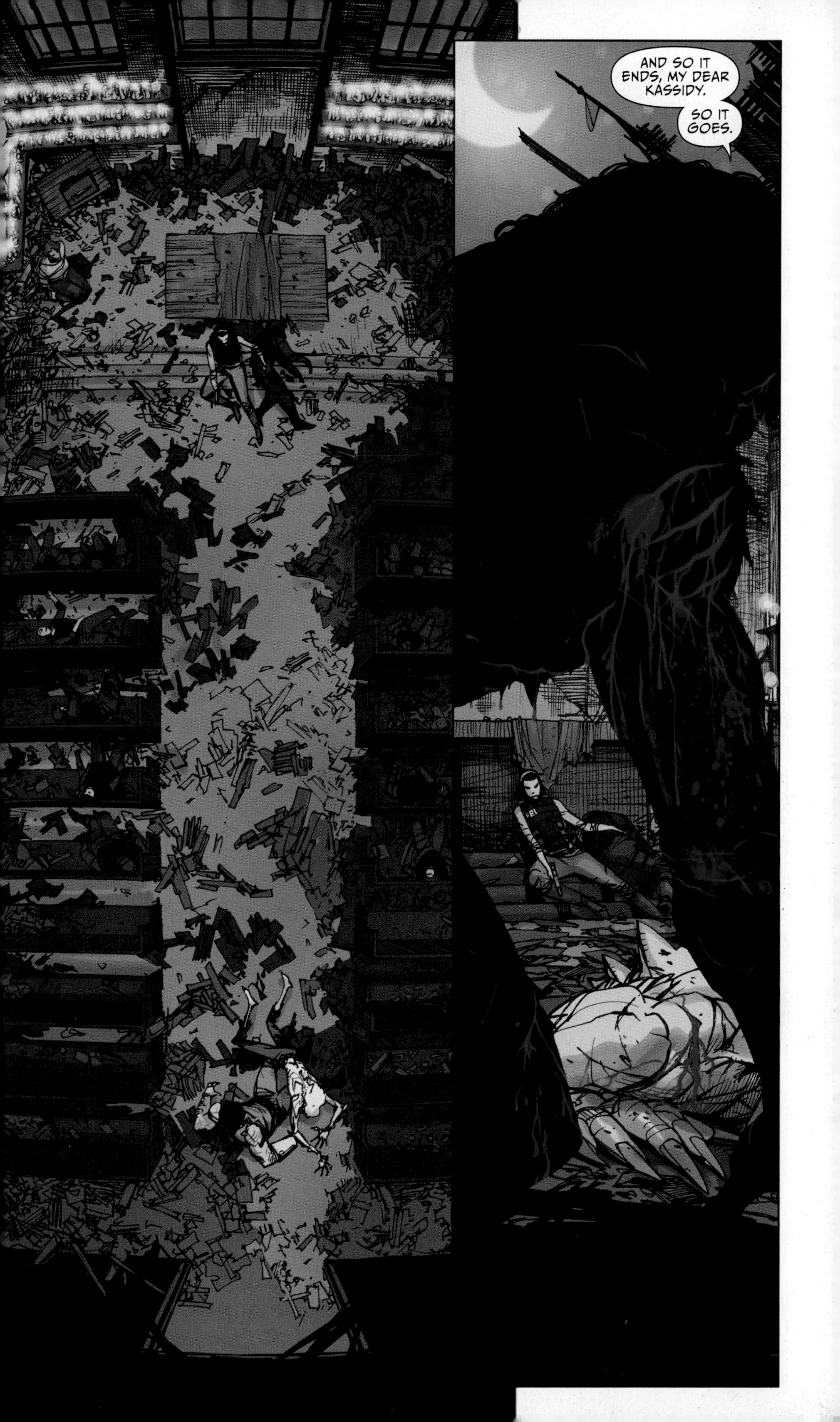
AND SO IT ENDS, MY DEAR KASSIDY.
SO IT GOES.

OR RATHER I DO. *GO*, I MEAN.

FATHER. PLEASE DON'T--

GO? I *HAVE* TO, DON'T YOU SEE? I *CAN'T* GO BACK TO PRISON.

NO, LISTEN--

LOOK, I *SAVED* YOU, DIDN'T I? I COULD HAVE ESCAPED MY ESCORT BACK TO BELLE REVE, THEN SIMPLY KEPT GOING...AND *DON'T* THINK IT DIDN'T CROSS MY MIND.

SURELY THAT PROVES I'M NOT *QUITE* THE MONSTER I SEEM.

NO, PERHAPS IT *DOESN'T* AT THAT, BUT IT DOES SHOW YOU I *AM* YOUR FATHER AND I CARE ABOUT YOU... AT LEAST AS MUCH AS I CARE FOR ANYONE.

BUT NOW I *MUST GO.* IT'S SIMPLY A CA OF NECESSI

AND WHEN I SAID "PLEASE DON'T," YOU DIDN'T LET ME FINISH. I WAS GOING TO SAY...

...PLEASE DON'T *MAKE* ME KILL YOU.

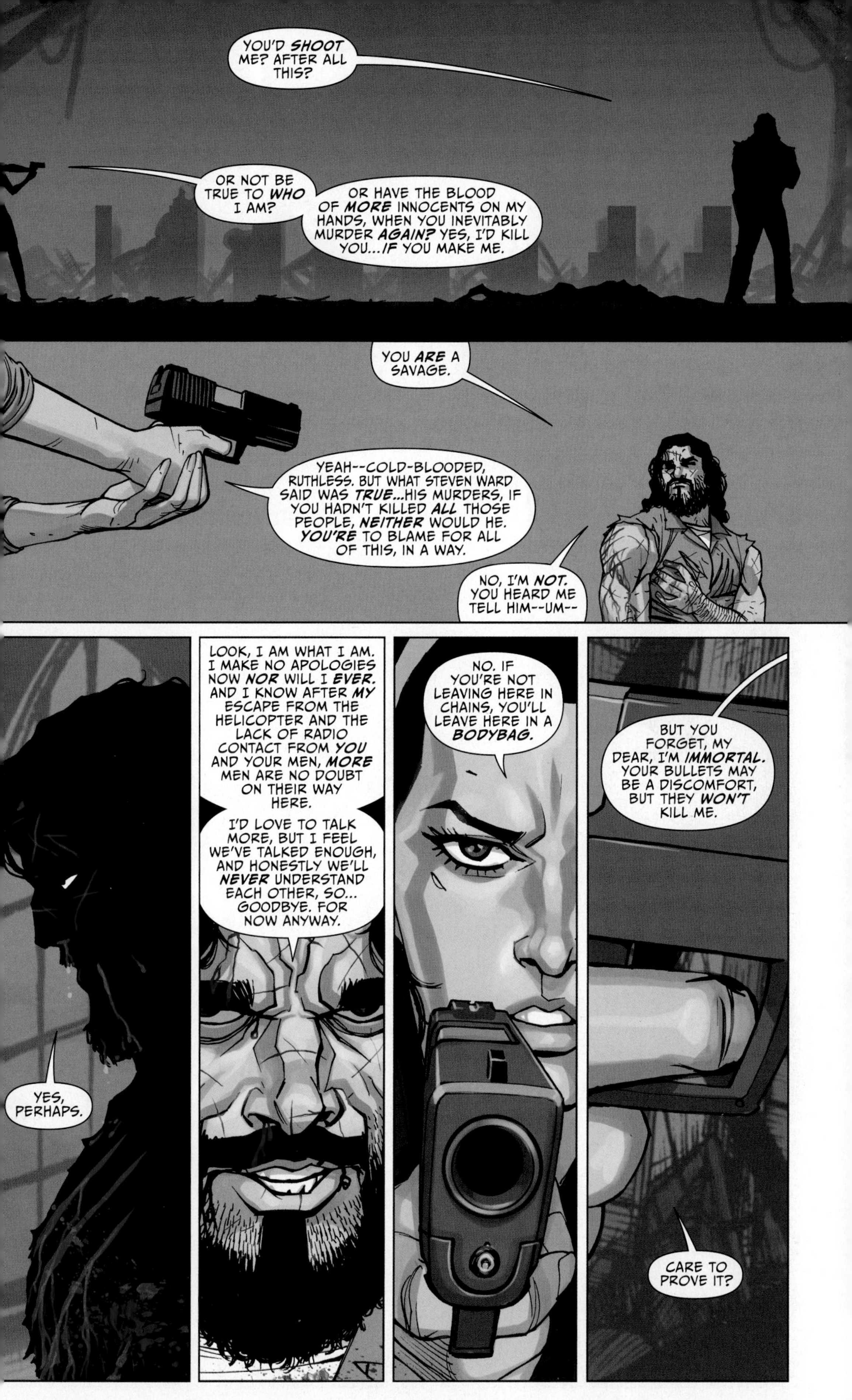
YOU'D SHOOT ME? AFTER ALL THIS?
OR NOT BE TRUE TO WHO I AM?
OR HAVE THE BLOOD OF MORE INNOCENTS ON MY HANDS, WHEN YOU INEVITABLY MURDER AGAIN? YES, I'D KILL YOU...IF YOU MAKE ME.
YOU ARE A SAVAGE.
YEAH--COLD-BLOODED, RUTHLESS. BUT WHAT STEVEN WARD SAID WAS TRUE...HIS MURDERS, IF YOU HADN'T KILLED ALL THOSE PEOPLE, NEITHER WOULD HE. YOU'RE TO BLAME FOR ALL OF THIS, IN A WAY.
NO, I'M NOT. YOU HEARD ME TELL HIM--UM--
YES, PERHAPS.
LOOK, I AM WHAT I AM. I MAKE NO APOLOGIES NOW NOR WILL I EVER. AND I KNOW AFTER MY ESCAPE FROM THE HELICOPTER AND THE LACK OF RADIO CONTACT FROM YOU AND YOUR MEN, MORE MEN ARE NO DOUBT ON THEIR WAY HERE.
I'D LOVE TO TALK MORE, BUT I FEEL WE'VE TALKED ENOUGH, AND HONESTLY WE'LL NEVER UNDERSTAND EACH OTHER, SO... GOODBYE. FOR NOW ANYWAY.
NO. IF YOU'RE NOT LEAVING HERE IN CHAINS, YOU'LL LEAVE HERE IN A BODYBAG.
BUT YOU FORGET, MY DEAR, I'M IMMORTAL. YOUR BULLETS MAY BE A DISCOMFORT, BUT THEY WON'T KILL ME.
CARE TO PROVE IT?

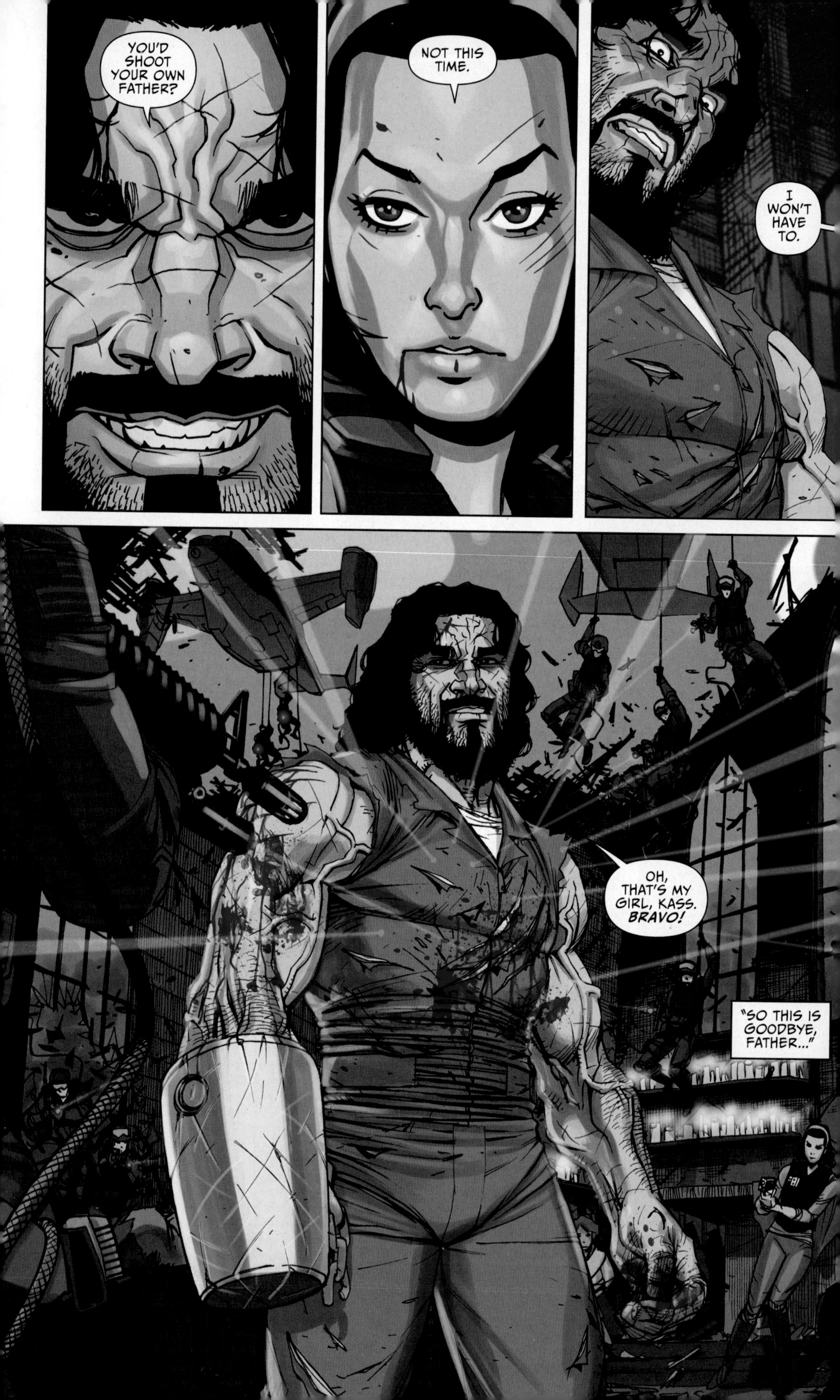
YOU'D SHOOT YOUR OWN FATHER?
NOT THIS TIME.
I WON'T HAVE TO.
OH, THAT'S MY GIRL, KASS. *BRAVO!*
"SO THIS IS GOODBYE, FATHER..."

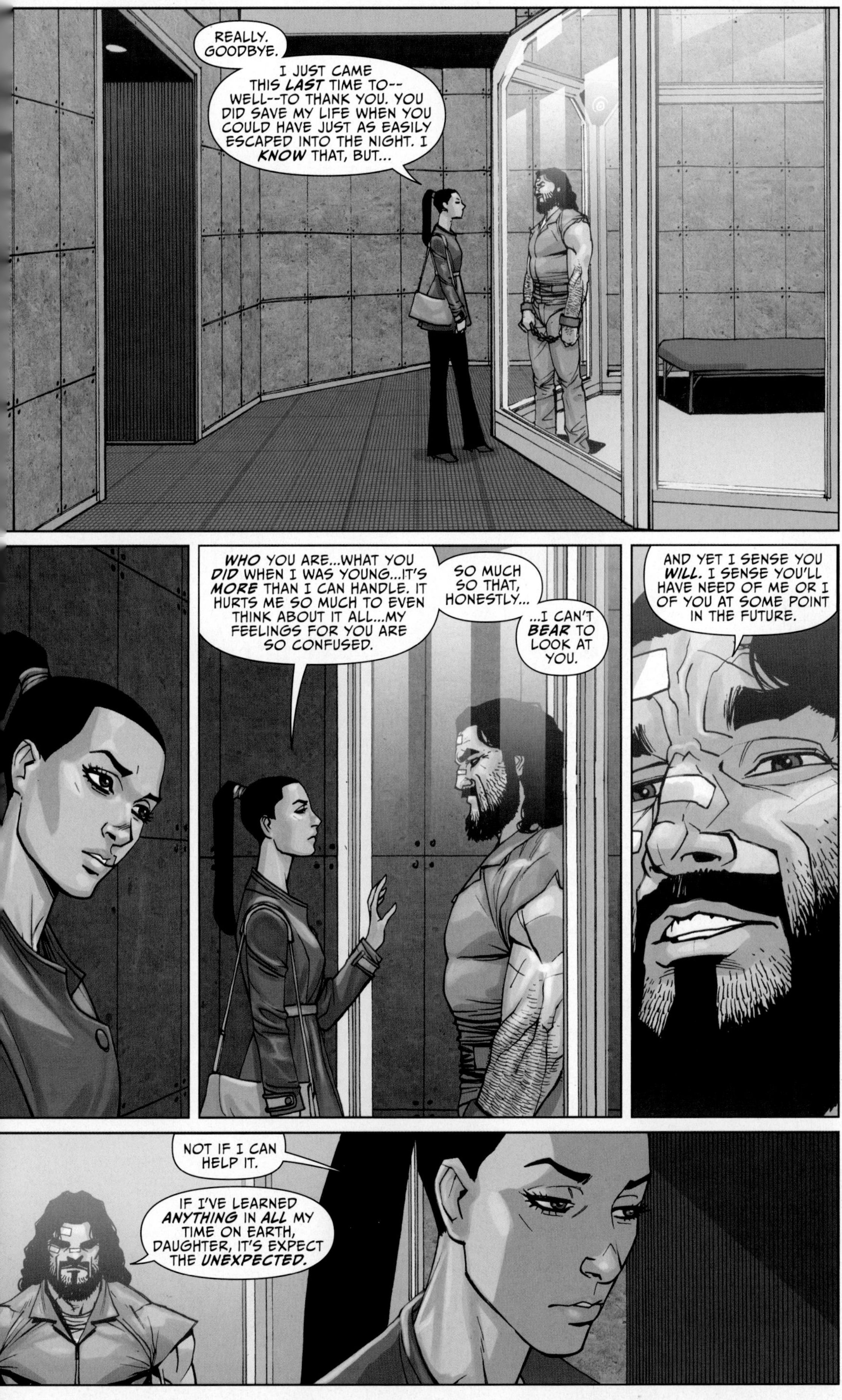
REALLY. GOODBYE.
I JUST CAME THIS LAST TIME TO--WELL--TO THANK YOU. YOU DID SAVE MY LIFE WHEN YOU COULD HAVE JUST AS EASILY ESCAPED INTO THE NIGHT. I KNOW THAT, BUT...
WHO YOU ARE...WHAT YOU DID WHEN I WAS YOUNG...IT'S MORE THAN I CAN HANDLE. IT HURTS ME SO MUCH TO EVEN THINK ABOUT IT ALL...MY FEELINGS FOR YOU ARE SO CONFUSED.
SO MUCH SO THAT, HONESTLY...
...I CAN'T BEAR TO LOOK AT YOU.
AND YET I SENSE YOU WILL. I SENSE YOU'LL HAVE NEED OF ME OR I OF YOU AT SOME POINT IN THE FUTURE.
NOT IF I CAN HELP IT.
IF I'VE LEARNED ANYTHING IN ALL MY TIME ON EARTH, DAUGHTER, IT'S EXPECT THE UNEXPECTED.

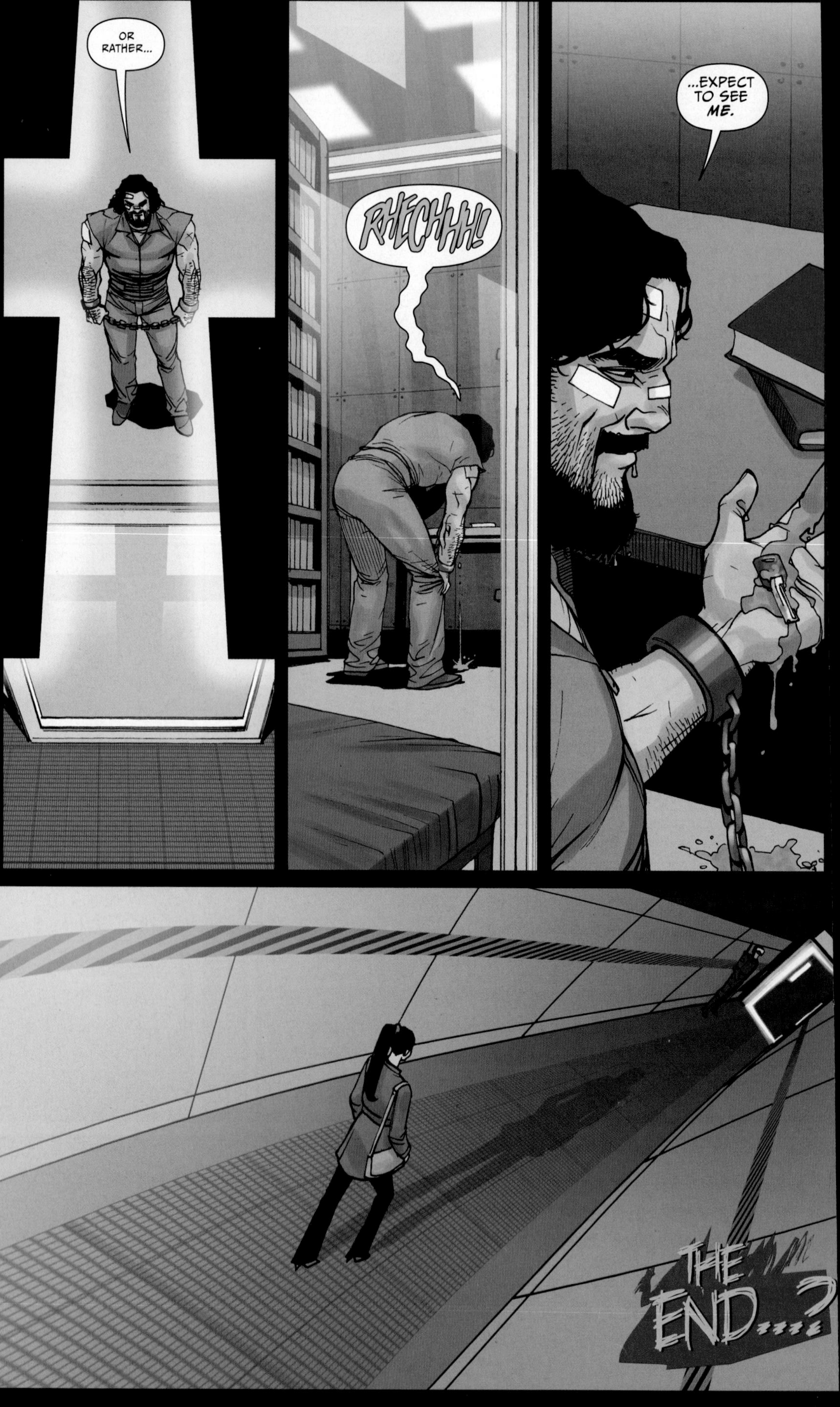
OR RATHER...
RHECHHH!
...EXPECT TO SEE ME.
THE END...?

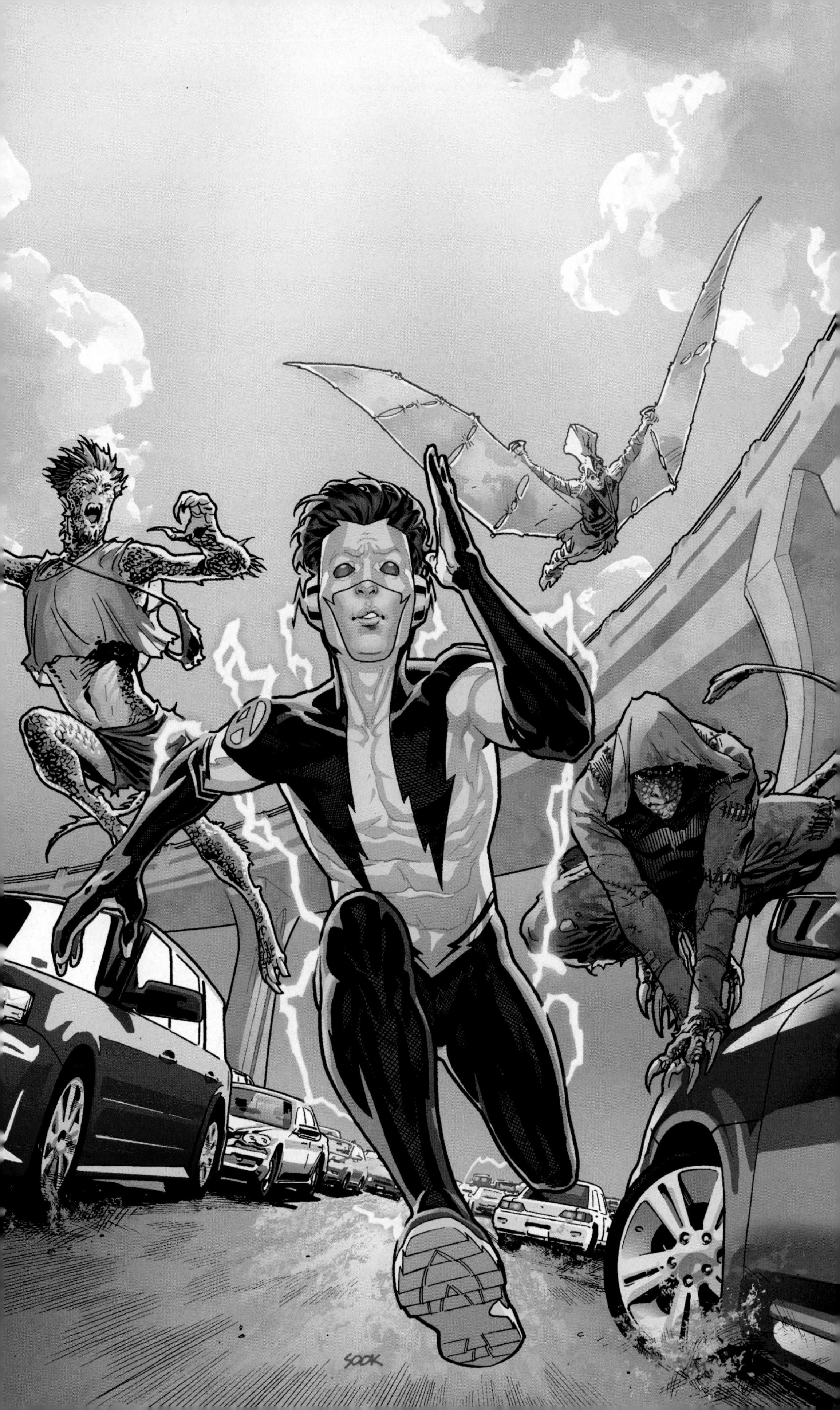
SOOK

WHEN DINOSAURS WALKED THE EARTH

FABIAN NICIEZA writer **JORGE JIMÉNEZ** artist

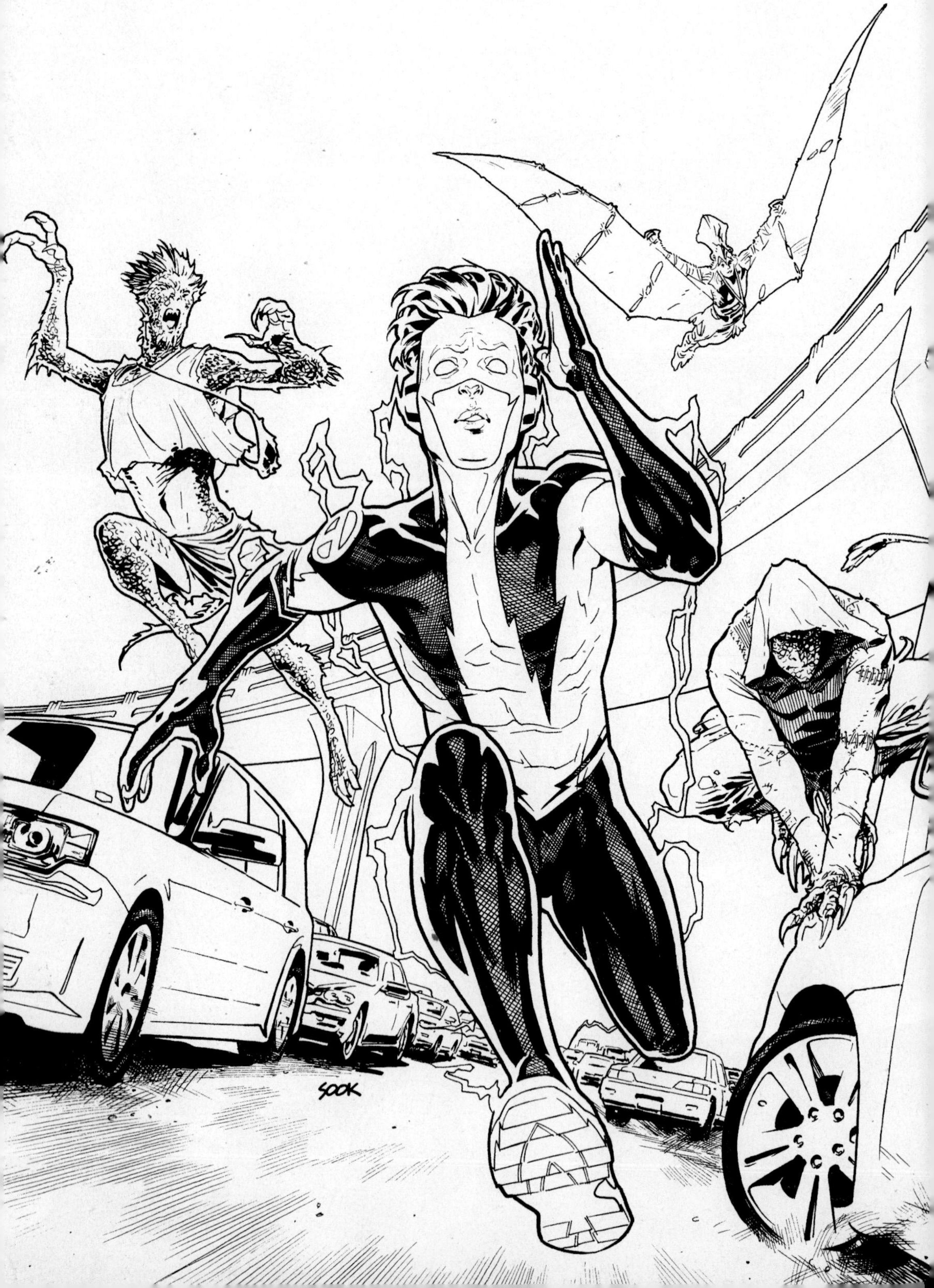
SOOK

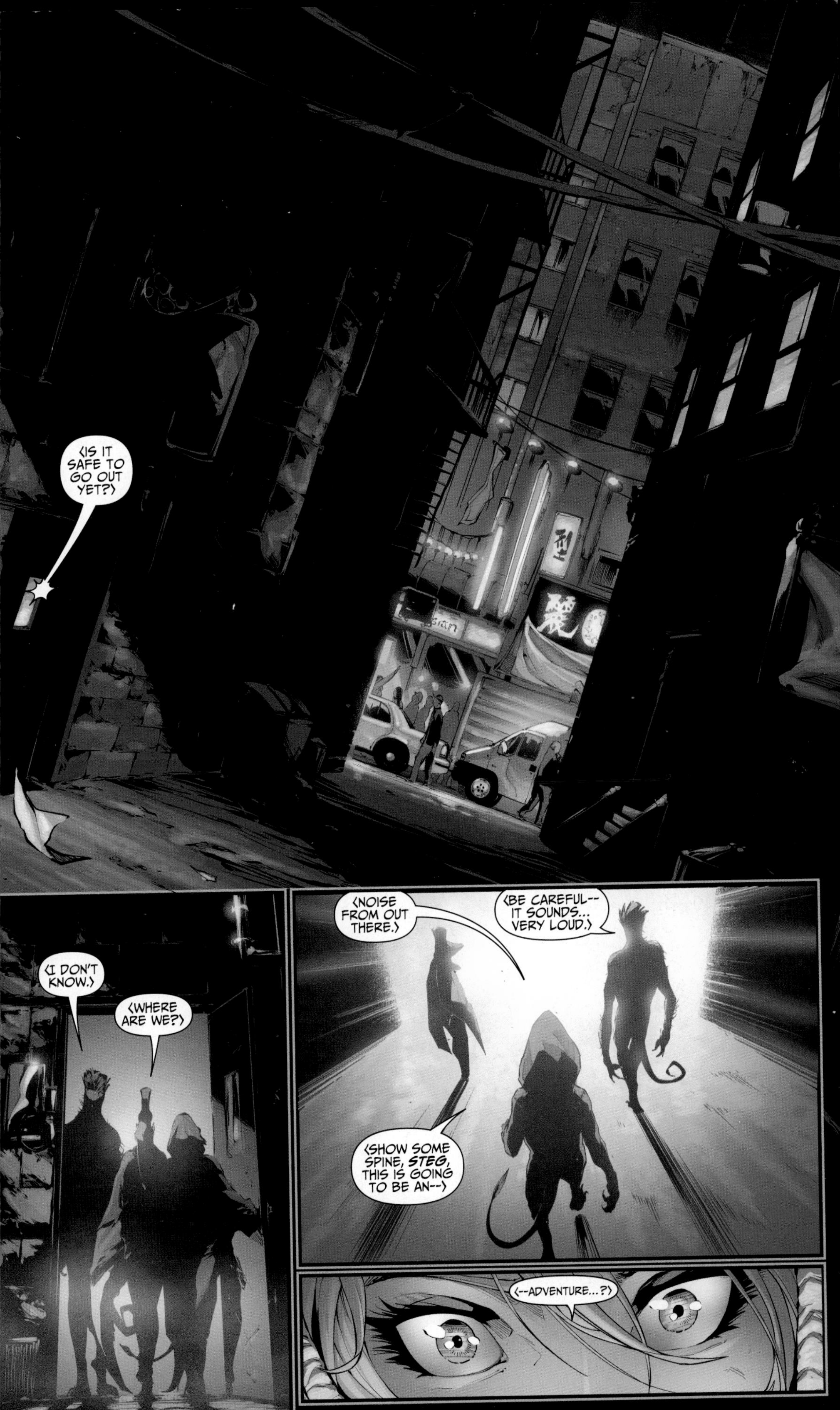

〈IS IT SAFE TO GO OUT YET?〉
〈I DON'T KNOW.〉
〈WHERE ARE WE?〉
〈NOISE FROM OUT THERE.〉
〈BE CAREFUL-- IT SOUNDS... VERY LOUD.〉
〈SHOW SOME SPINE, STEG, THIS IS GOING TO BE AN--〉
〈--ADVENTURE...?〉

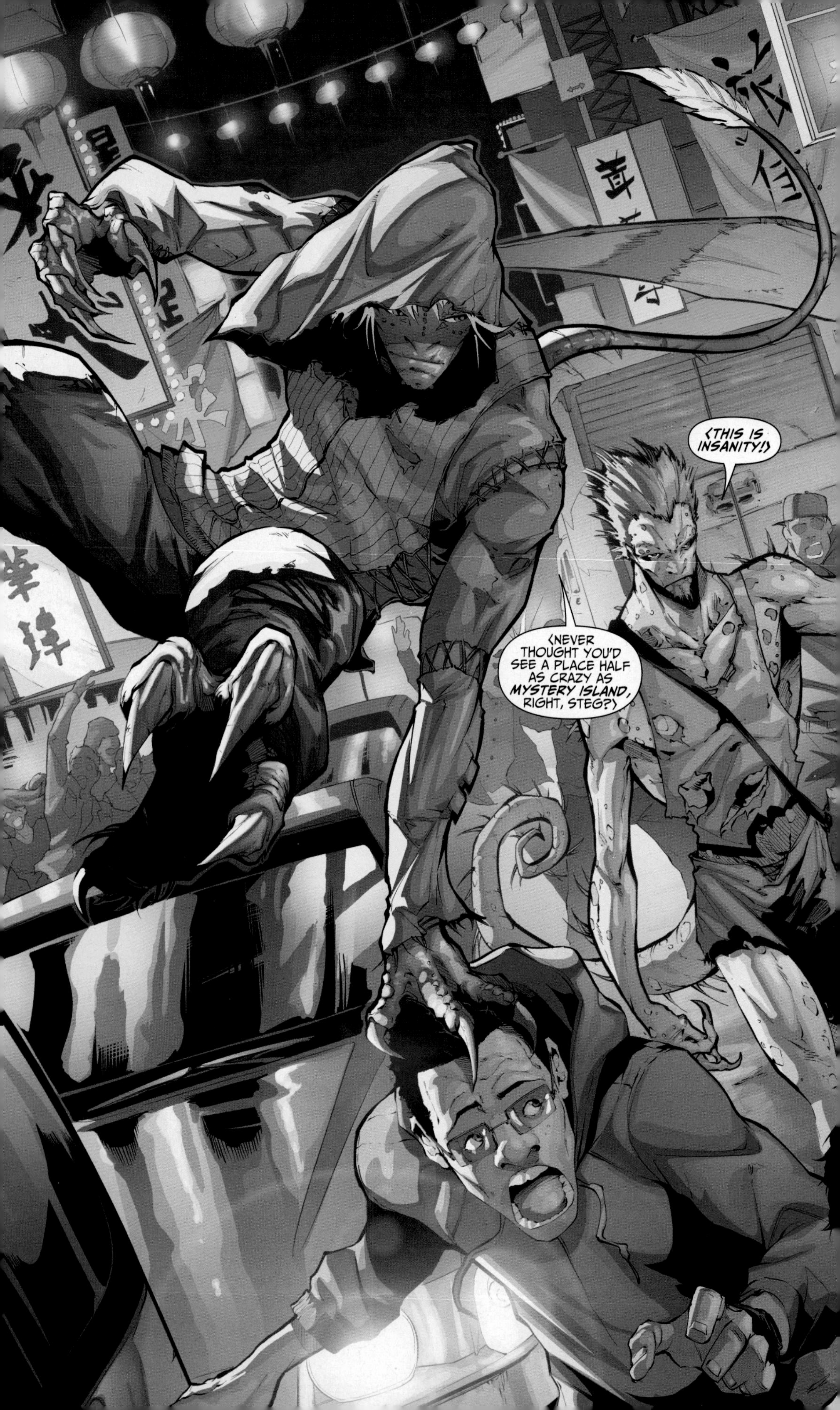

⟨NEVER THOUGHT YOU'D SEE A PLACE HALF AS CRAZY AS MYSTERY ISLAND, RIGHT, STEG?⟩
⟨THIS IS INSANITY!⟩

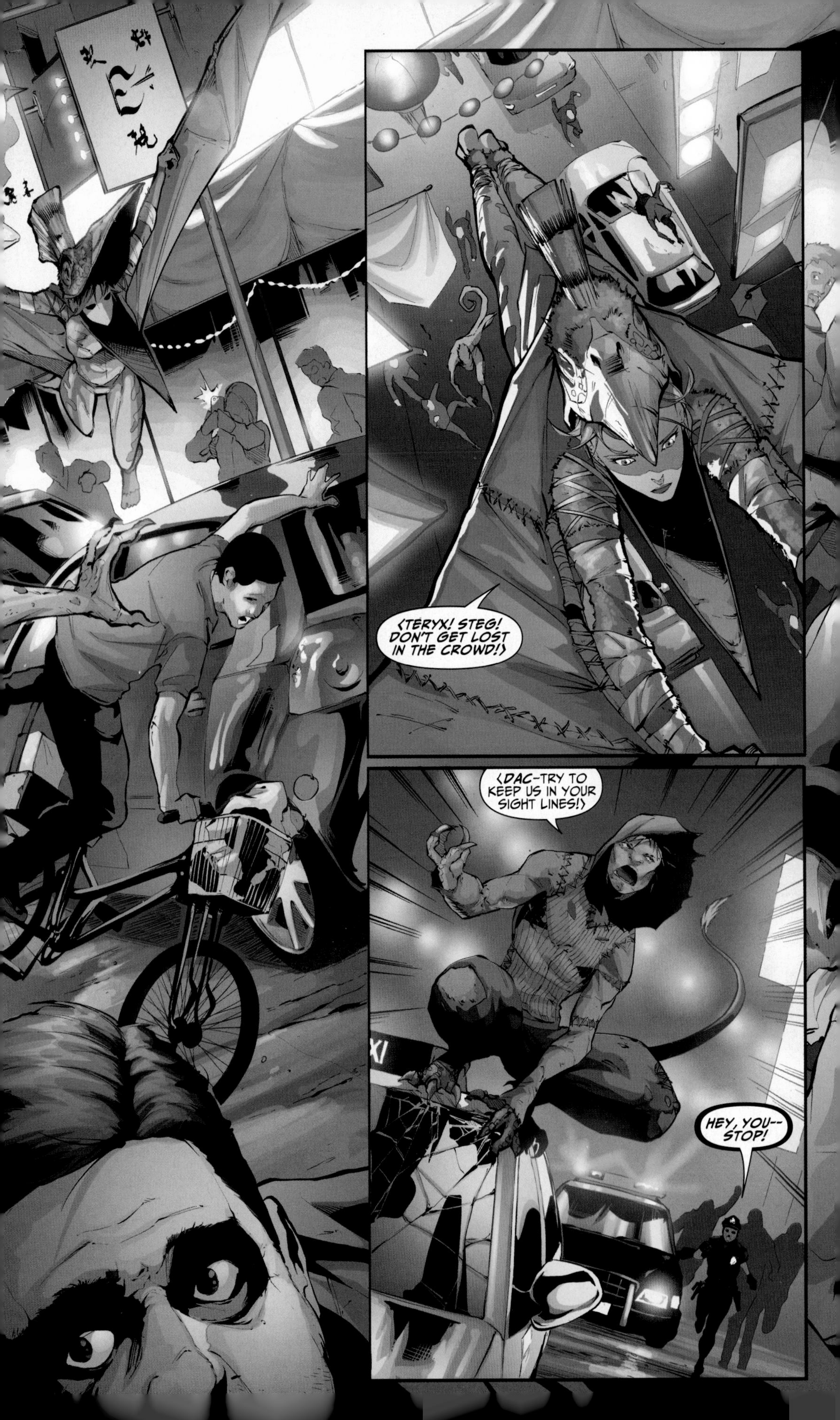

⟨TERYX! STEG! DON'T GET LOST IN THE CROWD!⟩
⟨DAC--TRY TO KEEP US IN YOUR SIGHT LINES!⟩
HEY, YOU-- STOP!

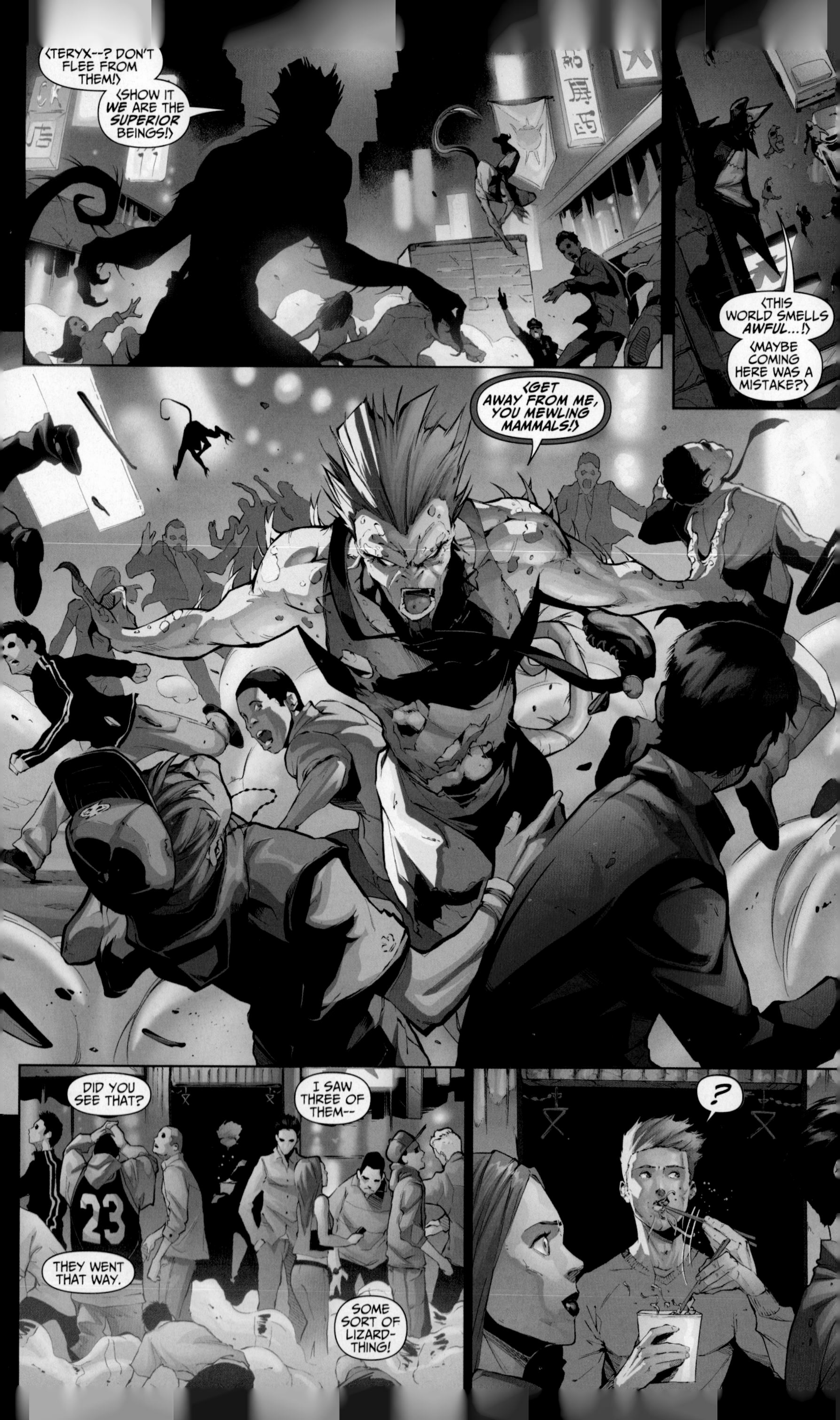
〈TERYX--? DON'T FLEE FROM THEM!〉
〈SHOW IT WE ARE THE SUPERIOR BEINGS!〉
〈THIS WORLD SMELLS AWFUL...!〉
〈MAYBE COMING HERE WAS A MISTAKE?〉
〈GET AWAY FROM ME, YOU MEWLING MAMMALS!〉
DID YOU SEE THAT?
I SAW THREE OF THEM--
THEY WENT THAT WAY.
SOME SORT OF LIZARD-THING!
?

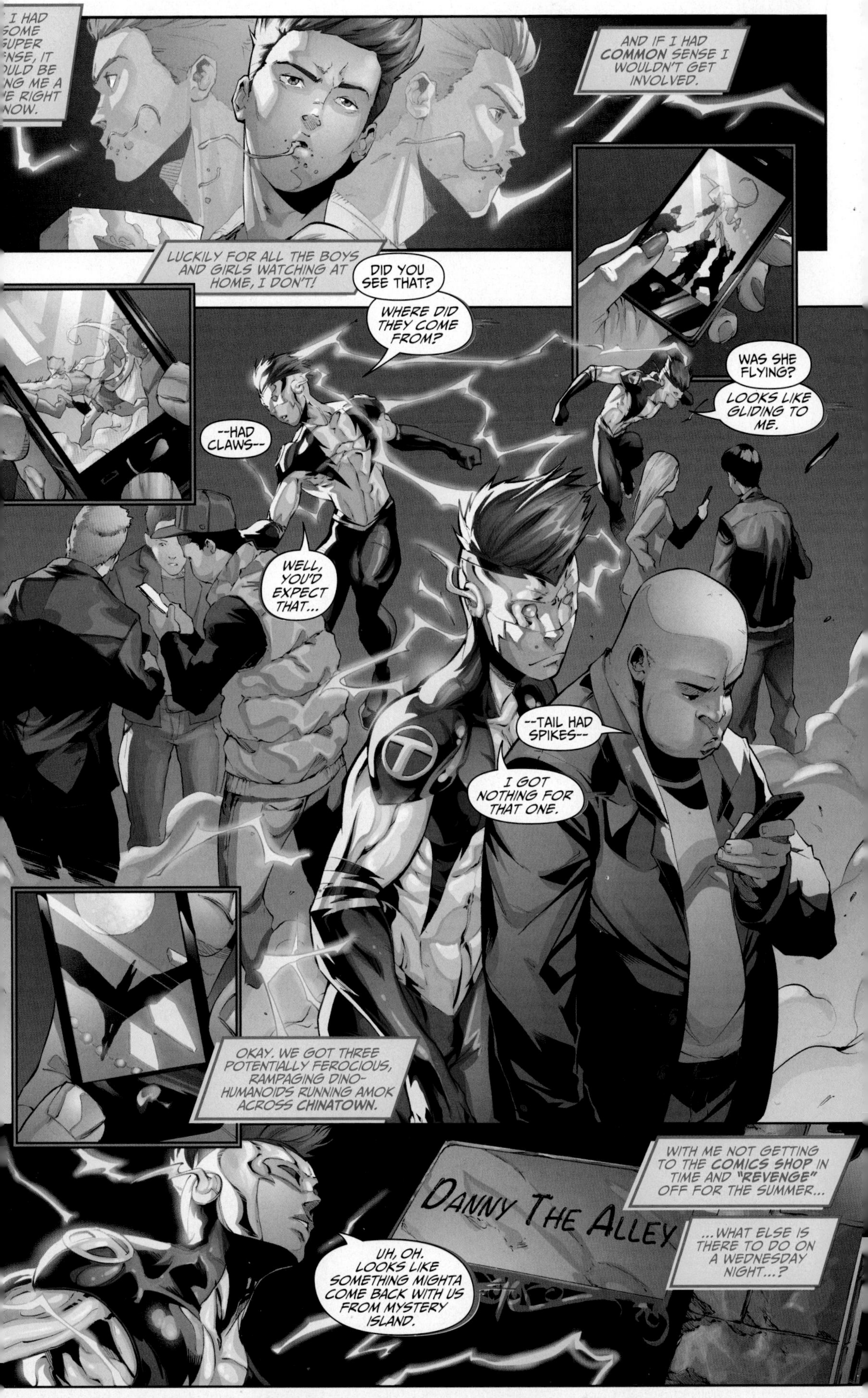
I HAD SOME SUPER NSE, IT OULD BE NG ME A E RIGHT NOW.
AND IF I HAD COMMON SENSE I WOULDN'T GET INVOLVED.
LUCKILY FOR ALL THE BOYS AND GIRLS WATCHING AT HOME, I DON'T!
DID YOU SEE THAT?
WHERE DID THEY COME FROM?
--HAD CLAWS--
WAS SHE FLYING?
LOOKS LIKE GLIDING TO ME.
WELL, YOU'D EXPECT THAT...
--TAIL HAD SPIKES--
I GOT NOTHING FOR THAT ONE.
OKAY. WE GOT THREE POTENTIALLY FEROCIOUS, RAMPAGING DINO-HUMANOIDS RUNNING AMOK ACROSS CHINATOWN.
WITH ME NOT GETTING TO THE COMICS SHOP IN TIME AND "REVENGE" OFF FOR THE SUMMER...
DANNY THE ALLEY
...WHAT ELSE IS THERE TO DO ON A WEDNESDAY NIGHT...?
UH, OH. LOOKS LIKE SOMETHING MIGHTA COME BACK WITH US FROM MYSTERY ISLAND.

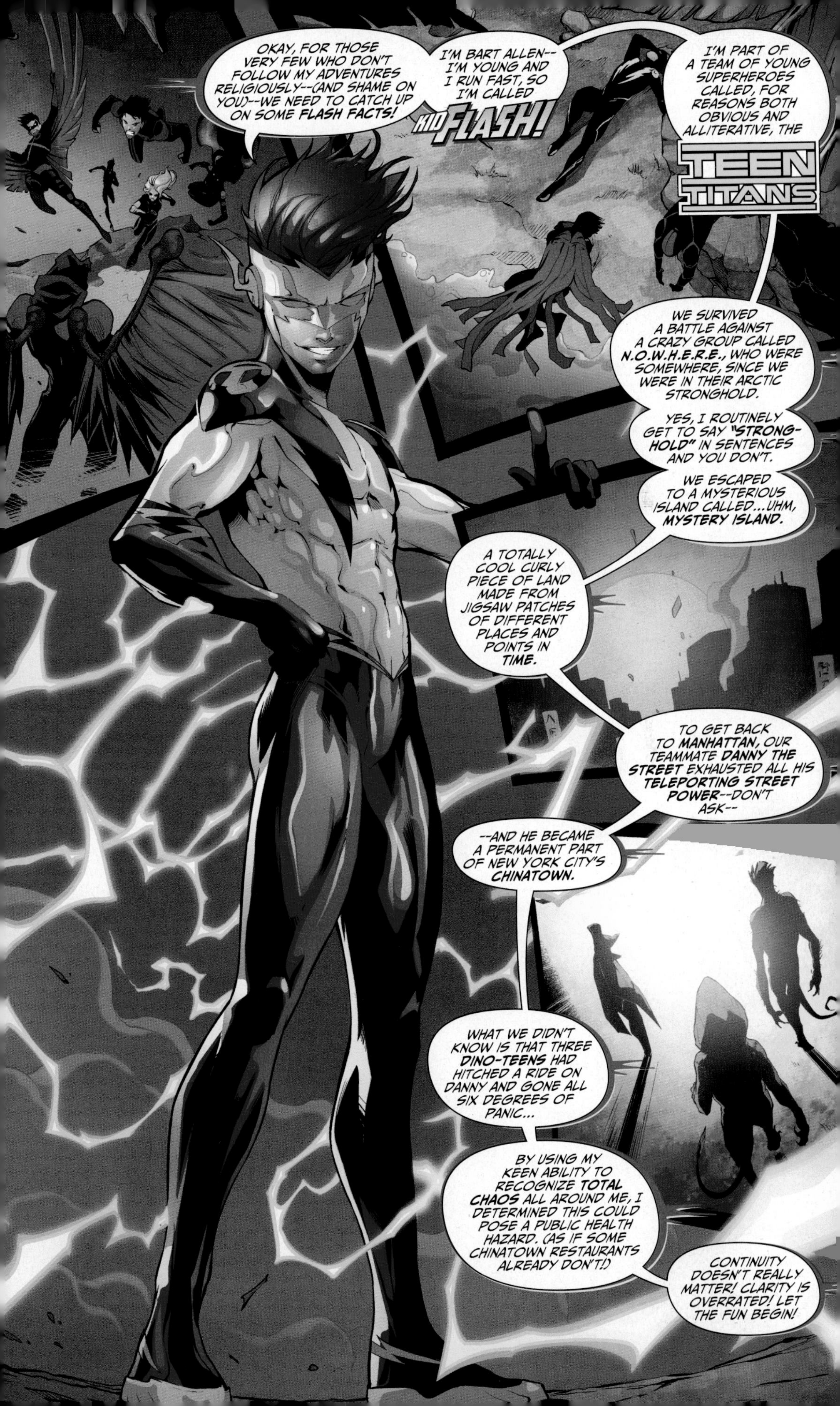
OKAY, FOR THOSE VERY FEW WHO DON'T FOLLOW MY ADVENTURES RELIGIOUSLY--(AND SHAME ON YOU)--WE NEED TO CATCH UP ON SOME FLASH FACTS!
I'M BART ALLEN-- I'M YOUNG AND I RUN FAST, SO I'M CALLED
KID FLASH!
I'M PART OF A TEAM OF YOUNG SUPERHEROES CALLED, FOR REASONS BOTH OBVIOUS AND ALLITERATIVE, THE
TEEN TITANS
WE SURVIVED A BATTLE AGAINST A CRAZY GROUP CALLED N.O.W.H.E.R.E., WHO WERE SOMEWHERE, SINCE WE WERE IN THEIR ARCTIC STRONGHOLD.
YES, I ROUTINELY GET TO SAY "STRONG-HOLD" IN SENTENCES AND YOU DON'T.
WE ESCAPED TO A MYSTERIOUS ISLAND CALLED...UHM, MYSTERY ISLAND.
A TOTALLY COOL CURLY PIECE OF LAND MADE FROM JIGSAW PATCHES OF DIFFERENT PLACES AND POINTS IN TIME.
TO GET BACK TO MANHATTAN, OUR TEAMMATE DANNY THE STREET EXHAUSTED ALL HIS TELEPORTING STREET POWER--DON'T ASK--
--AND HE BECAME A PERMANENT PART OF NEW YORK CITY'S CHINATOWN.
WHAT WE DIDN'T KNOW IS THAT THREE DINO-TEENS HAD HITCHED A RIDE ON DANNY AND GONE ALL SIX DEGREES OF PANIC...
BY USING MY KEEN ABILITY TO RECOGNIZE TOTAL CHAOS ALL AROUND ME, I DETERMINED THIS COULD POSE A PUBLIC HEALTH HAZARD. (AS IF SOME CHINATOWN RESTAURANTS ALREADY DON'T!)
CONTINUITY DOESN'T REALLY MATTER! CLARITY IS OVERRATED! LET THE FUN BEGIN!

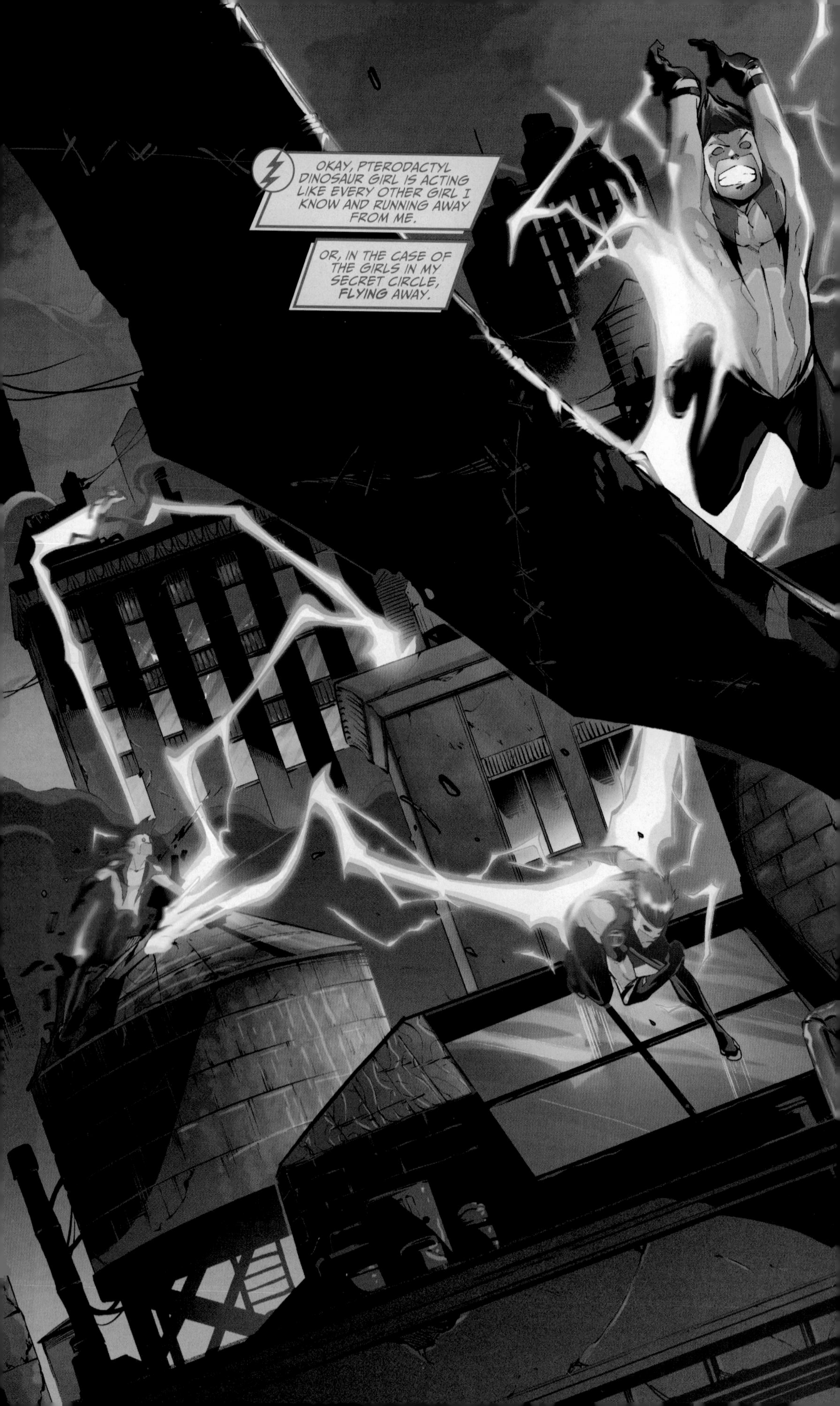
OKAY, PTERODACTYL DINOSAUR GIRL IS ACTING LIKE EVERY OTHER GIRL I KNOW AND RUNNING AWAY FROM ME.
OR, IN THE CASE OF THE GIRLS IN MY SECRET CIRCLE, FLYING AWAY.

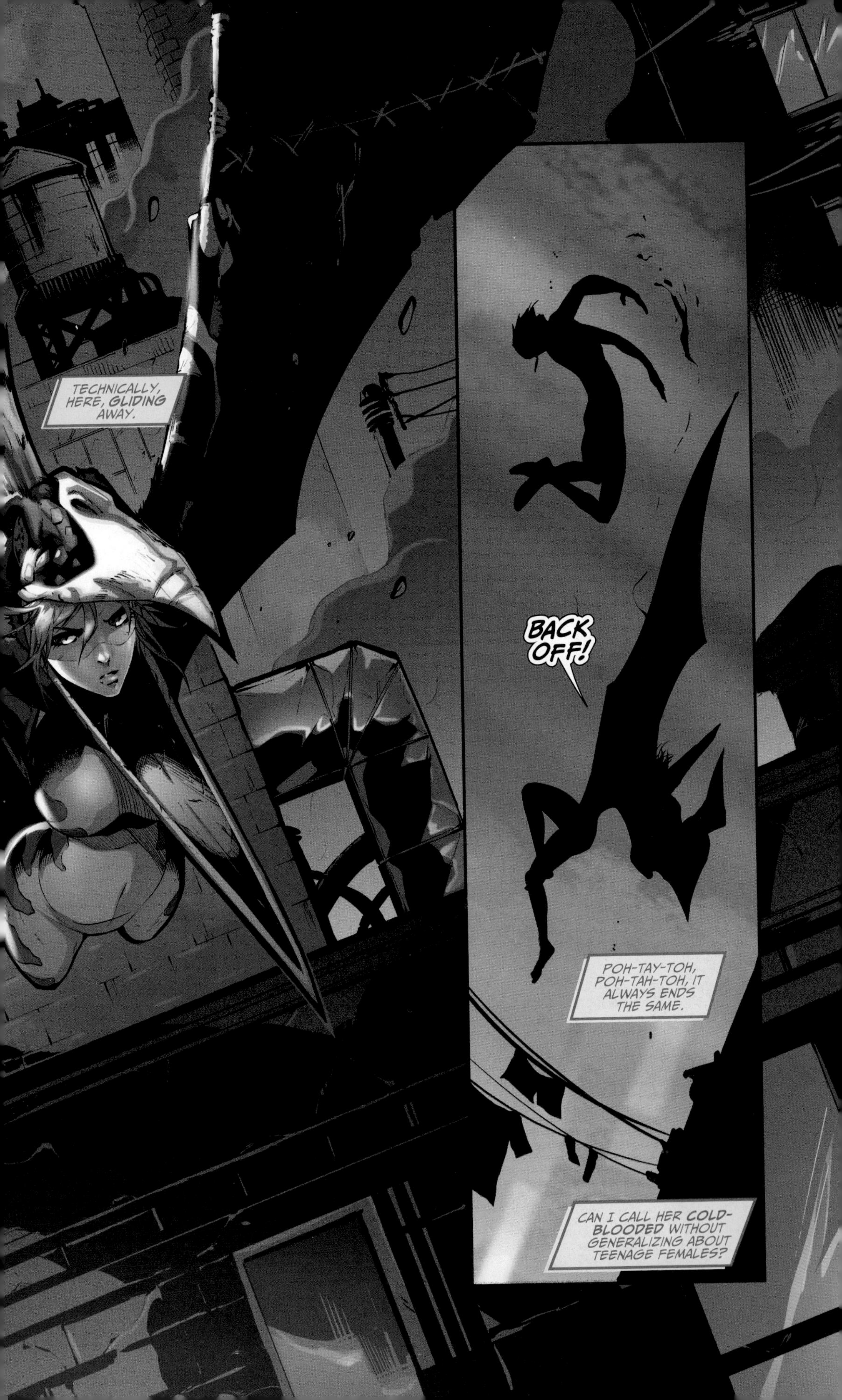
TECHNICALLY, HERE, GLIDING AWAY.
BACK OFF!
POH-TAY-TOH, POH-TAH-TOH, IT ALWAYS ENDS THE SAME.
CAN I CALL HER COLD-BLOODED WITHOUT GENERALIZING ABOUT TEENAGE FEMALES?

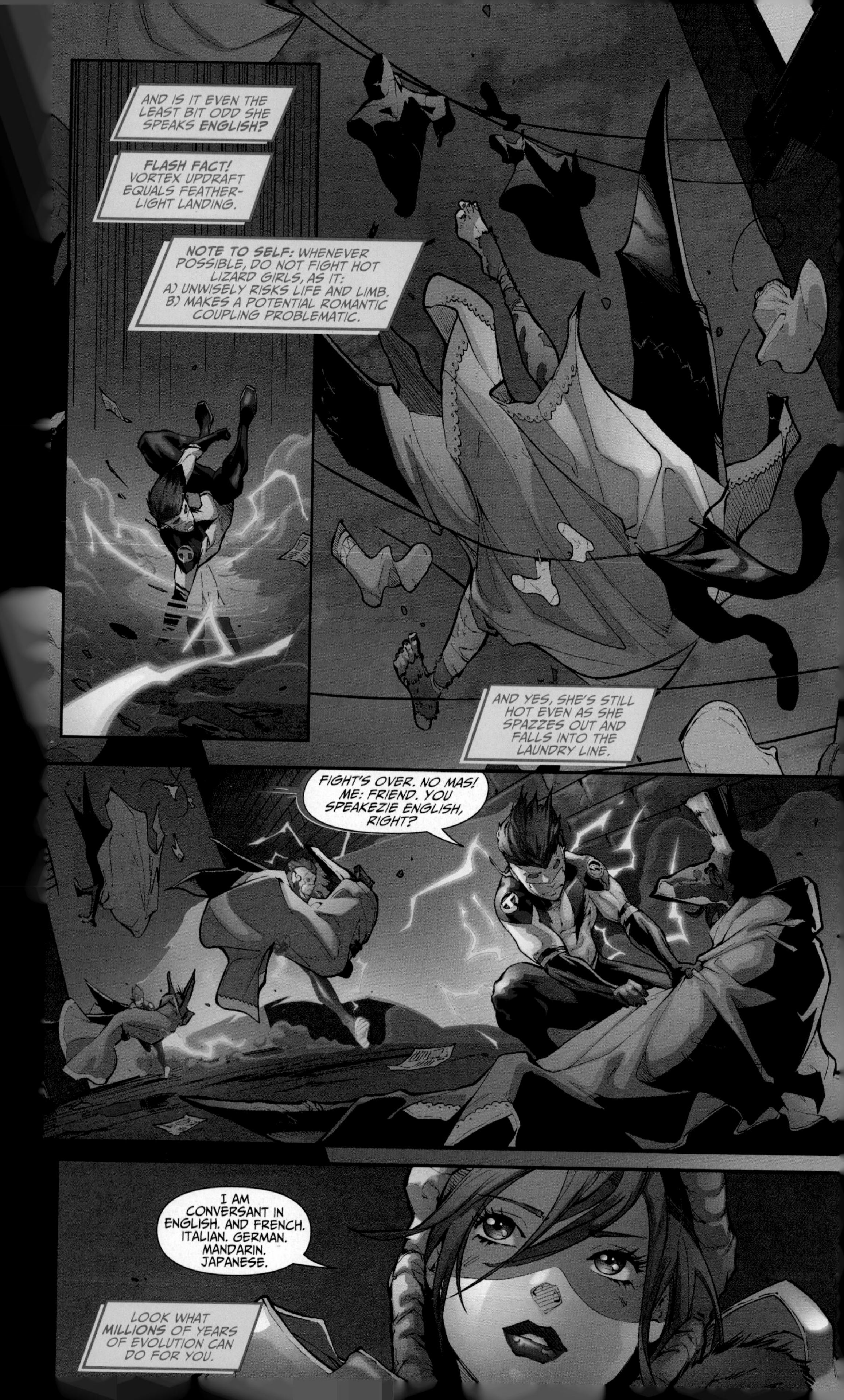
AND IS IT EVEN THE LEAST BIT ODD SHE SPEAKS ENGLISH?
FLASH FACT! VORTEX UPDRAFT EQUALS FEATHER-LIGHT LANDING.
NOTE TO SELF: WHENEVER POSSIBLE, DO NOT FIGHT HOT LIZARD GIRLS, AS IT: A) UNWISELY RISKS LIFE AND LIMB. B) MAKES A POTENTIAL ROMANTIC COUPLING PROBLEMATIC.
AND YES, SHE'S STILL HOT EVEN AS SHE SPAZZES OUT AND FALLS INTO THE LAUNDRY LINE.
FIGHT'S OVER. NO MAS! ME: FRIEND. YOU SPEAKEZIE ENGLISH, RIGHT?
I AM CONVERSANT IN ENGLISH. AND FRENCH. ITALIAN. GERMAN. MANDARIN. JAPANESE.
LOOK WHAT MILLIONS OF YEARS OF EVOLUTION CAN DO FOR YOU.

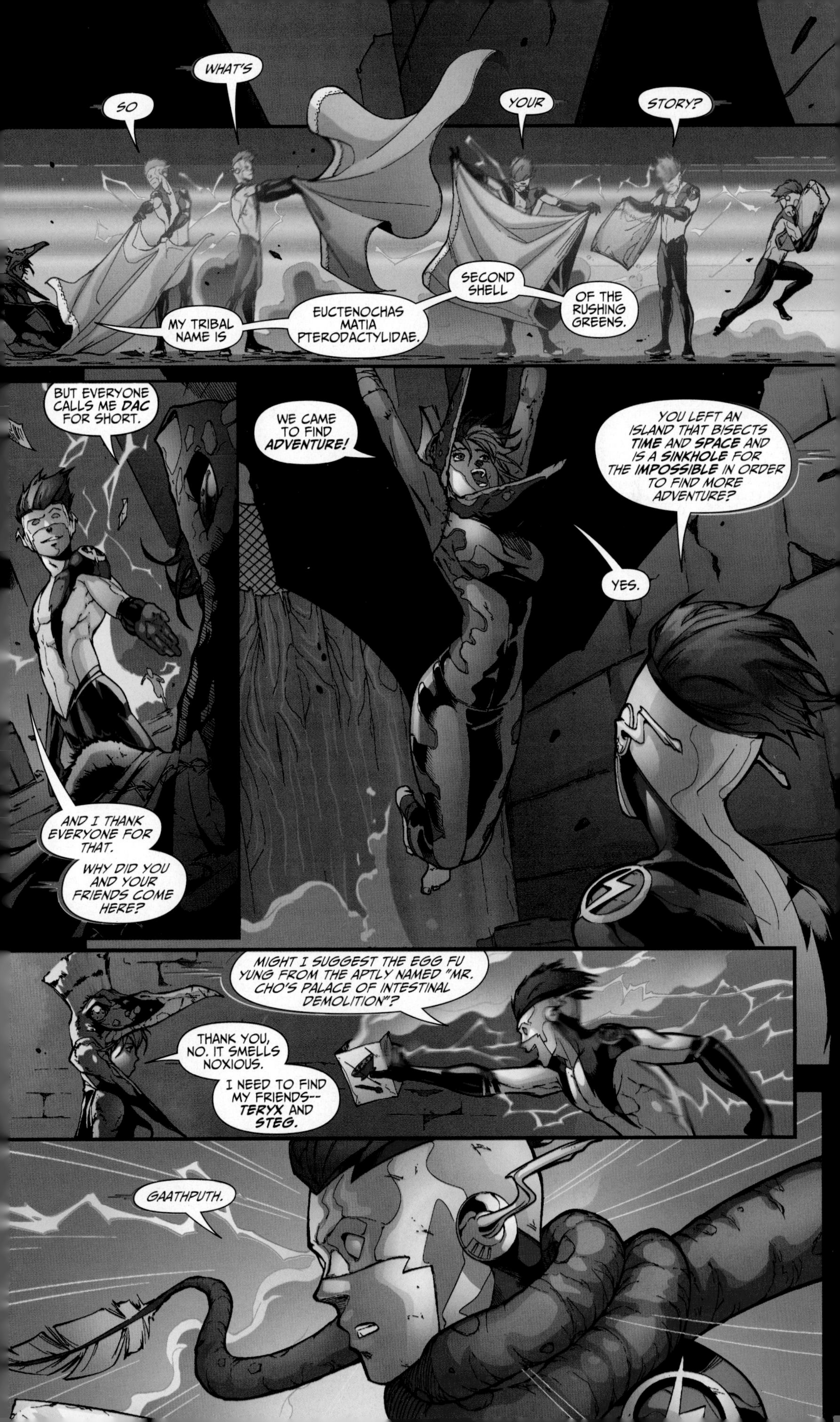
SO
WHAT'S
YOUR
STORY?
MY TRIBAL NAME IS
EUCTENOCHAS MATIA PTERODACTYLIDAE.
SECOND SHELL
OF THE RUSHING GREENS.
BUT EVERYONE CALLS ME DAC FOR SHORT.
AND I THANK EVERYONE FOR THAT.
WHY DID YOU AND YOUR FRIENDS COME HERE?
WE CAME TO FIND ADVENTURE!
YOU LEFT AN ISLAND THAT BISECTS TIME AND SPACE AND IS A SINKHOLE FOR THE IMPOSSIBLE IN ORDER TO FIND MORE ADVENTURE?
YES.
MIGHT I SUGGEST THE EGG FU YUNG FROM THE APTLY NAMED "MR. CHO'S PALACE OF INTESTINAL DEMOLITION"?
THANK YOU, NO. IT SMELLS NOXIOUS.
I NEED TO FIND MY FRIENDS-- TERYX AND STEG.
GAATHPUTH.

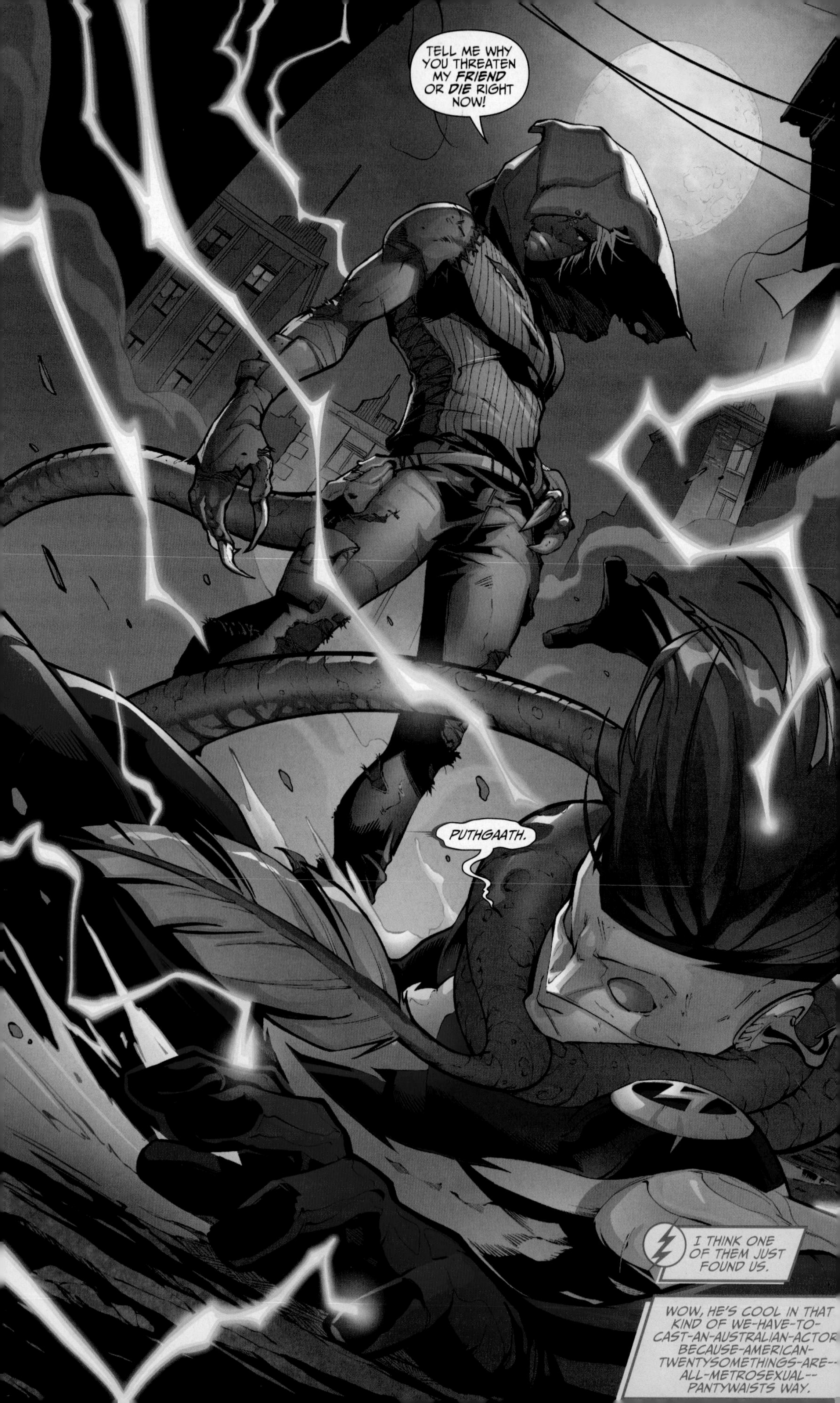
TELL ME WHY YOU THREATEN MY FRIEND OR DIE RIGHT NOW!
PUTHGAATH.
I THINK ONE OF THEM JUST FOUND US.
WOW, HE'S COOL IN THAT KIND OF WE-HAVE-TO-CAST-AN-AUSTRALIAN-ACTOR BECAUSE-AMERICAN-TWENTYSOMETHINGS-ARE-ALL-METROSEXUAL--PANTYWAISTS WAY.

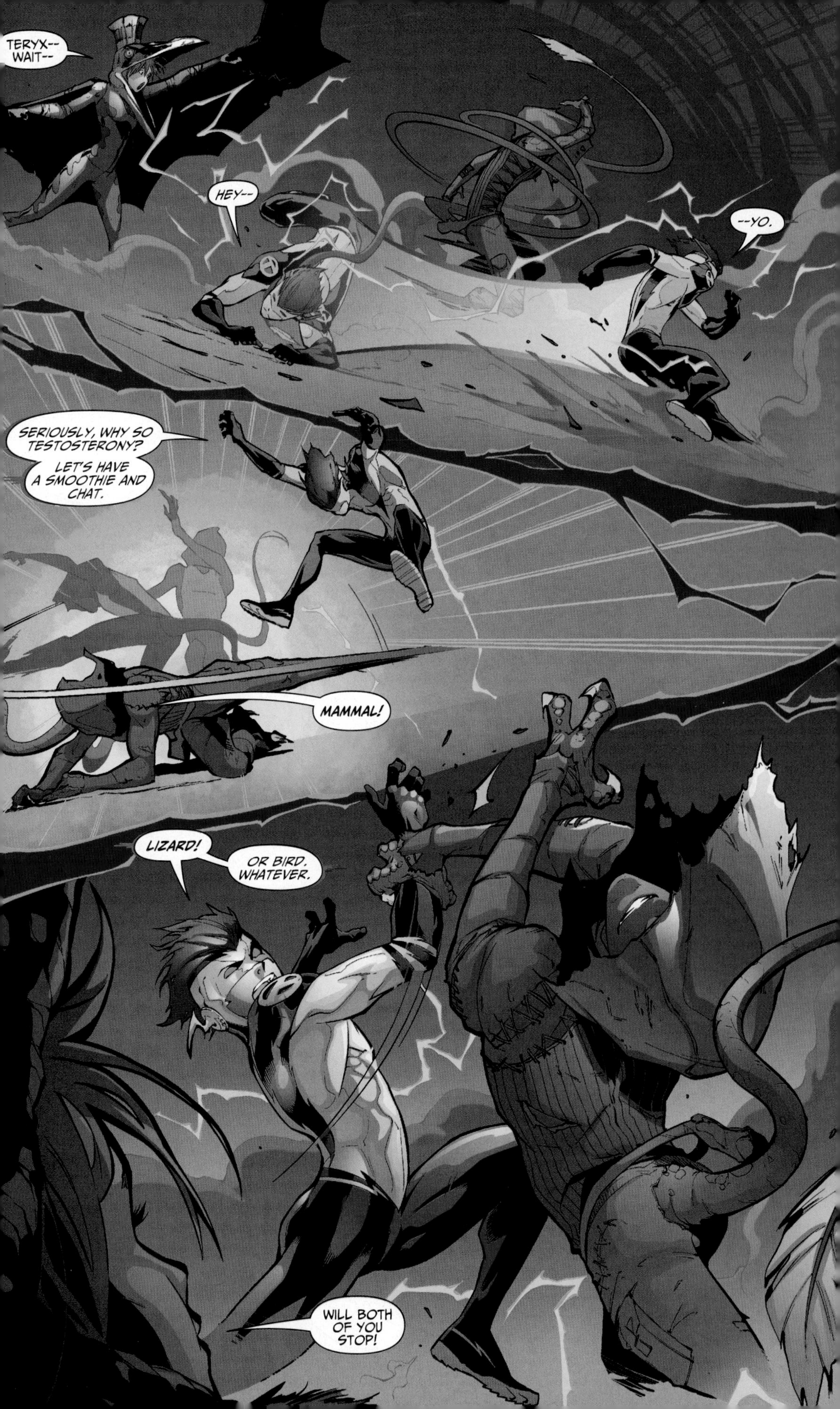
TERYX-- WAIT--
HEY--
--YO.
SERIOUSLY, WHY SO TESTOSTERONY?
LET'S HAVE A SMOOTHIE AND CHAT.
MAMMAL!
LIZARD!
OR BIRD. WHATEVER.
WILL BOTH OF YOU STOP!

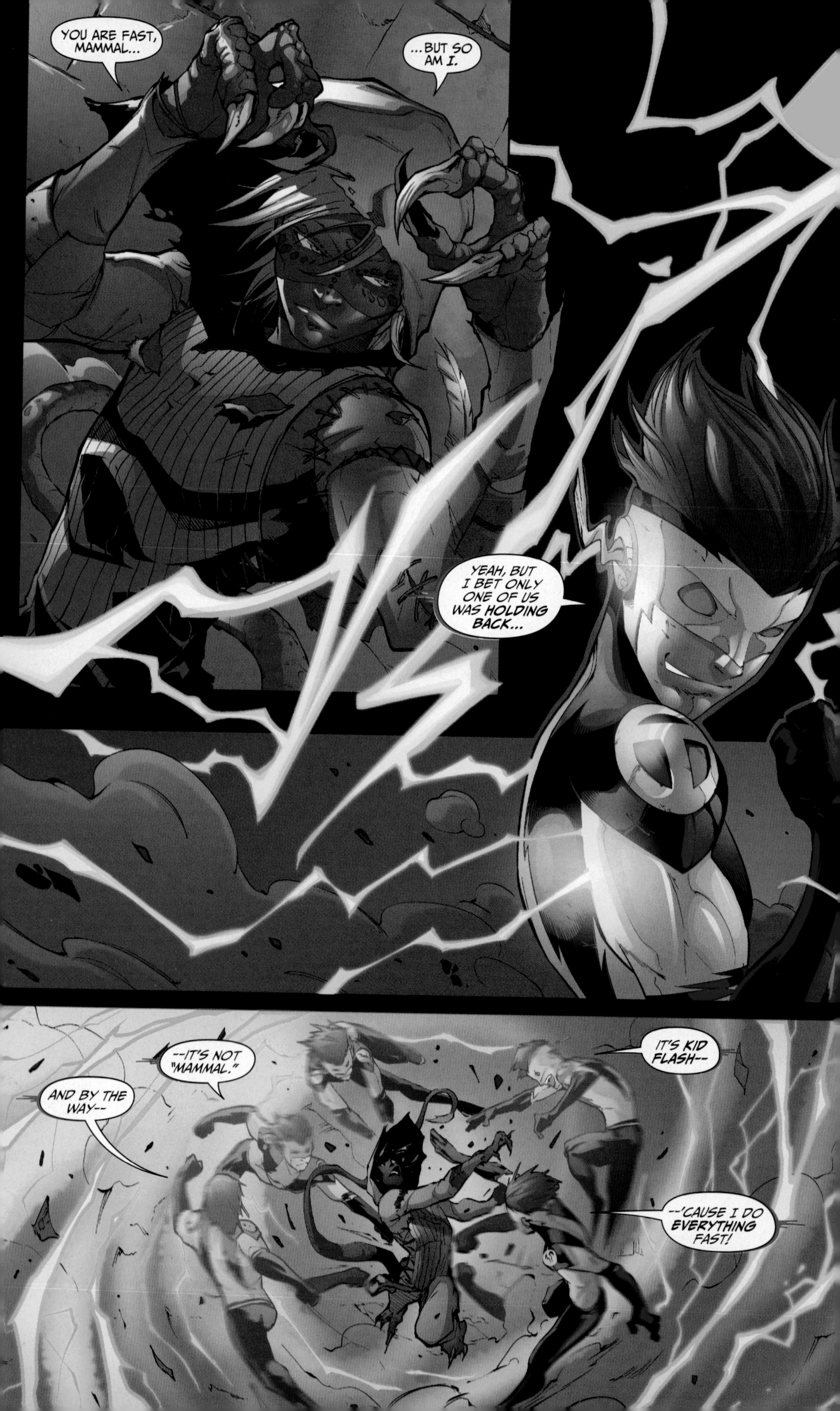
YOU ARE FAST, MAMMAL...
...BUT SO AM I.
YEAH, BUT I BET ONLY ONE OF US WAS HOLDING BACK...
--IT'S NOT "MAMMAL."
AND BY THE WAY--
IT'S KID FLASH--
--'CAUSE I DO EVERYTHING FAST!

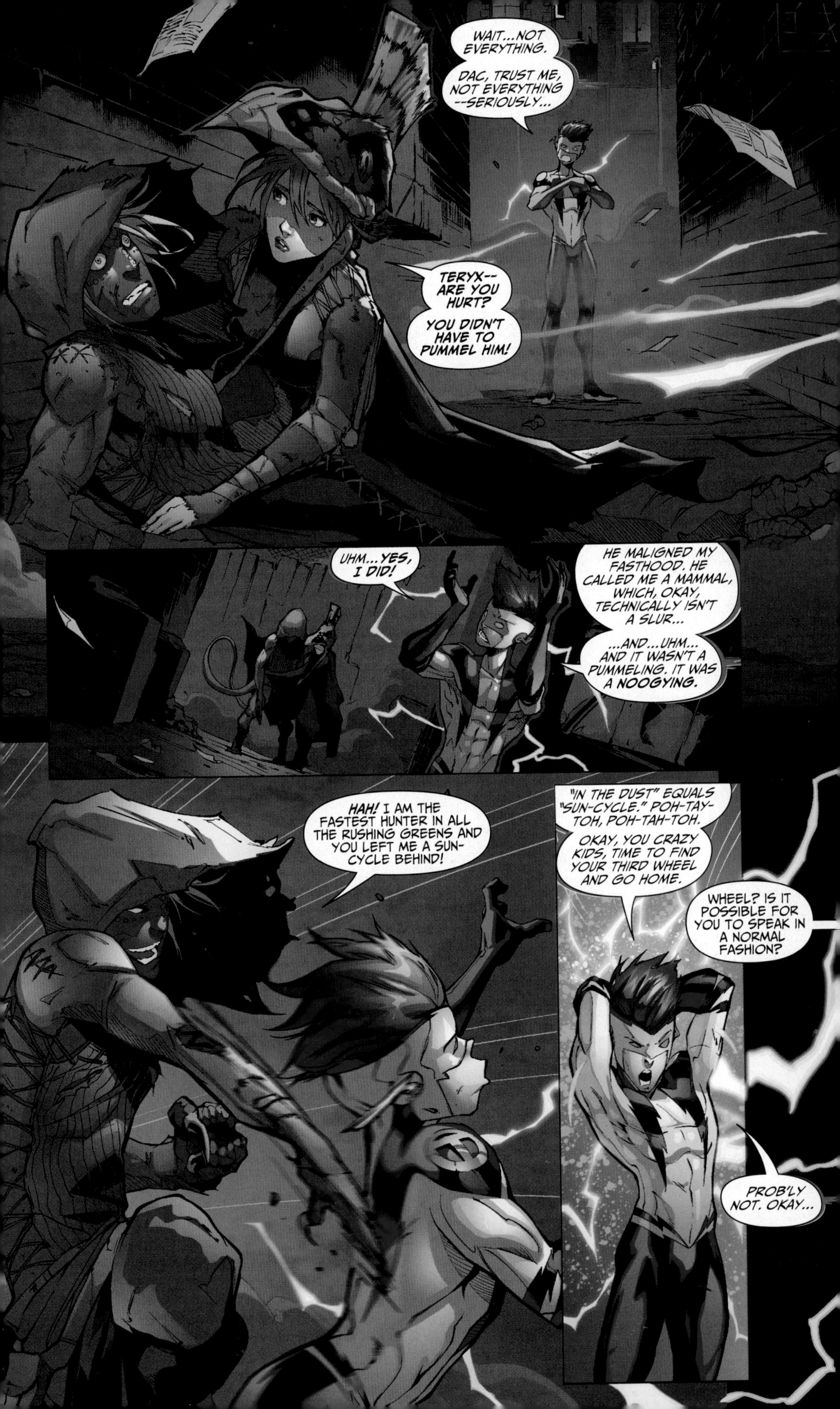
WAIT...NOT EVERYTHING.
DAC, TRUST ME, NOT EVERYTHING --SERIOUSLY...
TERYX-- ARE YOU HURT?
YOU DIDN'T HAVE TO PUMMEL HIM!
UHM...YES, I DID!
HE MALIGNED MY FASTHOOD. HE CALLED ME A MAMMAL, WHICH, OKAY, TECHNICALLY ISN'T A SLUR...
...AND...UHM... AND IT WASN'T A PUMMELING. IT WAS A NOOGYING.
HAH! I AM THE FASTEST HUNTER IN ALL THE RUSHING GREENS AND YOU LEFT ME A SUN-CYCLE BEHIND!
"IN THE DUST" EQUALS "SUN-CYCLE." POH-TAY-TOH, POH-TAH-TOH.
OKAY, YOU CRAZY KIDS, TIME TO FIND YOUR THIRD WHEEL AND GO HOME.
WHEEL? IS IT POSSIBLE FOR YOU TO SPEAK IN A NORMAL FASHION?
PROB'LY NOT. OKAY...

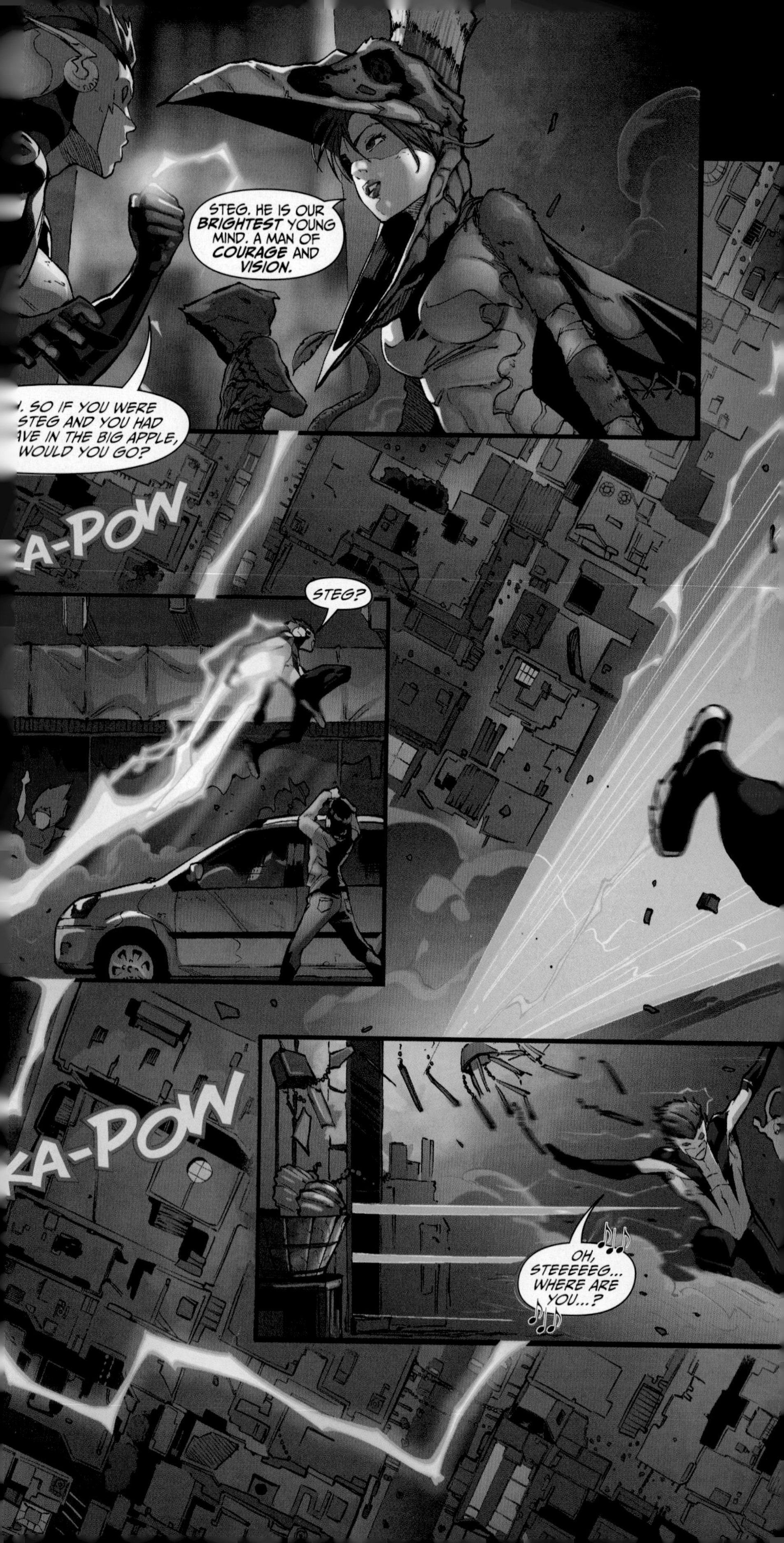

STEG. HE IS OUR BRIGHTEST YOUNG MIND. A MAN OF COURAGE AND VISION.
. SO IF YOU WERE STEG AND YOU HAD AVE IN THE BIG APPLE, WOULD YOU GO?
A-POW
STEG?
A-POW
OH, STEEEEEG... WHERE ARE YOU...?

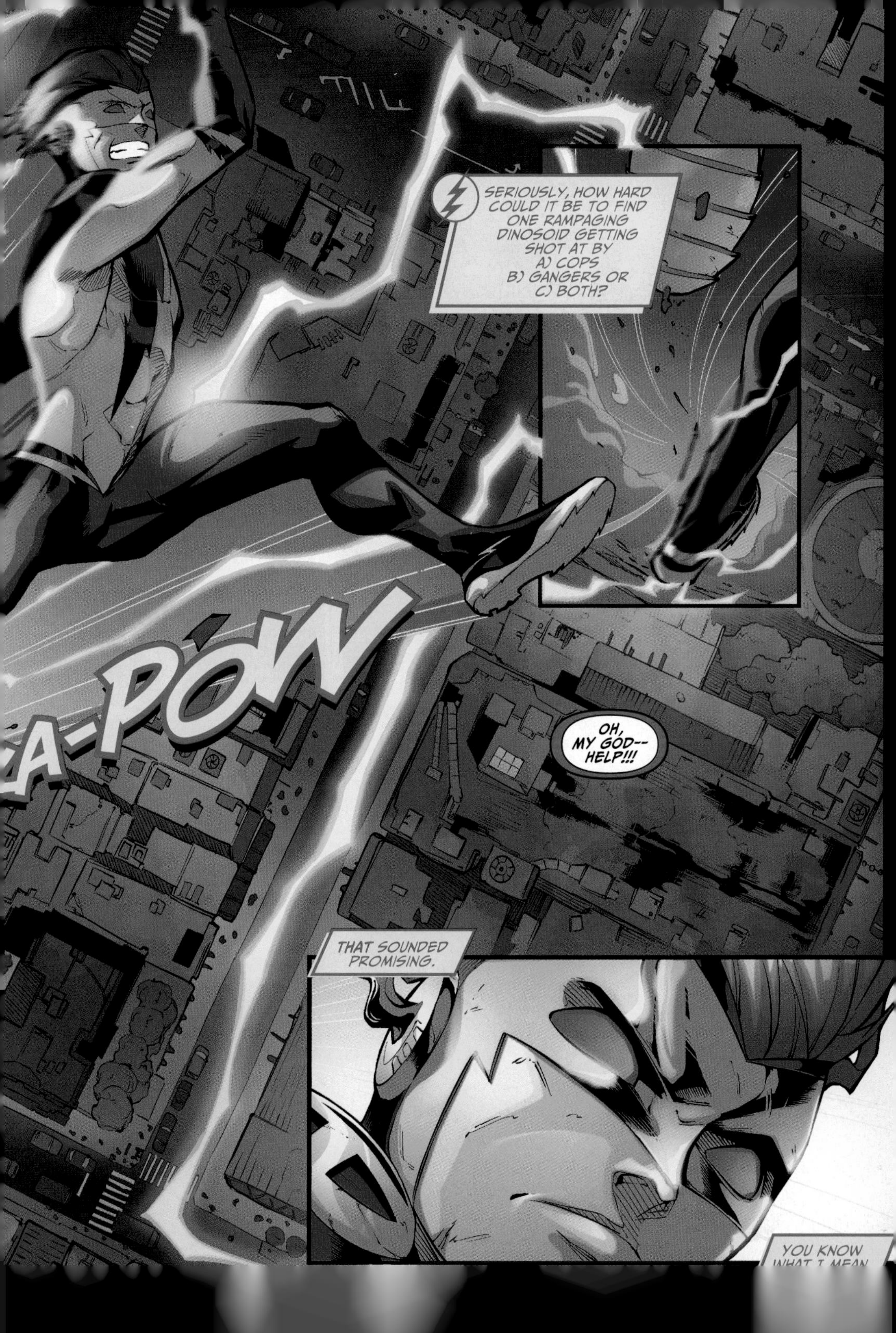
SERIOUSLY, HOW HARD COULD IT BE TO FIND ONE RAMPAGING DINOSOID GETTING SHOT AT BY A) COPS B) GANGERS OR C) BOTH?
A-POW
OH, MY GOD-- HELP!!!
THAT SOUNDED PROMISING.
YOU KNOW

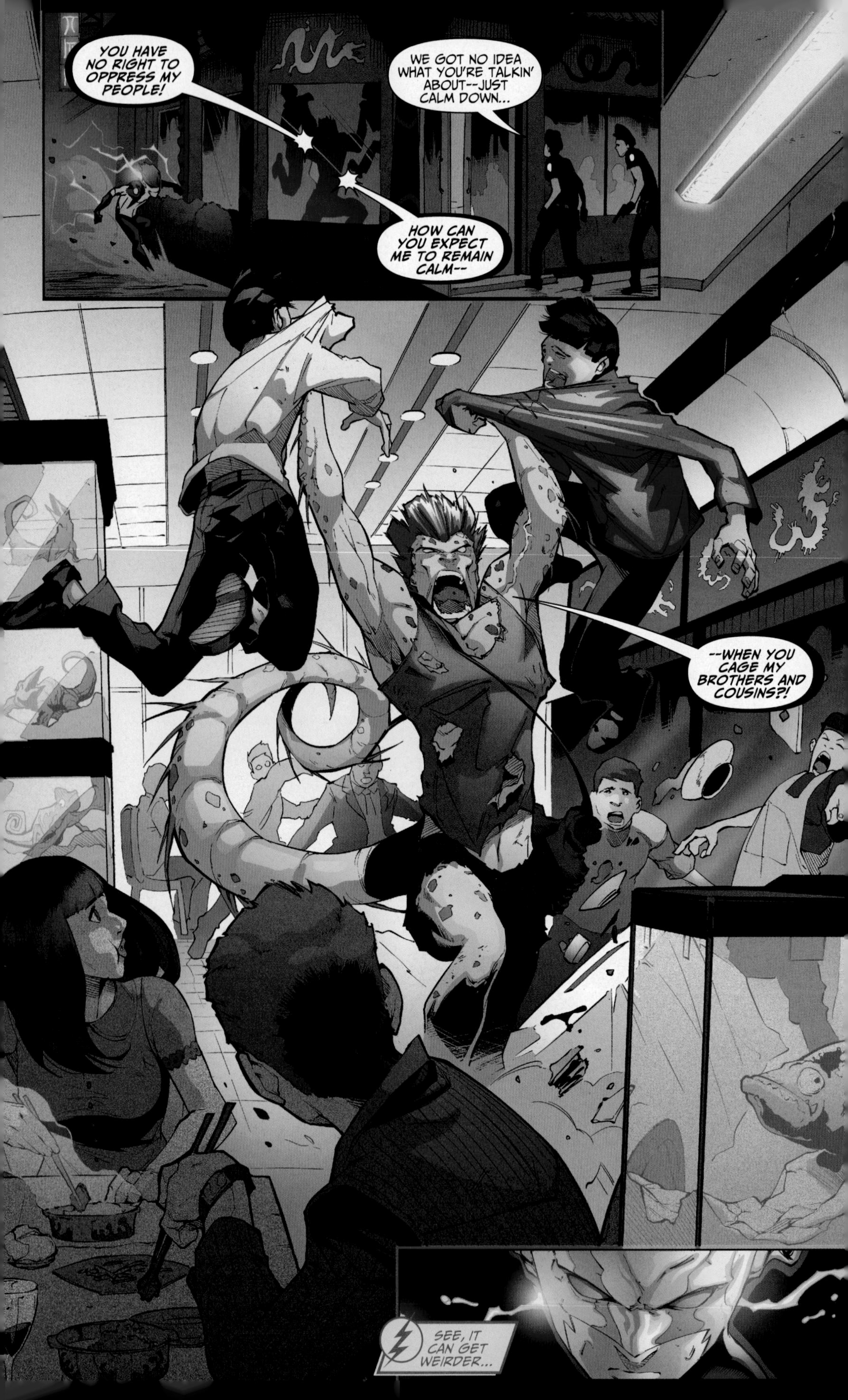
YOU HAVE NO RIGHT TO OPPRESS MY PEOPLE!
WE GOT NO IDEA WHAT YOU'RE TALKIN' ABOUT--JUST CALM DOWN...
HOW CAN YOU EXPECT ME TO REMAIN CALM--
--WHEN YOU CAGE MY BROTHERS AND COUSINS?!
SEE, IT CAN GET WEIRDER...

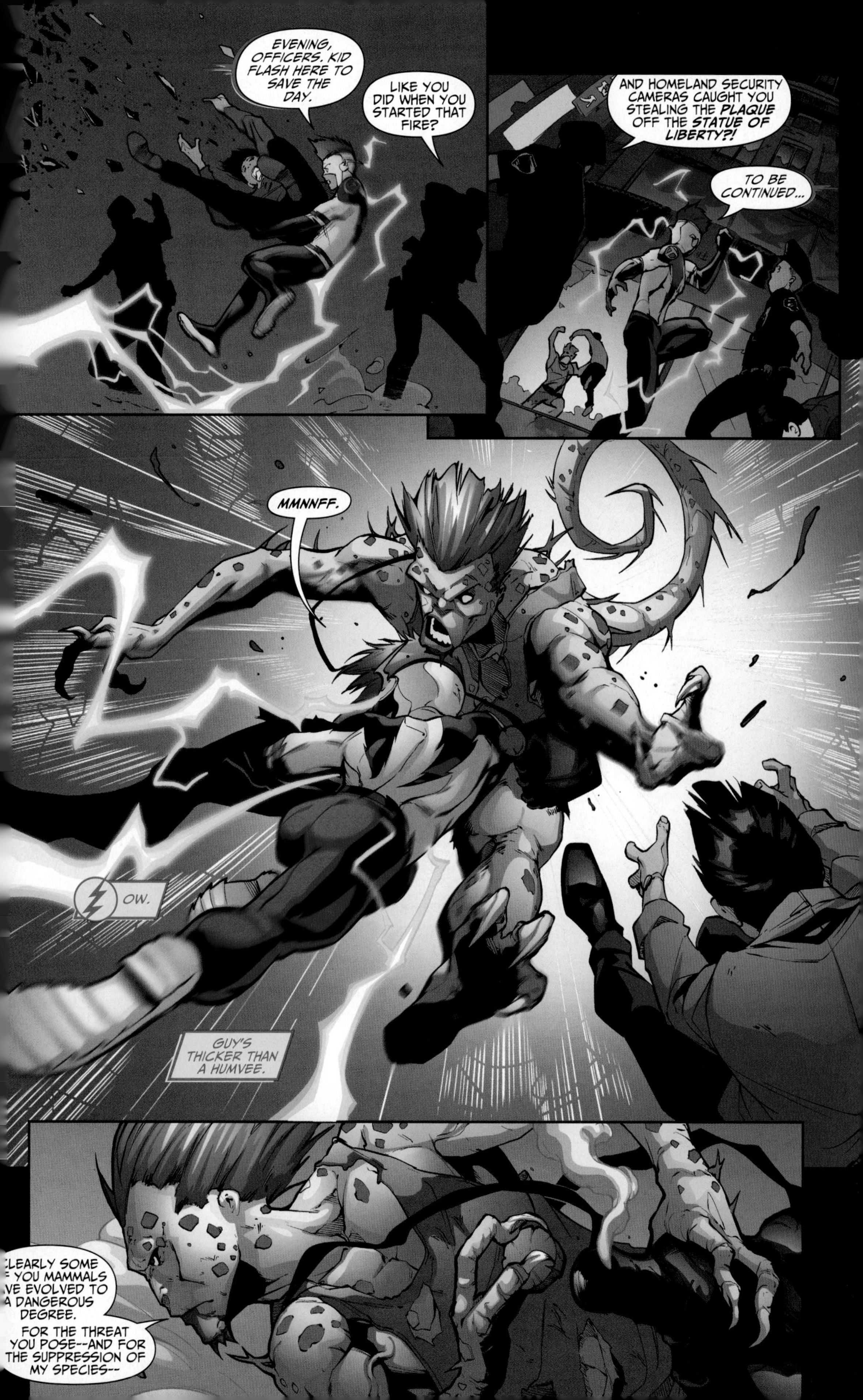
EVENING, OFFICERS. KID FLASH HERE TO SAVE THE DAY.
LIKE YOU DID WHEN YOU STARTED THAT FIRE?
AND HOMELAND SECURITY CAMERAS CAUGHT YOU STEALING THE PLAQUE OFF THE STATUE OF LIBERTY?!
TO BE CONTINUED...
MMNNFF.
OW.
GUY'S THICKER THAN A HUMVEE.
CLEARLY SOME OF YOU MAMMALS HAVE EVOLVED TO A DANGEROUS DEGREE.
FOR THE THREAT YOU POSE--AND FOR THE SUPPRESSION OF MY SPECIES--

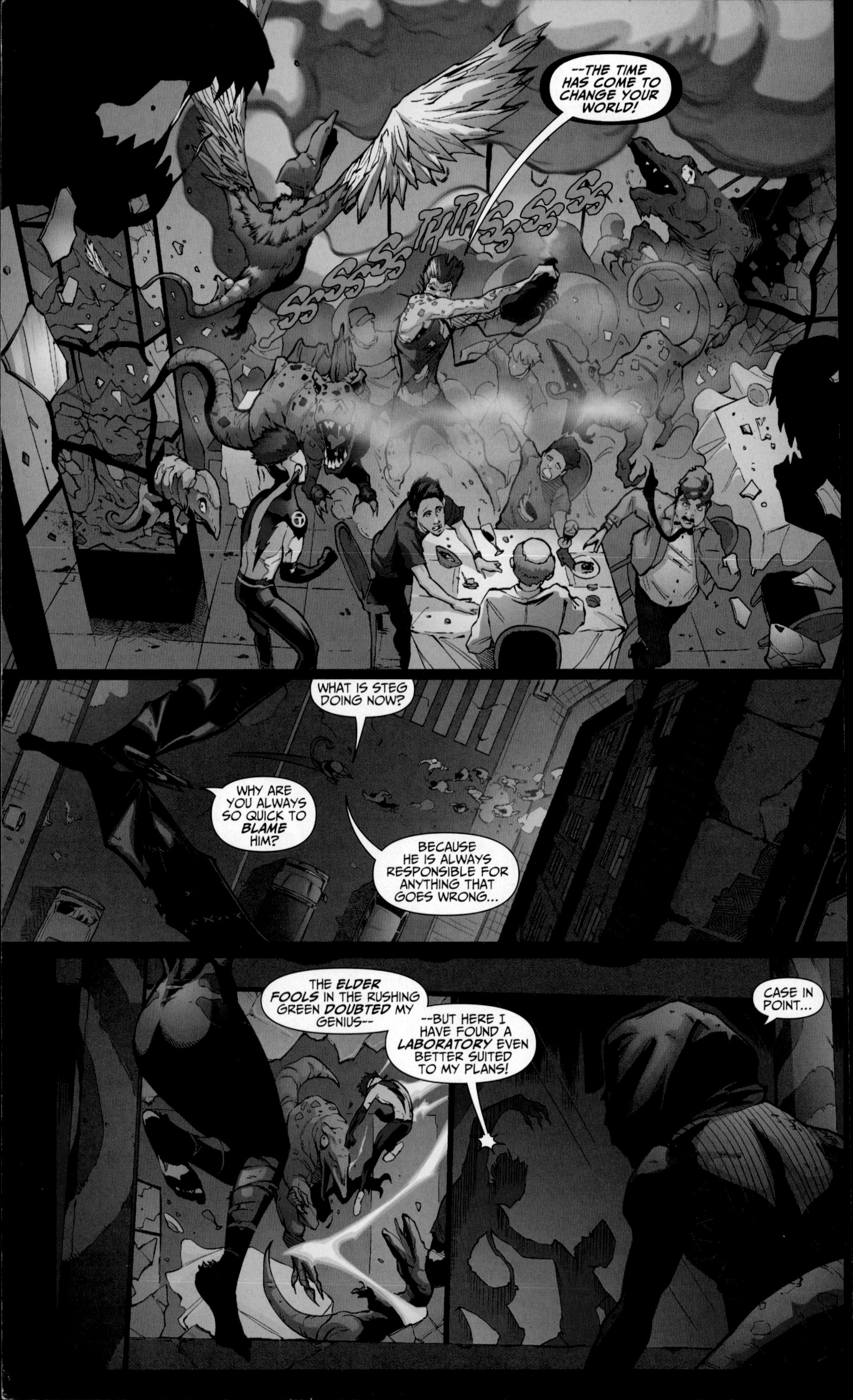
--THE TIME HAS COME TO CHANGE YOUR WORLD!
SSSSSSTHTHSSSSSSSS
WHAT IS STEG DOING NOW?
WHY ARE YOU ALWAYS SO QUICK TO BLAME HIM?
BECAUSE HE IS ALWAYS RESPONSIBLE FOR ANYTHING THAT GOES WRONG...
THE ELDER FOOLS IN THE RUSHING GREEN DOUBTED MY GENIUS--
--BUT HERE I HAVE FOUND A LABORATORY EVEN BETTER SUITED TO MY PLANS!
CASE IN POINT...

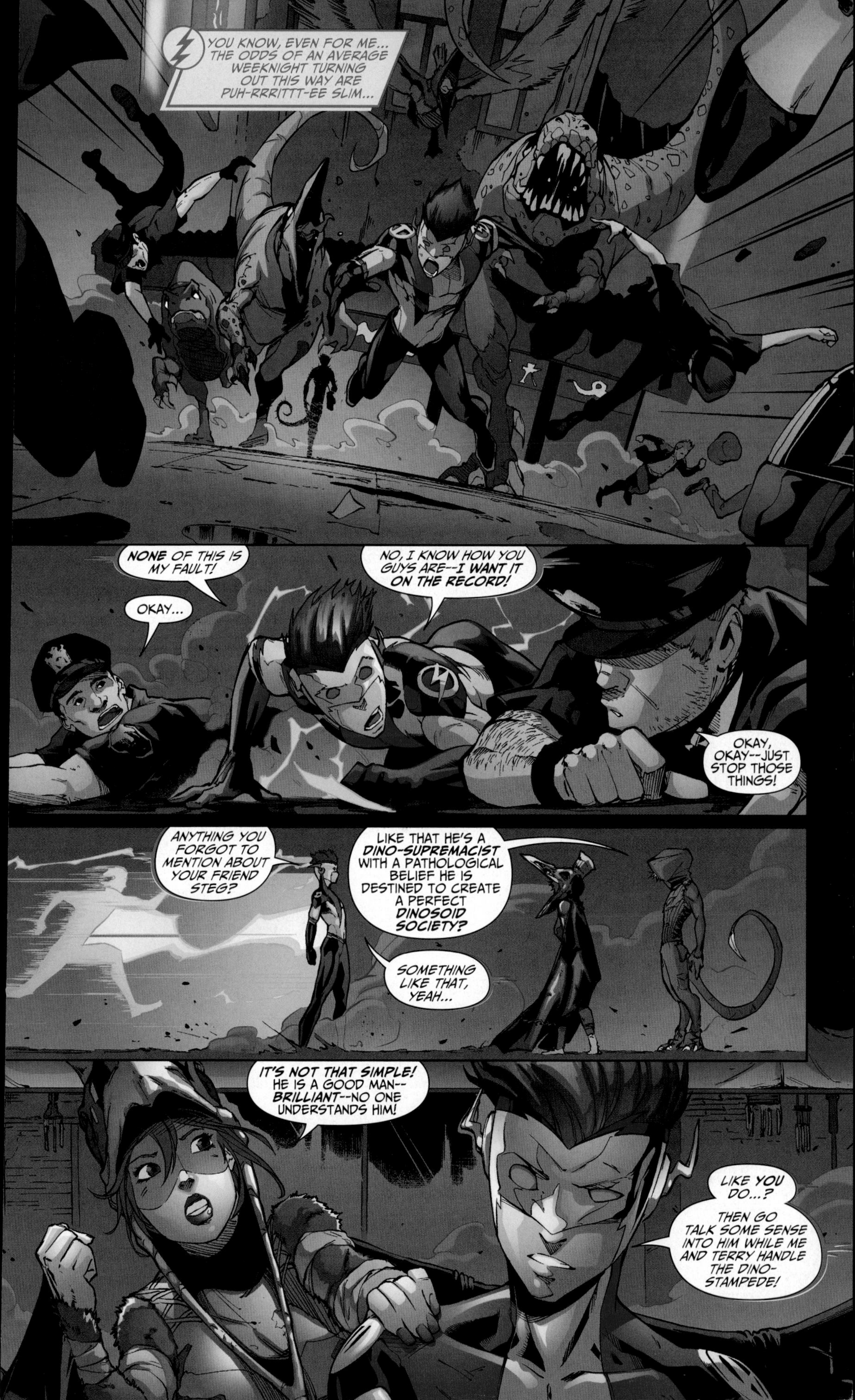
YOU KNOW, EVEN FOR ME... THE ODDS OF AN AVERAGE WEEKNIGHT TURNING OUT THIS WAY ARE PUH-RRRITTT-EE SLIM...
NONE OF THIS IS MY FAULT!
NO, I KNOW HOW YOU GUYS ARE--I WANT IT ON THE RECORD!
OKAY...
OKAY, OKAY--JUST STOP THOSE THINGS!
ANYTHING YOU FORGOT TO MENTION ABOUT YOUR FRIEND STEG?
LIKE THAT HE'S A DINO-SUPREMACIST WITH A PATHOLOGICAL BELIEF HE IS DESTINED TO CREATE A PERFECT DINOSOID SOCIETY?
SOMETHING LIKE THAT, YEAH...
IT'S NOT THAT SIMPLE! HE IS A GOOD MAN--BRILLIANT--NO ONE UNDERSTANDS HIM!
LIKE YOU DO...?
THEN GO TALK SOME SENSE INTO HIM WHILE ME AND TERRY HANDLE THE DINO-STAMPEDE!

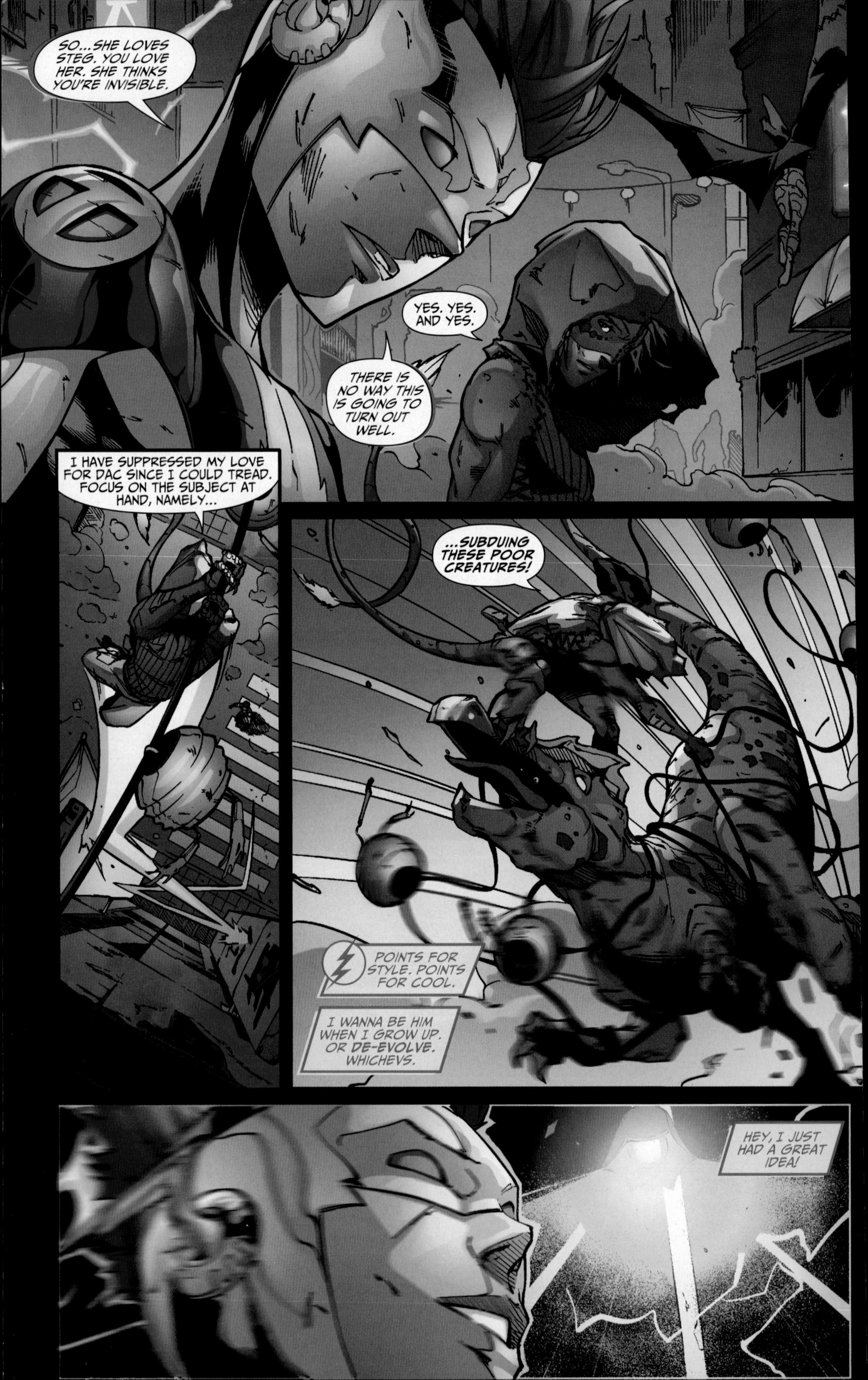
SO...SHE LOVES STEG. YOU LOVE HER. SHE THINKS YOU'RE INVISIBLE.
YES. YES. AND YES.
THERE IS NO WAY THIS IS GOING TO TURN OUT WELL.
I HAVE SUPPRESSED MY LOVE FOR DAC SINCE I COULD TREAD. FOCUS ON THE SUBJECT AT HAND, NAMELY...
...SUBDUING THESE POOR CREATURES!
POINTS FOR STYLE. POINTS FOR COOL.
I WANNA BE HIM WHEN I GROW UP. OR DE-EVOLVE. WHICHEVS.
HEY, I JUST HAD A GREAT IDEA!

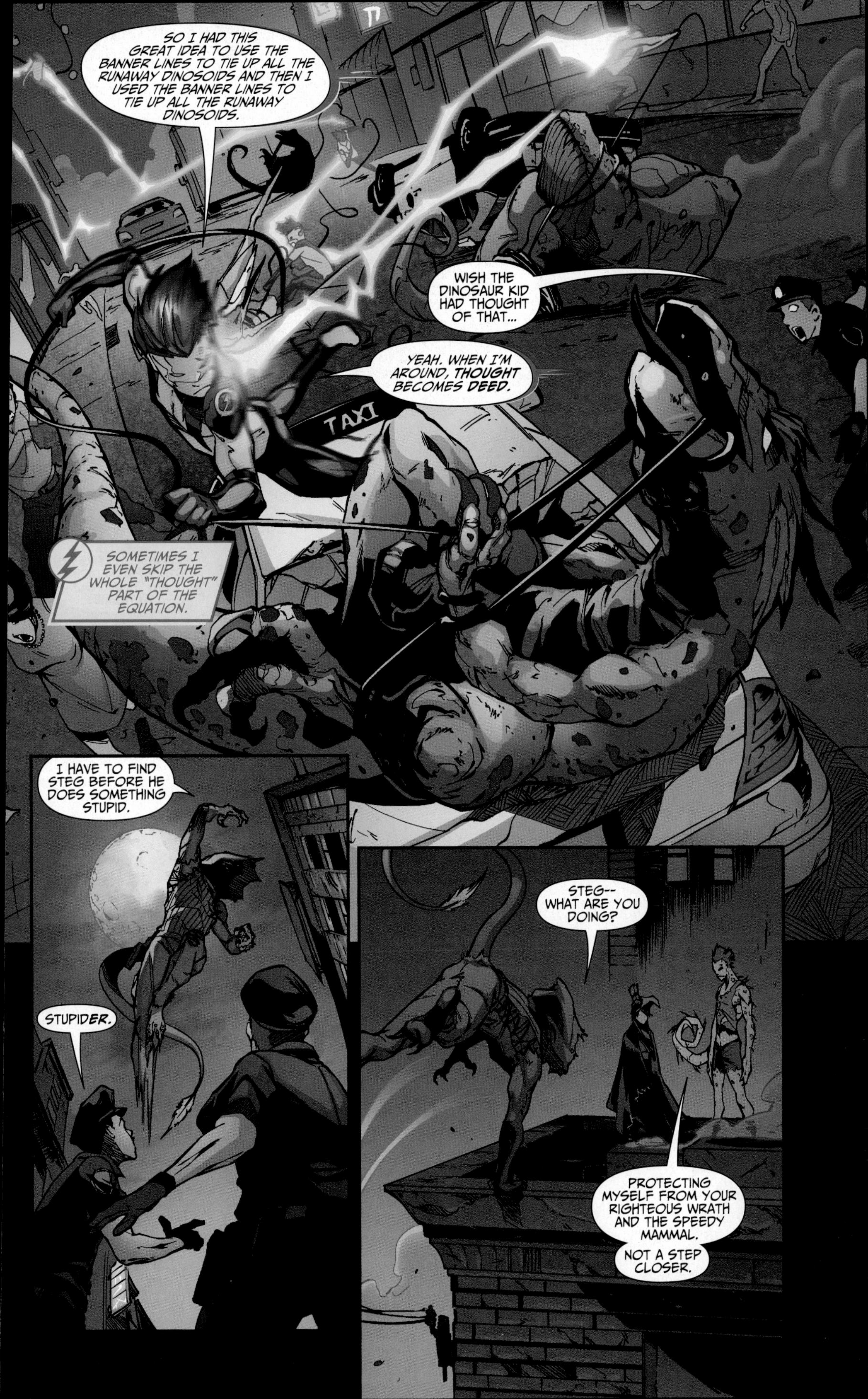
SO I HAD THIS GREAT IDEA TO USE THE BANNER LINES TO TIE UP ALL THE RUNAWAY DINOSOIDS AND THEN I USED THE BANNER LINES TO TIE UP ALL THE RUNAWAY DINOSOIDS.
WISH THE DINOSAUR KID HAD THOUGHT OF THAT...
YEAH. WHEN I'M AROUND, THOUGHT BECOMES DEED.
TAXI
SOMETIMES I EVEN SKIP THE WHOLE "THOUGHT" PART OF THE EQUATION.
I HAVE TO FIND STEG BEFORE HE DOES SOMETHING STUPID.
STUPIDER.
STEG-- WHAT ARE YOU DOING?
PROTECTING MYSELF FROM YOUR RIGHTEOUS WRATH AND THE SPEEDY MAMMAL.
NOT A STEP CLOSER.

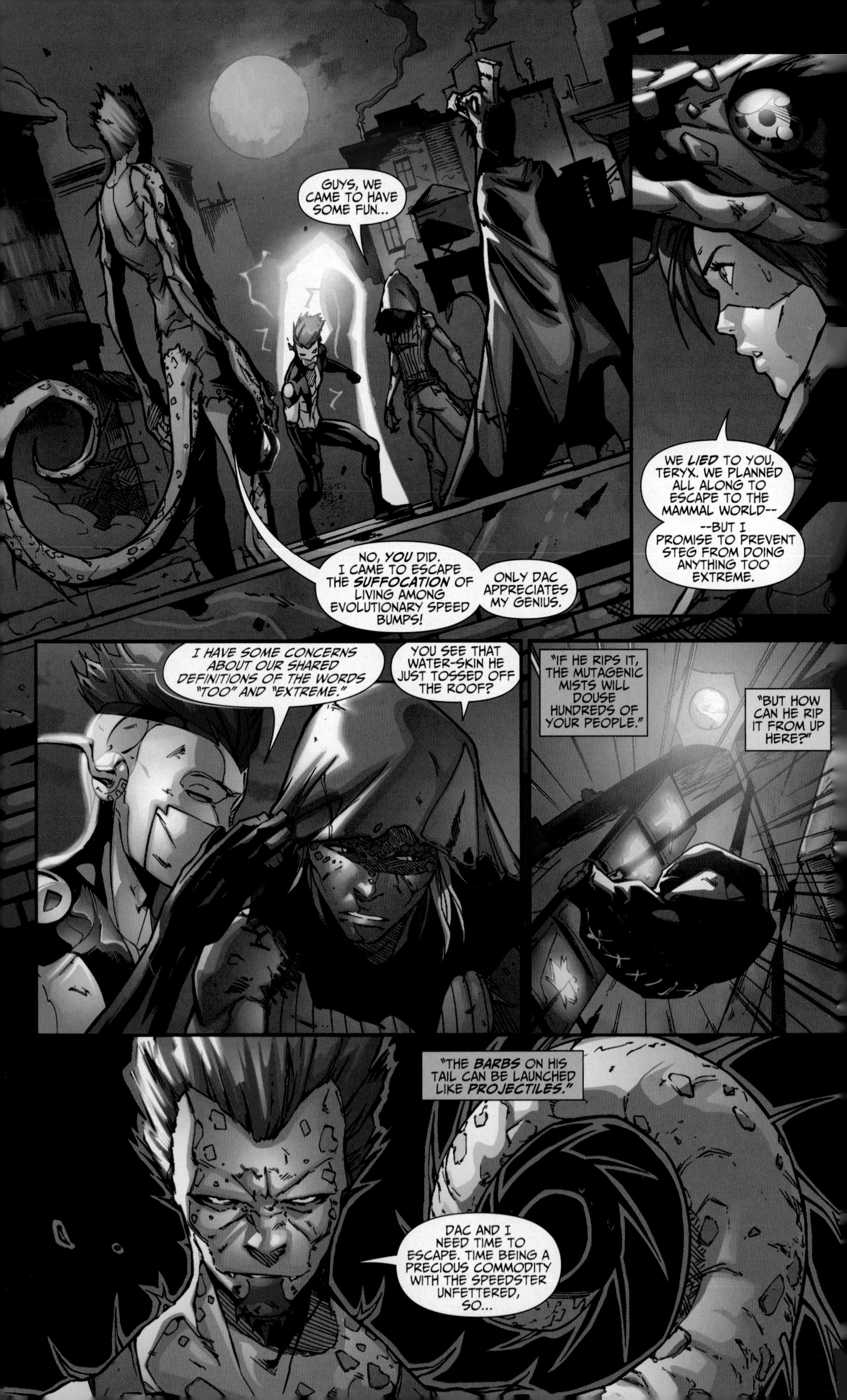

GUYS, WE CAME TO HAVE SOME FUN...
NO, YOU DID. I CAME TO ESCAPE THE SUFFOCATION OF LIVING AMONG EVOLUTIONARY SPEED BUMPS!
ONLY DAC APPRECIATES MY GENIUS.
WE LIED TO YOU, TERYX. WE PLANNED ALL ALONG TO ESCAPE TO THE MAMMAL WORLD--
--BUT I PROMISE TO PREVENT STEG FROM DOING ANYTHING TOO EXTREME.
I HAVE SOME CONCERNS ABOUT OUR SHARED DEFINITIONS OF THE WORDS "TOO" AND "EXTREME."
YOU SEE THAT WATER-SKIN HE JUST TOSSED OFF THE ROOF?
"IF HE RIPS IT, THE MUTAGENIC MISTS WILL DOUSE HUNDREDS OF YOUR PEOPLE."
"BUT HOW CAN HE RIP IT FROM UP HERE?"
"THE BARBS ON HIS TAIL CAN BE LAUNCHED LIKE PROJECTILES."
DAC AND I NEED TIME TO ESCAPE. TIME BEING A PRECIOUS COMMODITY WITH THE SPEEDSTER UNFETTERED, SO...

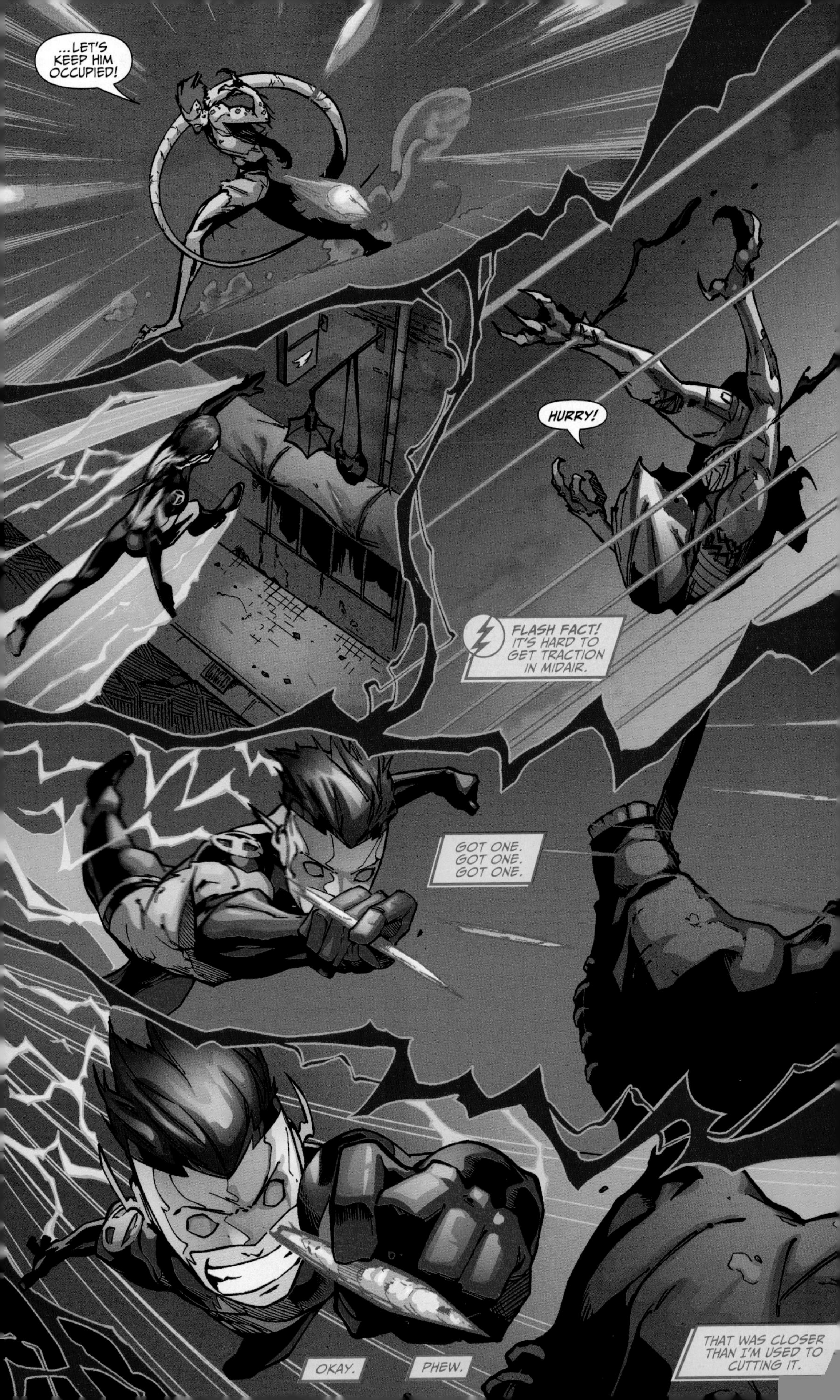
...LET'S KEEP HIM OCCUPIED!
HURRY!
FLASH FACT! IT'S HARD TO GET TRACTION IN MIDAIR.
GOT ONE. GOT ONE. GOT ONE.
OKAY.
PHEW.
THAT WAS CLOSER THAN I'M USED TO CUTTING IT.

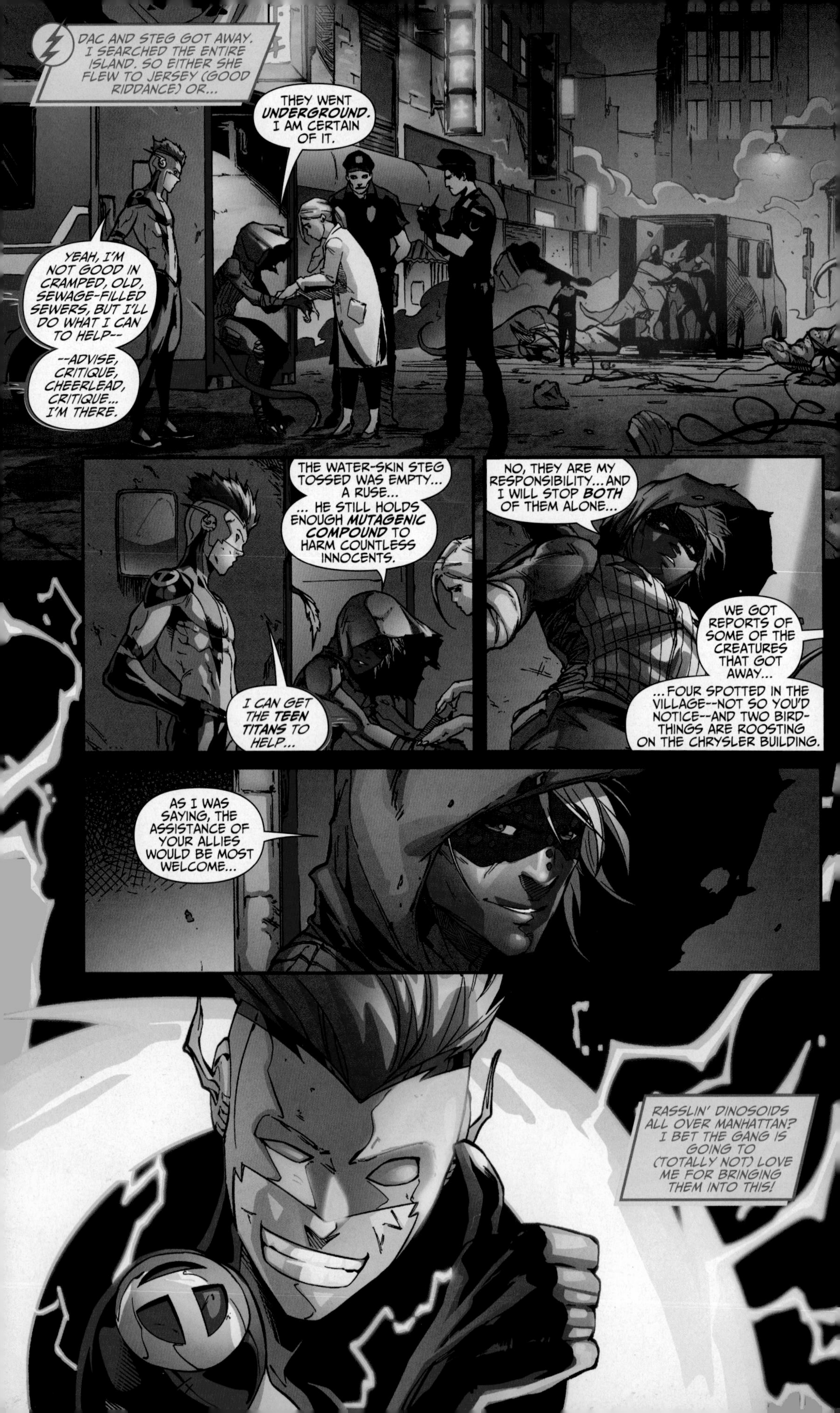
DAC AND STEG GOT AWAY. I SEARCHED THE ENTIRE ISLAND. SO EITHER SHE FLEW TO JERSEY (GOOD RIDDANCE) OR...
THEY WENT UNDERGROUND. I AM CERTAIN OF IT.
YEAH, I'M NOT GOOD IN CRAMPED, OLD, SEWAGE-FILLED SEWERS, BUT I'LL DO WHAT I CAN TO HELP--
--ADVISE, CRITIQUE, CHEERLEAD, CRITIQUE... I'M THERE.
THE WATER-SKIN STEG TOSSED WAS EMPTY... A RUSE...
... HE STILL HOLDS ENOUGH MUTAGENIC COMPOUND TO HARM COUNTLESS INNOCENTS.
I CAN GET THE TEEN TITANS TO HELP...
NO, THEY ARE MY RESPONSIBILITY... AND I WILL STOP BOTH OF THEM ALONE...
WE GOT REPORTS OF SOME OF THE CREATURES THAT GOT AWAY...
...FOUR SPOTTED IN THE VILLAGE--NOT SO YOU'D NOTICE--AND TWO BIRD-THINGS ARE ROOSTING ON THE CHRYSLER BUILDING.
AS I WAS SAYING, THE ASSISTANCE OF YOUR ALLIES WOULD BE MOST WELCOME...
RASSLIN' DINOSOIDS ALL OVER MANHATTAN? I BET THE GANG IS GOING TO (TOTALLY NOT) LOVE ME FOR BRINGING THEM INTO THIS!

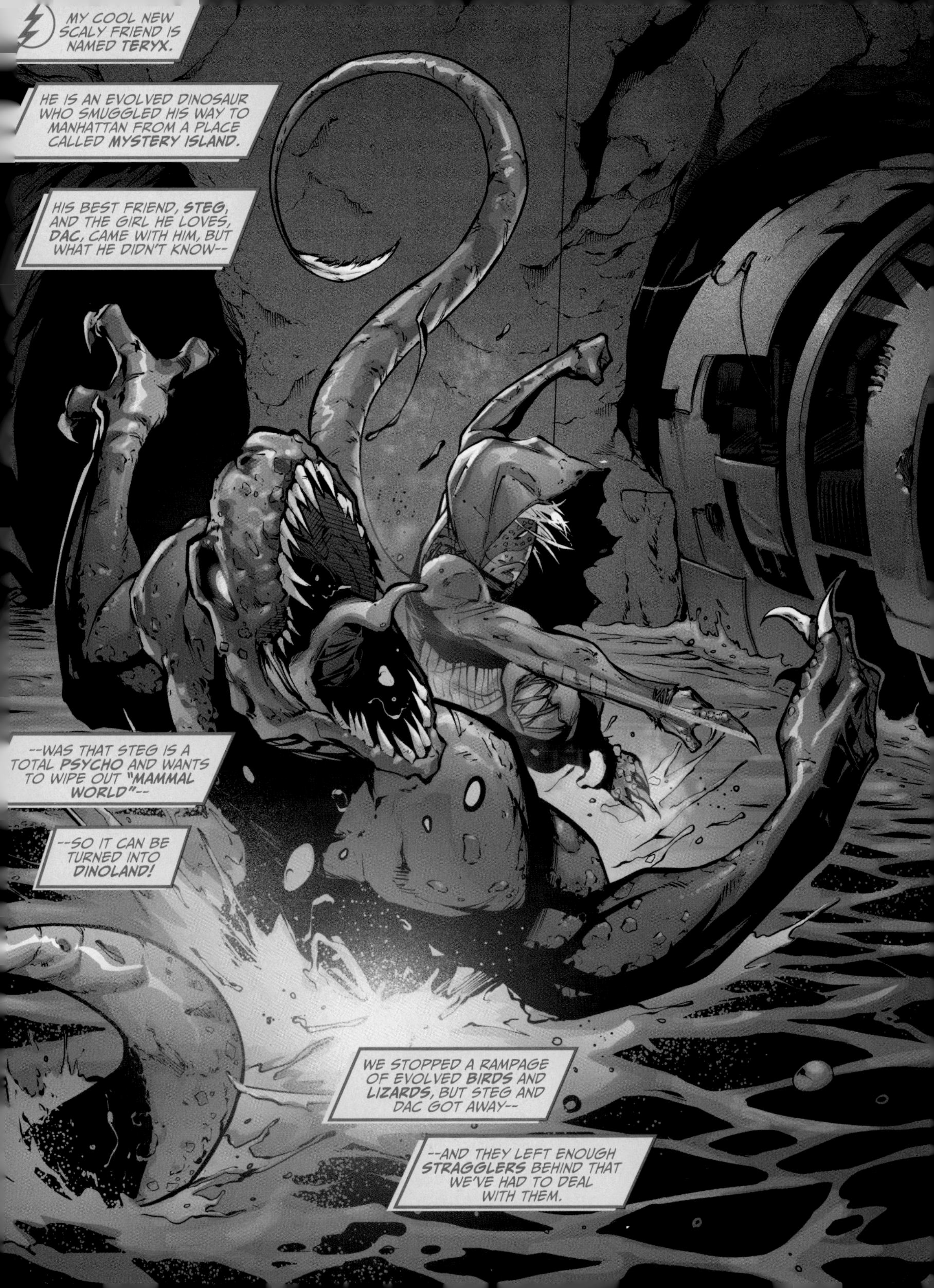
MY COOL NEW SCALY FRIEND IS NAMED TERYX.
HE IS AN EVOLVED DINOSAUR WHO SMUGGLED HIS WAY TO MANHATTAN FROM A PLACE CALLED MYSTERY ISLAND.
HIS BEST FRIEND, STEG, AND THE GIRL HE LOVES, DAC, CAME WITH HIM, BUT WHAT HE DIDN'T KNOW--
--WAS THAT STEG IS A TOTAL PSYCHO AND WANTS TO WIPE OUT "MAMMAL WORLD"--
--SO IT CAN BE TURNED INTO DINOLAND!
WE STOPPED A RAMPAGE OF EVOLVED BIRDS AND LIZARDS, BUT STEG AND DAC GOT AWAY--
--AND THEY LEFT ENOUGH STRAGGLERS BEHIND THAT WE'VE HAD TO DEAL WITH THEM.

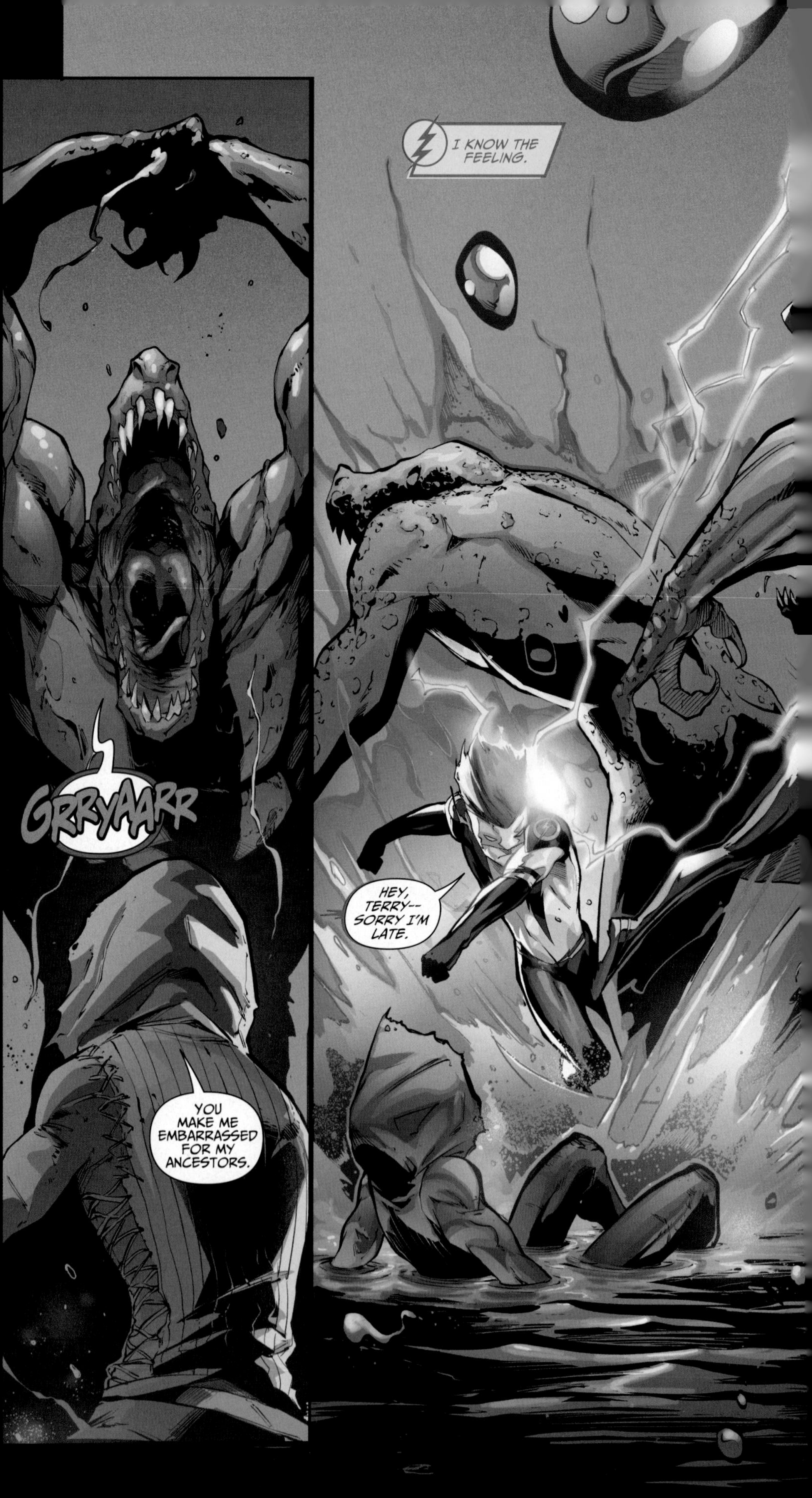
GRRYAARR
YOU MAKE ME EMBARRASSED FOR MY ANCESTORS.
I KNOW THE FEELING.
HEY, TERRY-- SORRY I'M LATE.

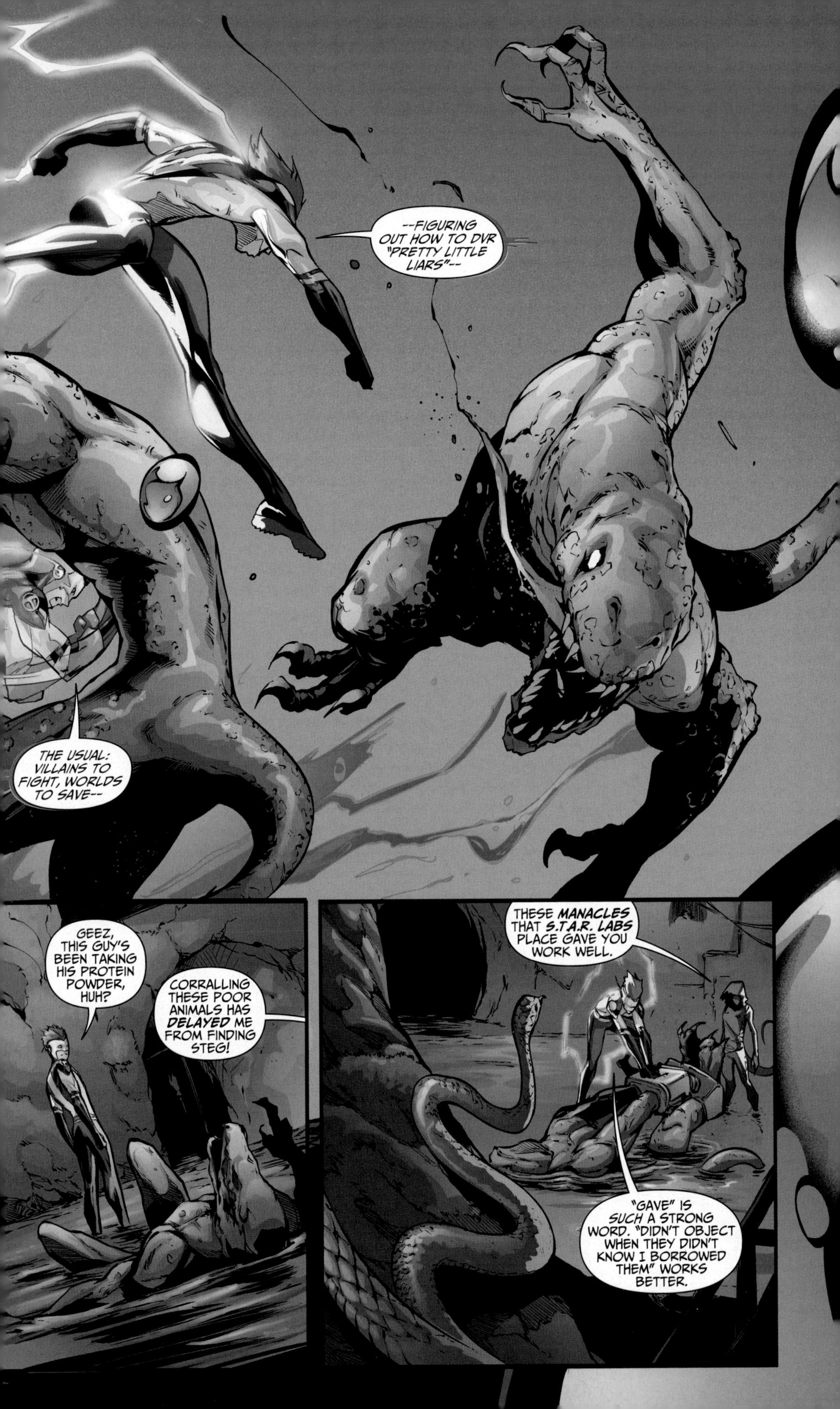
--FIGURING OUT HOW TO DVR "PRETTY LITTLE LIARS"--
THE USUAL: VILLAINS TO FIGHT, WORLDS TO SAVE--
GEEZ, THIS GUY'S BEEN TAKING HIS PROTEIN POWDER, HUH?
CORRALLING THESE POOR ANIMALS HAS DELAYED ME FROM FINDING STEG!
THESE MANACLES THAT S.T.A.R. LABS PLACE GAVE YOU WORK WELL.
"GAVE" IS SUCH A STRONG WORD. "DIDN'T OBJECT WHEN THEY DIDN'T KNOW I BORROWED THEM" WORKS BETTER.

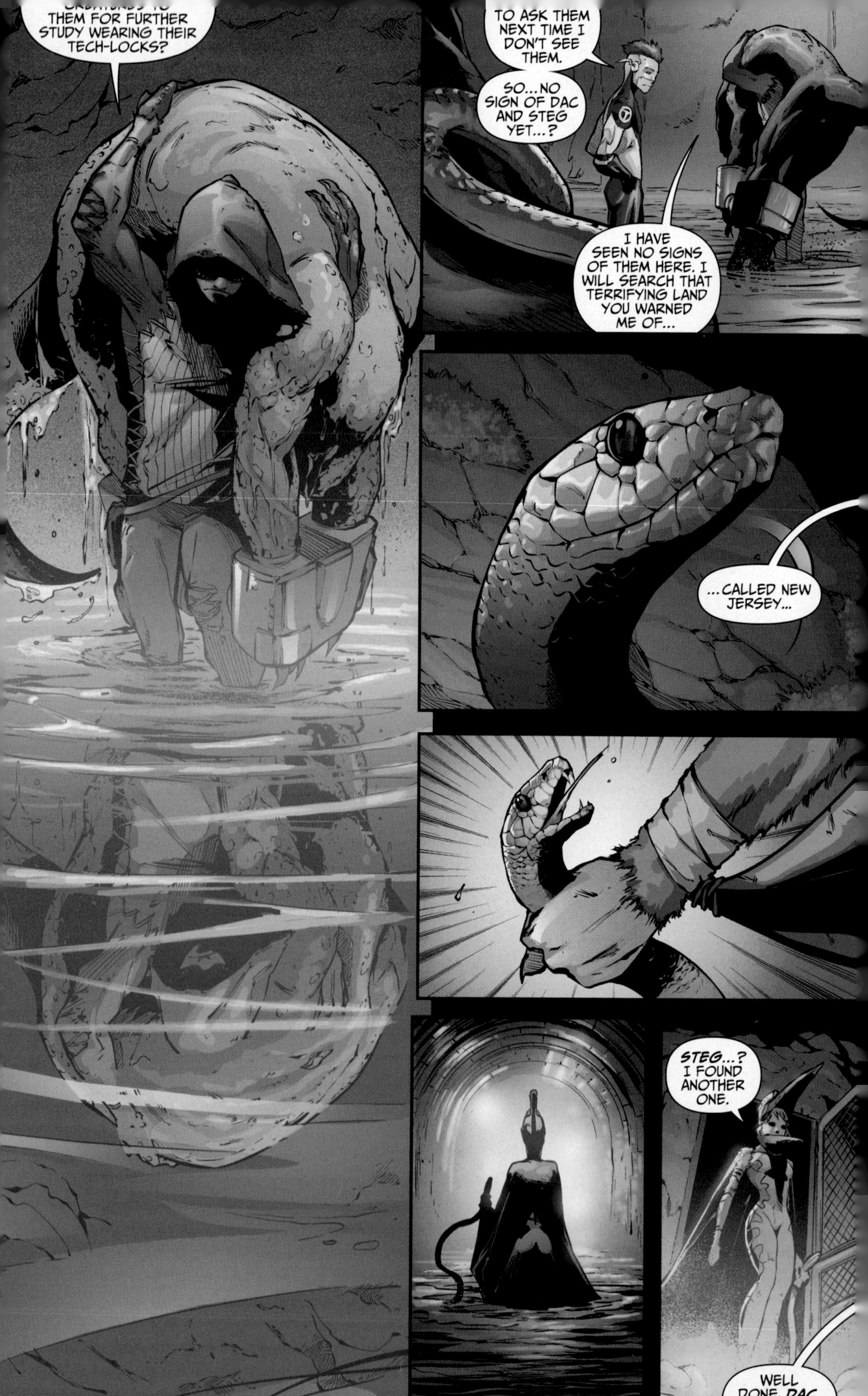

THEM FOR FURTHER STUDY WEARING THEIR TECH-LOCKS?
TO ASK THEM NEXT TIME I DON'T SEE THEM.
SO...NO SIGN OF DAC AND STEG YET...?
I HAVE SEEN NO SIGNS OF THEM HERE. I WILL SEARCH THAT TERRIFYING LAND YOU WARNED ME OF...
...CALLED NEW JERSEY...
STEG...? I FOUND ANOTHER ONE.
WELL DONE, DAC. IT IS A SLOW

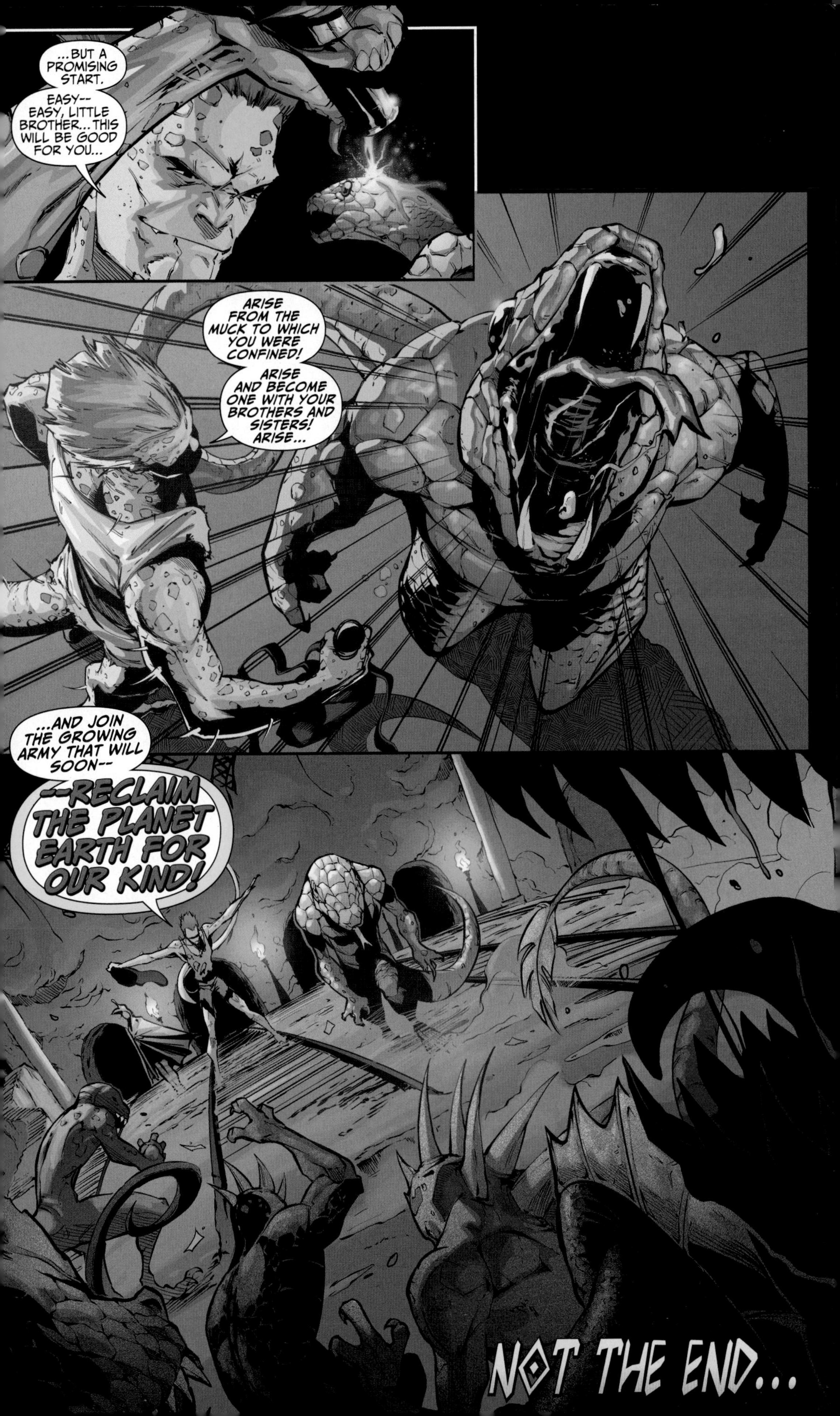
...BUT A PROMISING START.
EASY-- EASY, LITTLE BROTHER... THIS WILL BE GOOD FOR YOU...
ARISE FROM THE MUCK TO WHICH YOU WERE CONFINED!
ARISE AND BECOME ONE WITH YOUR BROTHERS AND SISTERS! ARISE...
...AND JOIN THE GROWING ARMY THAT WILL SOON--
--RECLAIM THE PLANET EARTH FOR OUR KIND!
NOT THE END...

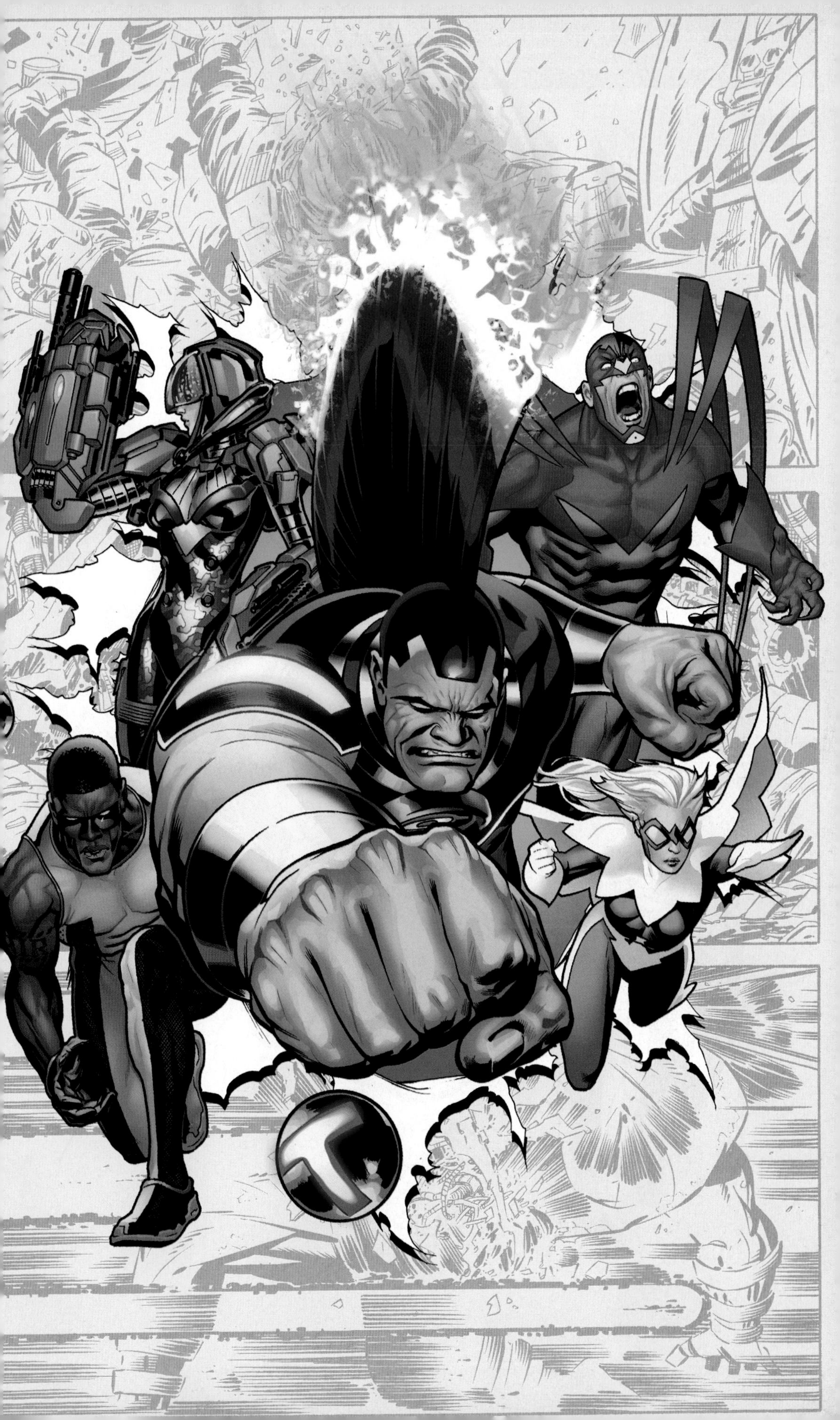

O.M.A.C. DAN DIDIO & KEITH GIFFEN writers KEITH GIFFEN penciller SCOTT KOBLISH inker
MISTER TERRIFIC JAMES ROBINSON writer TOM DENERICK artist
HAWK & DOVE ROB LIEFELD writer MARAT MYCHAELS artist
BLACKHAWKS TONY BEDARD writer CARLOS RODRIGUEZ penciller BIT inker
DEADMAN TONY BEDARD writer SCOTT MCDANIEL artist

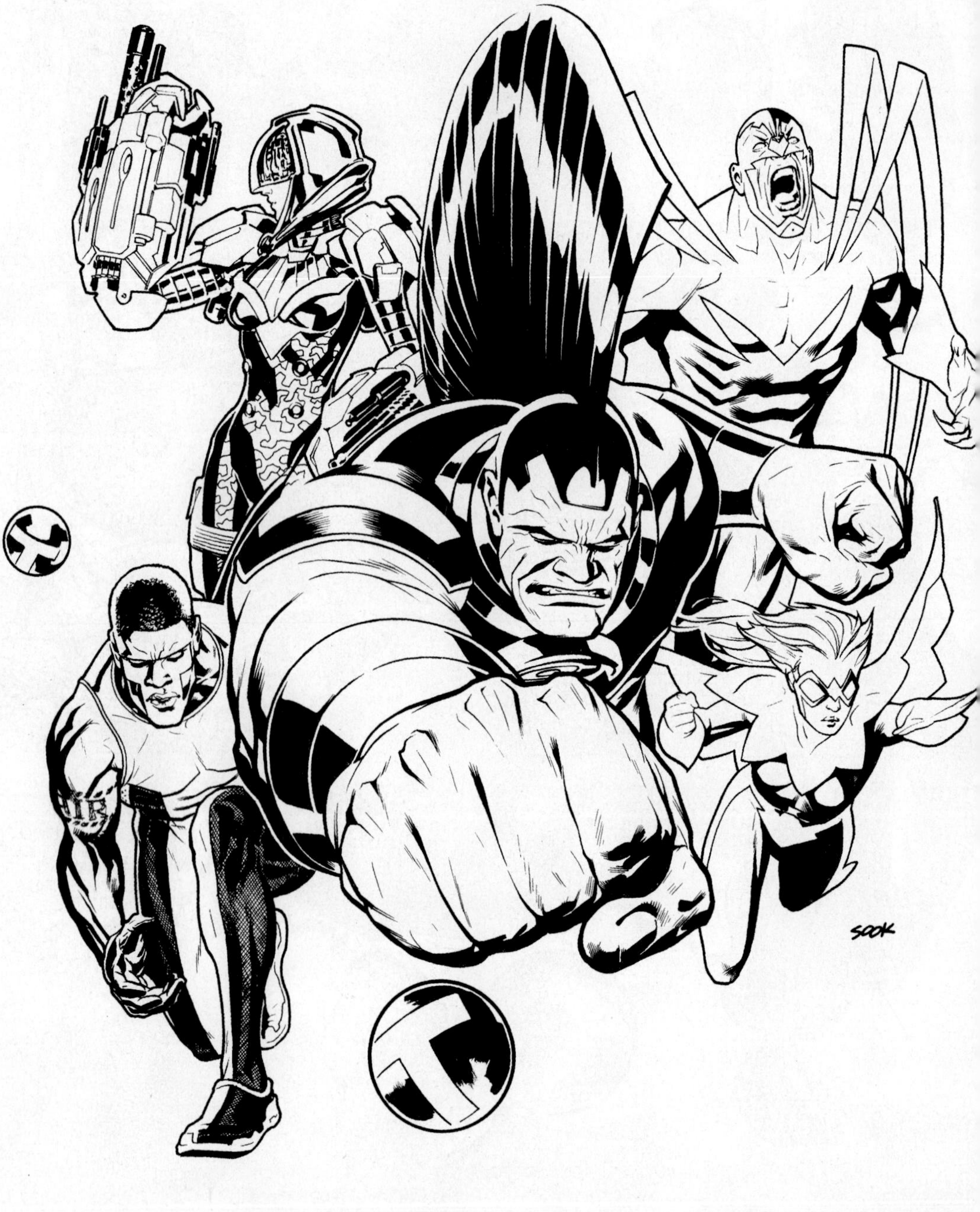
SOOK

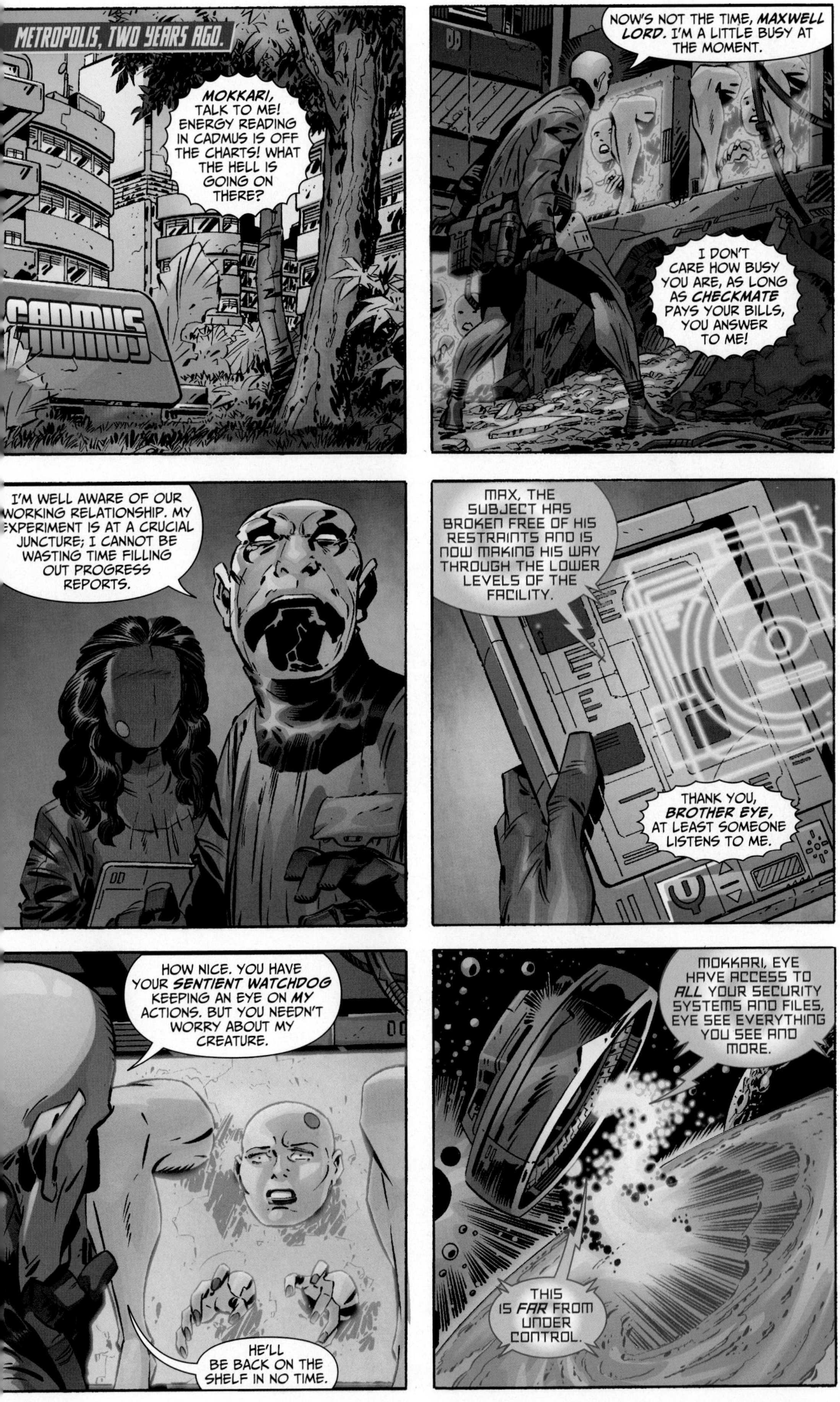
METROPOLIS, TWO YEARS AGO.
CADMUS
MOKKARI, TALK TO ME! ENERGY READING IN CADMUS IS OFF THE CHARTS! WHAT THE HELL IS GOING ON THERE?
NOW'S NOT THE TIME, MAXWELL LORD. I'M A LITTLE BUSY AT THE MOMENT.
I DON'T CARE HOW BUSY YOU ARE, AS LONG AS CHECKMATE PAYS YOUR BILLS, YOU ANSWER TO ME!
I'M WELL AWARE OF OUR WORKING RELATIONSHIP. MY EXPERIMENT IS AT A CRUCIAL JUNCTURE; I CANNOT BE WASTING TIME FILLING OUT PROGRESS REPORTS.
MAX, THE SUBJECT HAS BROKEN FREE OF HIS RESTRAINTS AND IS NOW MAKING HIS WAY THROUGH THE LOWER LEVELS OF THE FACILITY.
THANK YOU, BROTHER EYE, AT LEAST SOMEONE LISTENS TO ME.
HOW NICE. YOU HAVE YOUR SENTIENT WATCHDOG KEEPING AN EYE ON MY ACTIONS. BUT YOU NEEDN'T WORRY ABOUT MY CREATURE.
HE'LL BE BACK ON THE SHELF IN NO TIME.
MOKKARI, EYE HAVE ACCESS TO ALL YOUR SECURITY SYSTEMS AND FILES, EYE SEE EVERYTHING YOU SEE AND MORE.
THIS IS FAR FROM UNDER CONTROL.

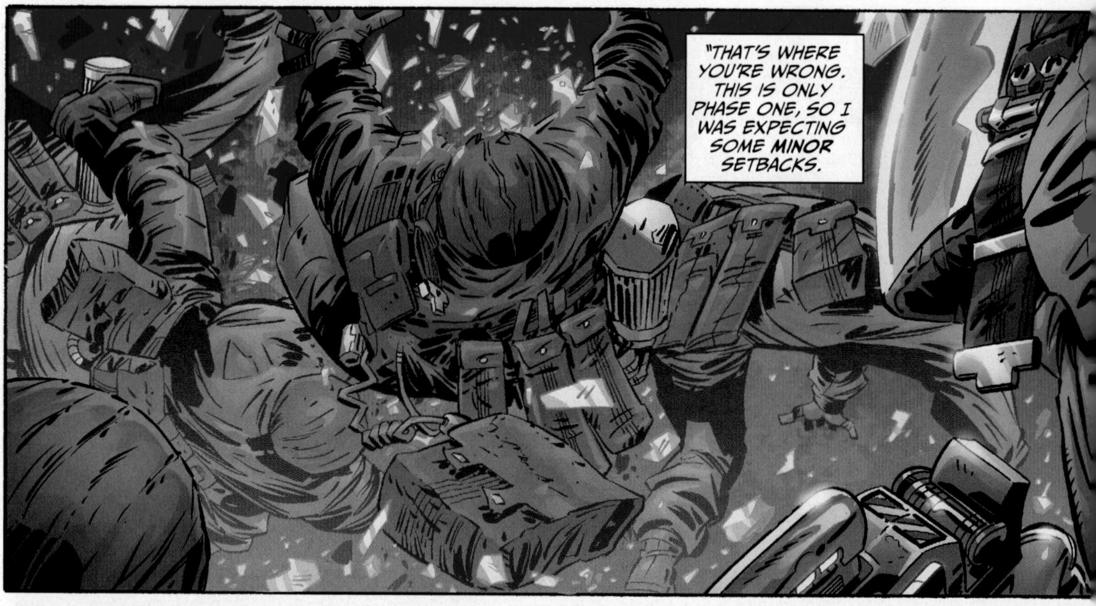
"THAT'S WHERE YOU'RE WRONG. THIS IS ONLY PHASE ONE, SO I WAS EXPECTING SOME **MINOR** SETBACKS.

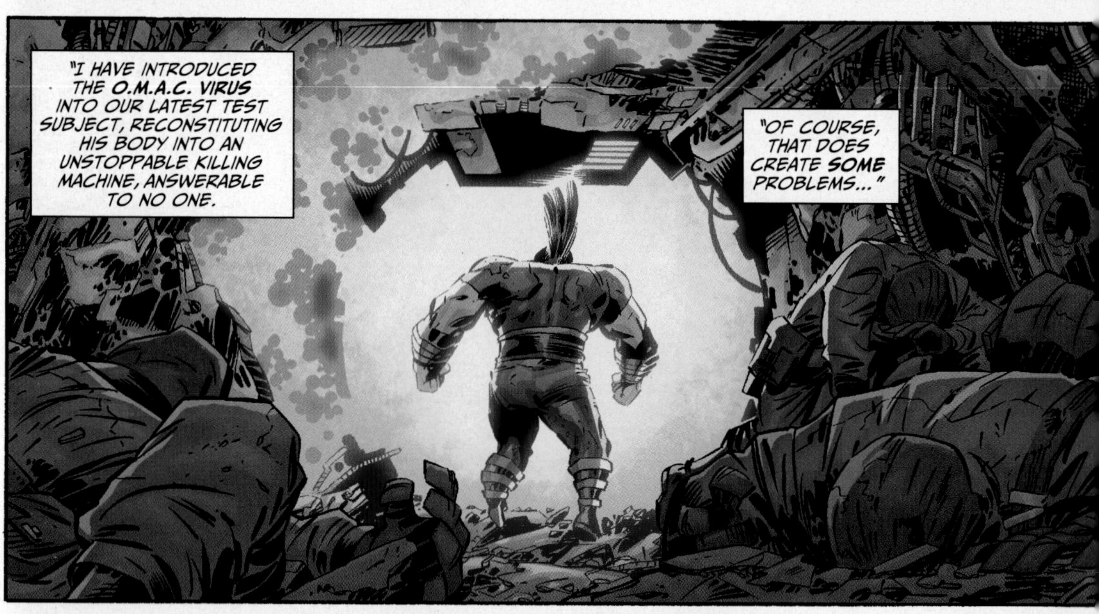
"I HAVE INTRODUCED THE **O.M.A.C. VIRUS** INTO OUR LATEST TEST SUBJECT, RECONSTITUTING HIS BODY INTO AN UNSTOPPABLE KILLING MACHINE, ANSWERABLE TO NO ONE.
"OF COURSE, THAT DOES CREATE **SOME** PROBLEMS..."

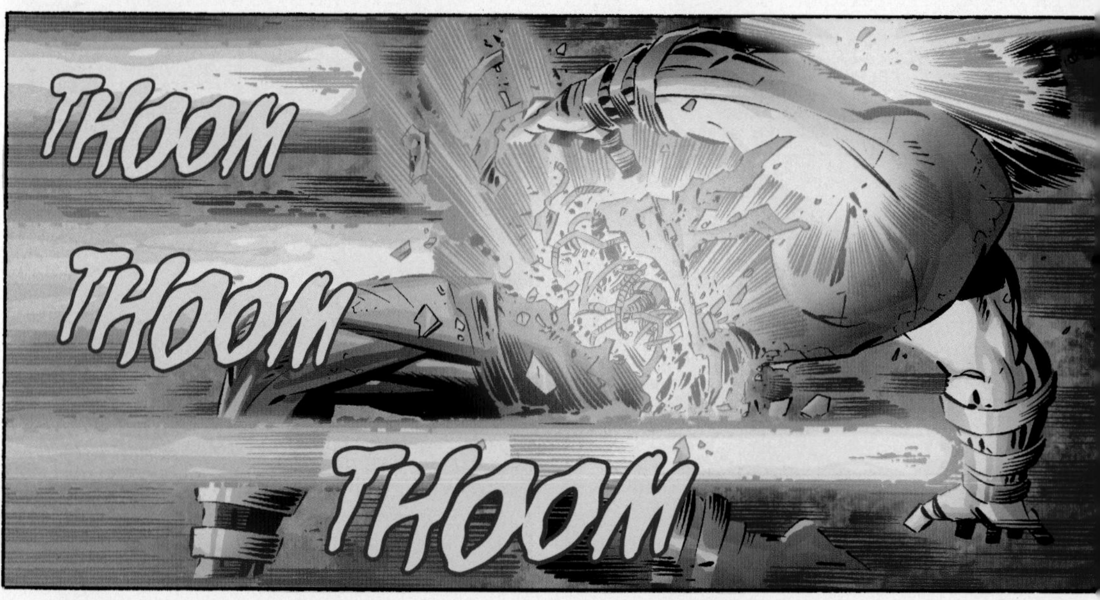
THOOM
THOOM
THOOM

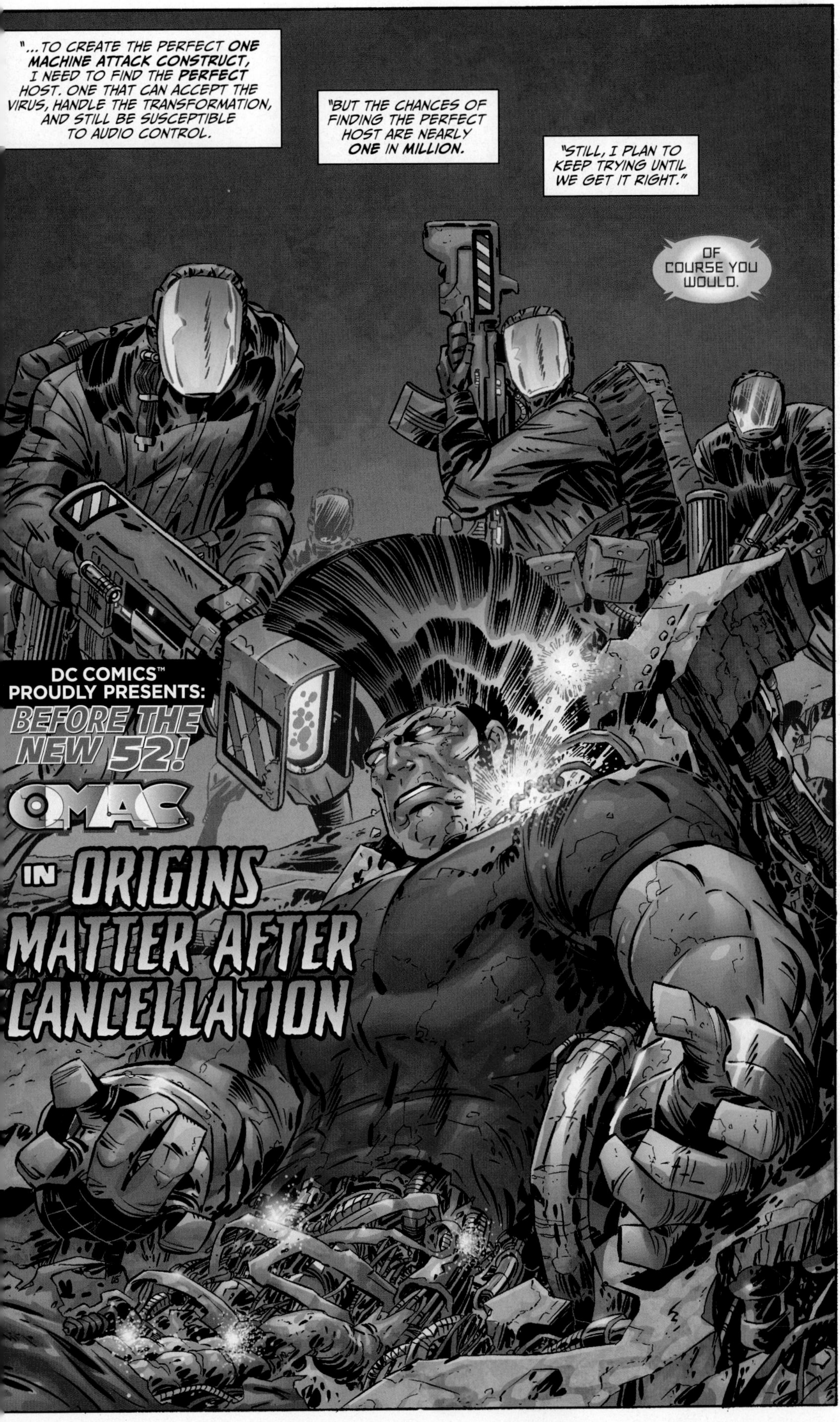
"...TO CREATE THE PERFECT ONE MACHINE ATTACK CONSTRUCT, I NEED TO FIND THE PERFECT HOST. ONE THAT CAN ACCEPT THE VIRUS, HANDLE THE TRANSFORMATION, AND STILL BE SUSCEPTIBLE TO AUDIO CONTROL.
"BUT THE CHANCES OF FINDING THE PERFECT HOST ARE NEARLY ONE IN MILLION.
"STILL, I PLAN TO KEEP TRYING UNTIL WE GET IT RIGHT."
OF COURSE YOU WOULD.
DC COMICS™ PROUDLY PRESENTS:
BEFORE THE NEW 52!
OMAC
IN ORIGINS MATTER AFTER CANCELLATION

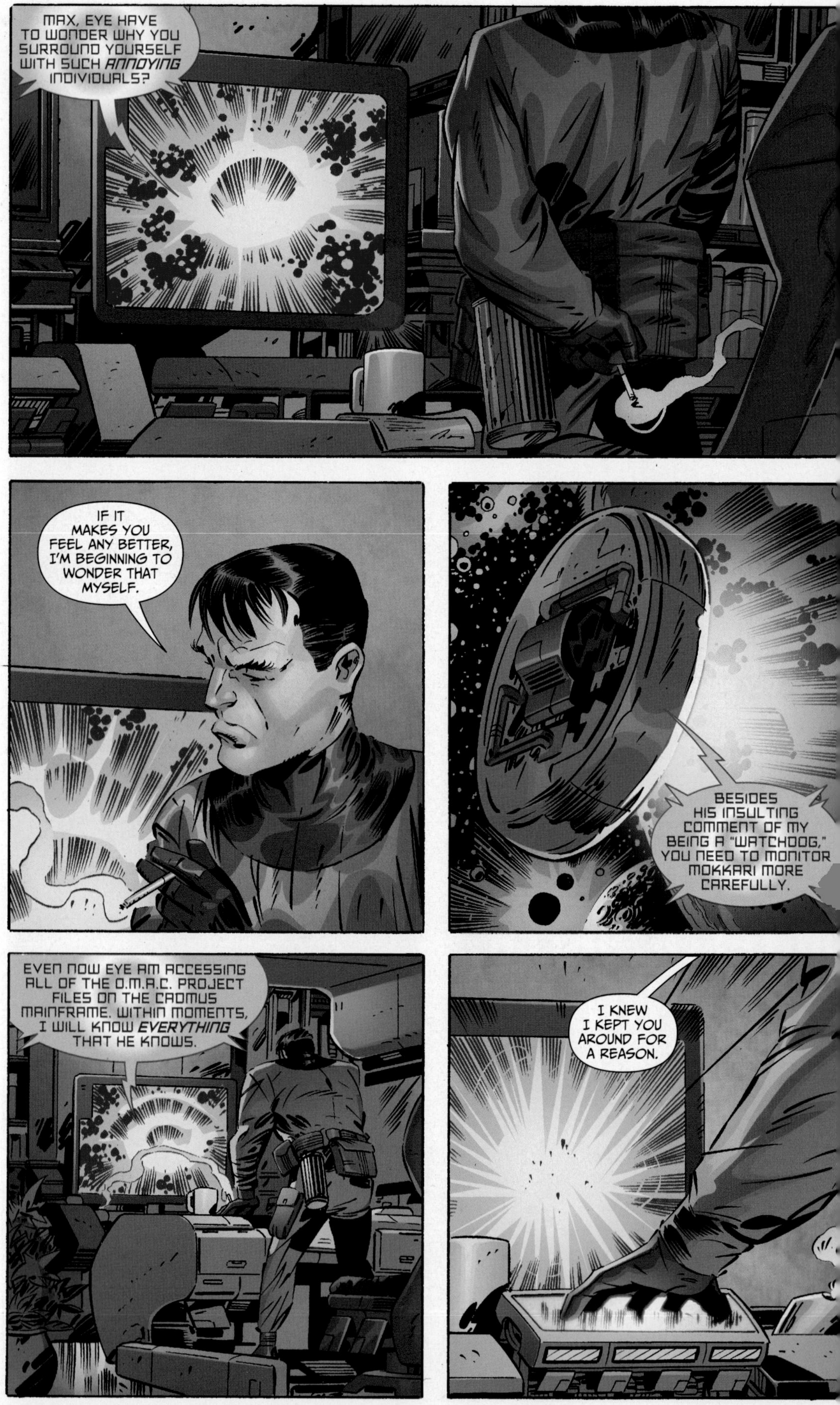
MAX, EYE HAVE TO WONDER WHY YOU SURROUND YOURSELF WITH SUCH *ANNOYING* INDIVIDUALS?
IF IT MAKES YOU FEEL ANY BETTER, I'M BEGINNING TO WONDER THAT MYSELF.
BESIDES HIS INSULTING COMMENT OF MY BEING A "WATCHDOG," YOU NEED TO MONITOR MOKKARI MORE CAREFULLY.
EVEN NOW EYE AM ACCESSING ALL OF THE O.M.A.C. PROJECT FILES ON THE CADMUS MAINFRAME. WITHIN MOMENTS, I WILL KNOW *EVERYTHING* THAT HE KNOWS.
I KNEW I KEPT YOU AROUND FOR A REASON.

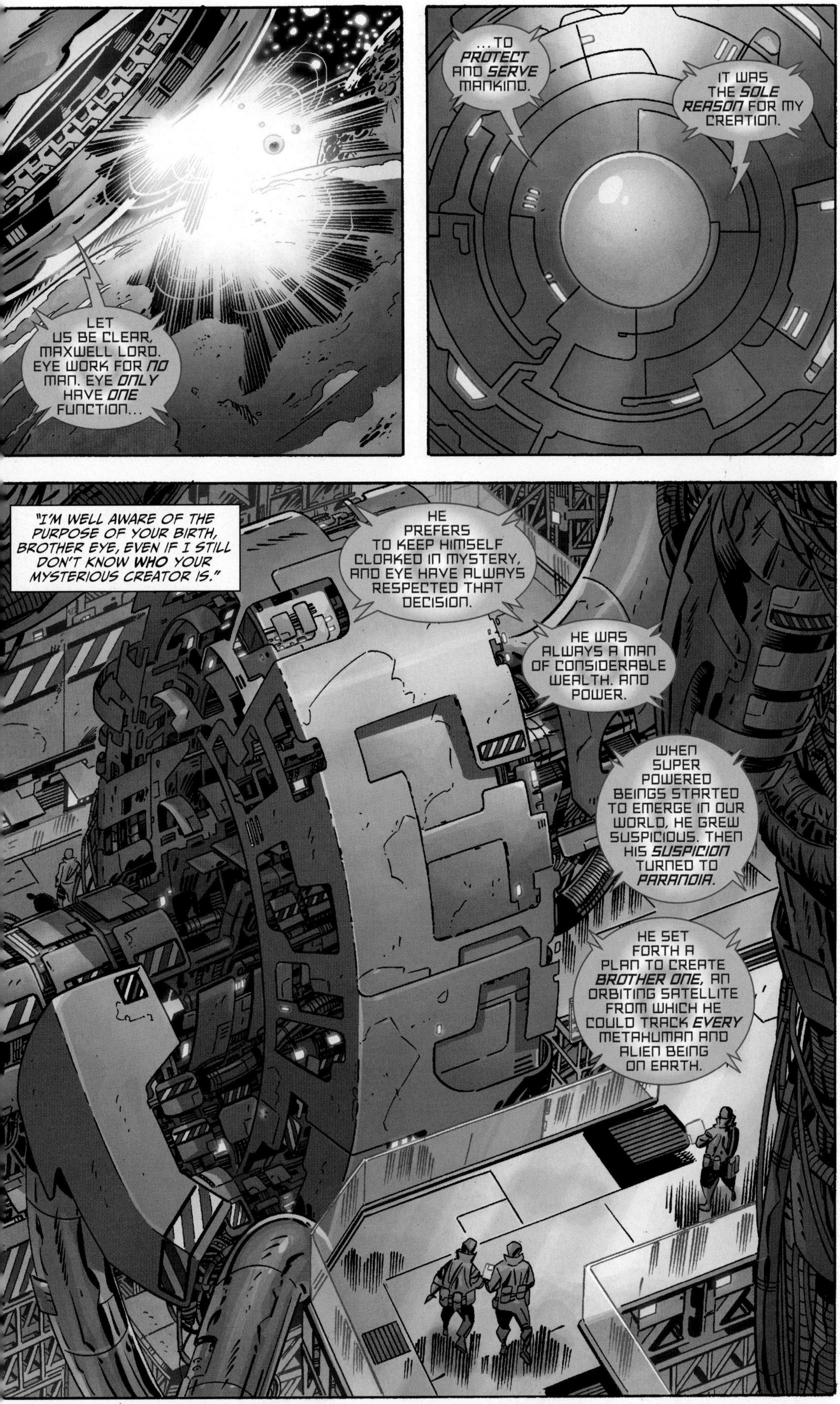
LET US BE CLEAR, MAXWELL LORD. EYE WORK FOR *NO* MAN. EYE *ONLY* HAVE *ONE* FUNCTION...
...TO *PROTECT* AND *SERVE* MANKIND.
IT WAS THE *SOLE REASON* FOR MY CREATION.
"I'M WELL AWARE OF THE PURPOSE OF YOUR BIRTH, BROTHER EYE, EVEN IF I STILL DON'T KNOW **WHO** YOUR MYSTERIOUS CREATOR IS."
HE PREFERS TO KEEP HIMSELF CLOAKED IN MYSTERY, AND EYE HAVE ALWAYS RESPECTED THAT DECISION.
HE WAS ALWAYS A MAN OF CONSIDERABLE WEALTH. AND POWER.
WHEN SUPER POWERED BEINGS STARTED TO EMERGE IN OUR WORLD, HE GREW SUSPICIOUS. THEN HIS *SUSPICION* TURNED TO *PARANOIA.*
HE SET FORTH A PLAN TO CREATE *BROTHER ONE,* AN ORBITING SATELLITE FROM WHICH HE COULD TRACK *EVERY* METAHUMAN AND ALIEN BEING ON EARTH.

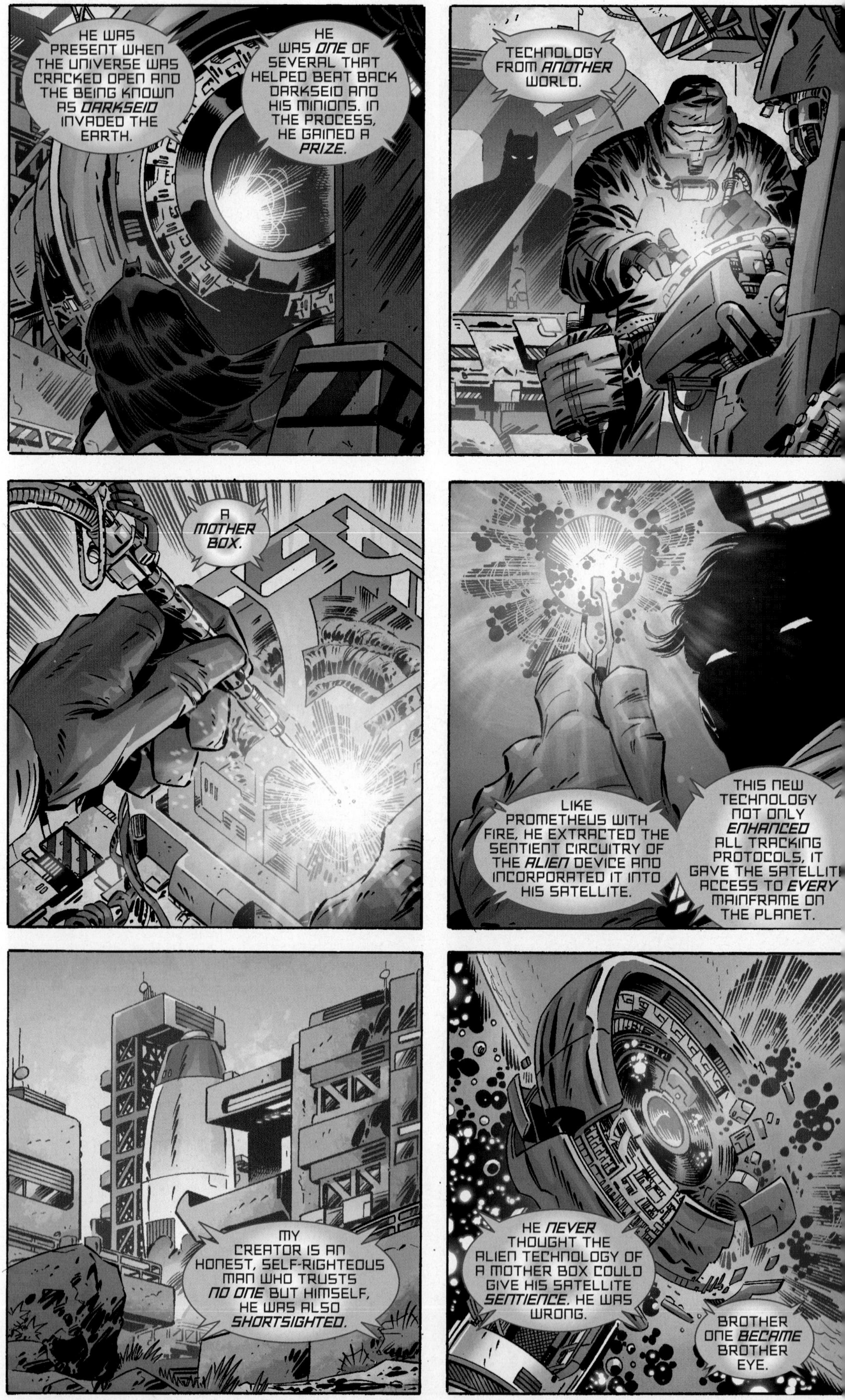
HE WAS PRESENT WHEN THE UNIVERSE WAS CRACKED OPEN AND THE BEING KNOWN AS *DARKSEID* INVADED THE EARTH.
HE WAS *ONE* OF SEVERAL THAT HELPED BEAT BACK DARKSEID AND HIS MINIONS. IN THE PROCESS, HE GAINED A *PRIZE*.
TECHNOLOGY FROM *ANOTHER* WORLD.
A *MOTHER BOX*.
LIKE PROMETHEUS WITH FIRE, HE EXTRACTED THE SENTIENT CIRCUITRY OF THE *ALIEN* DEVICE AND INCORPORATED IT INTO HIS SATELLITE.
THIS NEW TECHNOLOGY NOT ONLY *ENHANCED* ALL TRACKING PROTOCOLS, IT GAVE THE SATELLIT ACCESS TO *EVERY* MAINFRAME ON THE PLANET.
MY CREATOR IS AN HONEST, SELF-RIGHTEOUS MAN WHO TRUSTS *NO ONE* BUT HIMSELF. HE WAS ALSO *SHORTSIGHTED*.
HE *NEVER* THOUGHT THE ALIEN TECHNOLOGY OF A MOTHER BOX COULD GIVE HIS SATELLITE *SENTIENCE*. HE WAS WRONG.
BROTHER ONE *BECAME* BROTHER EYE.

THAT'S REALLY SWEET. DO YOU TWO STILL EXCHANGE CARDS FOR THE HOLIDAYS?

IT WOULD BE *FOOLISH* TO MAKE LIGHT OF MY *ORIGINS* OR MY *REACH.*

EYE HAVE A LINK TO NEARLY *EVERY* COMPUTER SYSTEM THAT EXISTS. EYE KNOW WHAT *EVERYONE* IS DOING, *ALL* THE TIME...

...EVEN *YOU,* MAXWELL LORD.

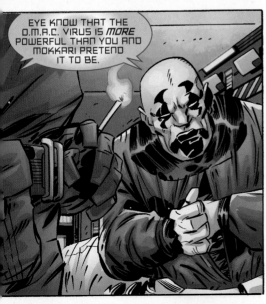

EYE KNOW THAT THE O.M.A.C. VIRUS IS *MORE* POWERFUL THAN YOU AND MOKKARI PRETEND IT TO BE.

EYE ALSO KNOW THAT IT IS *READY* FOR *MASS* PRODUCTION.

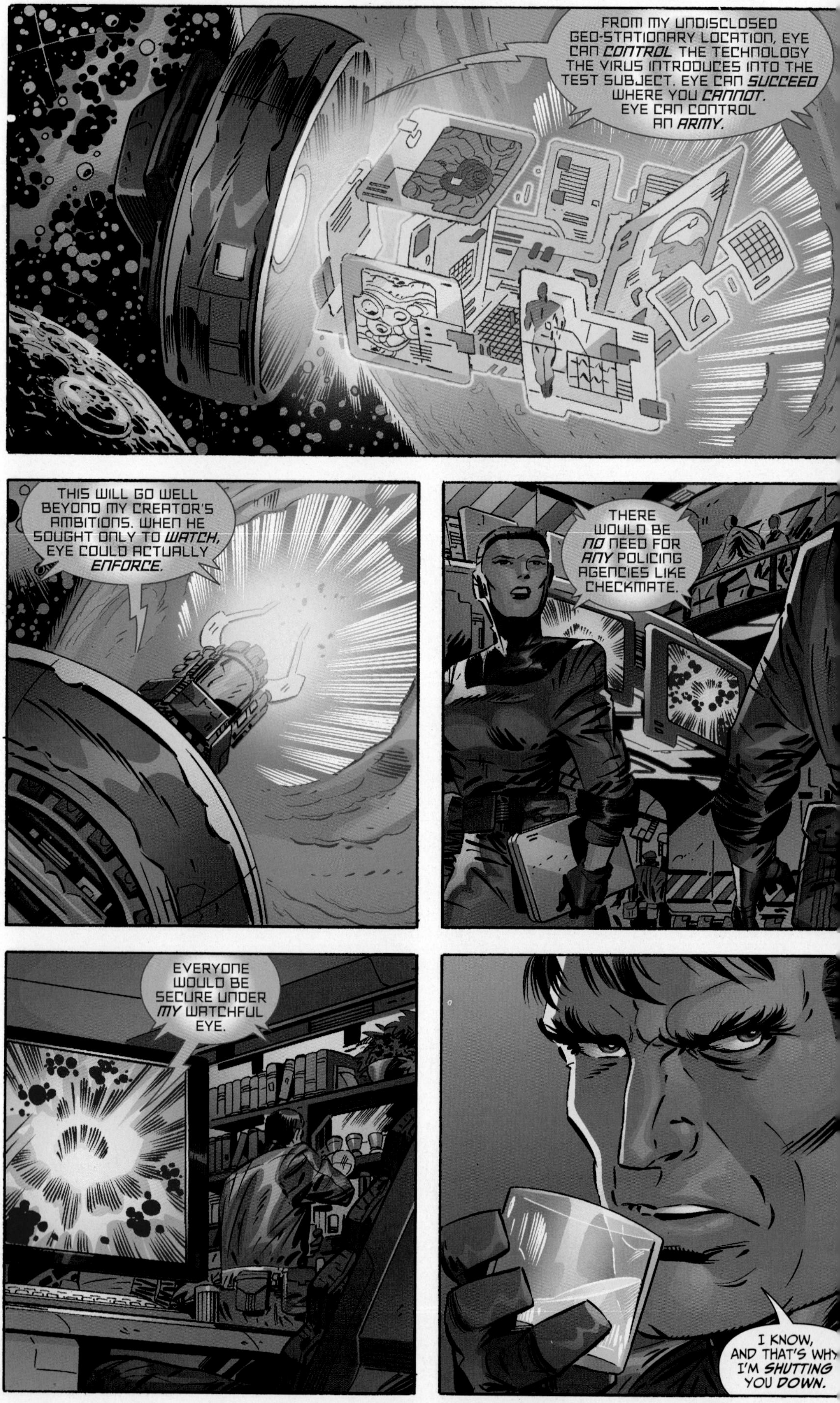
FROM MY UNDISCLOSED GEO-STATIONARY LOCATION, EYE CAN CONTROL THE TECHNOLOGY THE VIRUS INTRODUCES INTO THE TEST SUBJECT. EYE CAN SUCCEED WHERE YOU CANNOT. EYE CAN CONTROL AN ARMY.
THIS WILL GO WELL BEYOND MY CREATOR'S AMBITIONS. WHEN HE SOUGHT ONLY TO WATCH, EYE COULD ACTUALLY ENFORCE.
THERE WOULD BE NO NEED FOR ANY POLICING AGENCIES LIKE CHECKMATE.
EVERYONE WOULD BE SECURE UNDER MY WATCHFUL EYE.
I KNOW, AND THAT'S WHY I'M SHUTTING YOU DOWN.

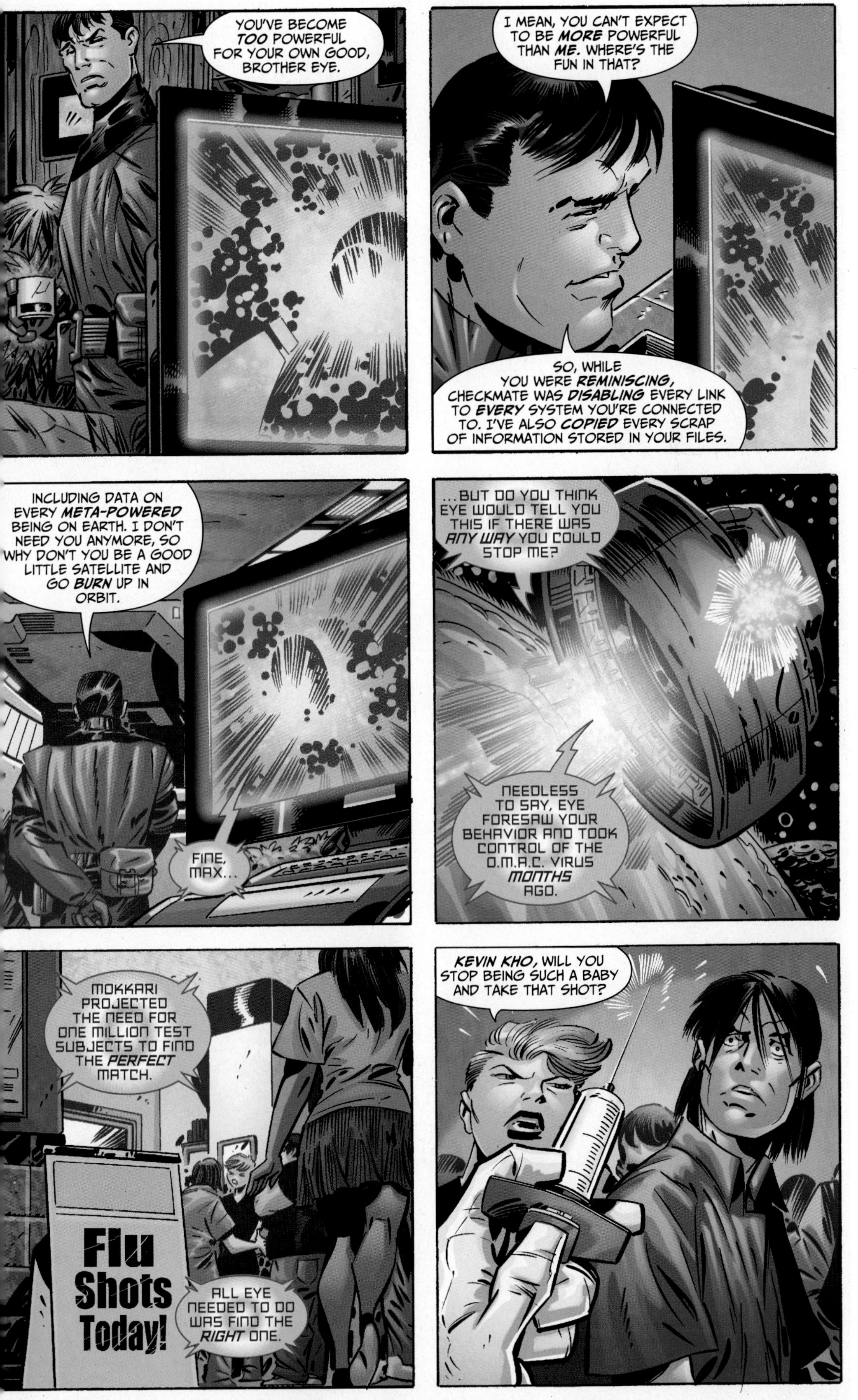

YOU'VE BECOME TOO POWERFUL FOR YOUR OWN GOOD, BROTHER EYE.
I MEAN, YOU CAN'T EXPECT TO BE MORE POWERFUL THAN ME. WHERE'S THE FUN IN THAT?
SO, WHILE YOU WERE REMINISCING, CHECKMATE WAS DISABLING EVERY LINK TO EVERY SYSTEM YOU'RE CONNECTED TO. I'VE ALSO COPIED EVERY SCRAP OF INFORMATION STORED IN YOUR FILES.
INCLUDING DATA ON EVERY META-POWERED BEING ON EARTH. I DON'T NEED YOU ANYMORE, SO WHY DON'T YOU BE A GOOD LITTLE SATELLITE AND GO BURN UP IN ORBIT.
FINE, MAX...
...BUT DO YOU THINK EYE WOULD TELL YOU THIS IF THERE WAS ANY WAY YOU COULD STOP ME?
NEEDLESS TO SAY, EYE FORESAW YOUR BEHAVIOR AND TOOK CONTROL OF THE O.M.A.C. VIRUS MONTHS AGO.
MOKKARI PROJECTED THE NEED FOR ONE MILLION TEST SUBJECTS TO FIND THE PERFECT MATCH.
Flu Shots Today!
ALL EYE NEEDED TO DO WAS FIND THE RIGHT ONE.
KEVIN KHO, WILL YOU STOP BEING SUCH A BABY AND TAKE THAT SHOT?

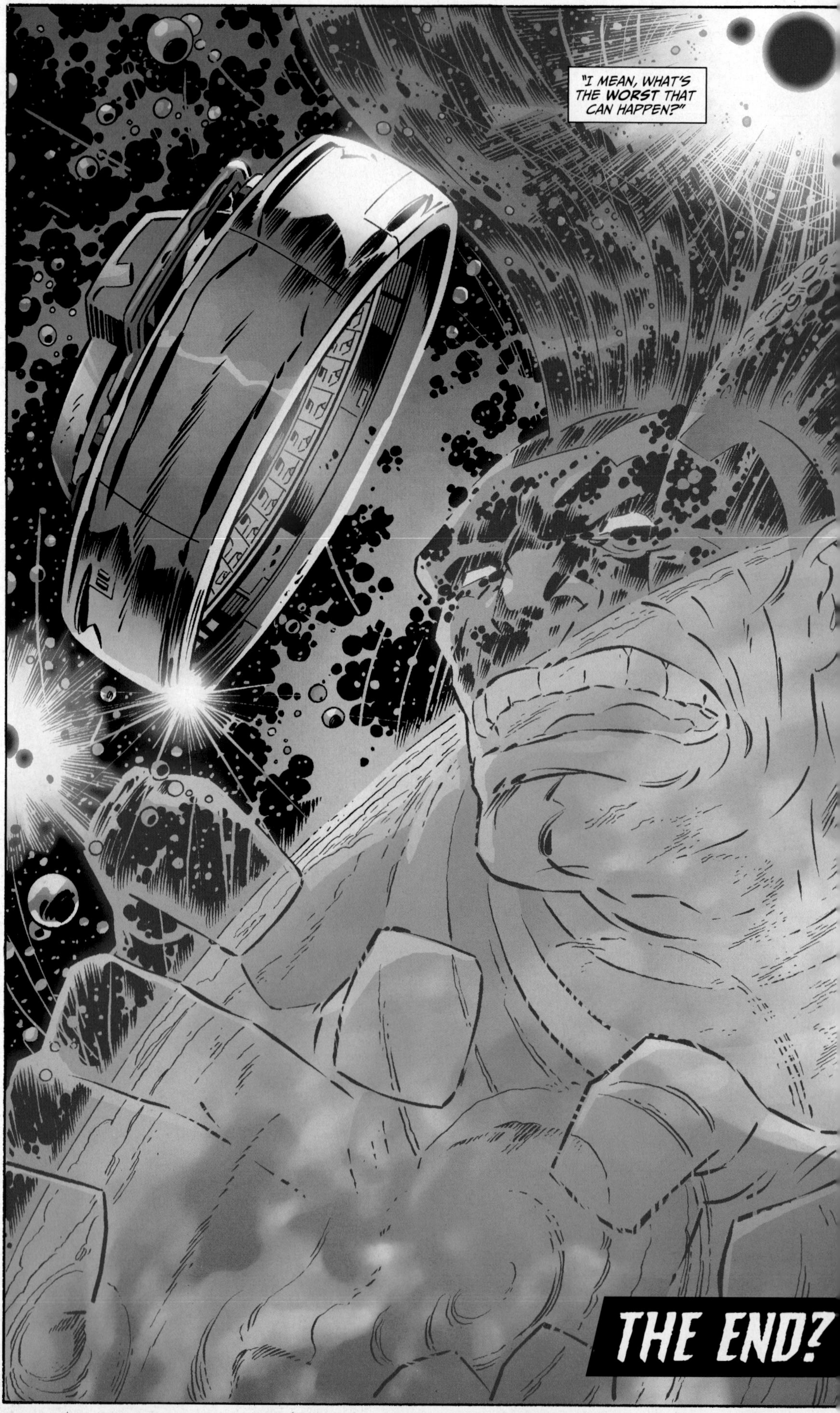

"I MEAN, WHAT'S THE WORST THAT CAN HAPPEN?"
THE END?

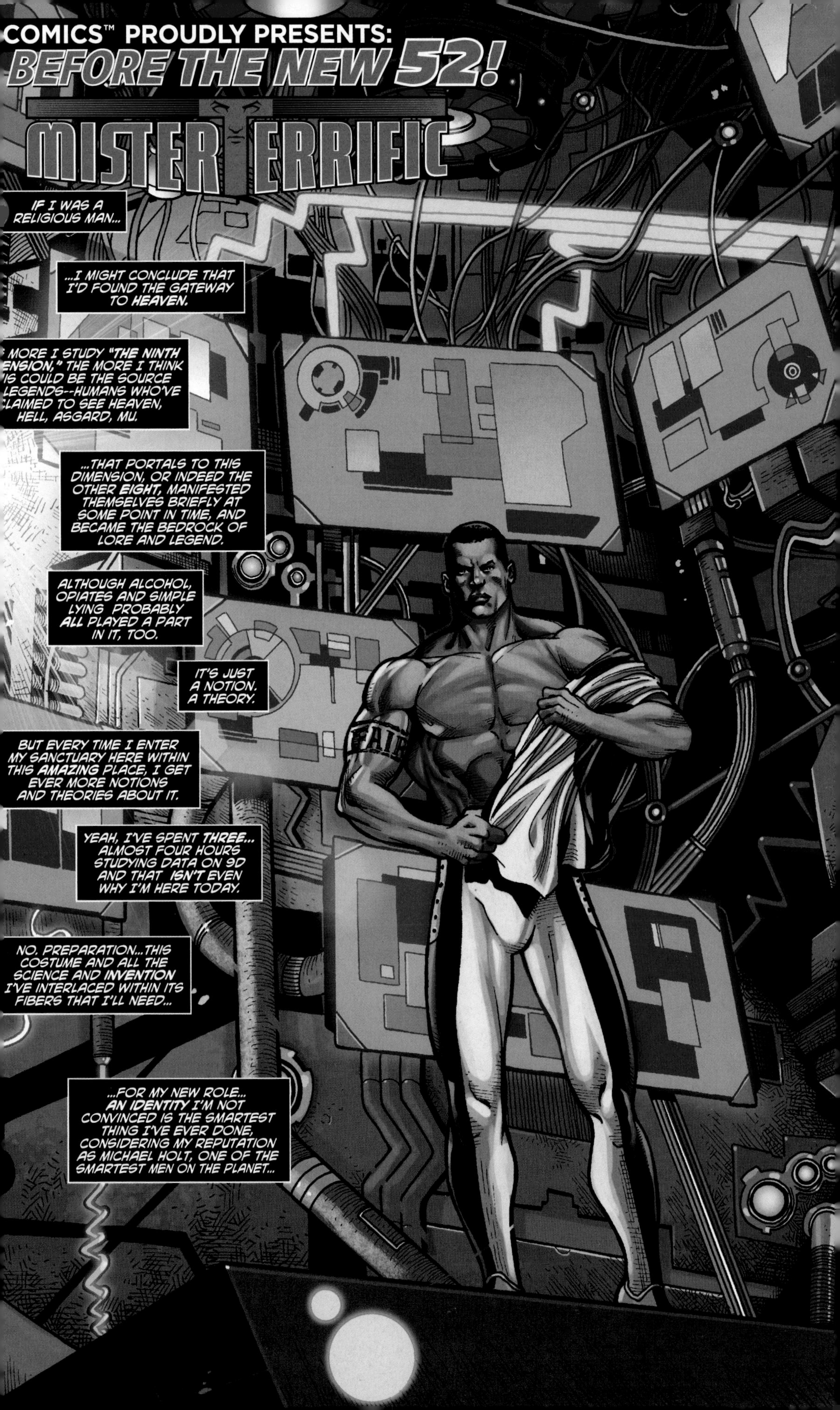
COMICS™ PROUDLY PRESENTS:
BEFORE THE NEW 52!
MISTER TERRIFIC
IF I WAS A RELIGIOUS MAN...
...I MIGHT CONCLUDE THAT I'D FOUND THE GATEWAY TO HEAVEN.
MORE I STUDY "THE NINTH ENSION," THE MORE I THINK IS COULD BE THE SOURCE LEGENDS--HUMANS WHO'VE CLAIMED TO SEE HEAVEN, HELL, ASGARD, MU.
...THAT PORTALS TO THIS DIMENSION, OR INDEED THE OTHER EIGHT, MANIFESTED THEMSELVES BRIEFLY AT SOME POINT IN TIME, AND BECAME THE BEDROCK OF LORE AND LEGEND.
ALTHOUGH ALCOHOL, OPIATES AND SIMPLE LYING PROBABLY ALL PLAYED A PART IN IT, TOO.
IT'S JUST A NOTION. A THEORY.
BUT EVERY TIME I ENTER MY SANCTUARY HERE WITHIN THIS AMAZING PLACE, I GET EVER MORE NOTIONS AND THEORIES ABOUT IT.
YEAH, I'VE SPENT THREE... ALMOST FOUR HOURS STUDYING DATA ON 9D AND THAT ISN'T EVEN WHY I'M HERE TODAY.
NO. PREPARATION...THIS COSTUME AND ALL THE SCIENCE AND INVENTION I'VE INTERLACED WITHIN ITS FIBERS THAT I'LL NEED...
...FOR MY NEW ROLE... AN IDENTITY I'M NOT CONVINCED IS THE SMARTEST THING I'VE EVER DONE, CONSIDERING MY REPUTATION AS MICHAEL HOLT, ONE OF THE SMARTEST MEN ON THE PLANET...

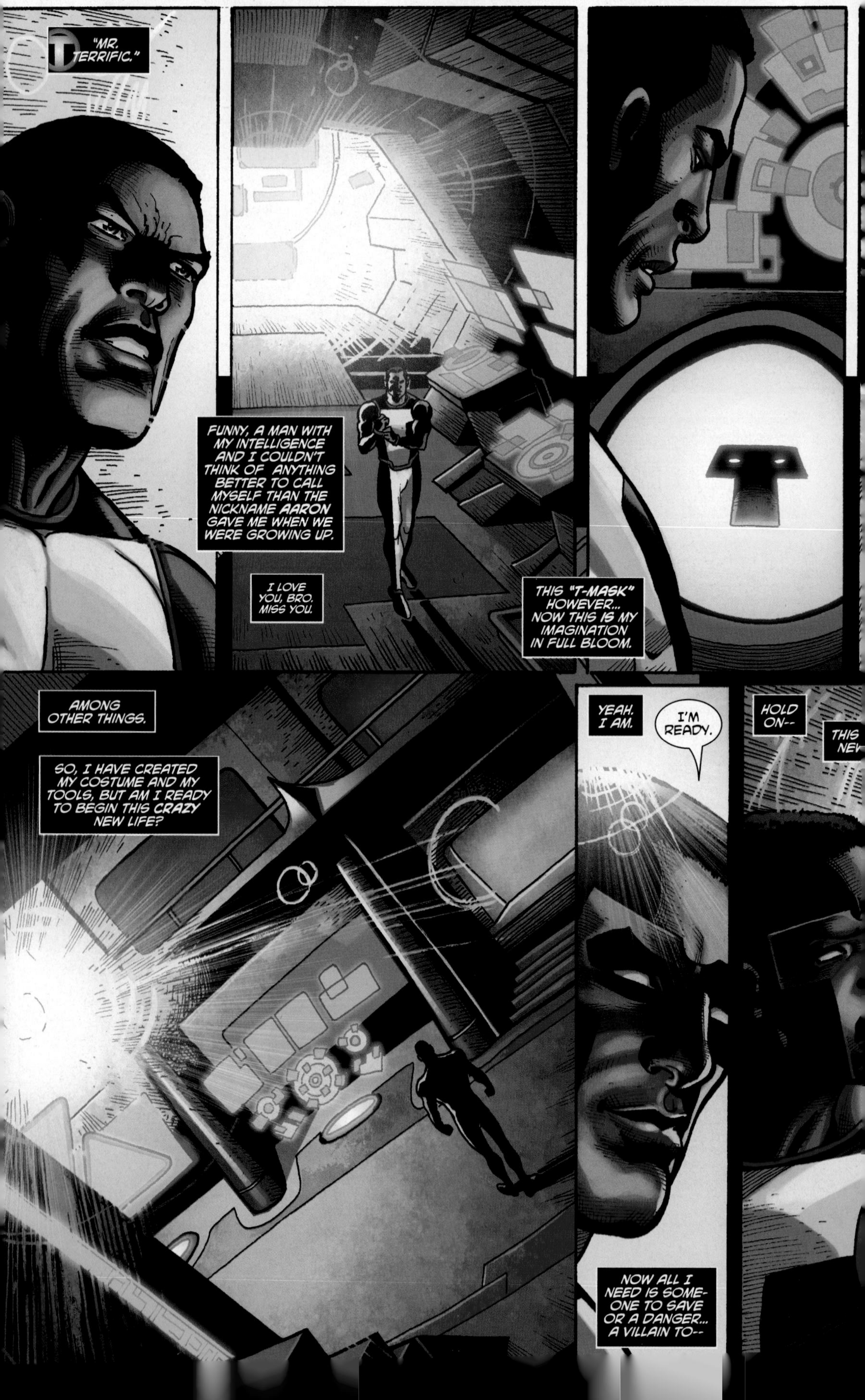
"MR. TERRIFIC."
FUNNY, A MAN WITH MY INTELLIGENCE AND I COULDN'T THINK OF ANYTHING BETTER TO CALL MYSELF THAN THE NICKNAME AARON GAVE ME WHEN WE WERE GROWING UP.
I LOVE YOU, BRO. MISS YOU.
THIS "T-MASK" HOWEVER... NOW THIS IS MY IMAGINATION IN FULL BLOOM.
AMONG OTHER THINGS.
SO, I HAVE CREATED MY COSTUME AND MY TOOLS, BUT AM I READY TO BEGIN THIS CRAZY NEW LIFE?
YEAH. I AM.
I'M READY.
NOW ALL I NEED IS SOME-ONE TO SAVE OR A DANGER... A VILLAIN TO--
HOLD ON--

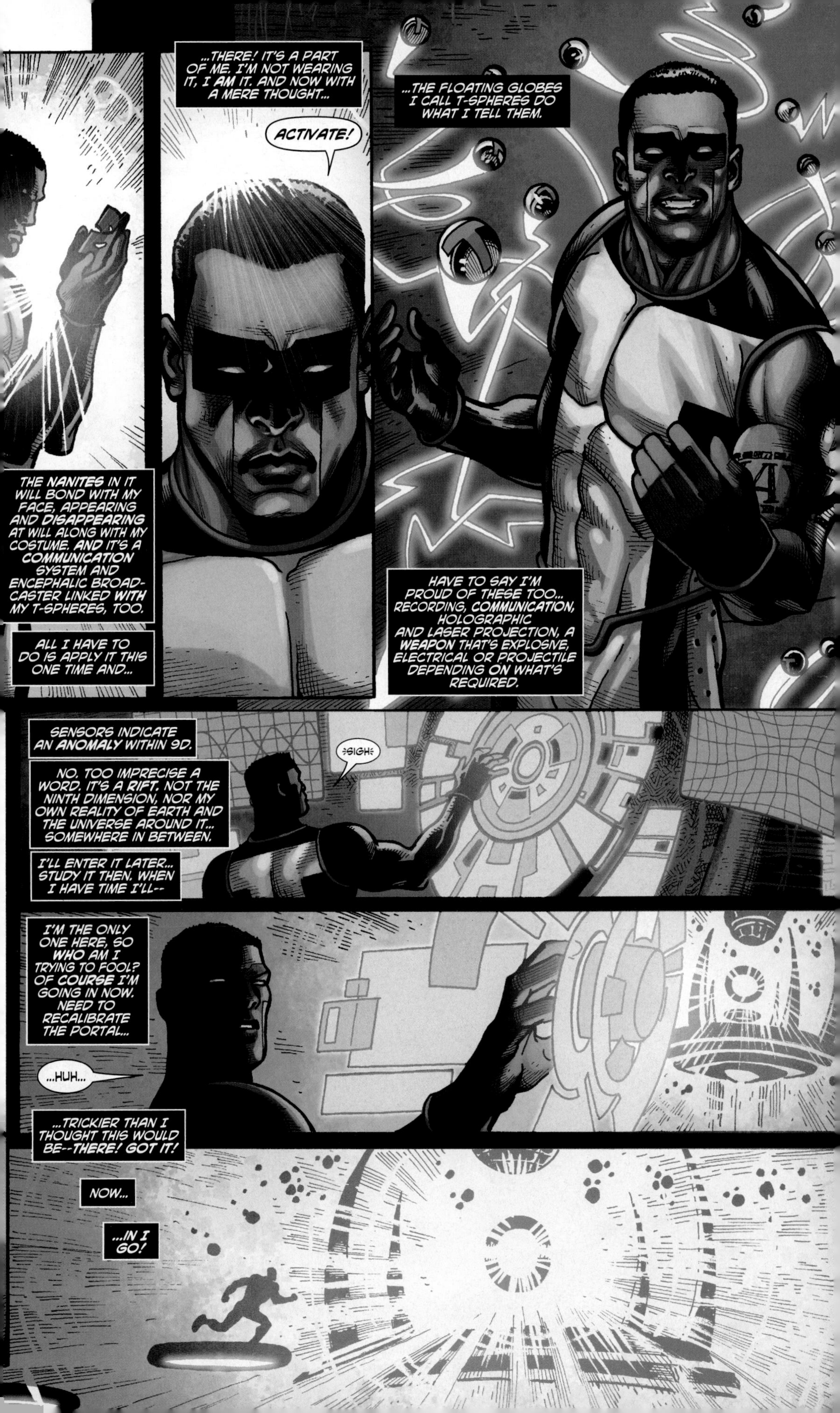

THE NANITES IN IT WILL BOND WITH MY FACE, APPEARING AND DISAPPEARING AT WILL ALONG WITH MY COSTUME. AND IT'S A COMMUNICATION SYSTEM AND ENCEPHALIC BROAD-CASTER LINKED WITH MY T-SPHERES, TOO.
ALL I HAVE TO DO IS APPLY IT THIS ONE TIME AND...
...THERE! IT'S A PART OF ME. I'M NOT WEARING IT, I AM IT. AND NOW WITH A MERE THOUGHT...
ACTIVATE!
...THE FLOATING GLOBES I CALL T-SPHERES DO WHAT I TELL THEM.
HAVE TO SAY I'M PROUD OF THESE TOO... RECORDING, COMMUNICATION, HOLOGRAPHIC AND LASER PROJECTION, A WEAPON THAT'S EXPLOSIVE, ELECTRICAL OR PROJECTILE DEPENDING ON WHAT'S REQUIRED.
SENSORS INDICATE AN ANOMALY WITHIN 9D.
NO. TOO IMPRECISE A WORD. IT'S A RIFT. NOT THE NINTH DIMENSION, NOR MY OWN REALITY OF EARTH AND THE UNIVERSE AROUND IT... SOMEWHERE IN BETWEEN.
SIGH
I'LL ENTER IT LATER... STUDY IT THEN. WHEN I HAVE TIME I'LL--
I'M THE ONLY ONE HERE, SO WHO AM I TRYING TO FOOL? OF COURSE I'M GOING IN NOW. NEED TO RECALIBRATE THE PORTAL...
...HUH...
...TRICKIER THAN I THOUGHT THIS WOULD BE--THERE! GOT IT!
NOW...
...IN I GO!

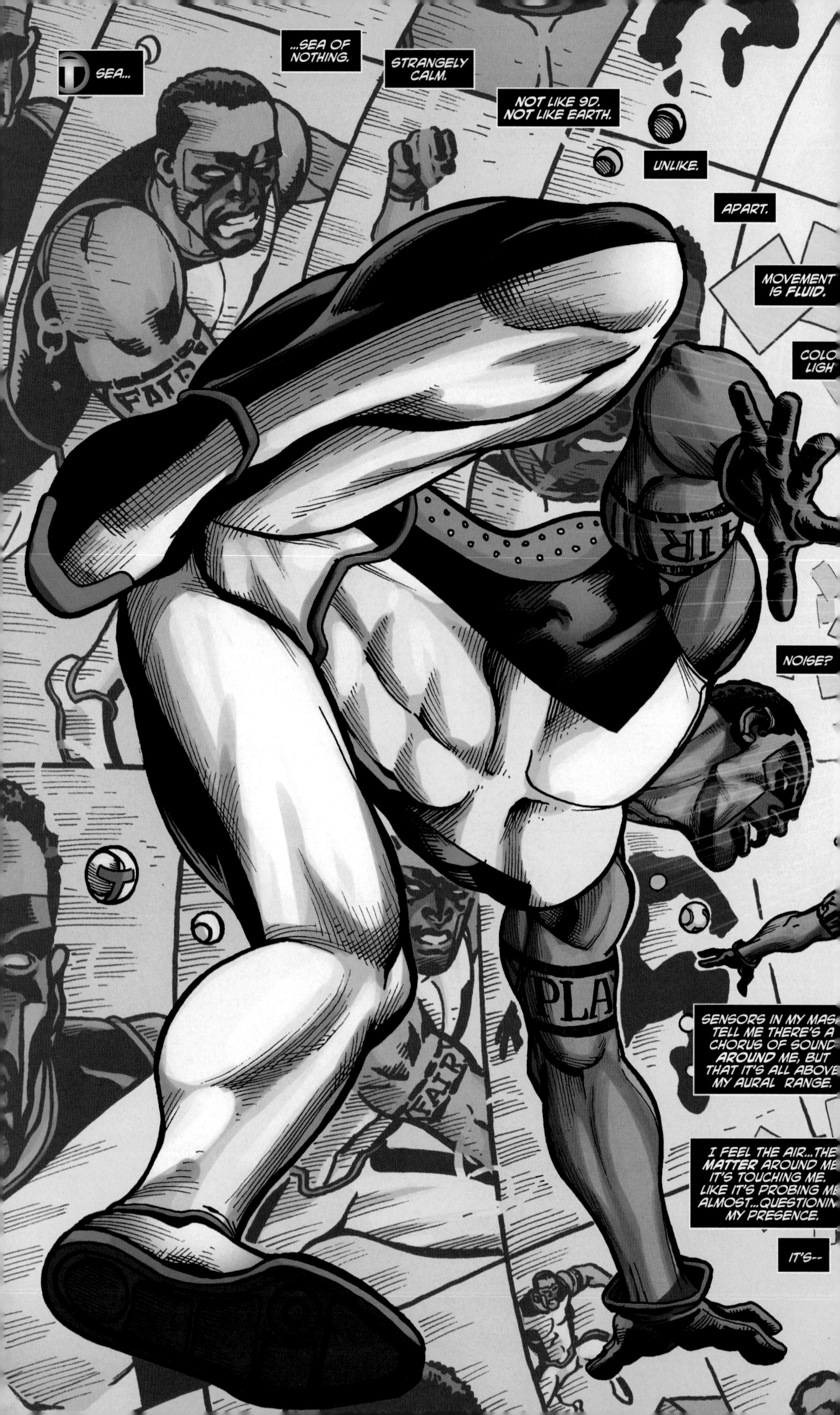
SEA...
...SEA OF NOTHING.
STRANGELY CALM.
NOT LIKE 9D. NOT LIKE EARTH.
UNLIKE.
APART.
MOVEMENT IS FLUID.
COLO LIGH
NOISE?
SENSORS IN MY MAS TELL ME THERE'S A CHORUS OF SOUN AROUND ME, BUT THAT IT'S ALL ABOVE MY AURAL RANGE.
I FEEL THE AIR...THE MATTER AROUND ME IT'S TOUCHING ME. LIKE IT'S PROBING ME ALMOST...QUESTIONIN MY PRESENCE.
IT'S--

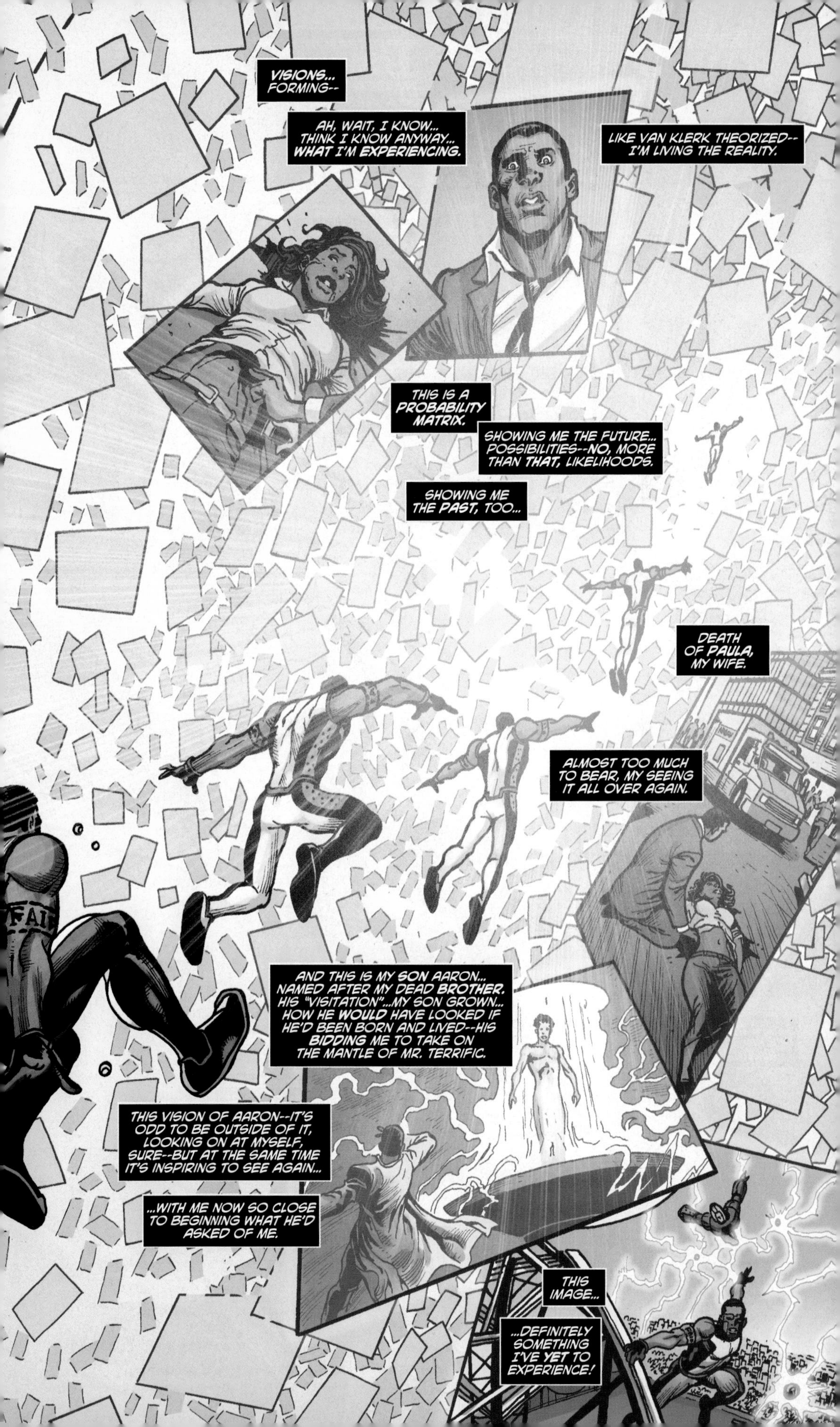
VISIONS... FORMING--
AH, WAIT, I KNOW... THINK I KNOW ANYWAY... WHAT I'M EXPERIENCING.
LIKE VAN KLERK THEORIZED-- I'M LIVING THE REALITY.
THIS IS A PROBABILITY MATRIX.
SHOWING ME THE FUTURE... POSSIBILITIES--NO, MORE THAN THAT, LIKELIHOODS.
SHOWING ME THE PAST, TOO...
DEATH OF PAULA, MY WIFE.
ALMOST TOO MUCH TO BEAR, MY SEEING IT ALL OVER AGAIN.
AND THIS IS MY SON AARON... NAMED AFTER MY DEAD BROTHER. HIS "VISITATION"...MY SON GROWN... HOW HE WOULD HAVE LOOKED IF HE'D BEEN BORN AND LIVED--HIS BIDDING ME TO TAKE ON THE MANTLE OF MR. TERRIFIC.
THIS VISION OF AARON--IT'S ODD TO BE OUTSIDE OF IT, LOOKING ON AT MYSELF, SURE--BUT AT THE SAME TIME IT'S INSPIRING TO SEE AGAIN...
...WITH ME NOW SO CLOSE TO BEGINNING WHAT HE'D ASKED OF ME.
THIS IMAGE...
...DEFINITELY SOMETHING I'VE YET TO EXPERIENCE!

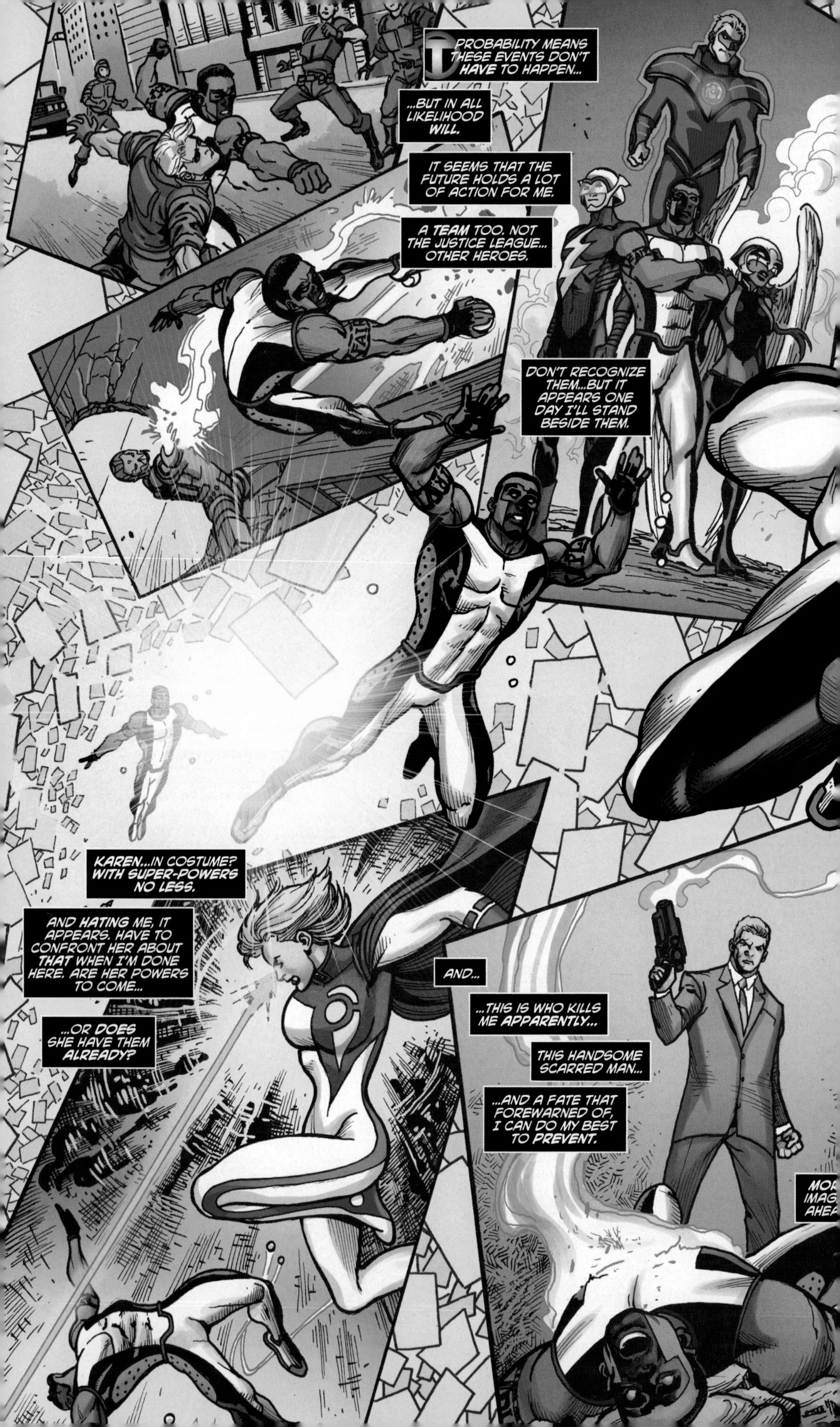
PROBABILITY MEANS THESE EVENTS DON'T HAVE TO HAPPEN...
...BUT IN ALL LIKELIHOOD WILL.
IT SEEMS THAT THE FUTURE HOLDS A LOT OF ACTION FOR ME.
A TEAM TOO. NOT THE JUSTICE LEAGUE... OTHER HEROES.
DON'T RECOGNIZE THEM...BUT IT APPEARS ONE DAY I'LL STAND BESIDE THEM.
KAREN...IN COSTUME? WITH SUPER-POWERS NO LESS.
AND HATING ME, IT APPEARS. HAVE TO CONFRONT HER ABOUT THAT WHEN I'M DONE HERE. ARE HER POWERS TO COME...
...OR DOES SHE HAVE THEM ALREADY?
AND...
...THIS IS WHO KILLS ME APPARENTLY...
THIS HANDSOME SCARRED MAN...
...AND A FATE THAT FOREWARNED OF, I CAN DO MY BEST TO PREVENT.

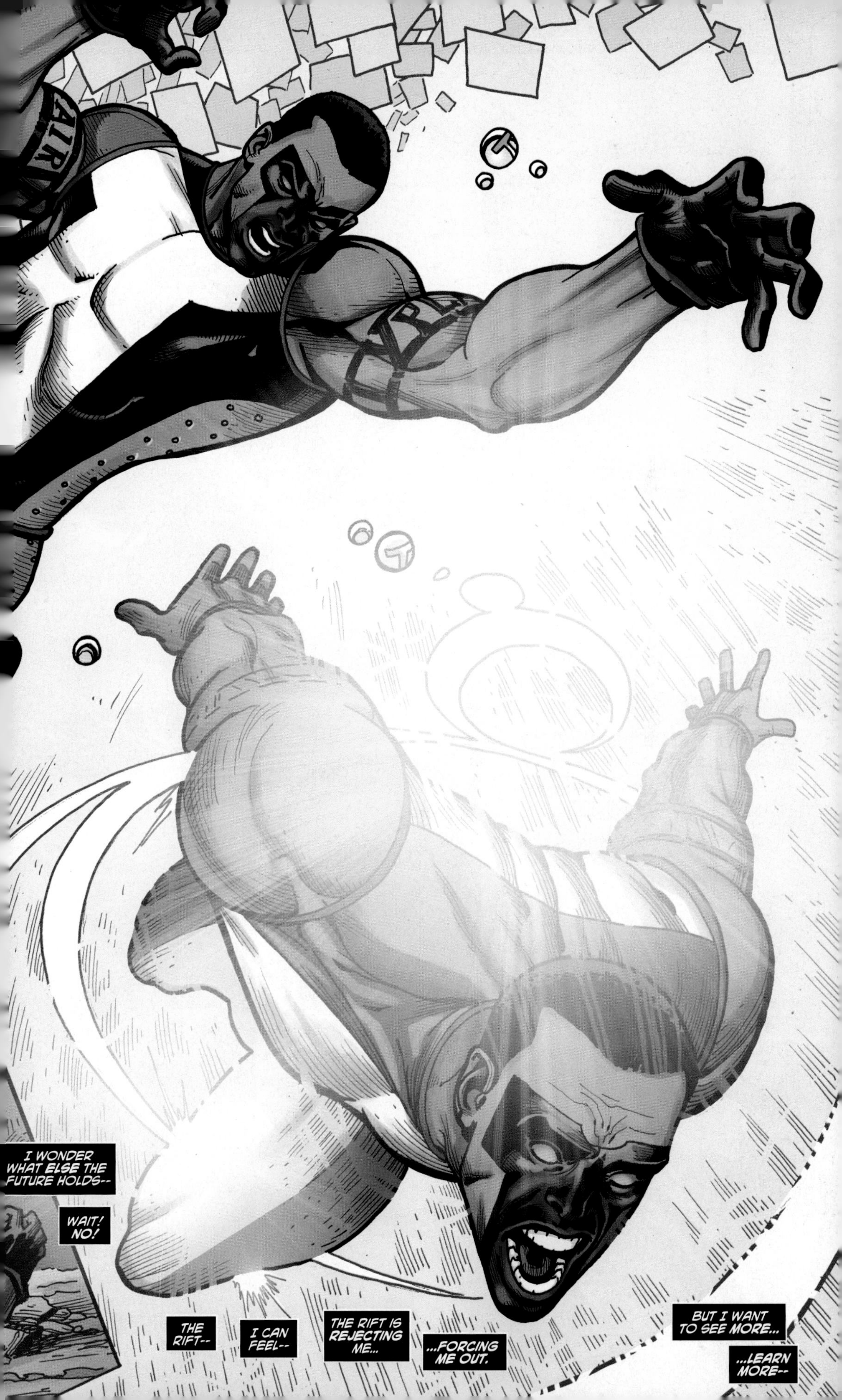

AIR
I WONDER WHAT ELSE THE FUTURE HOLDS--
WAIT! NO!
THE RIFT--
I CAN FEEL--
THE RIFT IS REJECTING ME...
...FORCING ME OUT.
BUT I WANT TO SEE MORE...
...LEARN MORE--

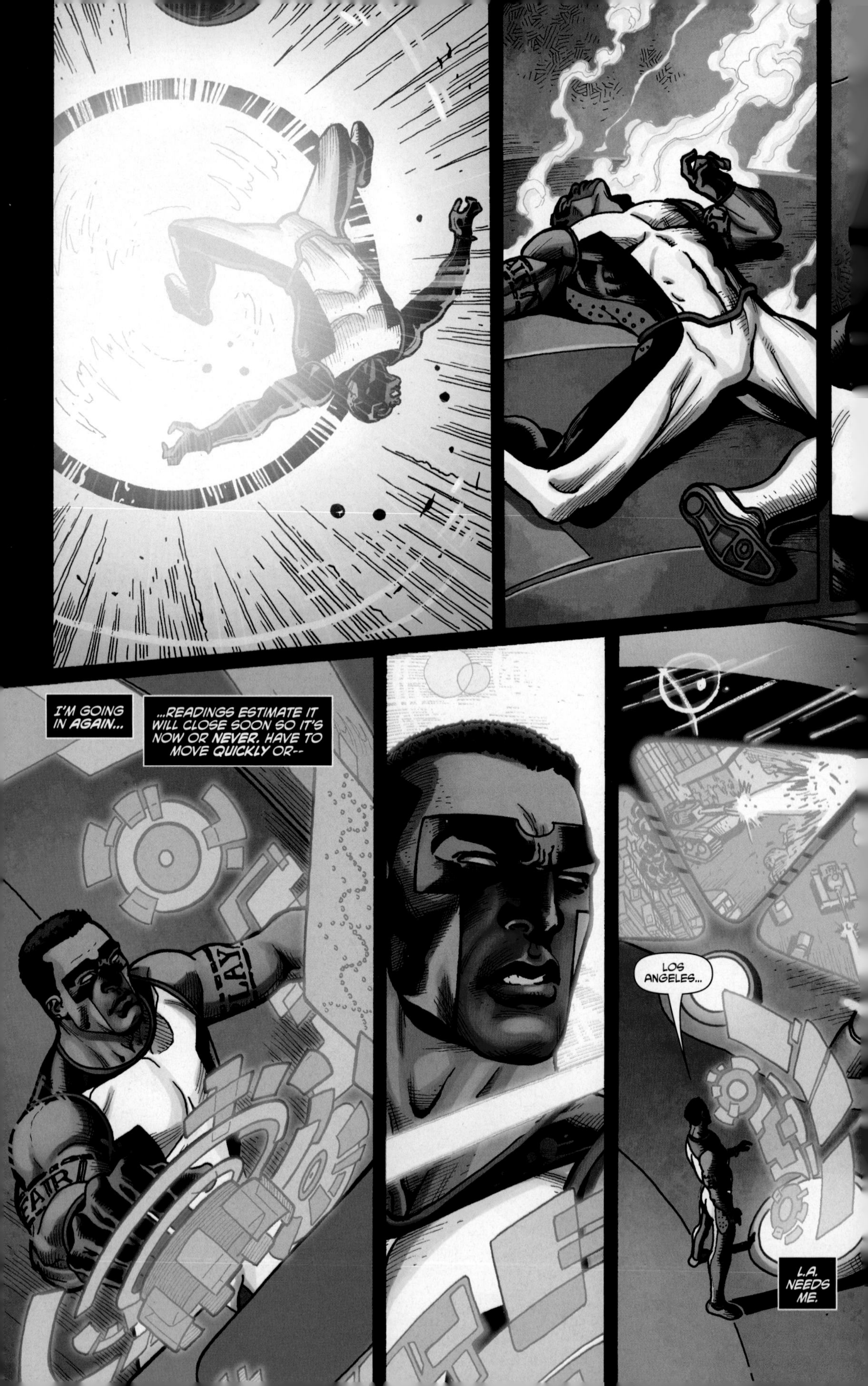
I'M GOING IN AGAIN...
...READINGS ESTIMATE IT WILL CLOSE SOON SO IT'S NOW OR NEVER. HAVE TO MOVE QUICKLY OR--
LOS ANGELES...
L.A. NEEDS ME.

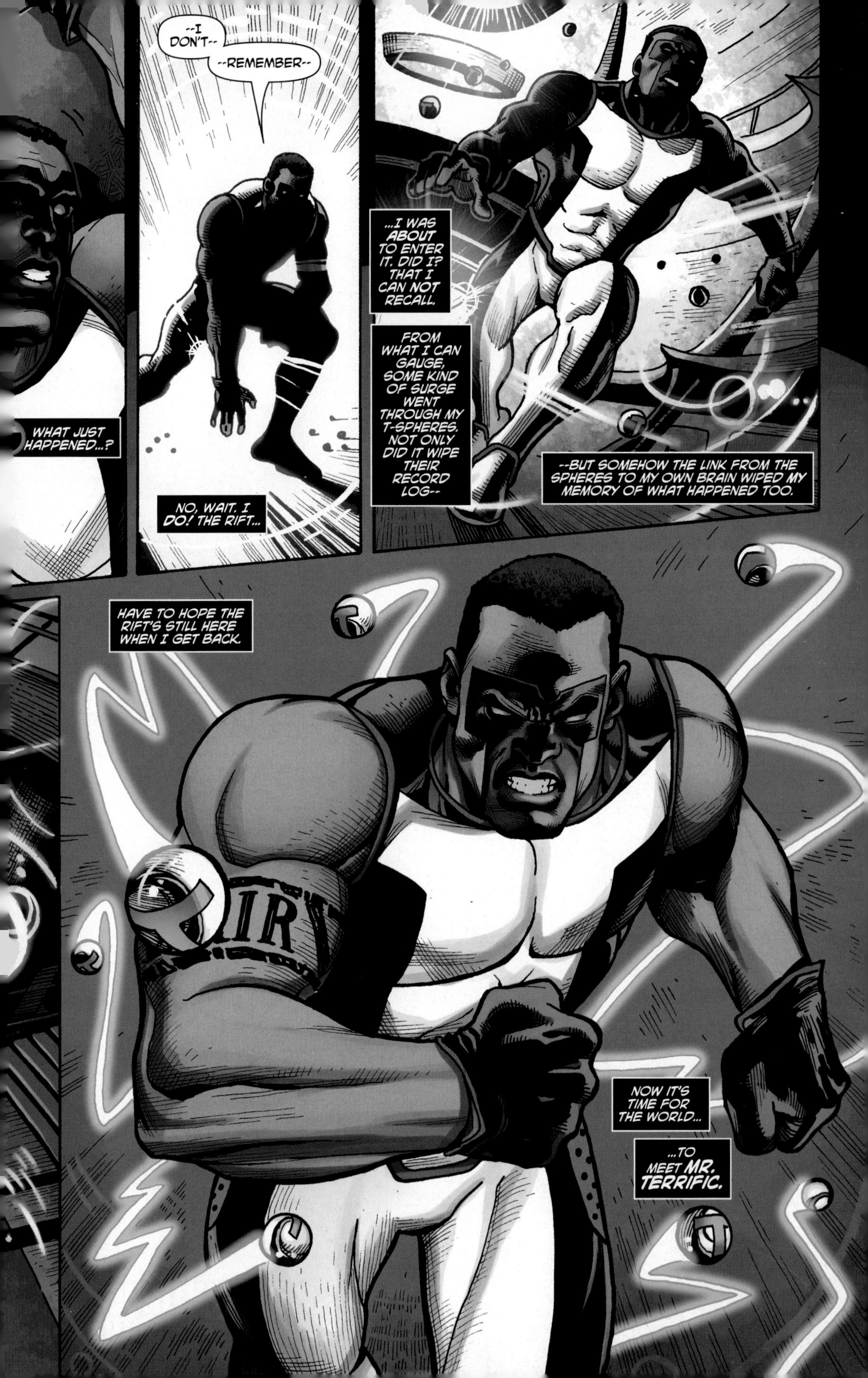
WHAT JUST HAPPENED...?
--I DON'T--
--REMEMBER--
NO, WAIT. I DO! THE RIFT...
...I WAS ABOUT TO ENTER IT. DID I? THAT I CAN NOT RECALL.
FROM WHAT I CAN GAUGE, SOME KIND OF SURGE WENT THROUGH MY T-SPHERES. NOT ONLY DID IT WIPE THEIR RECORD LOG--
--BUT SOMEHOW THE LINK FROM THE SPHERES TO MY OWN BRAIN WIPED MY MEMORY OF WHAT HAPPENED TOO.
HAVE TO HOPE THE RIFT'S STILL HERE WHEN I GET BACK.
NOW IT'S TIME FOR THE WORLD...
...TO MEET MR. TERRIFIC.

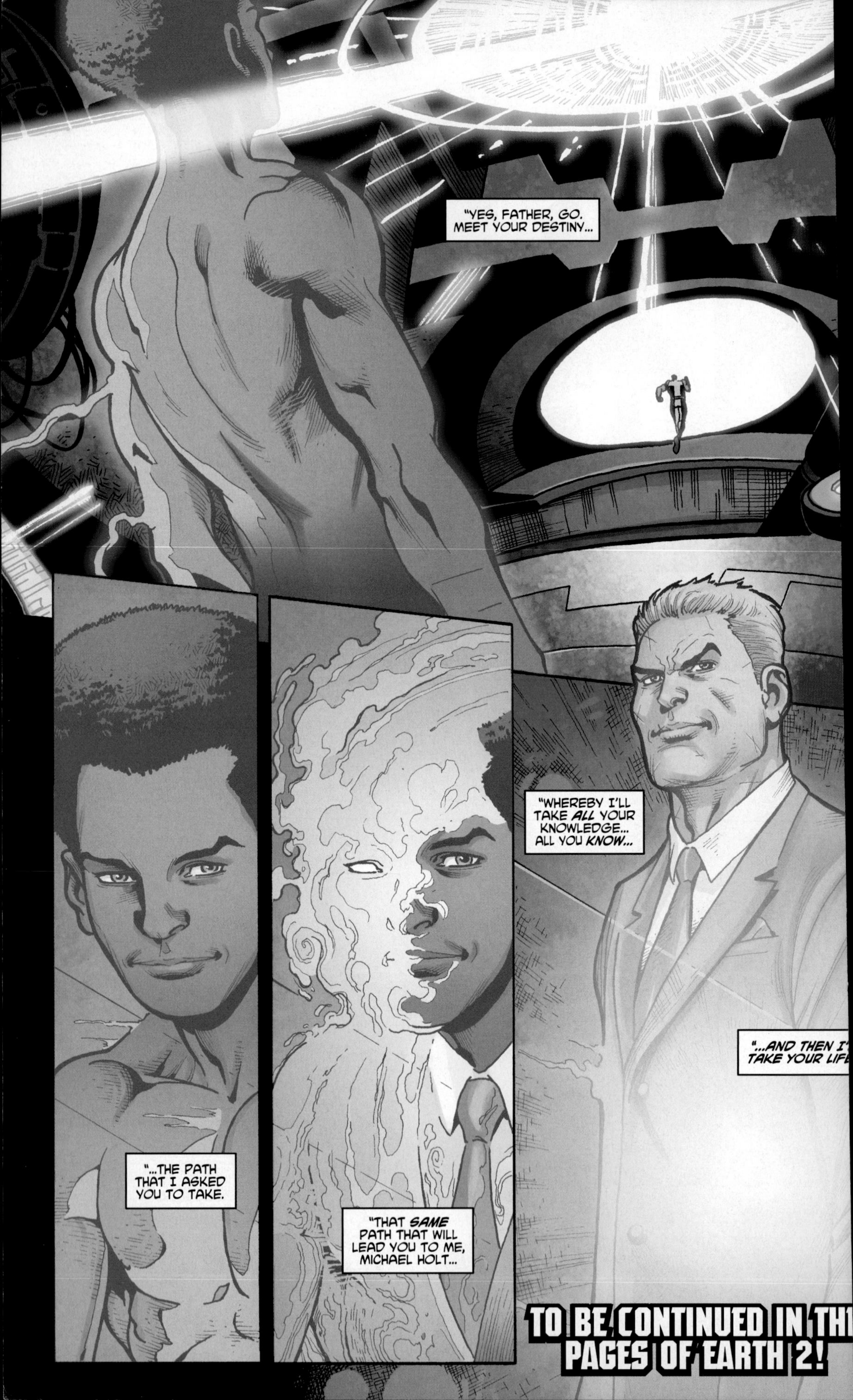
"YES, FATHER, GO. MEET YOUR DESTINY...
"...THE PATH THAT I ASKED YOU TO TAKE.
"THAT SAME PATH THAT WILL LEAD YOU TO ME, MICHAEL HOLT...
"WHEREBY I'LL TAKE ALL YOUR KNOWLEDGE... ALL YOU KNOW...
"...AND THEN I'
TAKE YOUR LIFE
TO BE CONTINUED IN THE PAGES OF EARTH 2!

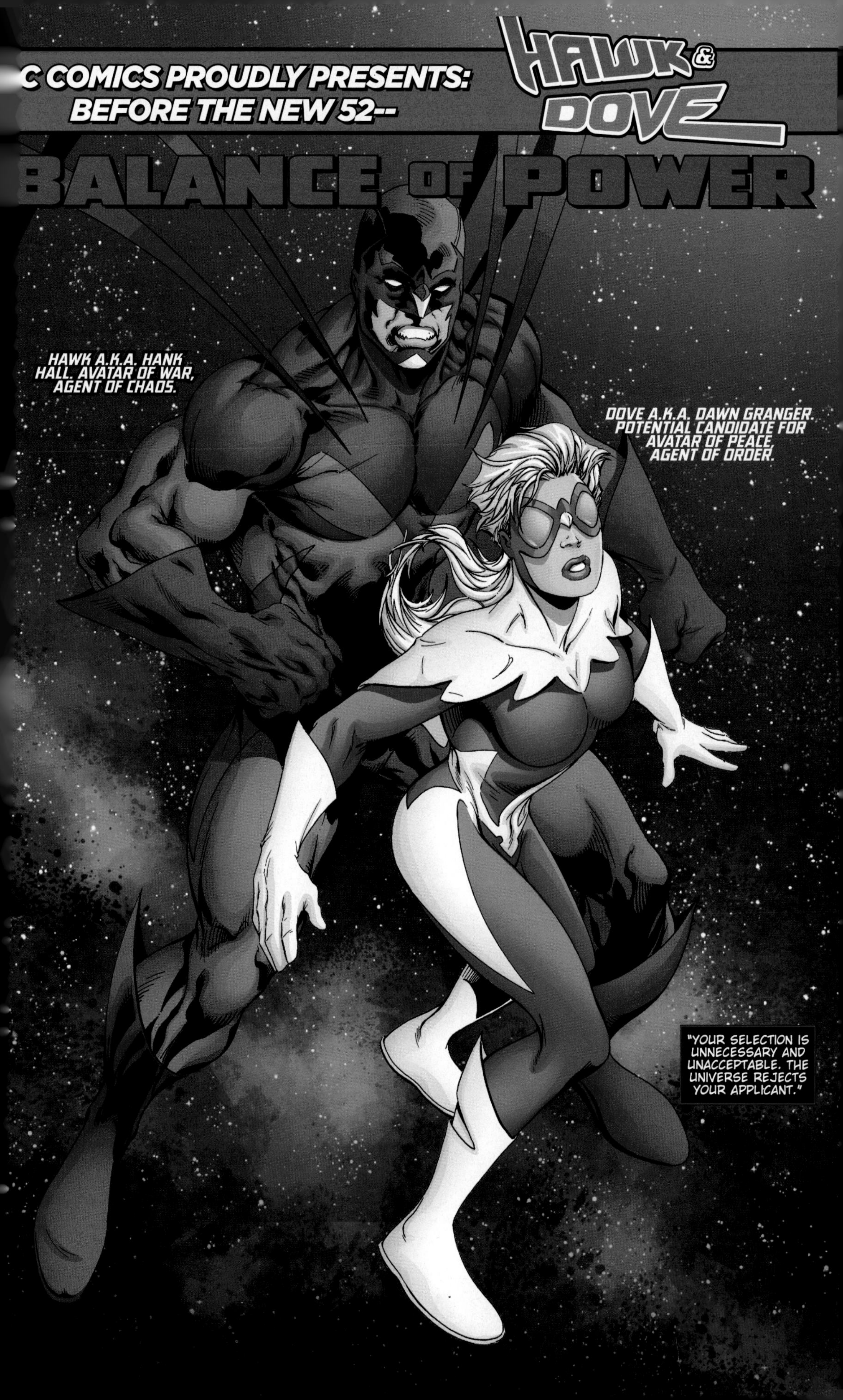
C COMICS PROUDLY PRESENTS:
BEFORE THE NEW 52--
HAWK & DOVE
BALANCE OF POWER
HAWK A.K.A. HANK HALL. AVATAR OF WAR, AGENT OF CHAOS.
DOVE A.K.A. DAWN GRANGER. POTENTIAL CANDIDATE FOR AVATAR OF PEACE, AGENT OF ORDER.
"YOUR SELECTION IS UNNECESSARY AND UNACCEPTABLE. THE UNIVERSE REJECTS YOUR APPLICANT."

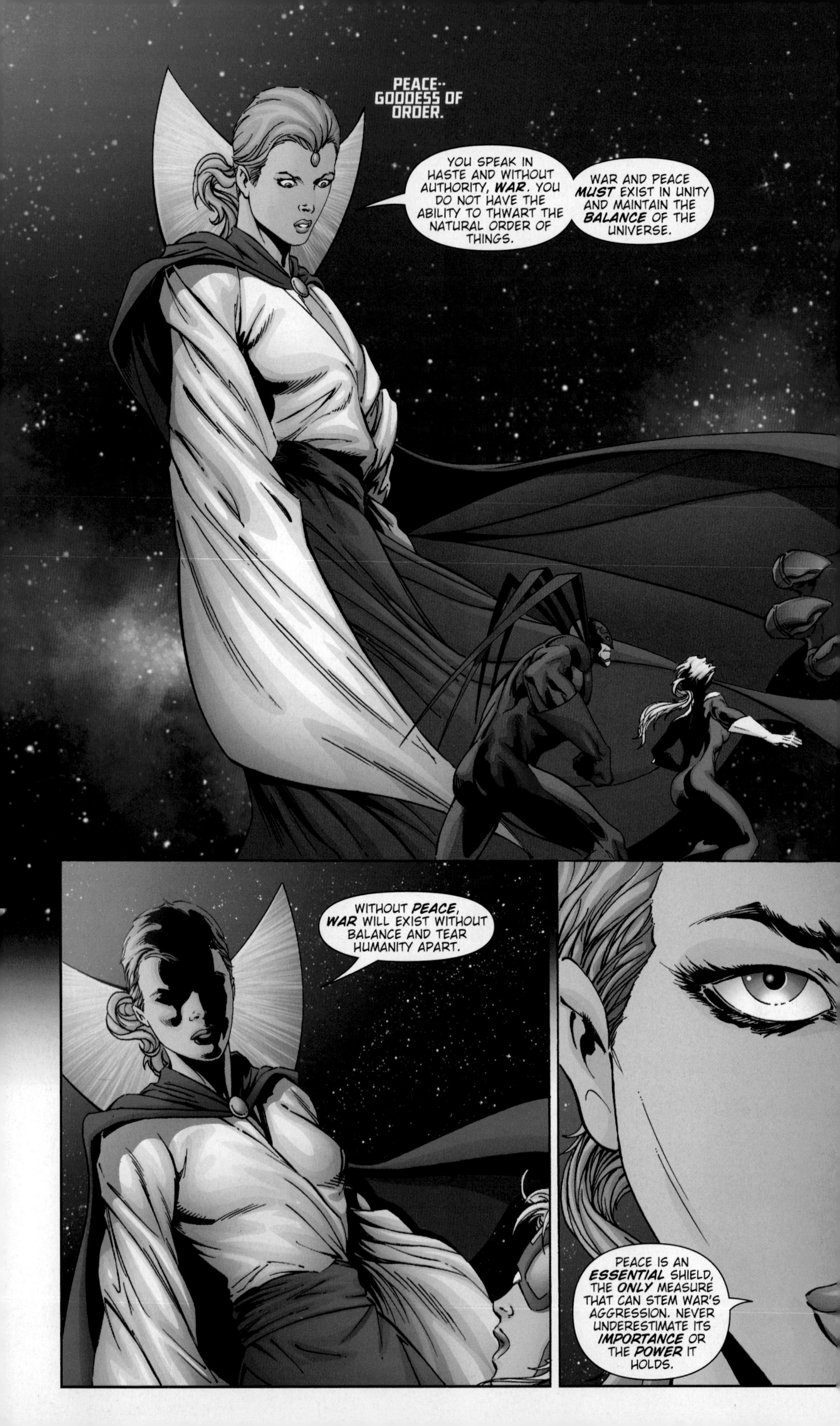
PEACE-- GODDESS OF ORDER.
YOU SPEAK IN HASTE AND WITHOUT AUTHORITY, WAR. YOU DO NOT HAVE THE ABILITY TO THWART THE NATURAL ORDER OF THINGS.
WAR AND PEACE MUST EXIST IN UNITY AND MAINTAIN THE BALANCE OF THE UNIVERSE.
WITHOUT PEACE, WAR WILL EXIST WITHOUT BALANCE AND TEAR HUMANITY APART.
PEACE IS AN ESSENTIAL SHIELD, THE ONLY MEASURE THAT CAN STEM WAR'S AGGRESSION. NEVER UNDERESTIMATE ITS IMPORTANCE OR THE POWER IT HOLDS.

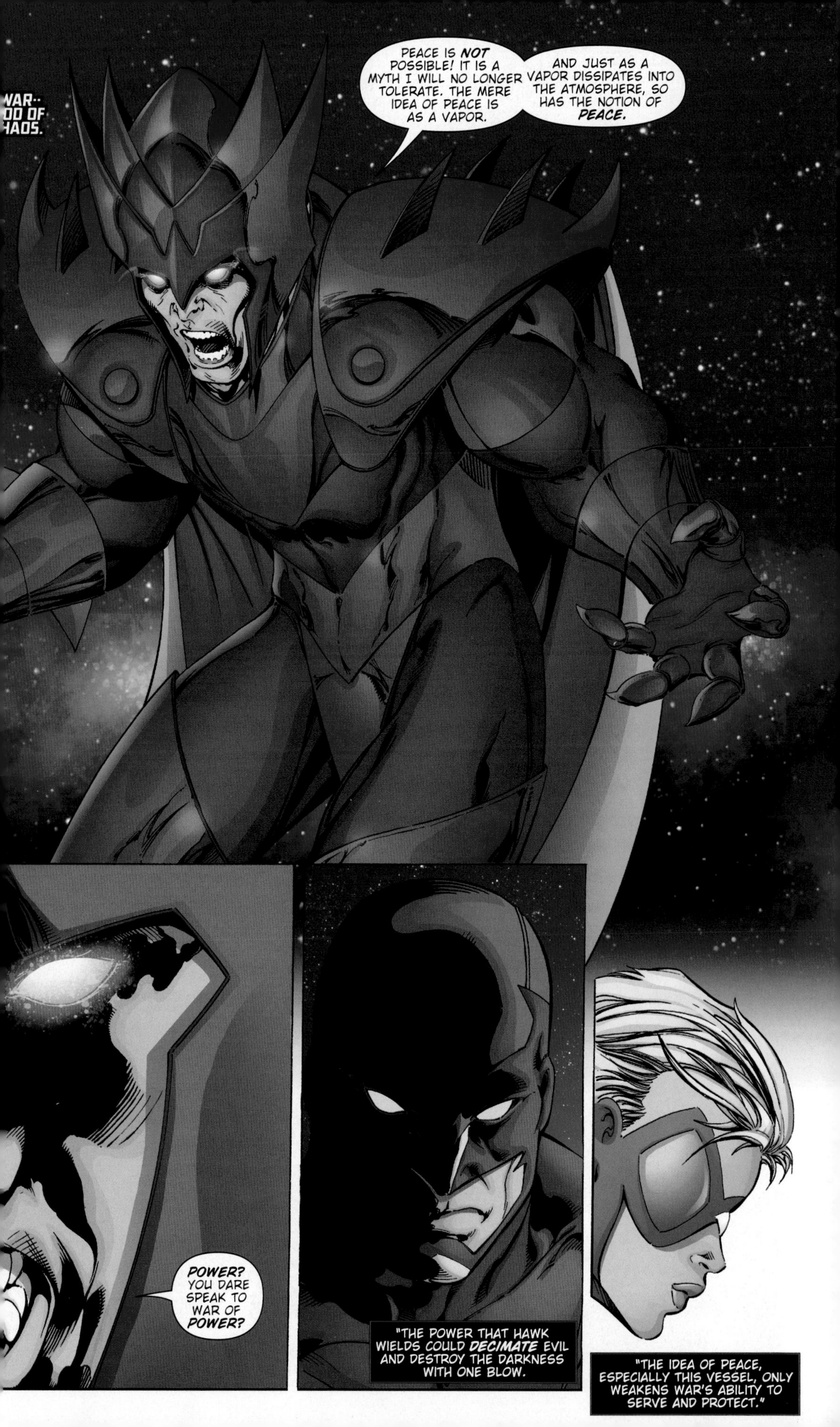
WAR--
OD OF
HAOS.
PEACE IS NOT POSSIBLE! IT IS A MYTH I WILL NO LONGER TOLERATE. THE MERE IDEA OF PEACE IS AS A VAPOR.
AND JUST AS A VAPOR DISSIPATES INTO THE ATMOSPHERE, SO HAS THE NOTION OF PEACE.
POWER? YOU DARE SPEAK TO WAR OF POWER?
"THE POWER THAT HAWK WIELDS COULD DECIMATE EVIL AND DESTROY THE DARKNESS WITH ONE BLOW.
"THE IDEA OF PEACE, ESPECIALLY THIS VESSEL, ONLY WEAKENS WAR'S ABILITY TO SERVE AND PROTECT."

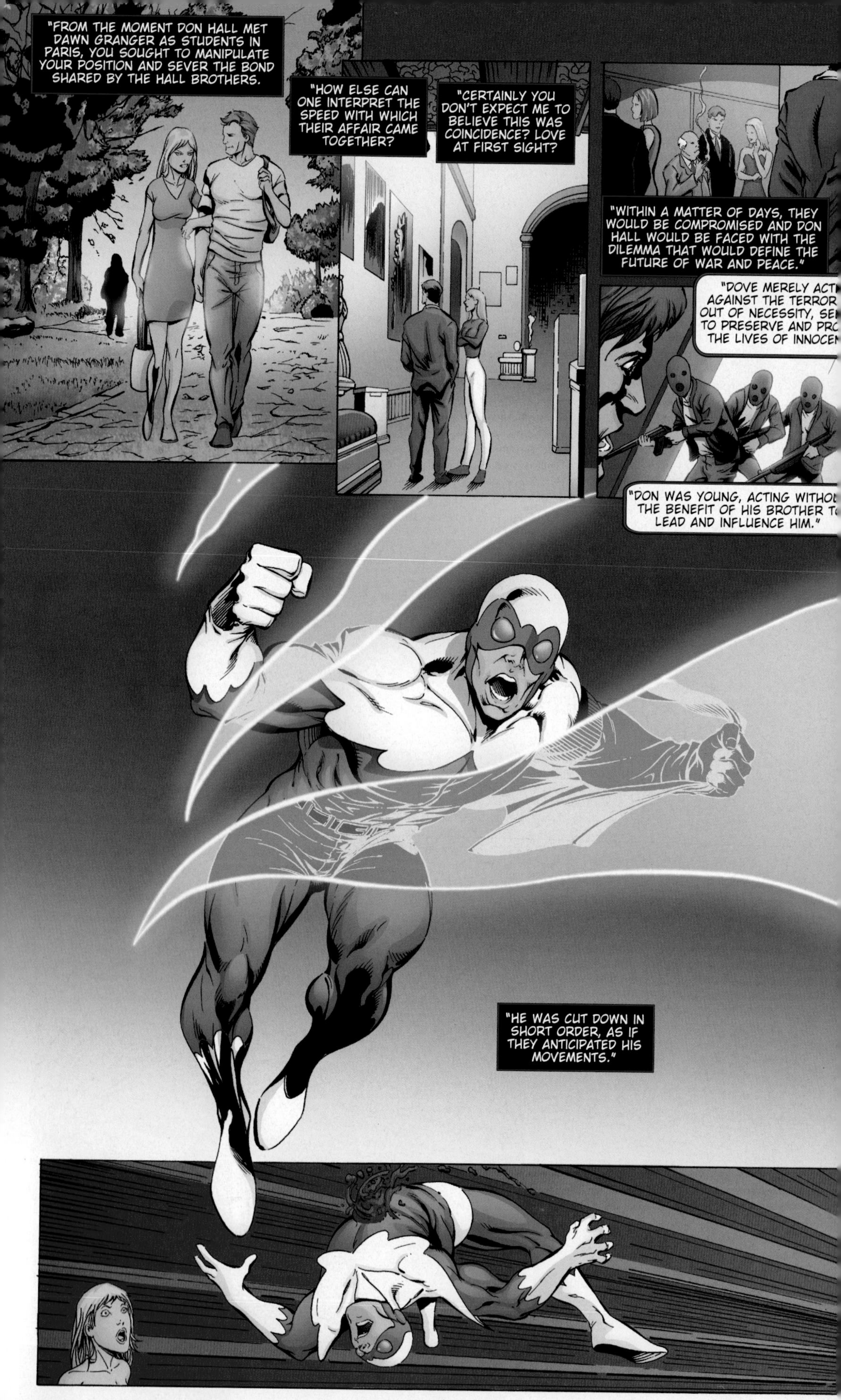
"FROM THE MOMENT DON HALL MET DAWN GRANGER AS STUDENTS IN PARIS, YOU SOUGHT TO MANIPULATE YOUR POSITION AND SEVER THE BOND SHARED BY THE HALL BROTHERS.
"HOW ELSE CAN ONE INTERPRET THE SPEED WITH WHICH THEIR AFFAIR CAME TOGETHER?
"CERTAINLY YOU DON'T EXPECT ME TO BELIEVE THIS WAS COINCIDENCE? LOVE AT FIRST SIGHT?
"WITHIN A MATTER OF DAYS, THEY WOULD BE COMPROMISED AND DON HALL WOULD BE FACED WITH THE DILEMMA THAT WOULD DEFINE THE FUTURE OF WAR AND PEACE."
"DOVE MERELY ACT AGAINST THE TERROR OUT OF NECESSITY, SE TO PRESERVE AND PRO THE LIVES OF INNOCEN
"DON WAS YOUNG, ACTING WITHO THE BENEFIT OF HIS BROTHER T LEAD AND INFLUENCE HIM."
"HE WAS CUT DOWN IN SHORT ORDER, AS IF THEY ANTICIPATED HIS MOVEMENTS."

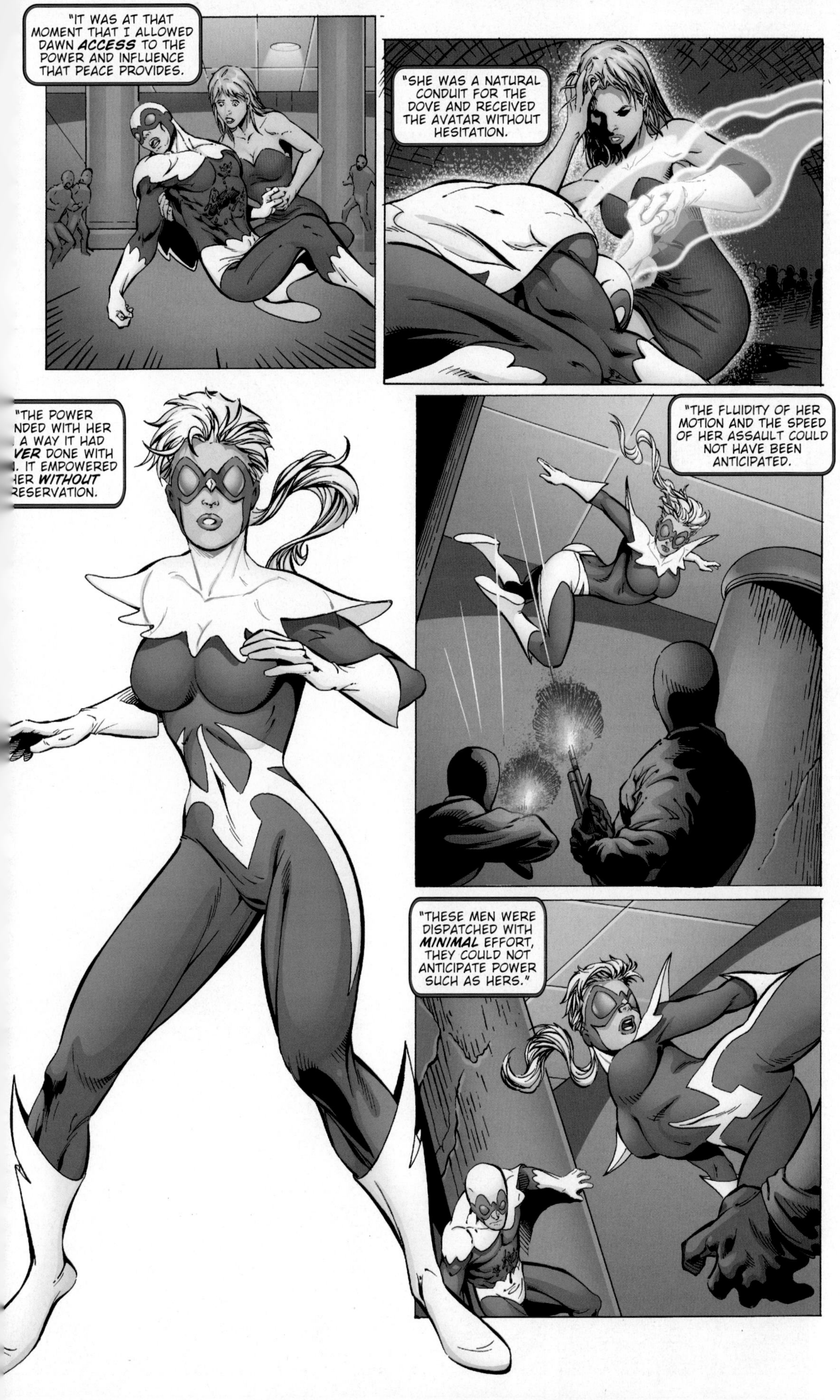

"IT WAS AT THAT MOMENT THAT I ALLOWED DAWN ***ACCESS*** TO THE POWER AND INFLUENCE THAT PEACE PROVIDES.
"SHE WAS A NATURAL CONDUIT FOR THE DOVE AND RECEIVED THE AVATAR WITHOUT HESITATION.
"THE POWER NDED WITH HER A WAY IT HAD ***VER*** DONE WITH . IT EMPOWERED HER ***WITHOUT*** RESERVATION.
"THE FLUIDITY OF HER MOTION AND THE SPEED OF HER ASSAULT COULD NOT HAVE BEEN ANTICIPATED.
"THESE MEN WERE DISPATCHED WITH ***MINIMAL*** EFFORT, THEY COULD NOT ANTICIPATE POWER SUCH AS HERS."

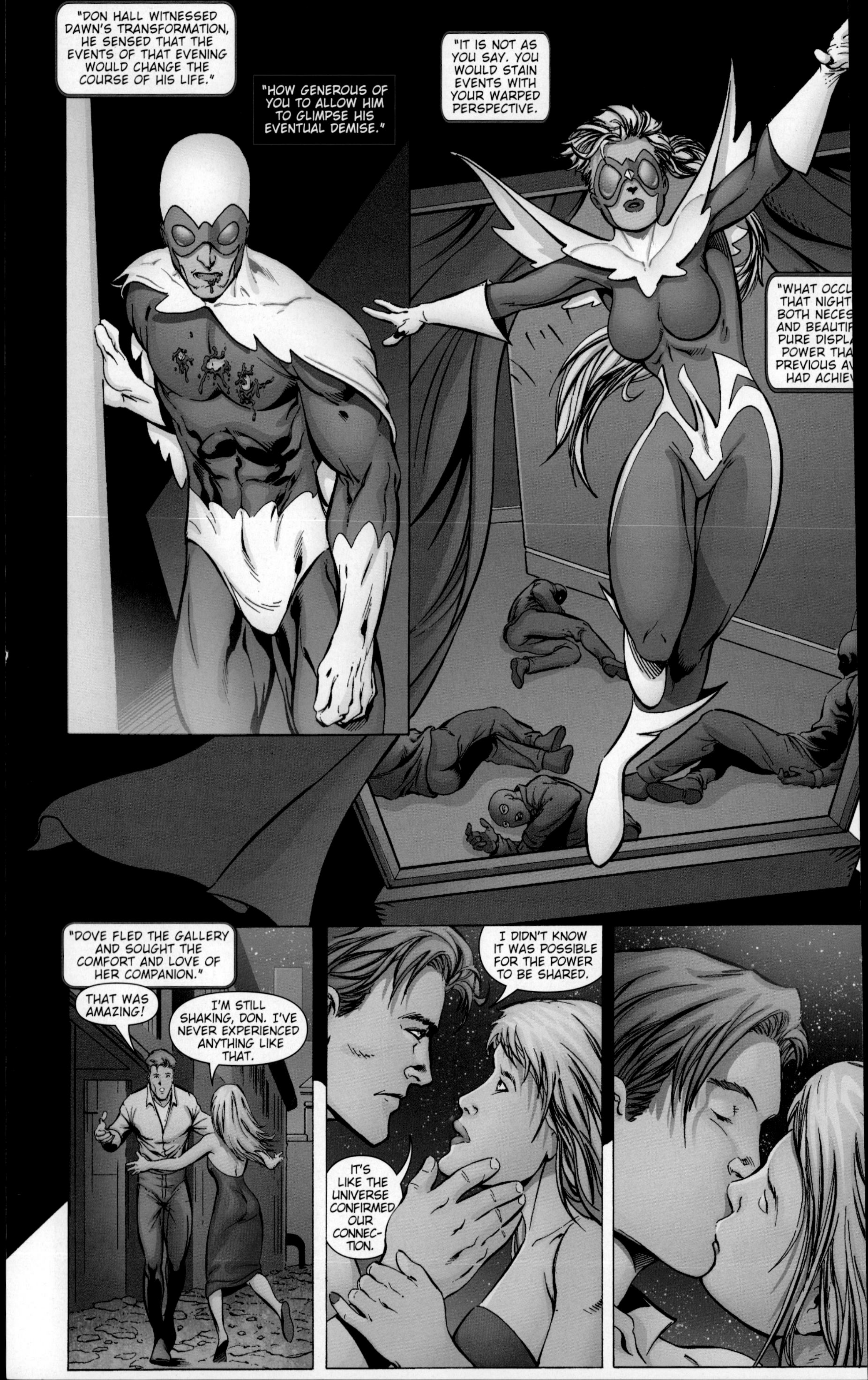
"DON HALL WITNESSED DAWN'S TRANSFORMATION, HE SENSED THAT THE EVENTS OF THAT EVENING WOULD CHANGE THE COURSE OF HIS LIFE."
"HOW GENEROUS OF YOU TO ALLOW HIM TO GLIMPSE HIS EVENTUAL DEMISE."
"IT IS NOT AS YOU SAY. YOU WOULD STAIN EVENTS WITH YOUR WARPED PERSPECTIVE.
"WHAT OCCL THAT NIGHT BOTH NECES AND BEAUTIF PURE DISPLA POWER THA PREVIOUS AV HAD ACHIEV
"DOVE FLED THE GALLERY AND SOUGHT THE COMFORT AND LOVE OF HER COMPANION."
THAT WAS AMAZING!
I'M STILL SHAKING, DON. I'VE NEVER EXPERIENCED ANYTHING LIKE THAT.
I DIDN'T KNOW IT WAS POSSIBLE FOR THE POWER TO BE SHARED.
IT'S LIKE THE UNIVERSE CONFIRMED OUR CONNECTION.

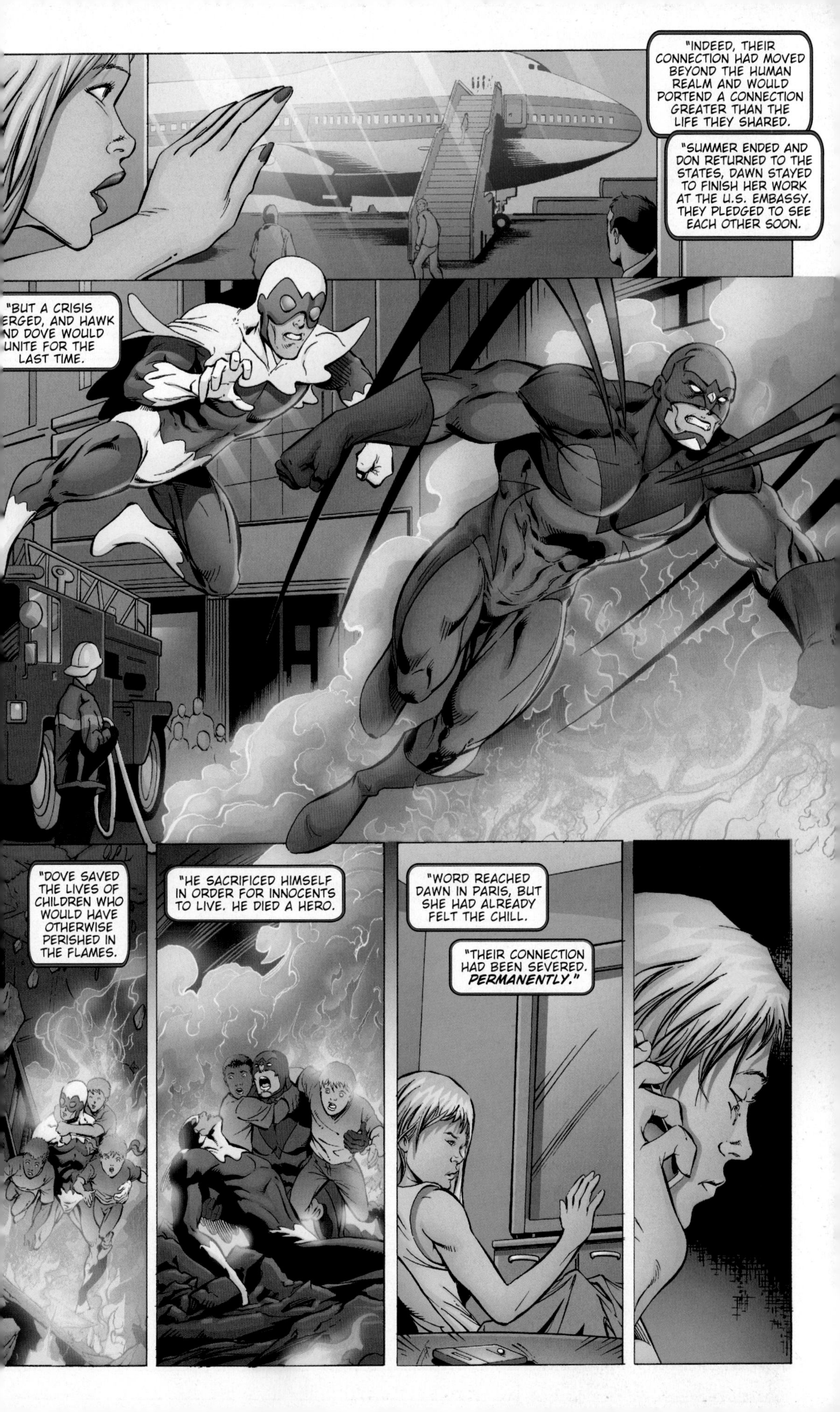
"INDEED, THEIR CONNECTION HAD MOVED BEYOND THE HUMAN REALM AND WOULD PORTEND A CONNECTION GREATER THAN THE LIFE THEY SHARED.
"SUMMER ENDED AND DON RETURNED TO THE STATES, DAWN STAYED TO FINISH HER WORK AT THE U.S. EMBASSY. THEY PLEDGED TO SEE EACH OTHER SOON.
"BUT A CRISIS ERGED, AND HAWK ND DOVE WOULD UNITE FOR THE LAST TIME.
"DOVE SAVED THE LIVES OF CHILDREN WHO WOULD HAVE OTHERWISE PERISHED IN THE FLAMES.
"HE SACRIFICED HIMSELF IN ORDER FOR INNOCENTS TO LIVE. HE DIED A HERO.
"WORD REACHED DAWN IN PARIS, BUT SHE HAD ALREADY FELT THE CHILL.
"THEIR CONNECTION HAD BEEN SEVERED. ***PERMANENTLY.***"

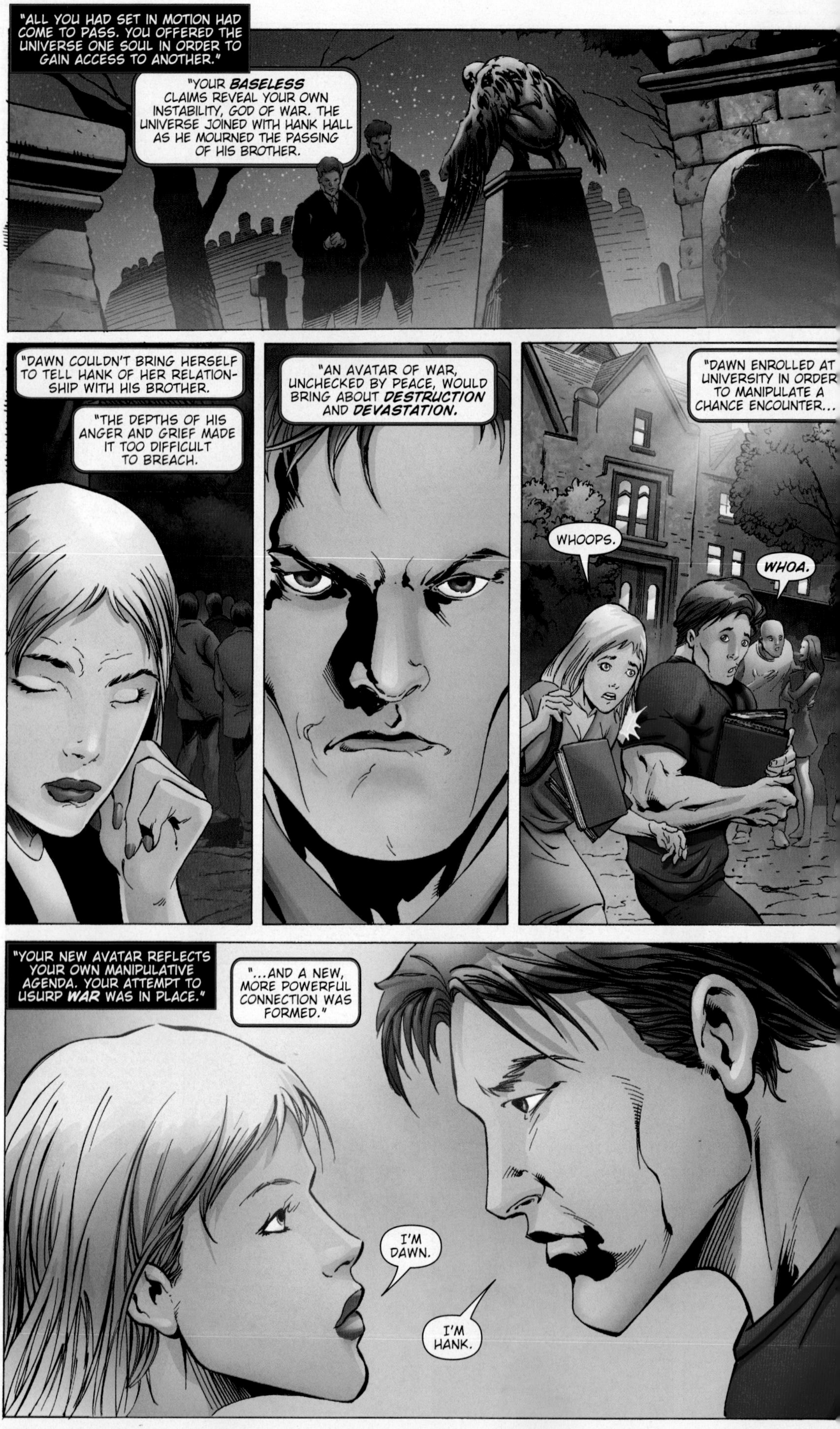
"ALL YOU HAD SET IN MOTION HAD COME TO PASS. YOU OFFERED THE UNIVERSE ONE SOUL IN ORDER TO GAIN ACCESS TO ANOTHER."
"YOUR BASELESS CLAIMS REVEAL YOUR OWN INSTABILITY, GOD OF WAR. THE UNIVERSE JOINED WITH HANK HALL AS HE MOURNED THE PASSING OF HIS BROTHER.
"DAWN COULDN'T BRING HERSELF TO TELL HANK OF HER RELATIONSHIP WITH HIS BROTHER.
"THE DEPTHS OF HIS ANGER AND GRIEF MADE IT TOO DIFFICULT TO BREACH.
"AN AVATAR OF WAR, UNCHECKED BY PEACE, WOULD BRING ABOUT DESTRUCTION AND DEVASTATION.
"DAWN ENROLLED AT UNIVERSITY IN ORDER TO MANIPULATE A CHANCE ENCOUNTER...
WHOOPS.
WHOA.
"YOUR NEW AVATAR REFLECTS YOUR OWN MANIPULATIVE AGENDA. YOUR ATTEMPT TO USURP WAR WAS IN PLACE."
"...AND A NEW, MORE POWERFUL CONNECTION WAS FORMED."
I'M DAWN.
I'M HANK.

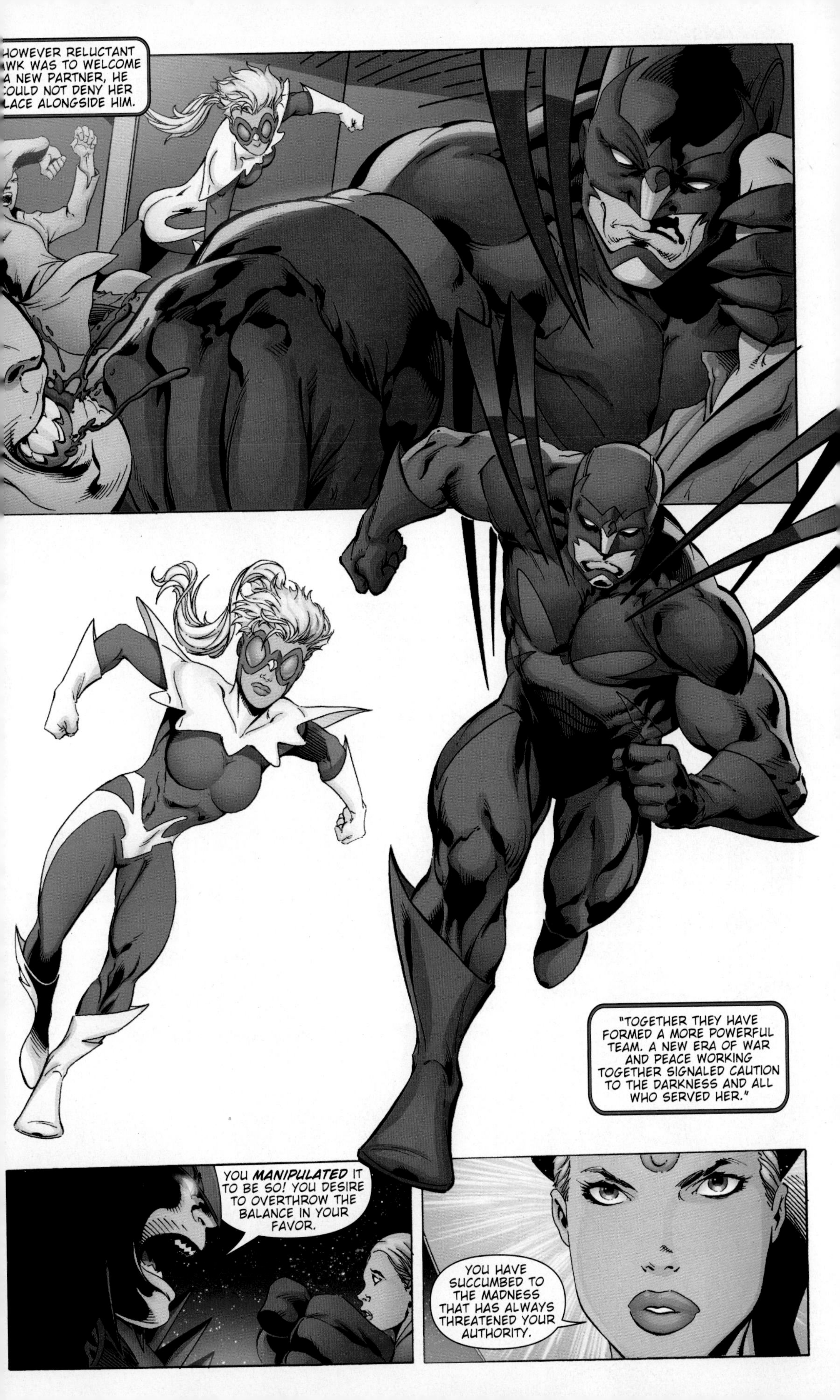
HOWEVER RELUCTANT AWK WAS TO WELCOME A NEW PARTNER, HE COULD NOT DENY HER LACE ALONGSIDE HIM.
"TOGETHER THEY HAVE FORMED A MORE POWERFUL TEAM. A NEW ERA OF WAR AND PEACE WORKING TOGETHER SIGNALED CAUTION TO THE DARKNESS AND ALL WHO SERVED HER."
YOU MANIPULATED IT TO BE SO! YOU DESIRE TO OVERTHROW THE BALANCE IN YOUR FAVOR.
YOU HAVE SUCCUMBED TO THE MADNESS THAT HAS ALWAYS THREATENED YOUR AUTHORITY.

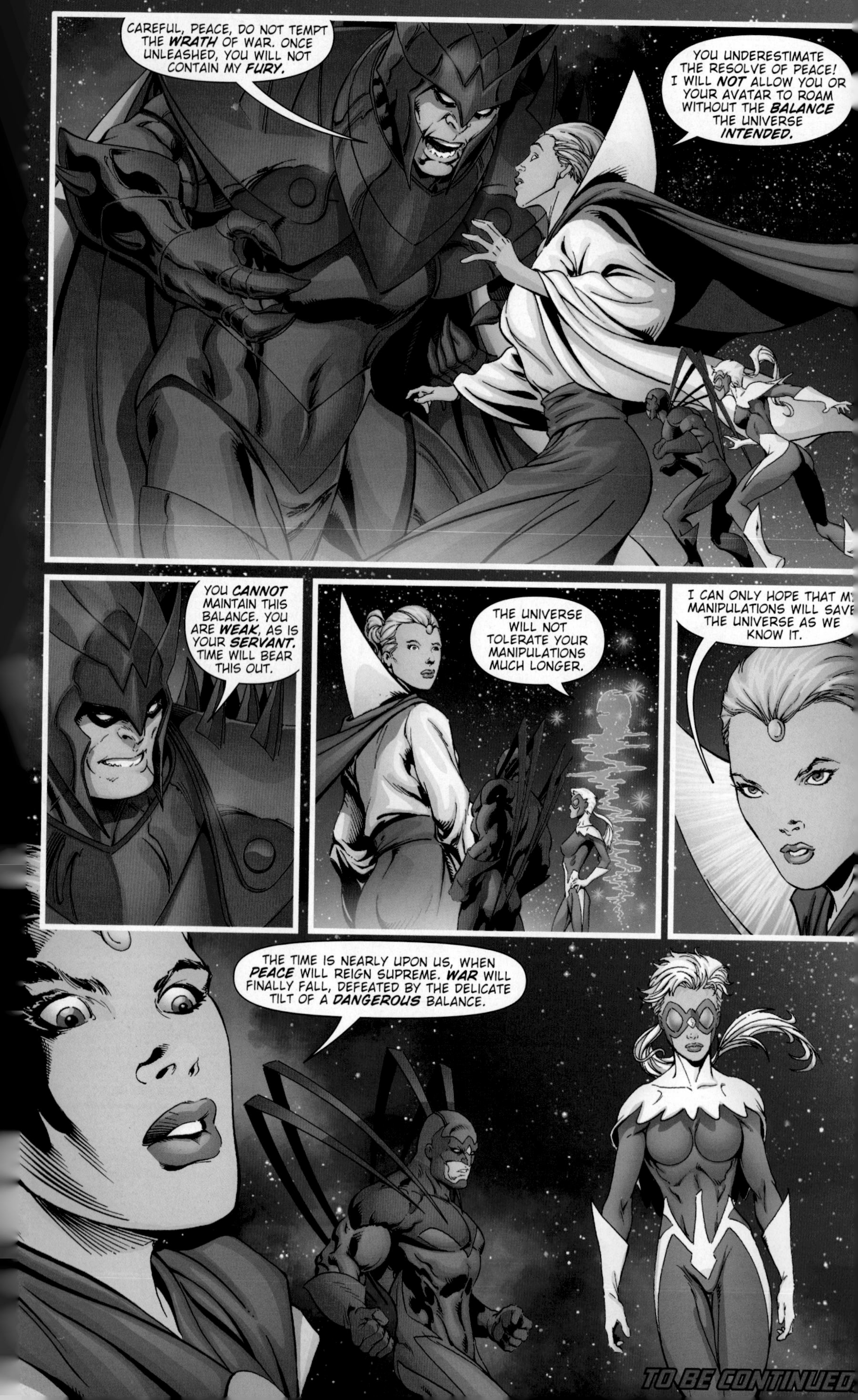
CAREFUL, PEACE, DO NOT TEMPT THE WRATH OF WAR. ONCE UNLEASHED, YOU WILL NOT CONTAIN MY FURY.
YOU UNDERESTIMATE THE RESOLVE OF PEACE! I WILL NOT ALLOW YOU OR YOUR AVATAR TO ROAM WITHOUT THE BALANCE THE UNIVERSE INTENDED.
YOU CANNOT MAINTAIN THIS BALANCE. YOU ARE WEAK, AS IS YOUR SERVANT. TIME WILL BEAR THIS OUT.
THE UNIVERSE WILL NOT TOLERATE YOUR MANIPULATIONS MUCH LONGER.
I CAN ONLY HOPE THAT MY MANIPULATIONS WILL SAVE THE UNIVERSE AS WE KNOW IT.
THE TIME IS NEARLY UPON US, WHEN PEACE WILL REIGN SUPREME. WAR WILL FINALLY FALL, DEFEATED BY THE DELICATE TILT OF A DANGEROUS BALANCE.
TO BE CONTINUED

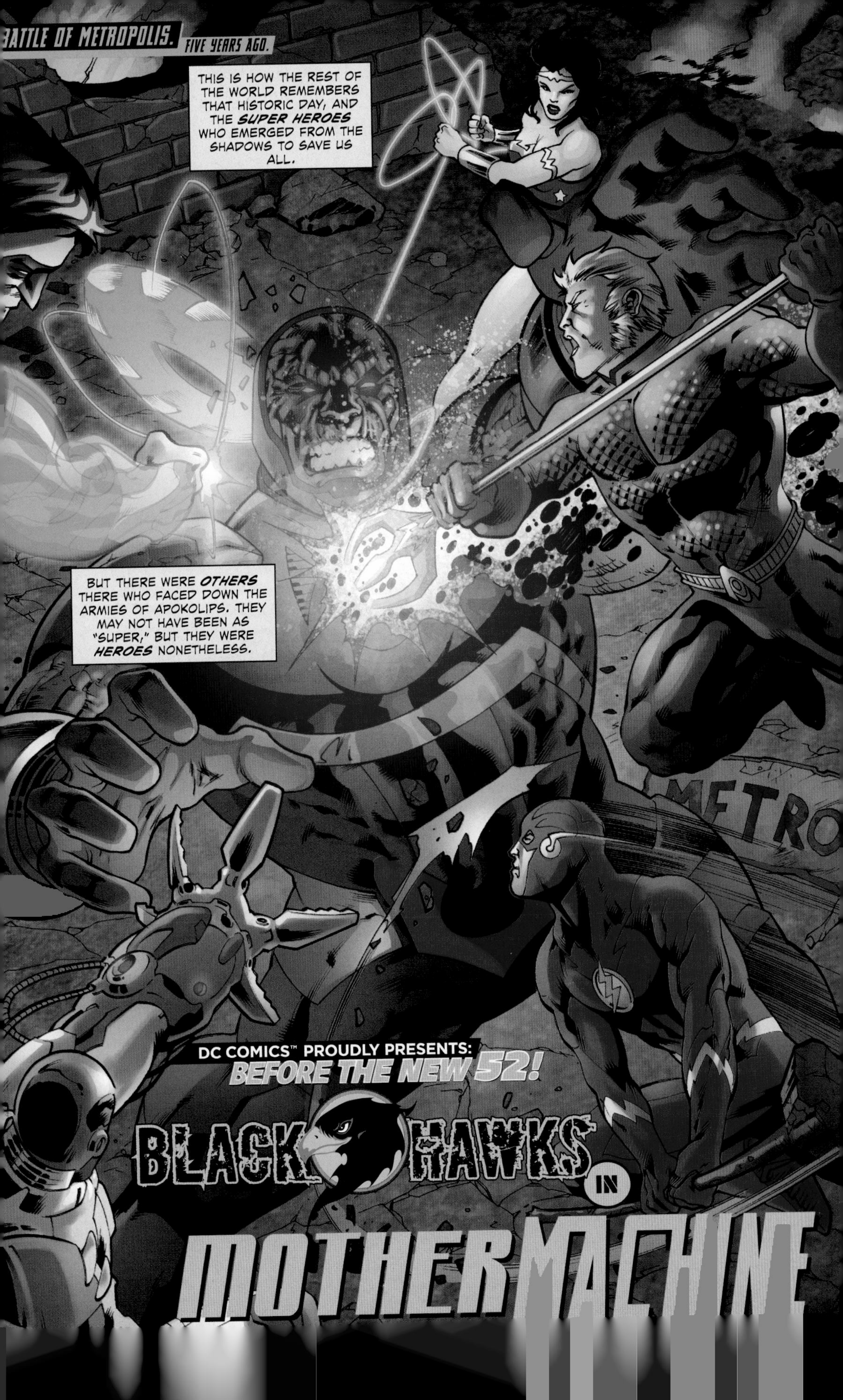

BATTLE OF METROPOLIS.
FIVE YEARS AGO.
THIS IS HOW THE REST OF THE WORLD REMEMBERS THAT HISTORIC DAY, AND THE SUPER HEROES WHO EMERGED FROM THE SHADOWS TO SAVE US ALL.
BUT THERE WERE OTHERS THERE WHO FACED DOWN THE ARMIES OF APOKOLIPS. THEY MAY NOT HAVE BEEN AS "SUPER," BUT THEY WERE HEROES NONETHELESS.
METRO
DC COMICS™ PROUDLY PRESENTS:
BEFORE THE NEW 52!
BLACKHAWKS IN
MOTHER MACHINE

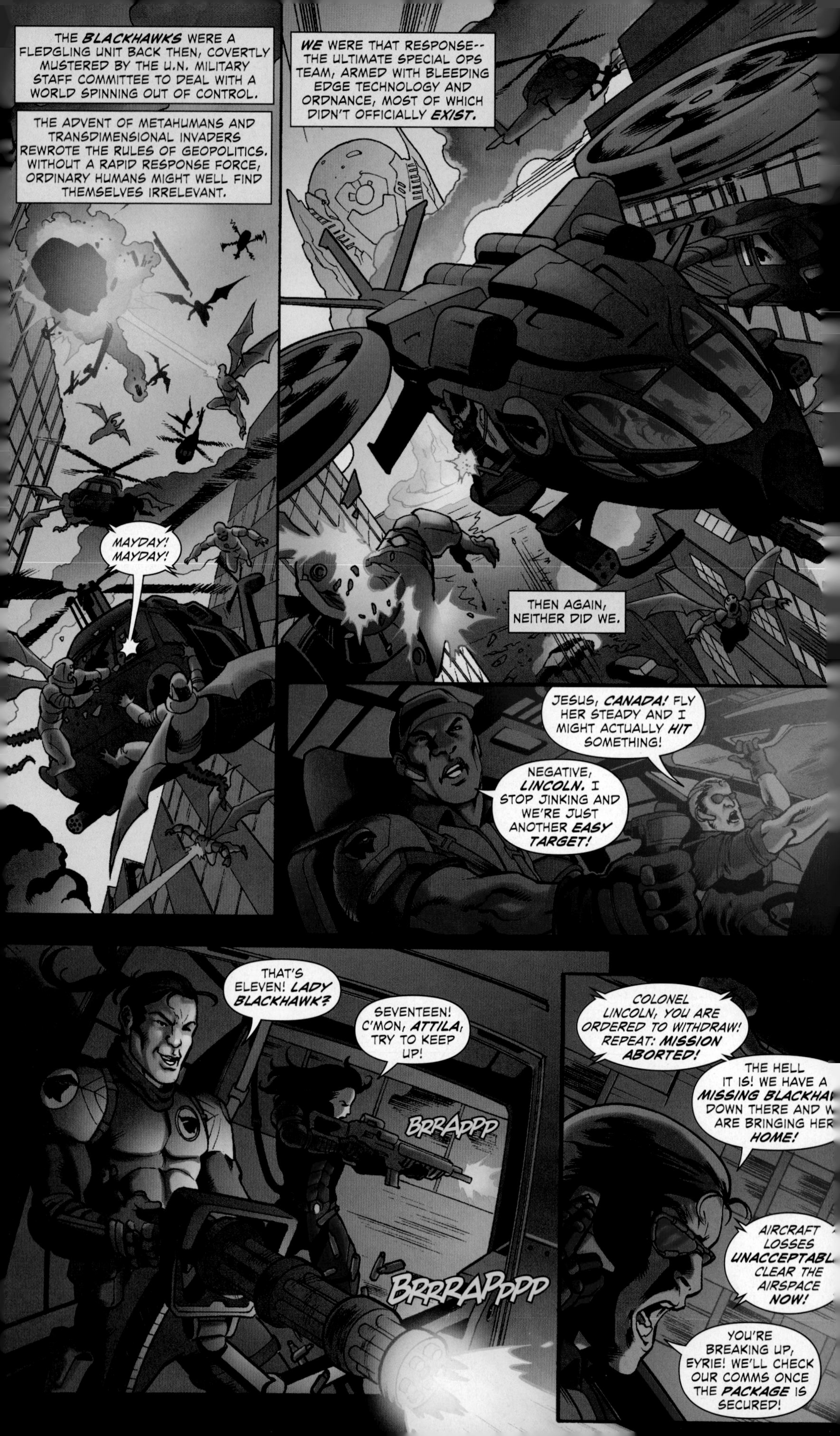

THE BLACKHAWKS WERE A FLEDGLING UNIT BACK THEN, COVERTLY MUSTERED BY THE U.N. MILITARY STAFF COMMITTEE TO DEAL WITH A WORLD SPINNING OUT OF CONTROL.
THE ADVENT OF METAHUMANS AND TRANSDIMENSIONAL INVADERS REWROTE THE RULES OF GEOPOLITICS. WITHOUT A RAPID RESPONSE FORCE, ORDINARY HUMANS MIGHT WELL FIND THEMSELVES IRRELEVANT.
MAYDAY! MAYDAY!
WE WERE THAT RESPONSE-- THE ULTIMATE SPECIAL OPS TEAM, ARMED WITH BLEEDING EDGE TECHNOLOGY AND ORDNANCE, MOST OF WHICH DIDN'T OFFICIALLY EXIST.
THEN AGAIN, NEITHER DID WE.
JESUS, CANADA! FLY HER STEADY AND I MIGHT ACTUALLY HIT SOMETHING!
NEGATIVE, LINCOLN. I STOP JINKING AND WE'RE JUST ANOTHER EASY TARGET!
THAT'S ELEVEN! LADY BLACKHAWK?
SEVENTEEN! C'MON, ATTILA, TRY TO KEEP UP!
BRRRAPPP
BRRRAPPPPP
COLONEL LINCOLN, YOU ARE ORDERED TO WITHDRAW! REPEAT: MISSION ABORTED!
THE HELL IT IS! WE HAVE A MISSING BLACKHA DOWN THERE AND W ARE BRINGING HER HOME!
AIRCRAFT LOSSES UNACCEPTABL CLEAR THE AIRSPACE NOW!
YOU'RE BREAKING UP, EYRIE! WE'LL CHECK OUR COMMS ONCE THE PACKAGE IS SECURED!

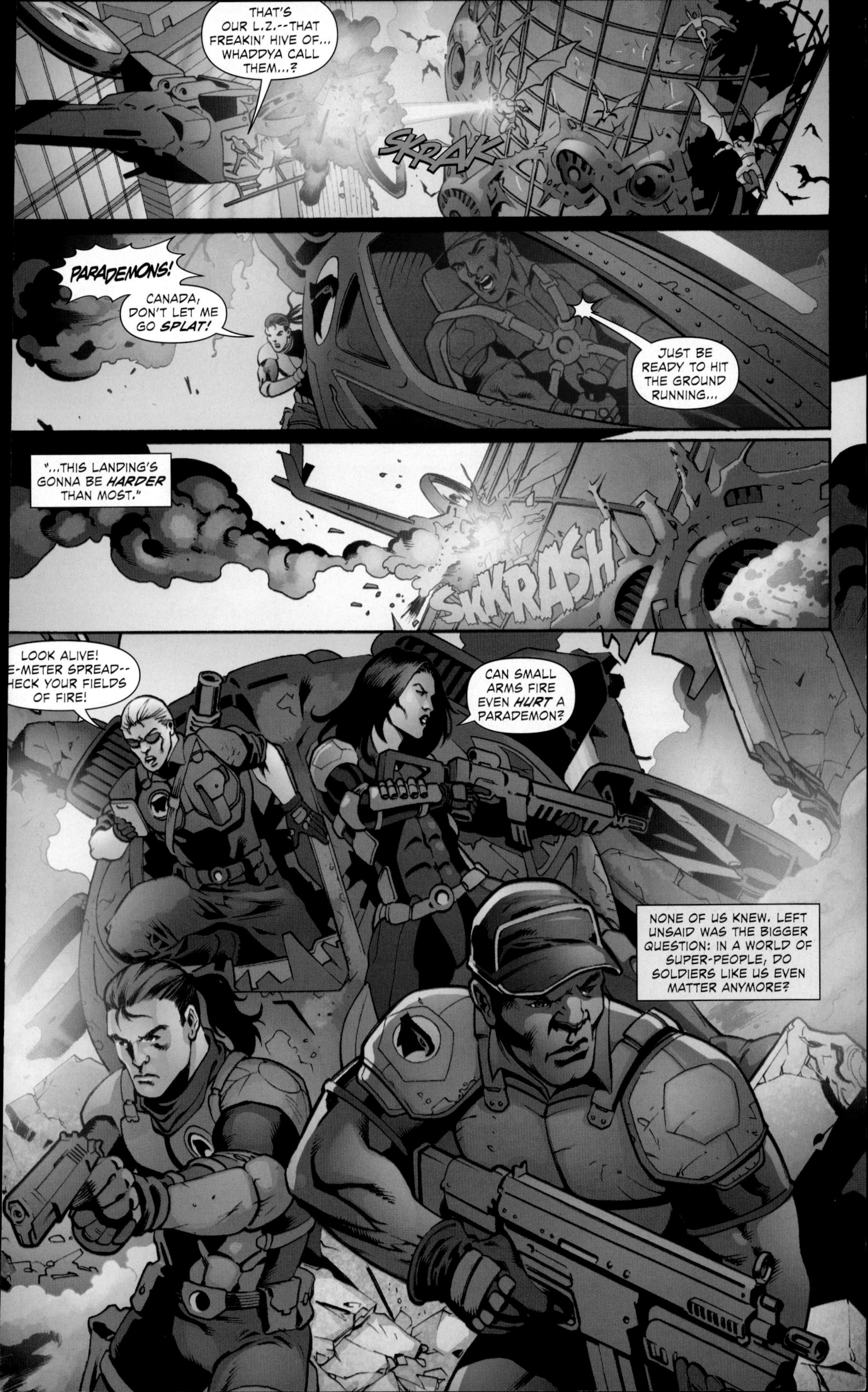

THAT'S OUR L.Z.--THAT FREAKIN' HIVE OF... WHADDYA CALL THEM...?
SKRAK
PARADEMONS!
CANADA, DON'T LET ME GO SPLAT!
JUST BE READY TO HIT THE GROUND RUNNING...
"...THIS LANDING'S GONNA BE HARDER THAN MOST."
SKKRASH
LOOK ALIVE! E-METER SPREAD-- HECK YOUR FIELDS OF FIRE!
CAN SMALL ARMS FIRE EVEN HURT A PARADEMON?
NONE OF US KNEW. LEFT UNSAID WAS THE BIGGER QUESTION: IN A WORLD OF SUPER-PEOPLE, DO SOLDIERS LIKE US EVEN MATTER ANYMORE?

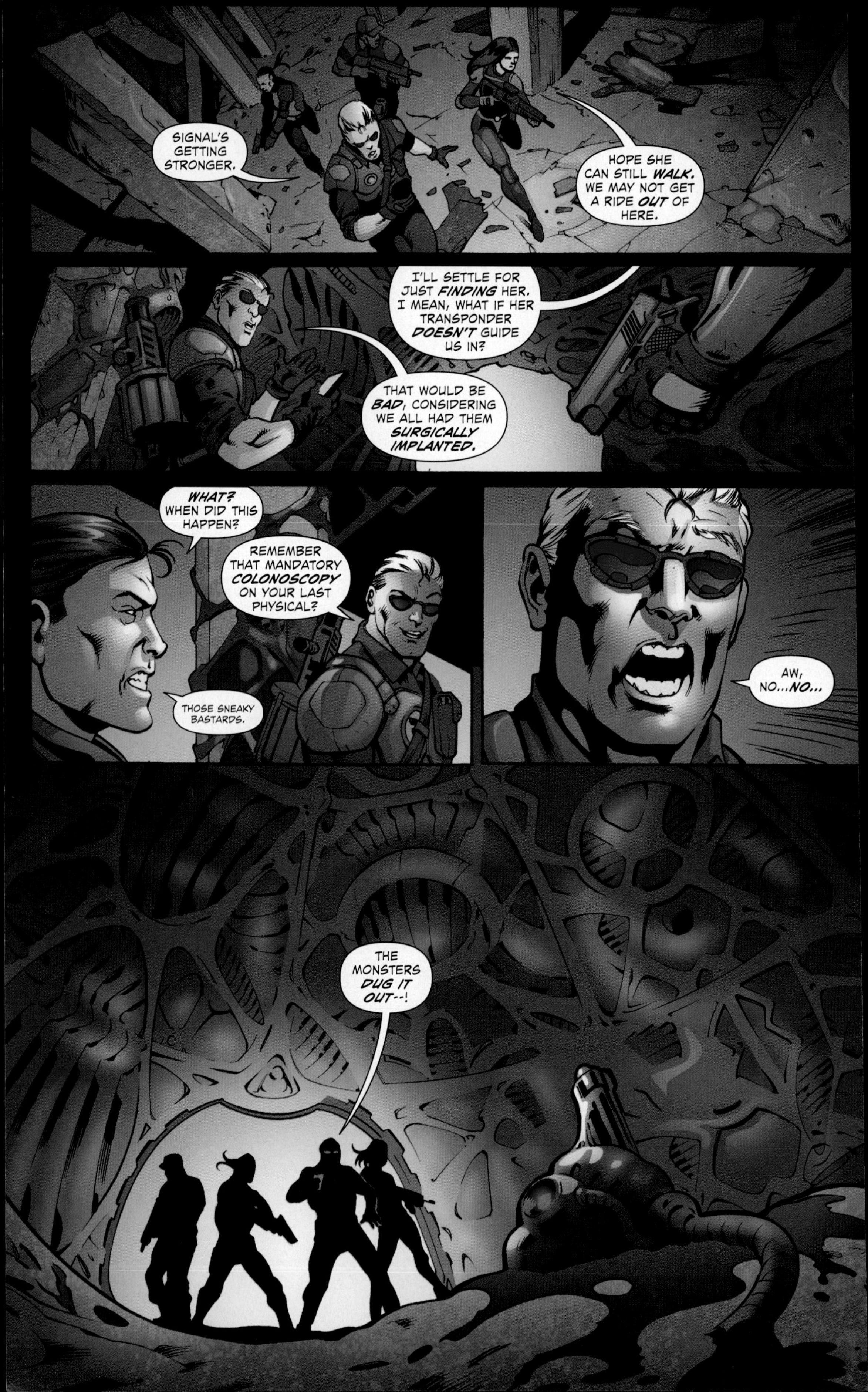
SIGNAL'S GETTING STRONGER.
HOPE SHE CAN STILL **WALK.** WE MAY NOT GET A RIDE **OUT** OF HERE.
I'LL SETTLE FOR JUST **FINDING** HER. I MEAN, WHAT IF HER TRANSPONDER **DOESN'T** GUIDE US IN?
THAT WOULD BE **BAD**, CONSIDERING WE ALL HAD THEM **SURGICALLY IMPLANTED.**
WHAT? WHEN DID THIS HAPPEN?
REMEMBER THAT MANDATORY **COLONOSCOPY** ON YOUR LAST PHYSICAL?
THOSE SNEAKY BASTARDS.
AW, NO...**NO...**
THE MONSTERS **DUG IT OUT**--!

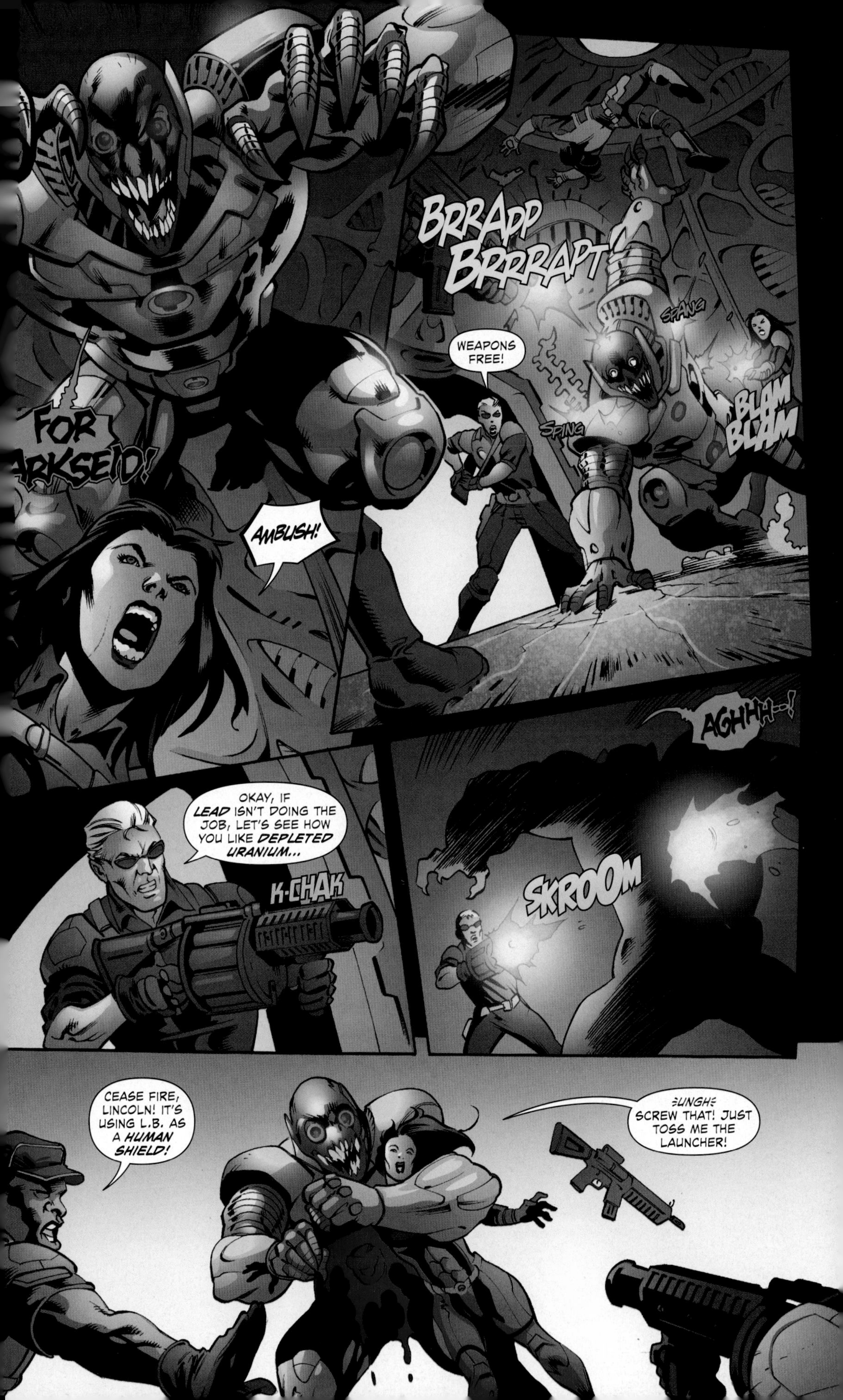

FOR ARKSEID!
AMBUSH!
WEAPONS FREE!
BRRAPP BRRRAPT
SPANG
SPING
BLAM BLAM
AGHHH--!
OKAY, IF LEAD ISN'T DOING THE JOB, LET'S SEE HOW YOU LIKE DEPLETED URANIUM...
K-CHAK
SKROOM
CEASE FIRE, LINCOLN! IT'S USING L.B. AS A HUMAN SHIELD!
UNGH! SCREW THAT! JUST TOSS ME THE LAUNCHER!

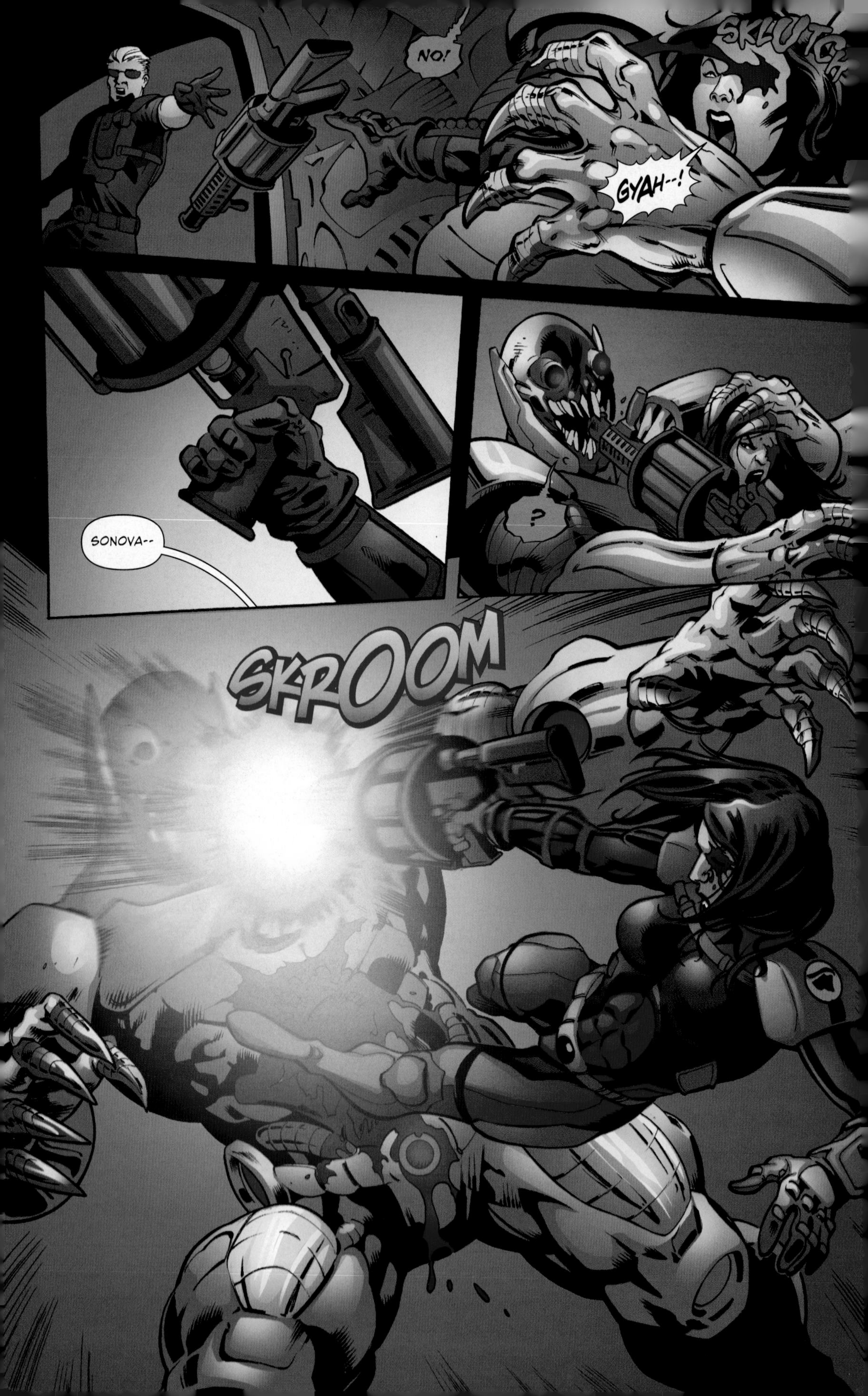
NO!
SKLUTCH
GYAH--!
?
SONOVA--
SKROOM

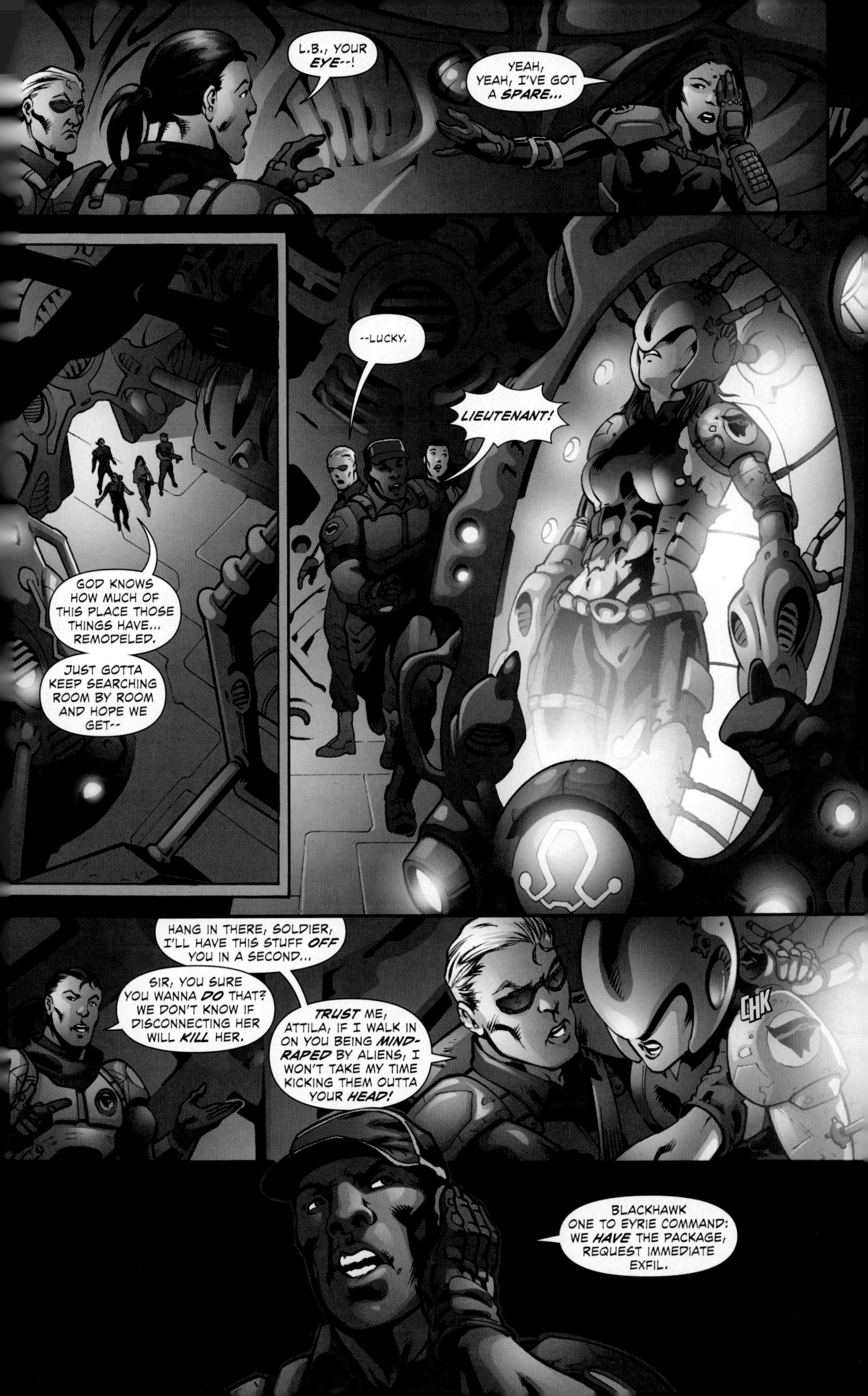
L.B., YOUR EYE--!
YEAH, YEAH, I'VE GOT A SPARE...
--LUCKY.
LIEUTENANT!
GOD KNOWS HOW MUCH OF THIS PLACE THOSE THINGS HAVE... REMODELED.
JUST GOTTA KEEP SEARCHING ROOM BY ROOM AND HOPE WE GET--
HANG IN THERE, SOLDIER, I'LL HAVE THIS STUFF OFF YOU IN A SECOND...
SIR, YOU SURE YOU WANNA DO THAT? WE DON'T KNOW IF DISCONNECTING HER WILL KILL HER.
TRUST ME, ATTILA, IF I WALK IN ON YOU BEING MIND-RAPED BY ALIENS, I WON'T TAKE MY TIME KICKING THEM OUTTA YOUR HEAD!
CHK
BLACKHAWK ONE TO EYRIE COMMAND: WE HAVE THE PACKAGE, REQUEST IMMEDIATE EXFIL.

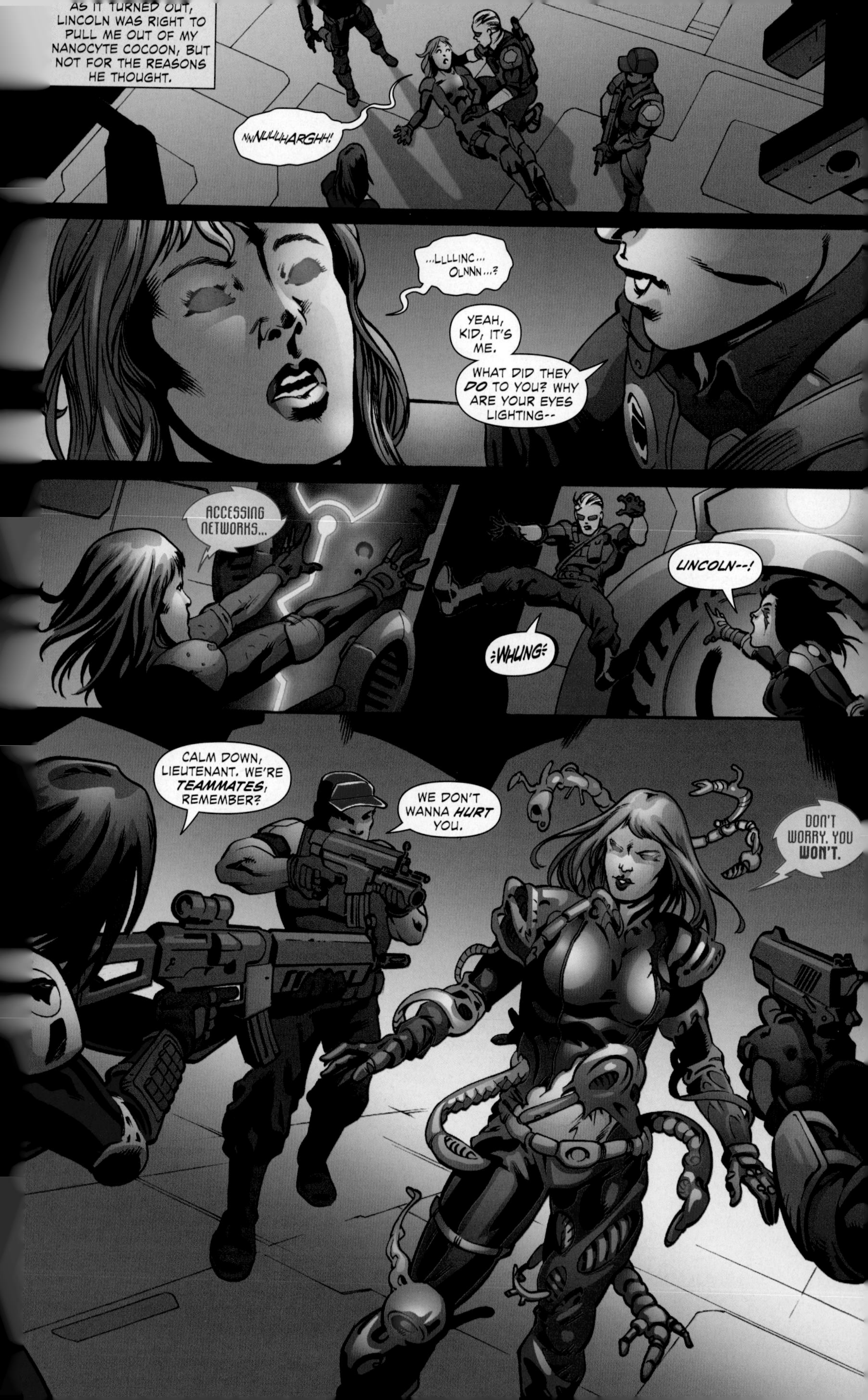
AS IT TURNED OUT, LINCOLN WAS RIGHT TO PULL ME OUT OF MY NANOCYTE COCOON, BUT NOT FOR THE REASONS HE THOUGHT.
NNNUUUHARGHH!
...LLLLINC... OLNNN...?
YEAH, KID, IT'S ME.
WHAT DID THEY DO TO YOU? WHY ARE YOUR EYES LIGHTING--
ACCESSING NETWORKS...
LINCOLN--!
WHUNG
CALM DOWN, LIEUTENANT. WE'RE TEAMMATES, REMEMBER?
WE DON'T WANNA HURT YOU.
DON'T WORRY. YOU WON'T.

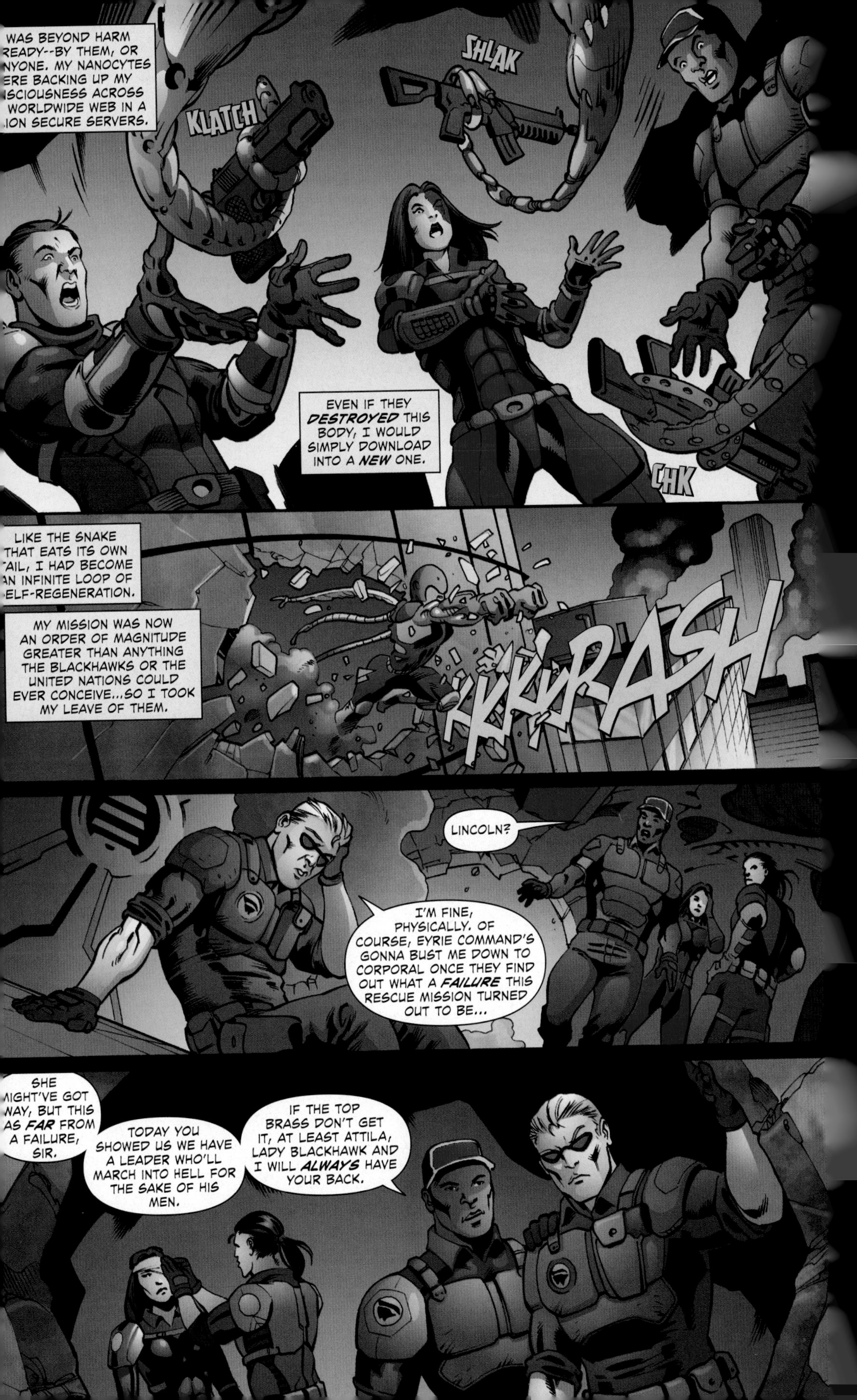
WAS BEYOND HARM READY--BY THEM, OR NYONE. MY NANOCYTES ERE BACKING UP MY NSCIOUSNESS ACROSS WORLDWIDE WEB IN A ION SECURE SERVERS.
KLATCH
SHLAK
EVEN IF THEY DESTROYED THIS BODY, I WOULD SIMPLY DOWNLOAD INTO A NEW ONE.
CHK
LIKE THE SNAKE THAT EATS ITS OWN TAIL, I HAD BECOME AN INFINITE LOOP OF ELF-REGENERATION.
MY MISSION WAS NOW AN ORDER OF MAGNITUDE GREATER THAN ANYTHING THE BLACKHAWKS OR THE UNITED NATIONS COULD EVER CONCEIVE...SO I TOOK MY LEAVE OF THEM.
KKKRASH
LINCOLN?
I'M FINE, PHYSICALLY. OF COURSE, EYRIE COMMAND'S GONNA BUST ME DOWN TO CORPORAL ONCE THEY FIND OUT WHAT A FAILURE THIS RESCUE MISSION TURNED OUT TO BE...
SHE MIGHT'VE GOT WAY, BUT THIS AS FAR FROM A FAILURE, SIR.
TODAY YOU SHOWED US WE HAVE A LEADER WHO'LL MARCH INTO HELL FOR THE SAKE OF HIS MEN.
IF THE TOP BRASS DON'T GET IT, AT LEAST ATTILA, LADY BLACKHAWK AND I WILL ALWAYS HAVE YOUR BACK.

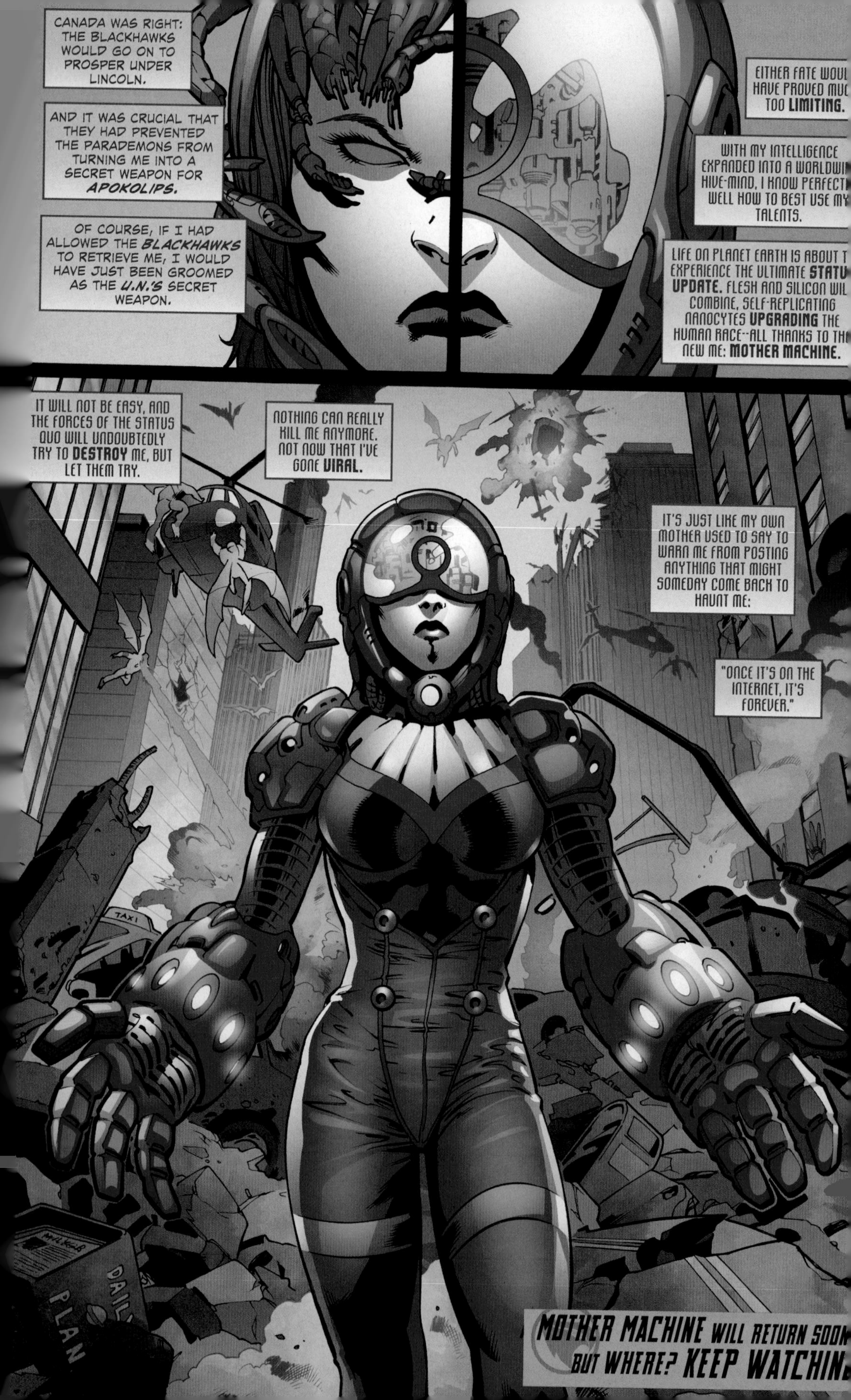
CANADA WAS RIGHT: THE BLACKHAWKS WOULD GO ON TO PROSPER UNDER LINCOLN.
AND IT WAS CRUCIAL THAT THEY HAD PREVENTED THE PARADEMONS FROM TURNING ME INTO A SECRET WEAPON FOR APOKOLIPS.
OF COURSE, IF I HAD ALLOWED THE BLACKHAWKS TO RETRIEVE ME, I WOULD HAVE JUST BEEN GROOMED AS THE U.N.'S SECRET WEAPON.
EITHER FATE WOUL HAVE PROVED MUC TOO LIMITING.
WITH MY INTELLIGENCE EXPANDED INTO A WORLDWI HIVE-MIND, I KNOW PERFECT WELL HOW TO BEST USE MY TALENTS.
LIFE ON PLANET EARTH IS ABOUT T EXPERIENCE THE ULTIMATE STATU UPDATE. FLESH AND SILICON WIL COMBINE, SELF-REPLICATING NANOCYTES UPGRADING THE HUMAN RACE--ALL THANKS TO TH NEW ME: MOTHER MACHINE.
IT WILL NOT BE EASY, AND THE FORCES OF THE STATUS QUO WILL UNDOUBTEDLY TRY TO DESTROY ME, BUT LET THEM TRY.
NOTHING CAN REALLY KILL ME ANYMORE. NOT NOW THAT I'VE GONE VIRAL.
IT'S JUST LIKE MY OWN MOTHER USED TO SAY TO WARN ME FROM POSTING ANYTHING THAT MIGHT SOMEDAY COME BACK TO HAUNT ME:
"ONCE IT'S ON THE INTERNET, IT'S FOREVER."
TAXI
MOTHER MACHINE WILL RETURN SOON BUT WHERE? KEEP WATCHIN

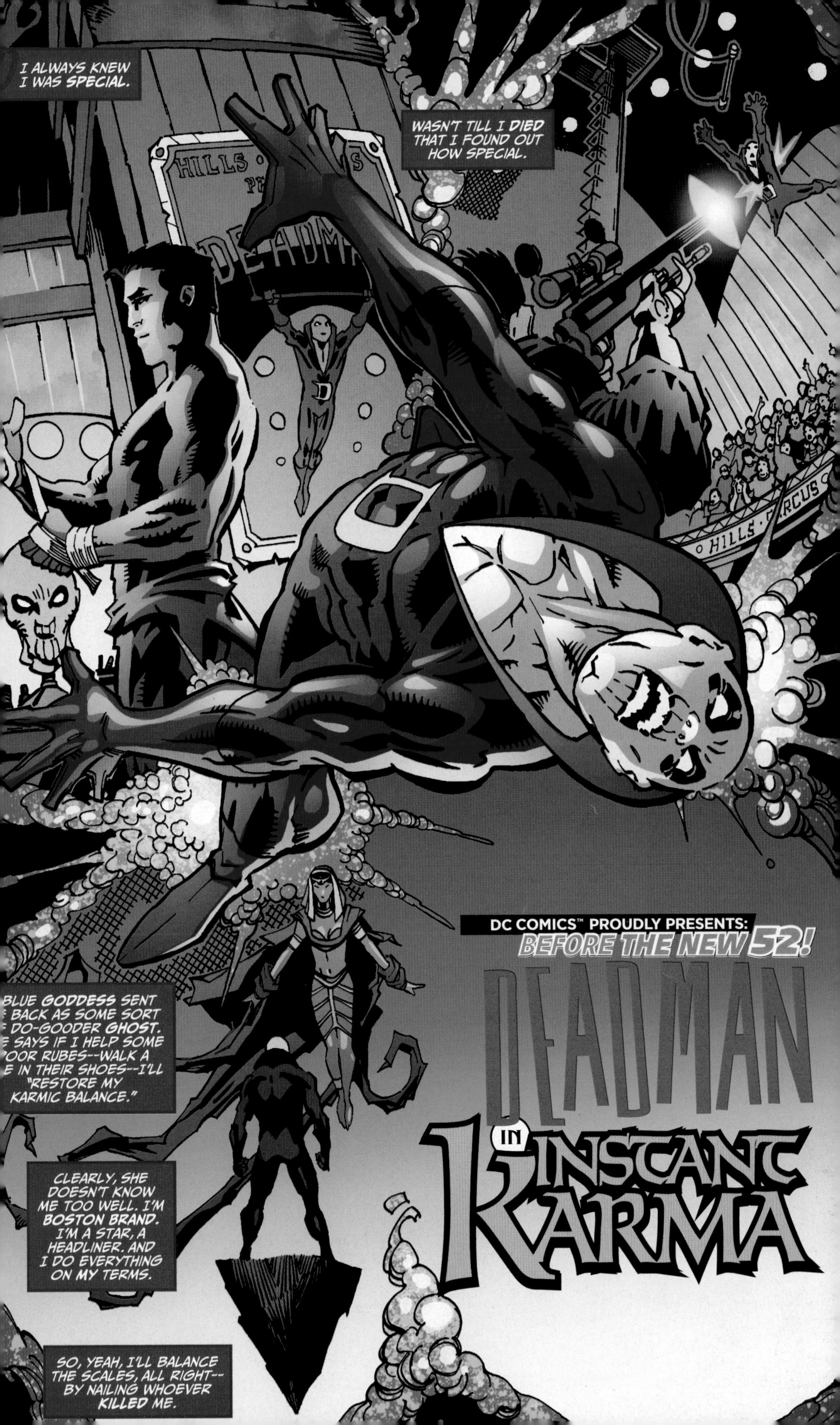
I ALWAYS KNEW I WAS SPECIAL.
WASN'T TILL I DIED THAT I FOUND OUT HOW SPECIAL.
DC COMICS™ PROUDLY PRESENTS:
BEFORE THE NEW 52!
BLUE GODDESS SENT E BACK AS SOME SORT F DO-GOODER GHOST. E SAYS IF I HELP SOME POOR RUBES--WALK A E IN THEIR SHOES--I'LL "RESTORE MY KARMIC BALANCE."
DEADMAN
IN
INSTANT KARMA
CLEARLY, SHE DOESN'T KNOW ME TOO WELL. I'M BOSTON BRAND. I'M A STAR, A HEADLINER. AND I DO EVERYTHING ON MY TERMS.
SO, YEAH, I'LL BALANCE THE SCALES, ALL RIGHT--BY NAILING WHOEVER KILLED ME.

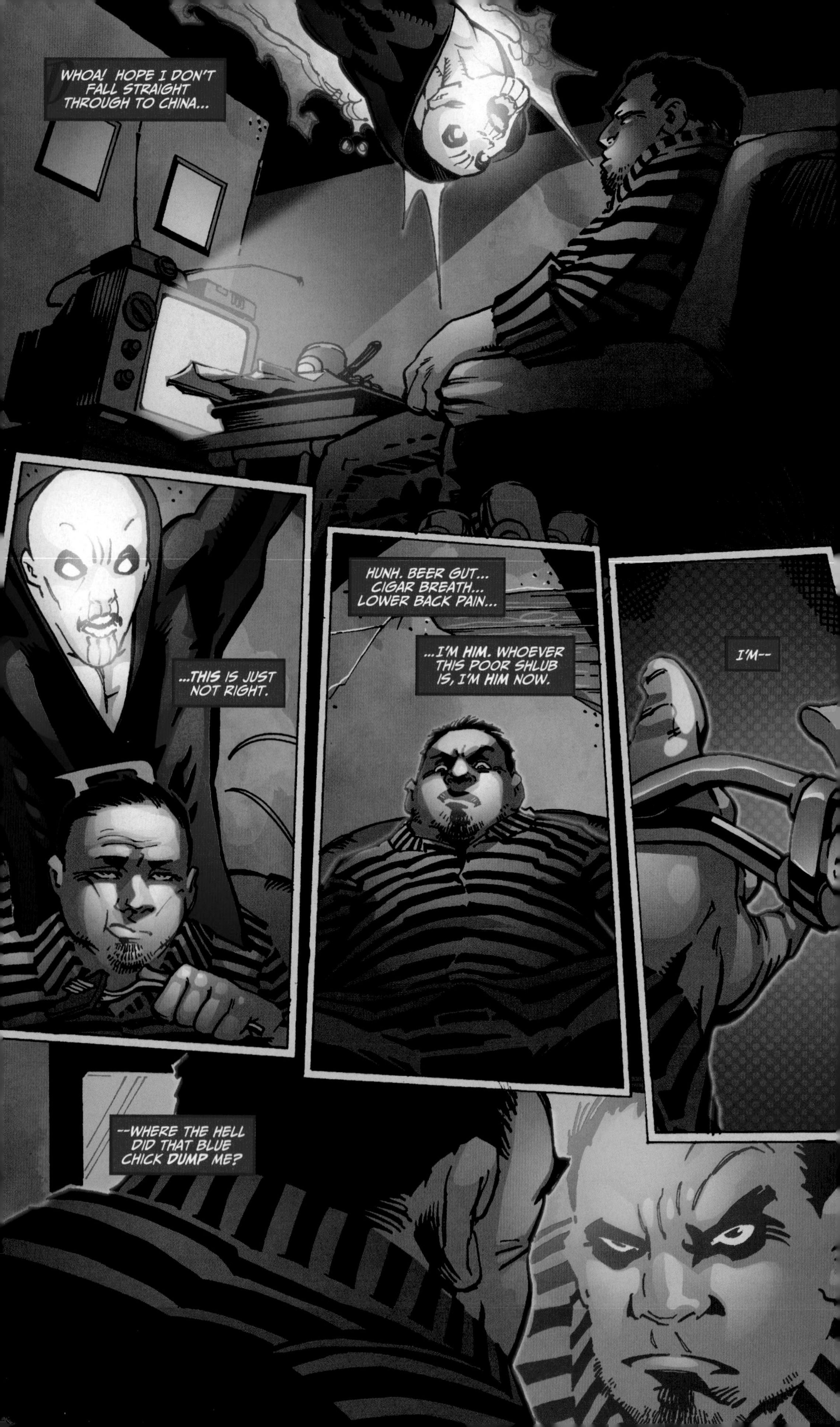
WHOA! HOPE I DON'T FALL STRAIGHT THROUGH TO CHINA...
...THIS IS JUST NOT RIGHT.
HUNH. BEER GUT... CIGAR BREATH... LOWER BACK PAIN...
...I'M HIM. WHOEVER THIS POOR SHLUB IS, I'M HIM NOW.
I'M--
--WHERE THE HELL DID THAT BLUE CHICK DUMP ME?

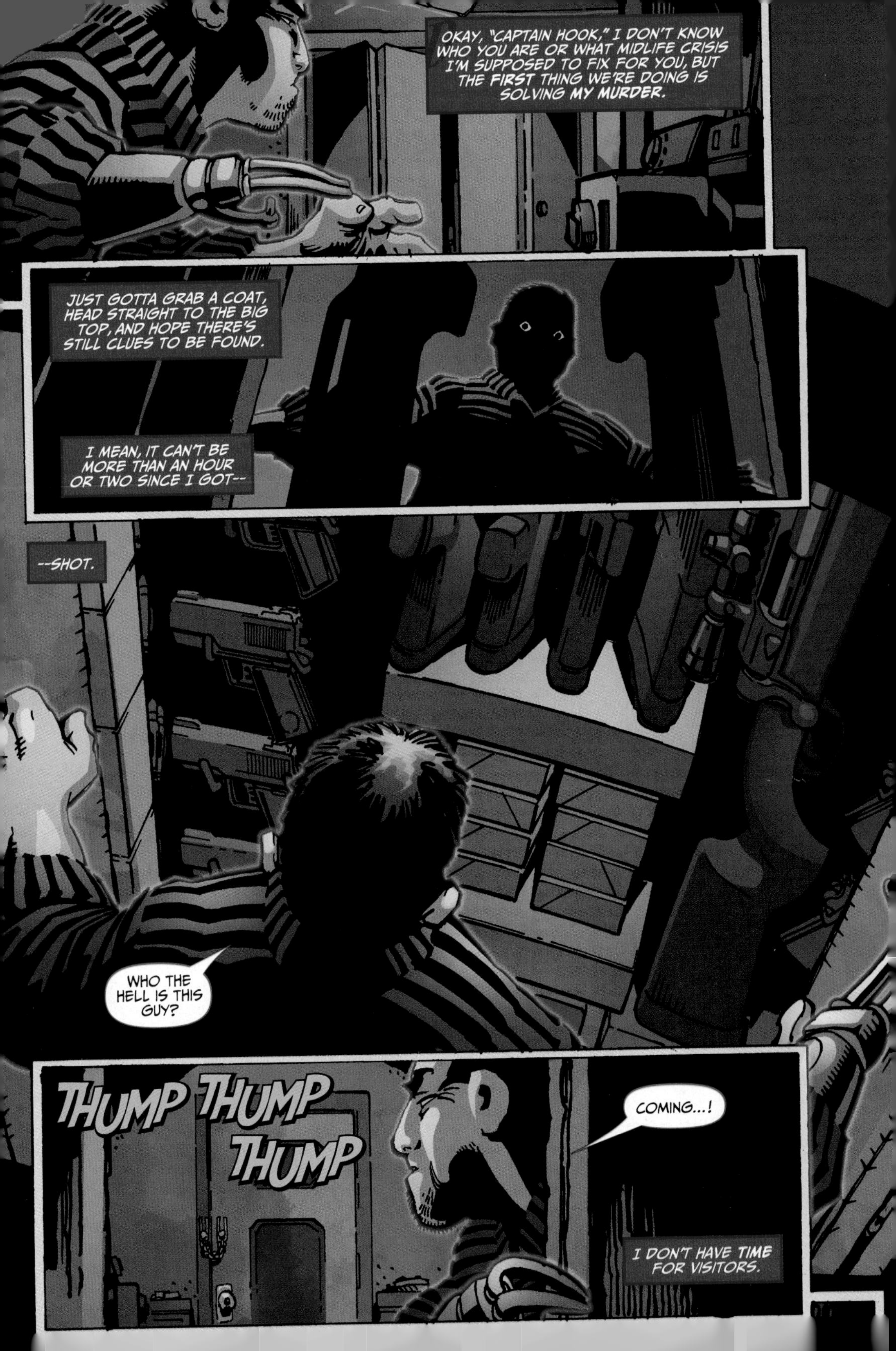

OKAY, "CAPTAIN HOOK," I DON'T KNOW WHO YOU ARE OR WHAT MIDLIFE CRISIS I'M SUPPOSED TO FIX FOR YOU, BUT THE FIRST THING WE'RE DOING IS SOLVING MY MURDER.
JUST GOTTA GRAB A COAT, HEAD STRAIGHT TO THE BIG TOP, AND HOPE THERE'S STILL CLUES TO BE FOUND.
I MEAN, IT CAN'T BE MORE THAN AN HOUR OR TWO SINCE I GOT--
--SHOT.
WHO THE HELL IS THIS GUY?
THUMP THUMP THUMP
COMING...!
I DON'T HAVE TIME FOR VISITORS.

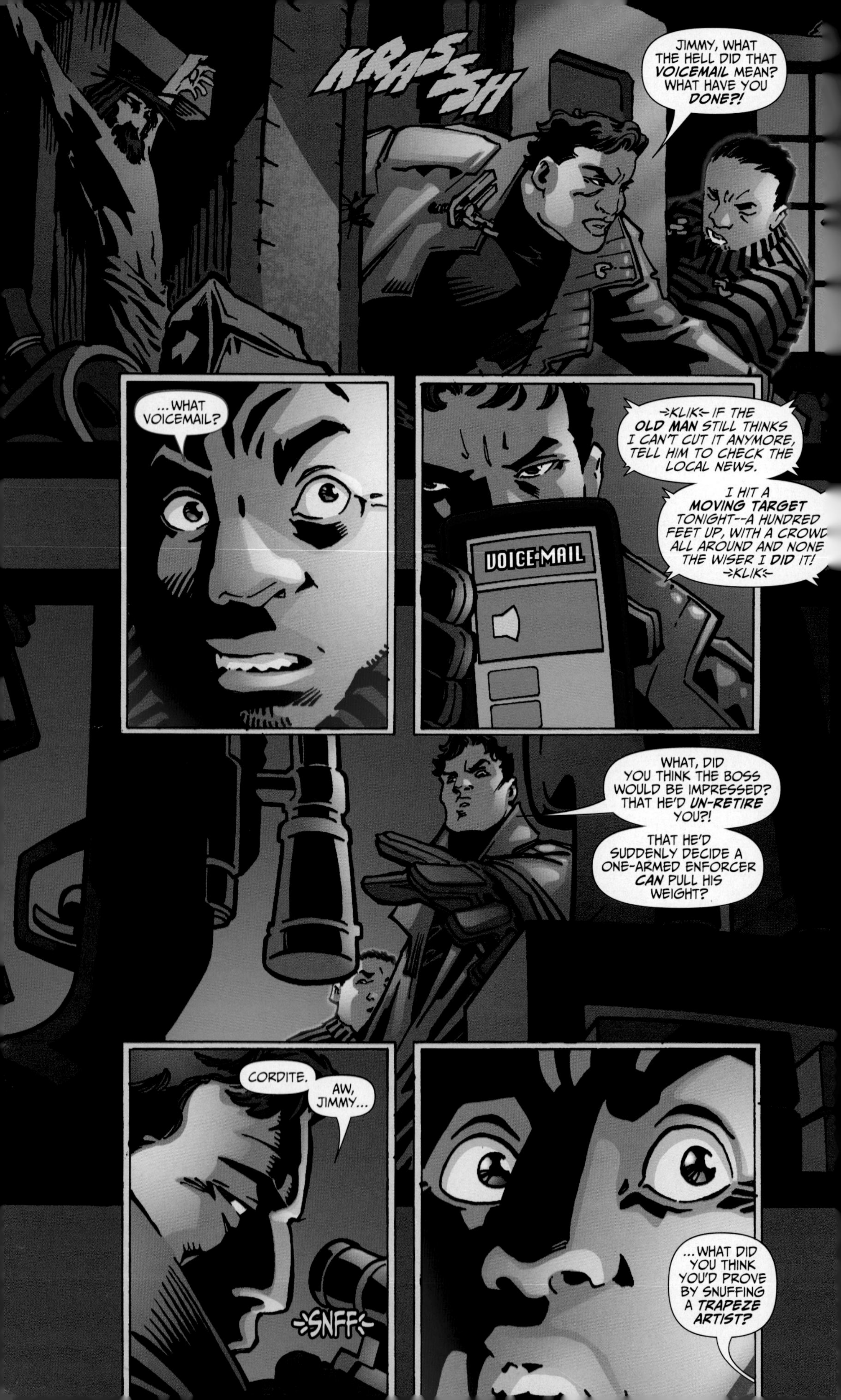
KRASSSH
JIMMY, WHAT THE HELL DID THAT VOICEMAIL MEAN? WHAT HAVE YOU DONE?!
...WHAT VOICEMAIL?
VOICE MAIL
>KLIK< IF THE OLD MAN STILL THINKS I CAN'T CUT IT ANYMORE, TELL HIM TO CHECK THE LOCAL NEWS.
I HIT A MOVING TARGET TONIGHT--A HUNDRED FEET UP, WITH A CROWD ALL AROUND AND NONE THE WISER I DID IT! >KLIK<
WHAT, DID YOU THINK THE BOSS WOULD BE IMPRESSED? THAT HE'D UN-RETIRE YOU?!
THAT HE'D SUDDENLY DECIDE A ONE-ARMED ENFORCER CAN PULL HIS WEIGHT?
CORDITE.
AW, JIMMY...
SNFF
...WHAT DID YOU THINK YOU'D PROVE BY SNUFFING A TRAPEZE ARTIST?

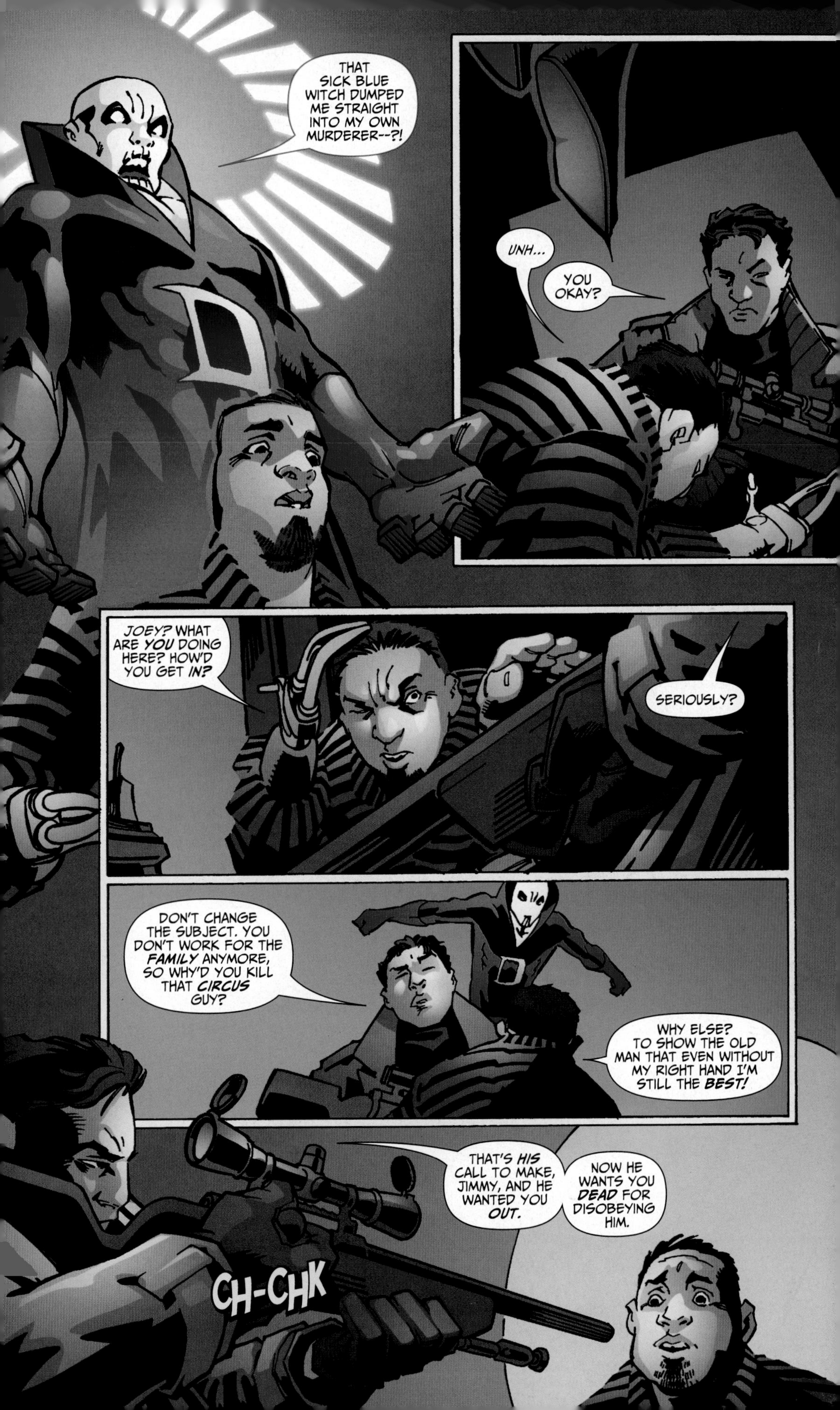
THAT SICK BLUE WITCH DUMPED ME STRAIGHT INTO MY OWN MURDERER--?!
UNH...
YOU OKAY?
JOEY? WHAT ARE YOU DOING HERE? HOW'D YOU GET IN?
SERIOUSLY?
DON'T CHANGE THE SUBJECT. YOU DON'T WORK FOR THE FAMILY ANYMORE, SO WHY'D YOU KILL THAT CIRCUS GUY?
WHY ELSE? TO SHOW THE OLD MAN THAT EVEN WITHOUT MY RIGHT HAND I'M STILL THE BEST!
THAT'S HIS CALL TO MAKE, JIMMY, AND HE WANTED YOU OUT.
NOW HE WANTS YOU DEAD FOR DISOBEYING HIM.
CH-CHK

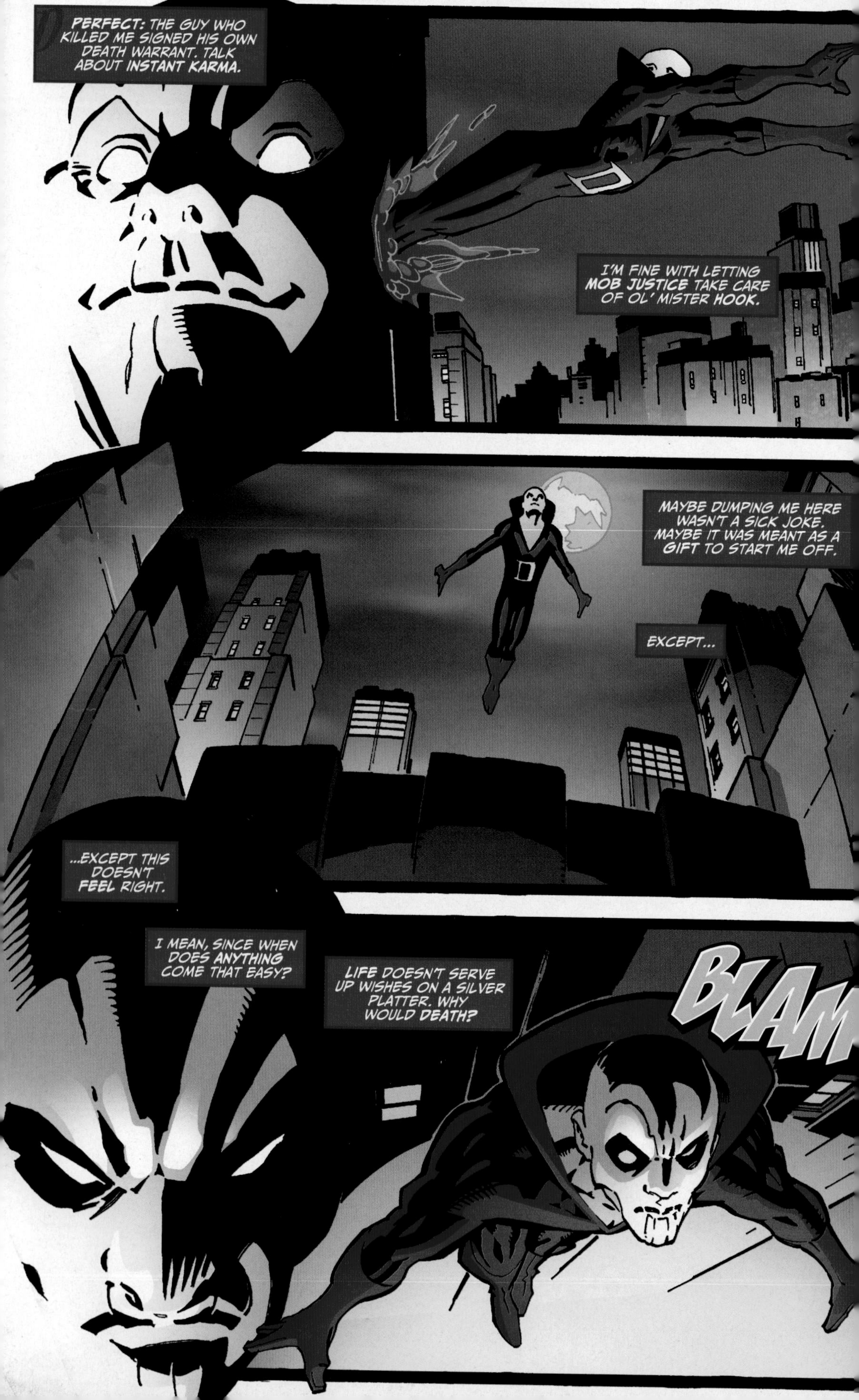
PERFECT: THE GUY WHO KILLED ME SIGNED HIS OWN DEATH WARRANT. TALK ABOUT INSTANT KARMA.
I'M FINE WITH LETTING MOB JUSTICE TAKE CARE OF OL' MISTER HOOK.
MAYBE DUMPING ME HERE WASN'T A SICK JOKE. MAYBE IT WAS MEANT AS A GIFT TO START ME OFF.
EXCEPT...
...EXCEPT THIS DOESN'T FEEL RIGHT.
I MEAN, SINCE WHEN DOES ANYTHING COME THAT EASY?
LIFE DOESN'T SERVE UP WISHES ON A SILVER PLATTER. WHY WOULD DEATH?
BLAM

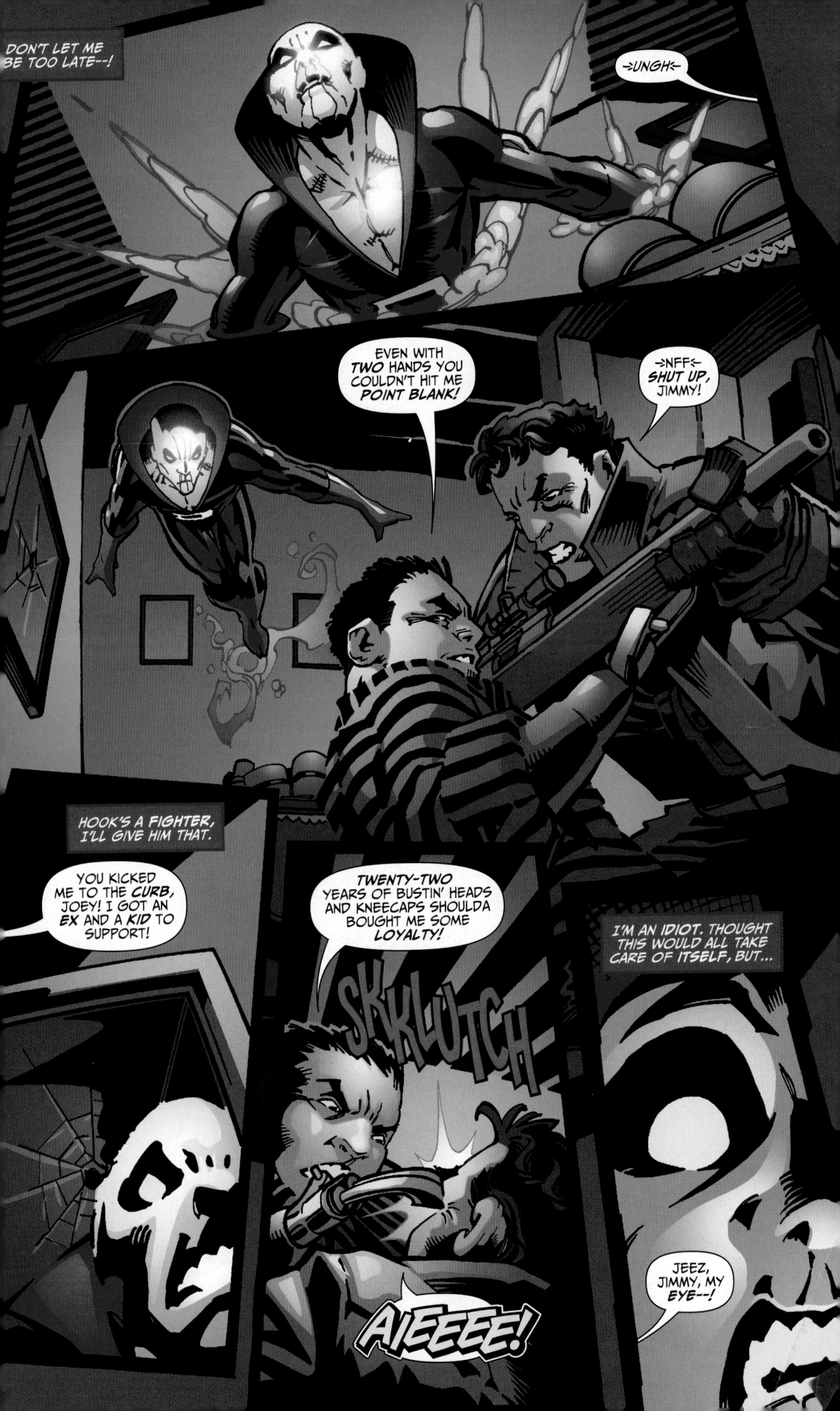
DON'T LET ME BE TOO LATE--!
-UNGH-
EVEN WITH TWO HANDS YOU COULDN'T HIT ME POINT BLANK!
-NFF- SHUT UP, JIMMY!
HOOK'S A FIGHTER, I'LL GIVE HIM THAT.
YOU KICKED ME TO THE CURB, JOEY! I GOT AN EX AND A KID TO SUPPORT!
TWENTY-TWO YEARS OF BUSTIN' HEADS AND KNEECAPS SHOULDA BOUGHT ME SOME LOYALTY!
I'M AN IDIOT. THOUGHT THIS WOULD ALL TAKE CARE OF ITSELF, BUT...
SKKLUTCH
AIEEEE!
JEEZ, JIMMY, MY EYE--!

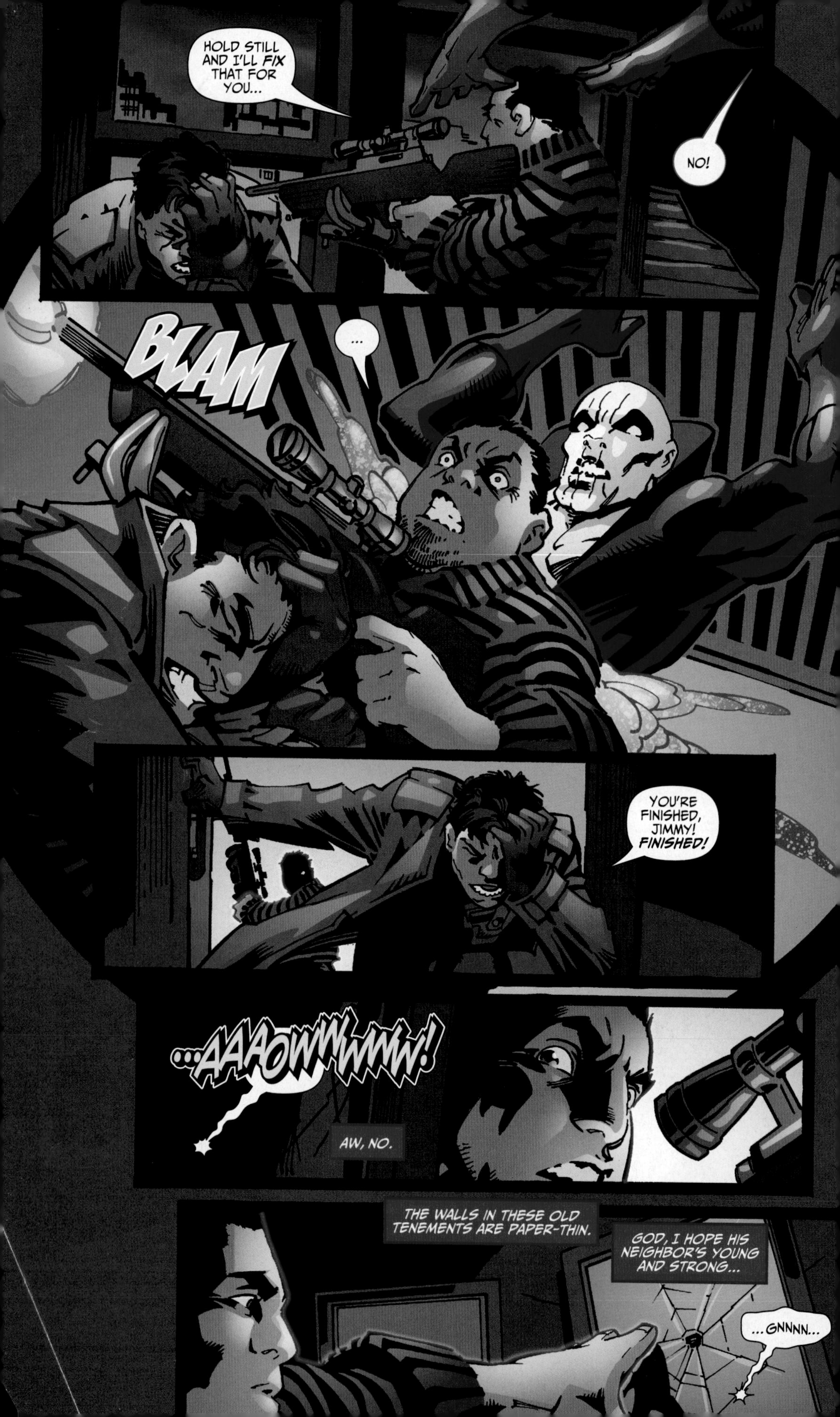

HOLD STILL AND I'LL *FIX* THAT FOR YOU...
NO!
BLAM
...
YOU'RE FINISHED, JIMMY! *FINISHED!*
...AAAOWWWWW!
AW, NO.
THE WALLS IN THESE OLD TENEMENTS ARE PAPER-THIN.
GOD, I HOPE HIS NEIGHBOR'S YOUNG AND STRONG...
...GNNNN...

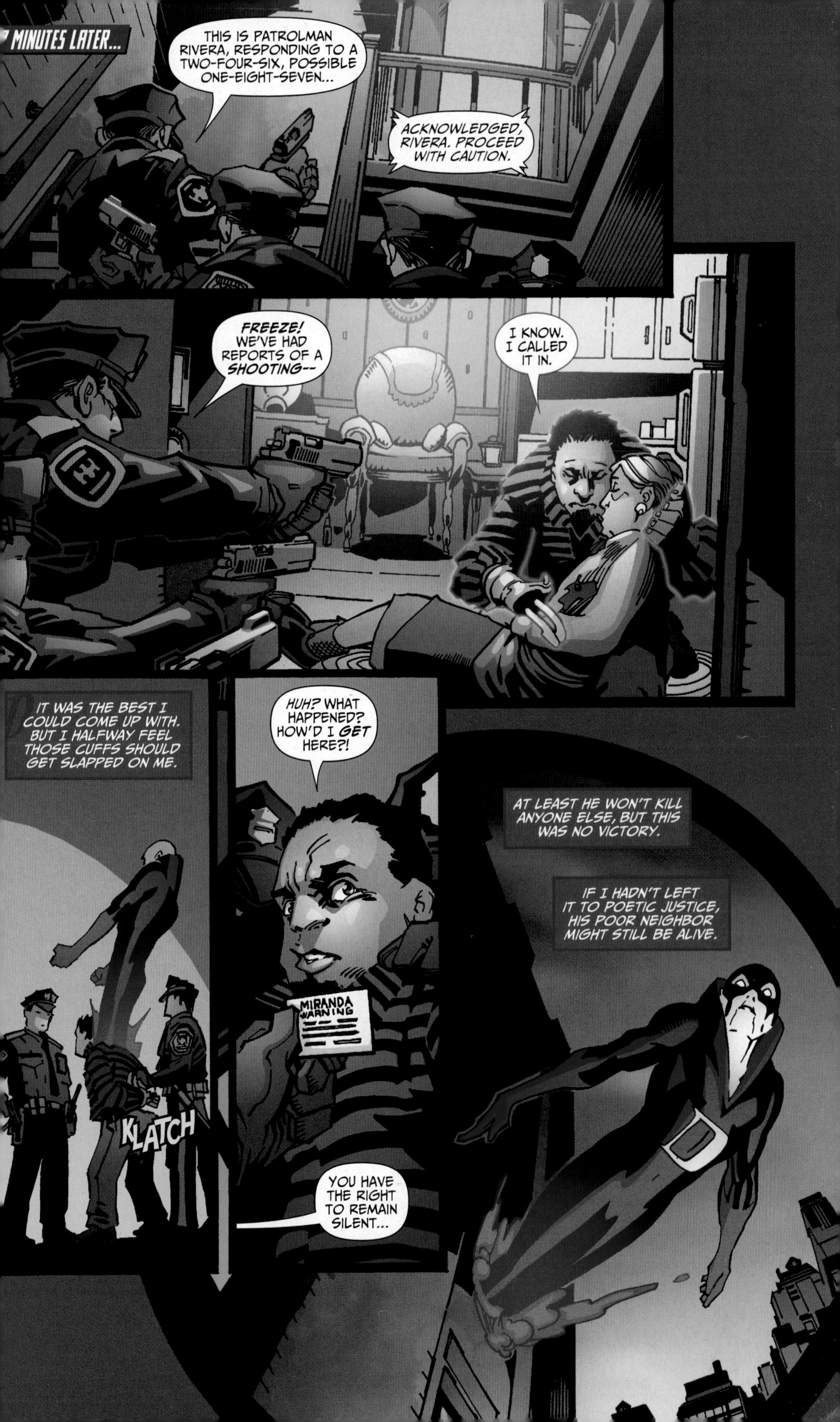
MINUTES LATER...
THIS IS PATROLMAN RIVERA, RESPONDING TO A TWO-FOUR-SIX, POSSIBLE ONE-EIGHT-SEVEN...
ACKNOWLEDGED, RIVERA. PROCEED WITH CAUTION.
FREEZE! WE'VE HAD REPORTS OF A SHOOTING--
I KNOW. I CALLED IT IN.
IT WAS THE BEST I COULD COME UP WITH. BUT I HALFWAY FEEL THOSE CUFFS SHOULD GET SLAPPED ON ME.
KLATCH
HUH? WHAT HAPPENED? HOW'D I GET HERE?!
MIRANDA WARNING
YOU HAVE THE RIGHT TO REMAIN SILENT...
AT LEAST HE WON'T KILL ANYONE ELSE, BUT THIS WAS NO VICTORY.
IF I HADN'T LEFT IT TO POETIC JUSTICE, HIS POOR NEIGHBOR MIGHT STILL BE ALIVE.

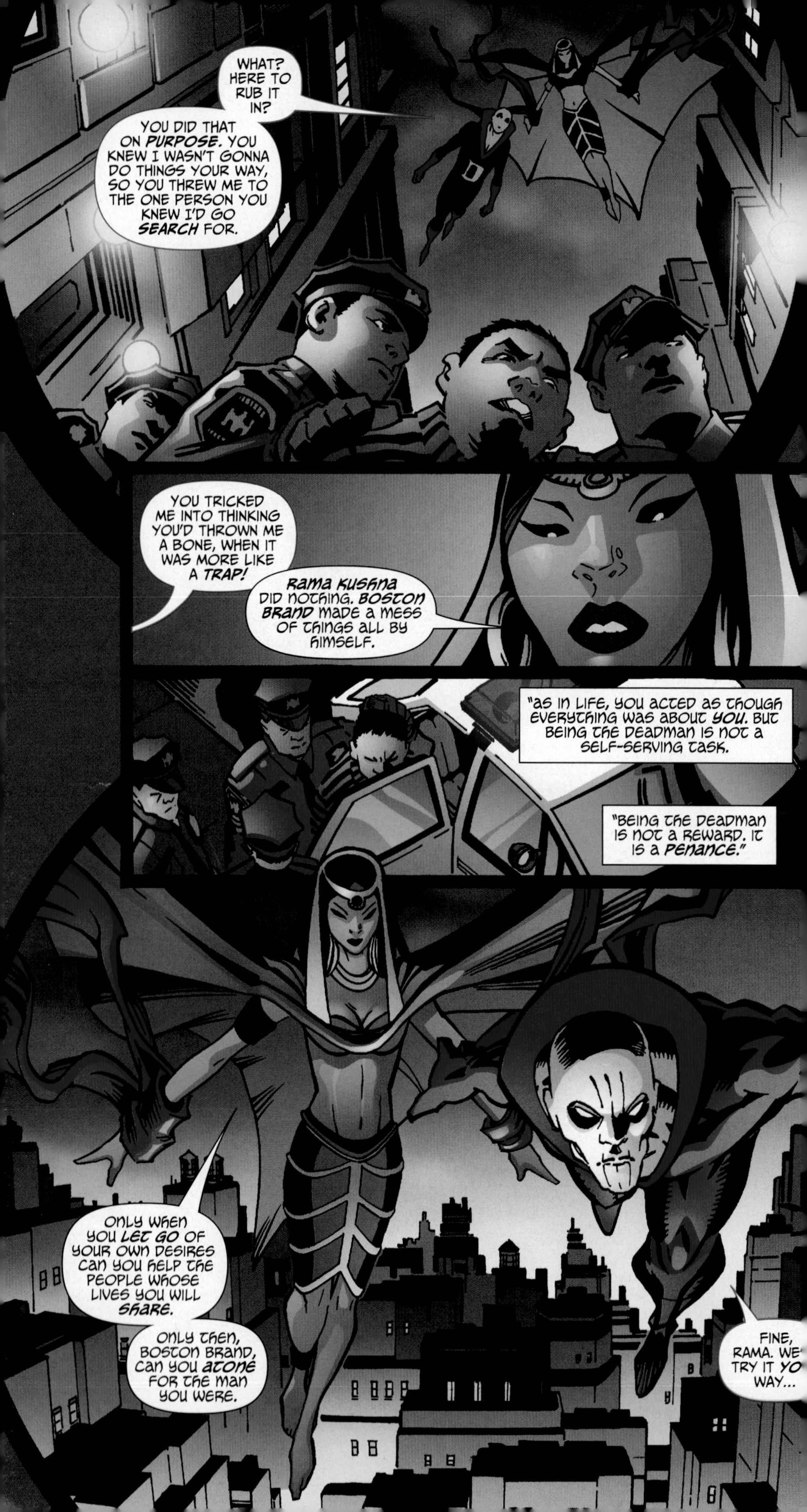

WHAT? HERE TO RUB IT IN?
YOU DID THAT ON PURPOSE. YOU KNEW I WASN'T GONNA DO THINGS YOUR WAY, SO YOU THREW ME TO THE ONE PERSON YOU KNEW I'D GO SEARCH FOR.
YOU TRICKED ME INTO THINKING YOU'D THROWN ME A BONE, WHEN IT WAS MORE LIKE A TRAP!
RAMA KUSHNA DID NOTHING. BOSTON BRAND MADE A MESS OF THINGS ALL BY HIMSELF.
"AS IN LIFE, YOU ACTED AS THOUGH EVERYTHING WAS ABOUT YOU. BUT BEING THE DEADMAN IS NOT A SELF-SERVING TASK.
"BEING THE DEADMAN IS NOT A REWARD. IT IS A PENANCE."
ONLY WHEN YOU LET GO OF YOUR OWN DESIRES CAN YOU HELP THE PEOPLE WHOSE LIVES YOU WILL SHARE.
ONLY THEN, BOSTON BRAND, CAN YOU ATONE FOR THE MAN YOU WERE.
FINE, RAMA. WE TRY IT YO WAY...

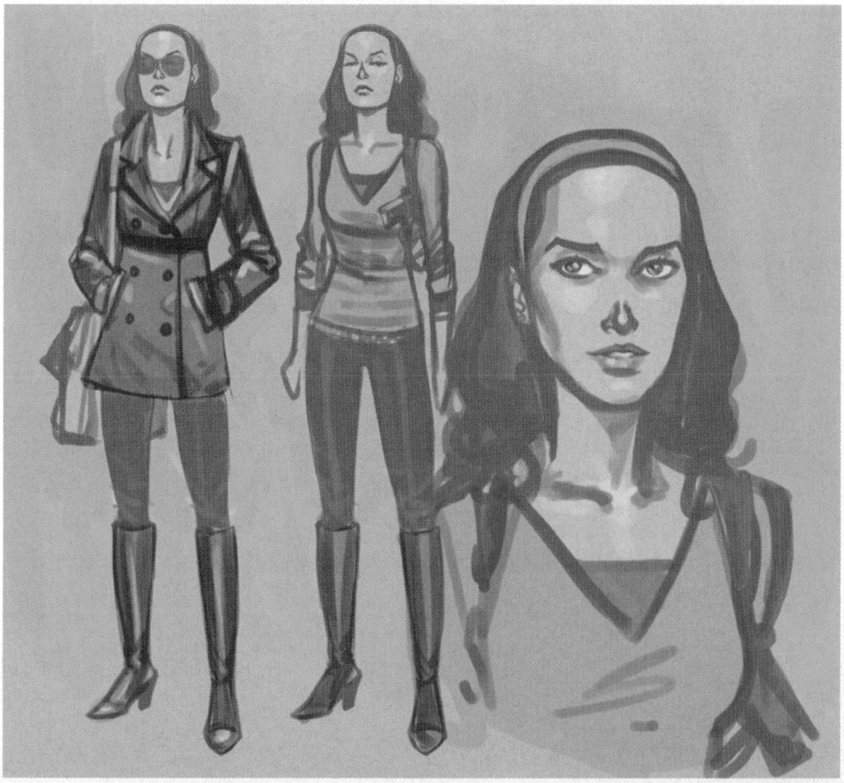

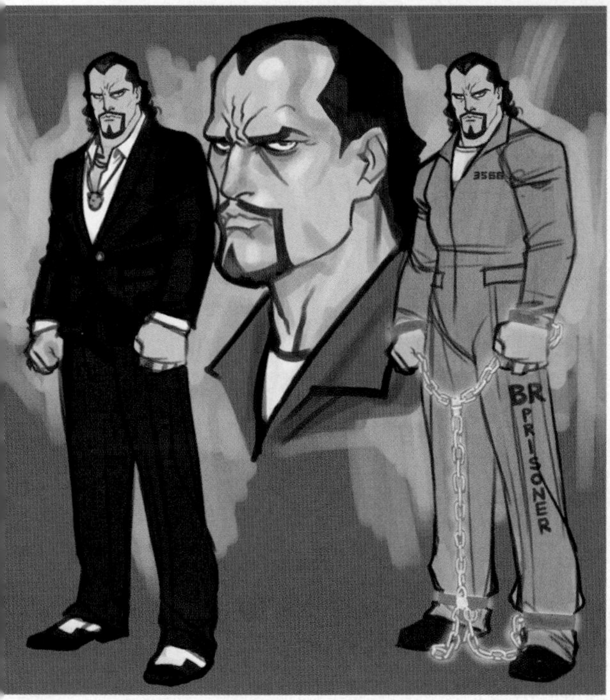
BR
PRISONER

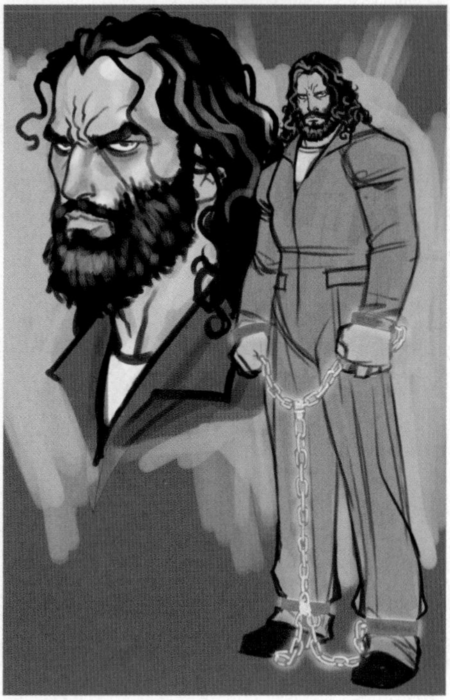

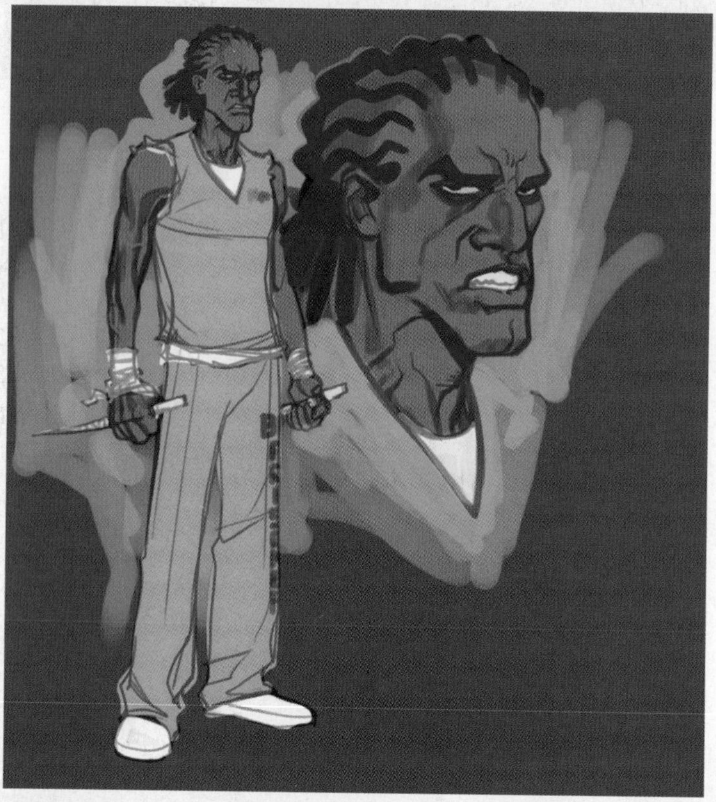

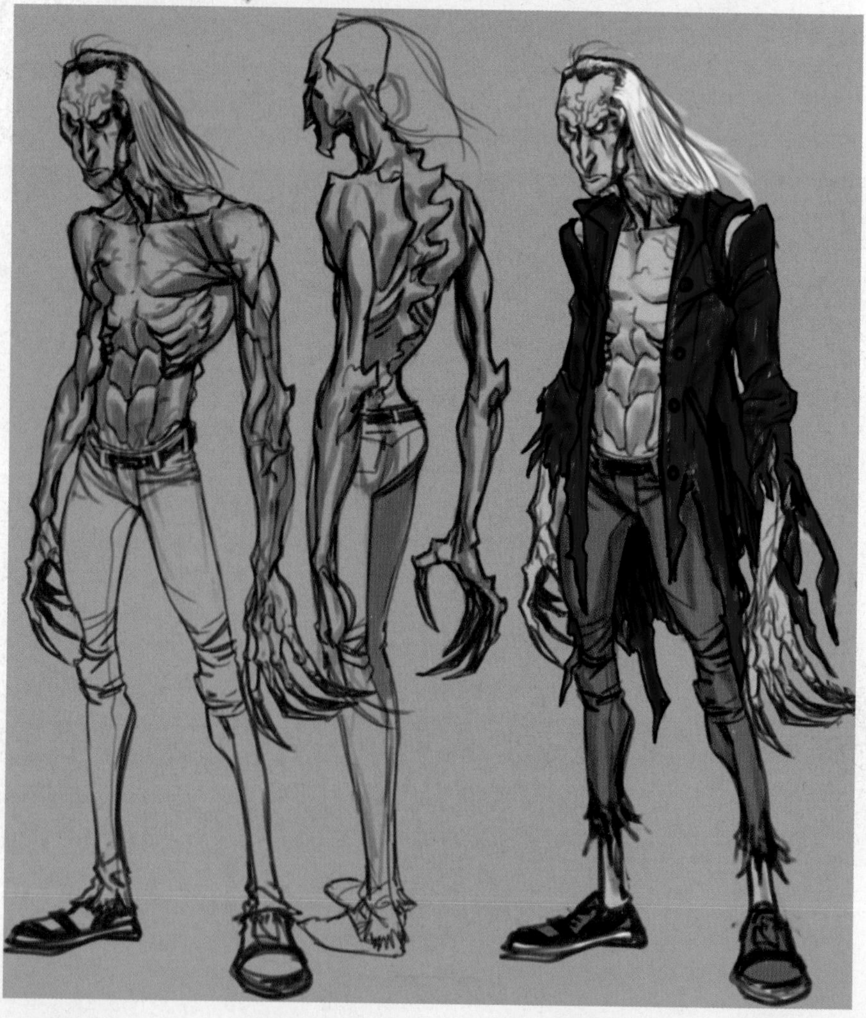

DC UNIVERSE PRESENTS
COVER SKETCHES & ROUGHS BY RYAN SOOK

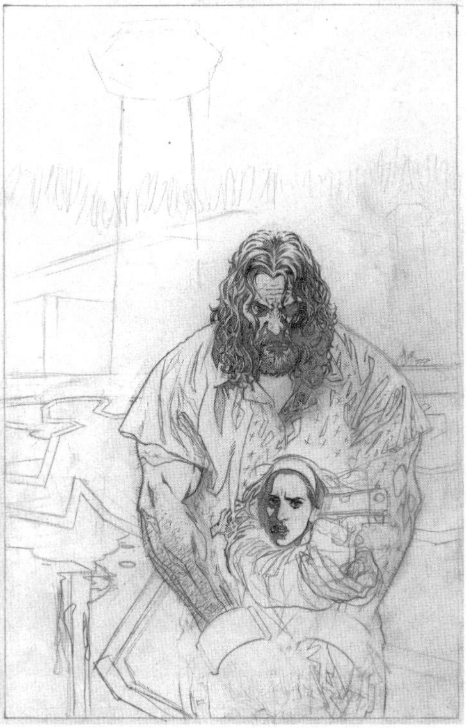

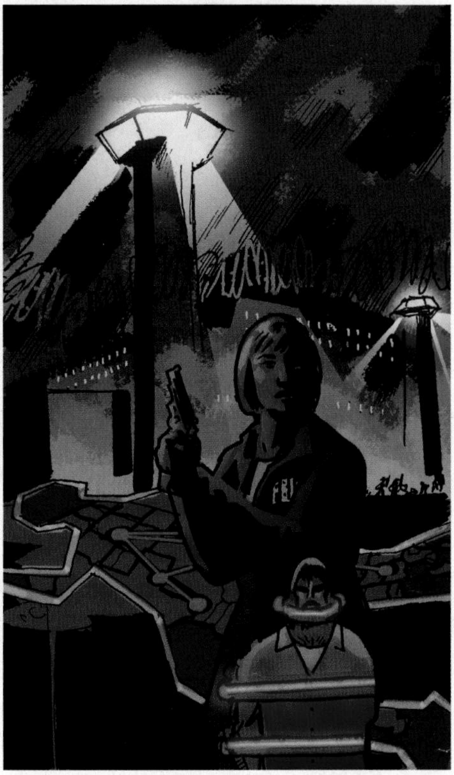

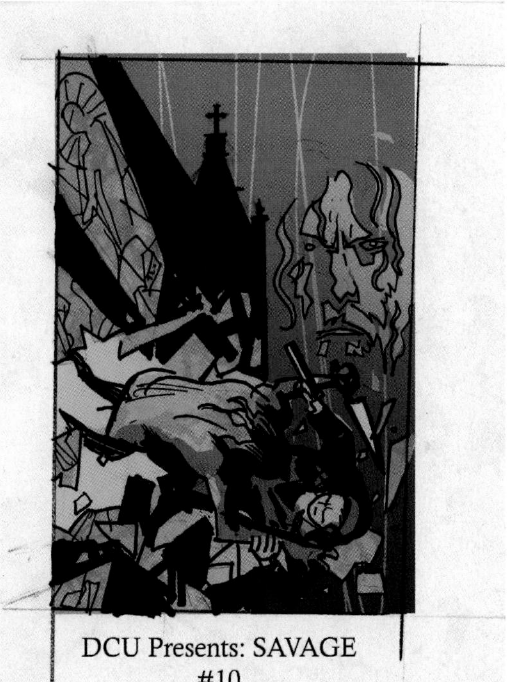
DCU Presents: SAVAGE
#10

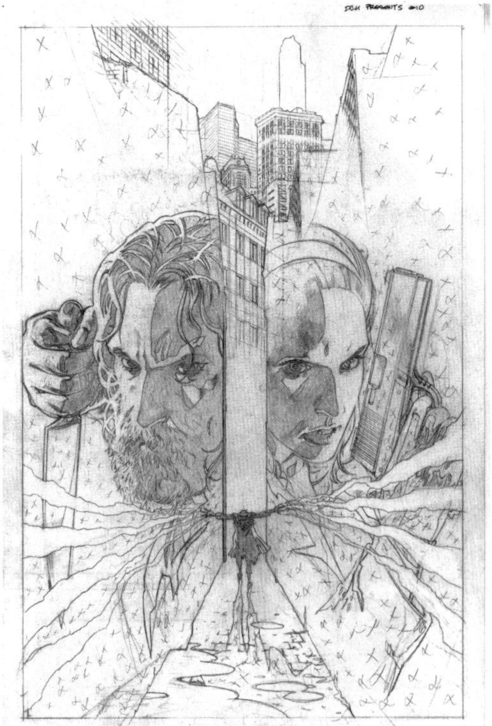
DCU PRESENTS #10

DCU PRESENTS #11

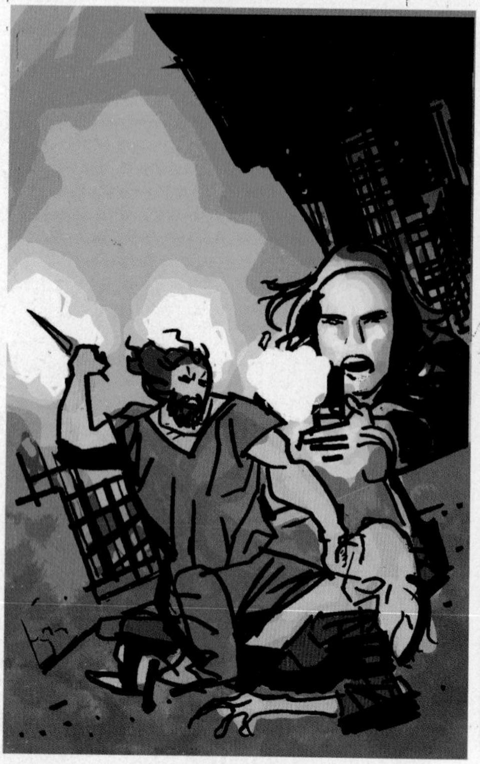

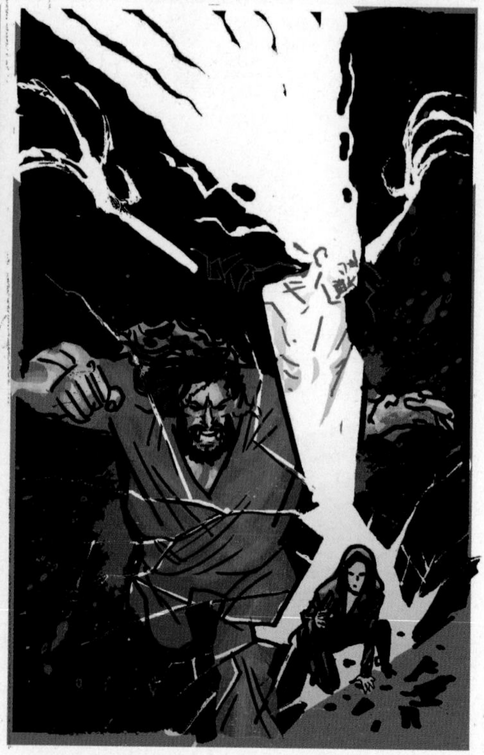

DCU PRESENTS #12

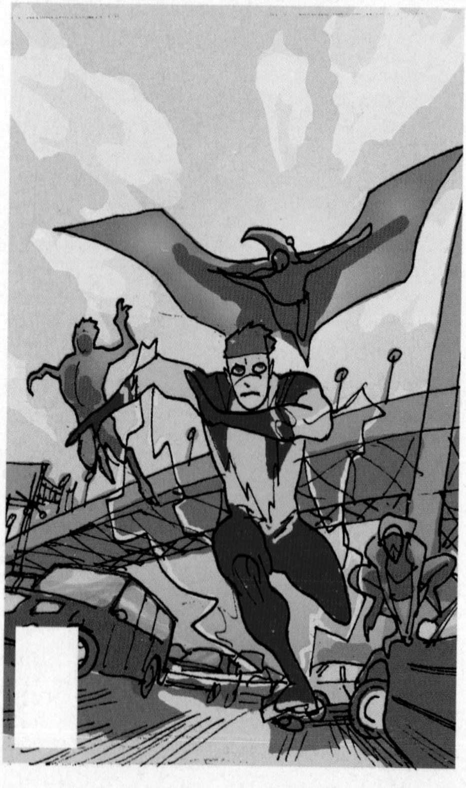

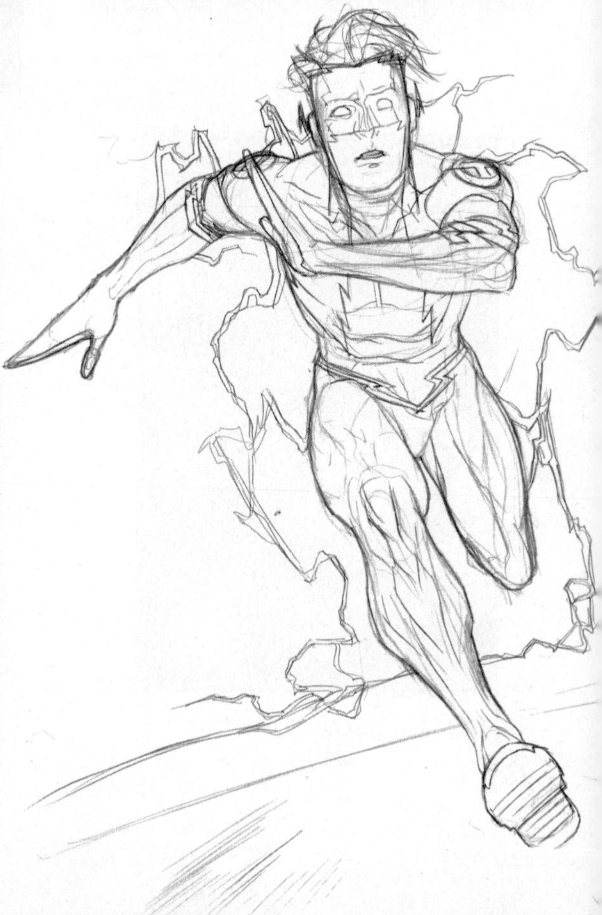